John Bradshaw

The Letters of Philip Dormer Stanhope, Earl of Chesterfield, With the Characters

Vol. II

John Bradshaw

The Letters of Philip Dormer Stanhope, Earl of Chesterfield, With the Characters
Vol. II

ISBN/EAN: 9783744766555

Printed in Europe, USA, Canada, Australia, Japan

Cover: Foto ©ninafisch / pixelio.de

More available books at **www.hansebooks.com**

THE

LETTERS

OF

PHILIP DORMER STANHOPE

EARL OF CHESTERFIELD

WITH THE

CHARACTERS

EDITED WITH INTRODUCTION, NOTES, AND INDEX

BY

JOHN BRADSHAW, M.A., LL.D.

*Inspector of Schools, Madras; Editor of Milton's
Poetical Works, A Concordance to Milton,
Gray's Poems, etc.*

IN THREE VOLUMES—VOL. II.

London

SWAN SONNENSCHEIN & CO.

PATERNOSTER SQUARE

1893

CONTENTS OF THE SECOND VOLUME.

LETTERS TO HIS SON, 1751-1754.

1751.

LETTERS TO HIS GODSON ON THE ART OF PLEASING.

POLITICAL AND MISCELLANEOUS LETTERS, 1712-1772.

1712.

1713.

1714.

1716.

1720.

1740.

1746.

1747.

* Now first published.

LORD CHESTERFIELD'S LETTERS.

(LETTERS TO HIS SON: 1739–1754.)

CLXXXI.

LONDON, *December* 19, O.S. 1751.

MY DEAR FRIEND,

You are now entered upon a scene of business, where I hope you will one day make a figure. Use does a great deal, but care and attention must be joined to it. The first thing necessary in writing letters of business is extreme clearness and perspicuity; every paragraph should be so clear and unambiguous, that the dullest fellow in the world may not be able to mistake it, nor obliged to read it twice in order to understand it. This necessary clearness implies a correctness, without excluding an elegancy of style. Tropes, figures, antitheses, epigrams, etc., would be as misplaced and as impertinent in letters of business, as they are sometimes (if judiciously used) proper and pleasing in familiar letters, upon common and trite subjects. In business, an elegant simplicity, the result of care, not of labour, is required. Business must be well, not affectedly, dressed, but by no means negligently. Let your first attention be to clearness, and read every paragraph after you have written it, in the critical view of discovering whether it is possible that any one man can mistake the true sense of it; and correct it accordingly.

Our pronouns and relatives often create obscurity or ambiguity; be therefore exceedingly attentive to them, and take care to mark out with precision their particular relations. For example: Mr. Johnson acquainted me that he had seen Mr. Smith, who had promised him to speak to Mr. Clarke, to return him (Mr. Johnson) those papers which he (Mr. Smith) had left some time ago with him (Mr. Clarke); it is better to repeat a name, though unnecessarily, ten times, than to have the person mistaken once.

Who, you know, is singly relative to persons, and cannot be applied to things; *which* and *that* are chiefly relative to things, but not absolutely exclusive of persons; for one may say, the man *that* robbed or killed such-a-one; but it is much better to say, the man *who* robbed or killed. One never says, the man or the woman *which*. *Which* and *that*, though chiefly relative to things, cannot be always used indifferently as to things; and the ευφονια must sometimes determine their place. For instance: The letter *which* I received from you, *which* you referred to in your last, *which* came by Lord Albemarle's messenger, and *which* I showed to such-a-one; I would change it thus: The letter *that* I received from you, *which* you referred to in your last, *that* came by Lord Albemarle's messenger, and *which* I showed to such-a-one.

Business does not exclude (as possibly you wish it did) the usual terms of politeness and good-breeding, but, on the contrary, strictly requires them; such as, *I have the honour to acquaint your Lordship ; Permit me to assure you ; If I may be allowed to give my opinion, etc.* For the Minister abroad, who writes to the Minister at home, writes to his superior; possibly to his patron, or at least to one who he desires should be so.

Letters of business will not only admit of, but be the better for *certain graces ;* but then, they must be scattered with a sparing and a skilful hand; they must fit their place exactly. They must decently adorn without encumbering, and modestly shine without glaring. But as this is the utmost degree of perfection in letters of business, I would not advise you to attempt those embellishments till you have first laid your foundation well.

Cardinal d'Ossat's letters are the true letters of business; those of Monsieur D'Avaux are excellent; Sir William Temple's are very pleasing, but I fear too affected. Carefully avoid all Greek or Latin quotations; and bring no precedents from the *virtuous Spartans, the polite Athenians, and the brave Romans.* Leave all that to futile pedants. No flourishes, no declamation. But (I repeat it again) there is an elegant simplicity and dignity of style absolutely necessary for good letters of business; attend to that carefully. Let your periods be harmonious, without seeming to be laboured; and let them not be too long, for that always occasions a degree of obscurity. I should not mention correct orthography, but that you very often fail in that particular, which will bring ridicule upon you; for no man is allowed to spell ill. I wish too that your handwriting were much better, and I cannot conceive why it is not, since every man may certainly write whatever hand he pleases. Neatness in folding up, sealing, and directing your packets, is by no means to be neglected; though I dare say you think it is. But there is something in the exterior, even of a packet, that may please or displease; and consequently worth some attention.

You say that your time is very well employed, and so it is, though as yet only in the outlines, and first *routine* of business. They are previously necessary to be known; they smooth the way for parts and dexterity. Business requires no conjuration nor supernatural talents, as people unacquainted with it are apt to think. Method, diligence, and discretion, will carry a man of good strong common sense much higher than the finest parts, without them, can do. *Par negotiis, neque supra,** is the true character of a man of business; but then it implies ready attention, and no *absences;* and a flexibility and versatility of attention from one object to another, without being engrossed by any one.

Be upon your guard against the pedantry and affectation of business, which young people are apt to fall into, from the pride of being concerned in it young. They look thoughtful, complain of the weight of business, throw out mysterious hints, and seem big with secrets which they do not know. Do you on the contrary never talk of business but to those with whom you are to transact it; and learn to seem *vacuus* and idle when you have the most business. Of all things, the *volto sciolto* and the *pensieri stretti* are necessary. Adieu!

CLXXXII.

LONDON, *December* 30, O.S. 1751.

MY DEAR FRIEND,

The Parliaments are the courts of justice of France, and are what our courts of justice in Westminster-Hall are here. They used anciently to follow the Court, and administer justice in the presence of the king. Philip le Bel first fixed it at Paris by an edict of 1302. It consisted then of but one *chambre*, which was called *La Chambre des Prélats*, most of the members being ecclesi-

---

* Tacitus—*Annals*, vi. 39. See Letter CLXXVI.

astics; but the multiplicity of business made it by degrees necessary to create several other *chambres ;* it consists now of seven *chambres.*

La Grand-Chambre, which is the highest court of justice, and to which appeals lie from the others.

Les cinq Chambres des Enquêtes, which are like our Common Pleas and Court of Exchequer.

La Tournelle, which is the court for criminal justice, and answers to our Old Bailey and King's Bench.

There are in all twelve Parliaments in France.

1. Paris. 2. Toulouse. 3. Grenoble. 4. Bourdeaux. 5. Dijon. 6. Rouen. 7. Aix en Provence. 8. Rennes en Bretagne. 9. Pau en Navarre. 10. Metz. 11. Dole en Franche Comté. 12. Douay.

There are three *Conseils Souverains,* which may almost be called Parliaments ; they are those of Perpignan, Arras, Alsace.

For further particulars of the French Parliaments, read Bernard de la Rochefavin *des Parlemens de France,* and other authors, who have treated that subject constitutionally. But what will be still better, converse upon it with people of sense and knowledge, who will inform you of the particular objects of the several *Chambres,* and the businesses of the respective members, as, *les Présidens, les Présidens à Mortier* (these last so called from their black velvet caps laced with gold), *les Maitres des Requêtes, les Greffiers, le Procureur Général, les Avocats Généraux, les Conseillers, etc.* The great point in dispute is, concerning the powers of the Parliament of Paris, in matters of state, and relatively to the Crown. They pretend to the powers of the States General of France, when they used to be assembled (which, I think, they have not been since the reign of Louis XIII., in the year 1615). The Crown denies those pretensions, and considers them only as courts of justice. Mezeray seems to be on the side of the Parliament in this question, which is very well worth your inquiry. But, be that as it will, the Parliament of Paris is certainly a very respectable body, and much regarded by the whole kingdom. The edicts of the Crown, especially those for levying money on the subjects, ought to be registered in Parliament ; I do not say to have their effect, for the Crown would take good care of that ; but to have a decent appearance, and to procure a willing acquiescence in the nation. And the Crown itself, absolute as it is, does not love that strong opposition, and those admirable remonstrances, which it sometimes meets with from the Parliaments. Many of those detached pieces are very well worth your collecting ; and I remember, a year or two ago, a remonstrance of the Parliament of Douay, upon the subject, as I think, of the *vingtiême*, which was, in my mind, one of the finest and most moving compositions I ever read. They owned themselves, indeed, to be slaves, and showed their chains ; but humbly begged of his Majesty to make them a little lighter and less galling.

The *States of France* were general assemblies of the three states or orders of the kingdom ; the clergy, the nobility, and the *Tiers Etat*, that is, the people. They used to be called together by the king, upon the most important affairs of state, like our Lords and Commons in Parliament, and our clergy in Convocation. Our Parliament is our States, and the French Parliaments are only their Courts of Justice. The nobility consisted of all those of noble extraction, whether belonging to the *sword*, or to the *robe ;* excepting such as were chosen (which sometimes happened) by the *tiers état*, as their deputies to the States General.* The *tiers état* was exactly our House of Commons, that is, the people, represented by deputies of their own choosing. Those who had the most considerable places, *dans la robe*, assisted at those assemblies, as commissioners on the part of the Crown. The States met, for the first time that I can find (I mean by the name of *les Etats*), in the reign of Pharamond, 424, when they confirmed the Salic law. From that time they have been very frequently assembled, sometimes upon important occasions, as making war and peace, reforming abuses, etc. ; at other times, upon seemingly trifling ones, as coronations, marriages, etc. Francis I. assembled them, in 1526, to declare null and void his famous treaty of Madrid, signed and sworn to by him, during his captivity there. They grew troublesome to the kings and to their Ministers, and were but seldom called, after the power of the Crown grew strong ; and they have never been heard of since

---

* As was afterwards the case with Mirabeau : " Il aspirait à être un des représentans du Tiers Etat par un pressentiment qu'il y jouerait un plus grand rôle, et que sa noblesse même ajouterait un nouveau mérito à ses principes populaires."—Dumont, *Souvenirs sur Mirabeau*, ch. i.—M.

the year 1615. Richelieu came and shackled the nation, and Mazarin and Louis XIV. riveted the shackles.

There still subsist in some provinces in France, which are called *pays d'états,* an humble local imitation, or rather mimicry, of the great *états,* as in *Languedoc, Bretagne, etc.* They meet, they speak, they grumble, and finally submit to whatever the king orders.

Independently of the intrinsic utility of this kind of knowledge to every man of business, it is a shame for any man to be ignorant of it, especially relatively to any country he has been long in. Adieu.

CLXXXIII.

LONDON, *January* 2, O.S. 1752.

MY DEAR FRIEND,

Laziness of mind, or inattention, are as great enemies to knowledge, as incapacity ; for, in truth, what difference is there between a man who will not, and a man who cannot, be informed ? This difference only, that the former is justly to be blamed, the latter to be pitied. And yet how many are there, very capable of receiving knowledge, who from laziness, inattention, and incuriousness, will not so much as ask for it, much less take the least pains to acquire it.

Our young English travellers generally distinguish themselves by a voluntary privation of all that useful knowledge for which they are sent abroad ; and yet at that age, the most useful knowledge is the most easy to be acquired; conversation being the book, and the best book, in which it is contained. The drudgery of dry grammatical learning is over, and the fruits of it are mixed with, and adorned by, the flowers of conversation. How many of our young men have been a year at Rome, and as long at . Paris, without knowing the meaning and institution of the Conclave in the former, and of the Parliament in the latter ? and this merely for want of asking the first people they met with in those several places, who could at least have given them some general notions of those matters.

You will, I hope, be wiser, and omit no opportunity (for opportunities present themselves every hour in the day) of acquainting

yourself with all those political and constitutional particulars of
the kingdom and government of France; for instance, when you
hear people mention *le Chancelier,* or *le Garde des Sçeaux,* is it
any great trouble for you to ask, or for others to tell you, what
is the nature, the powers, the objects, and the profits of those
two employments, either when joined together, as they often are,
or when separate, as they are at present? When you hear of a
Gouverneur, a *Lieutenant du Roi,* a *Commandant,* and an *Intendant* of the same province, is it not natural, is it not becoming, is
it not necessary, for a stranger to inquire into their respective
rights and privileges? And yet I dare say there are very few
Englishmen who know the difference between the civil department of the Intendant and the military powers of the others.
When you hear (as I am persuaded you must) every day of the
Vingtiême, which is one in twenty, and consequently five *per cent.,*
inquire upon what that tax is laid—whether upon lands, money,
merchandise, or upon all three; how levied, and what it is supposed to produce. When you find in books (as you will sometimes) allusion to particular laws and customs, do not rest till
you have traced them up to their *source.* To give you two
examples; you will meet in some French comedies, *Cri* or *Clameur
de Haro;* ask what it means, and you will be told that it is a
term of the law in Normandy, and means citing, arresting, or
obliging any person to appear in the courts of justice, either upon
a civil or a criminal account; and that it is derived from *à Raoul,*
which Raoul was anciently Duke of Normandy, and a Prince
eminent for his justice—insomuch, that when any injustice was
committed, the cry immediately was *venez à Raoul, à Raoul;*
which words are now corrupted and jumbled into *haro.* Another,
Le vol du Chapon—that is, a certain district of ground immediately contiguous to the mansion seat of a family, and answers
to what we call in English *demesnes.* It is in France computed
at about 1,600 feet round the house, that being supposed to be
the extent of the capon's flight from *la basse cour.* This little
district must go along with the mansion seat; however the rest
of the estate may be divided.

I do not mean that you should be a French lawyer, but I
would not have you be unacquainted with the general principles
of their law in matters that occur every day. Such is the nature

of their descents—that is, the inheritance of lands. Do they all go to the eldest son, or are they equally divided among the children of the deceased? In England, all lands unsettled descend to the eldest son, as heir at law, unless otherwise disposed of by the father's will: except in the county of Kent, where a particular custom prevails, called Gavel-kind, by which, if the father dies intestate, all his children divide his lands equally among them.* In Germany, as you know, all lands that are not fiefs are equally divided among all the children, which ruins those families; but all male fiefs of the empire descend unalienably to the next male heir, which preserves those families. In France, I believe, descents vary in different provinces.

The nature of marriage contracts deserves inquiry. In England, the general practice is, the husband takes all the wife's fortune, and, in consideration of it, settles upon her a proper pin-money, as it is called, that is, an annuity during his life, and a jointure after his death. In France it is not so, particularly at Paris, where *la communauté des biens* is established. Any married woman at Paris (*if you are acquainted with one*) can inform you of all these particulars.

These, and other things of the same nature, are the useful and rational objects of the curiosity of a man of sense and business. Could they only be attained by laborious researches in folio books and worm-eaten manuscripts, I should not wonder at a young fellow's being ignorant of them; but as they are the frequent topics of conversation, and to be known by a very little degree of curiosity, inquiry, and attention, it is unpardonable not to know them.

Thus I have given you some hints only for your inquiries; *l'Etat de la France, L'Almanach Royal,* and twenty other such superficial books, will furnish you with a thousand more. *Approfondissez.*

How often, and how justly, have I since regretted negligences of this kind in my youth! And how often have I since been at great trouble to learn many things, which I could then have learned without any! Save yourself now, then, I beg of you,

---

* See Blackstone's *Commentaries*, book ii. ch. 6. According to Seldon's opinion, Gravel-kind before the Norman conquest was the general custom of the realm.—M.

that regret and trouble hereafter. Ask questions, and many questions, and leave nothing till you are thoroughly informed of it. Such pertinent questions are far from being ill-bred, or troublesome to those of whom you ask them; on the contrary, they are a tacit compliment to their knowledge; and people have a better opinion of a young man when they see him desirous to be informed.

I have, by last post, received your two letters of the 1st and 5th January, N.S. I am very glad that you have been at all the shows at Versailles; frequent the Courts. I can conceive the murmurs of the French at the poorness of the fireworks, by which they thought their king or their country degraded; and, in truth, were things always as they should be, when Kings give shows, they ought to be magnificent.

I thank you for the *Thèse de la Sorbonne*, which you intend to send me, and which I am impatient to receive; but pray read it carefully yourself first, and inform yourself what the Sorbonne is, by whom founded, and for what purposes.

Since you have time, you have done very well, to take an Italian and German master; but pray take care to leave yourself time enough for company; for it is in company only that you can learn what will be much more useful to you than either Italian or German; I mean *la politesse, les manières, et les graces*, without which, as I told you long ago, and I told you true, *ogni fatica è vana*. Adieu.

Pray make my compliments to Lady Brown.

CLXXXIV

London, *January* 6, O.S. 1752.

My dear Friend,

I recommended to you, in my last, some inquiries into the constitution of that famous society the *Sorbonne*; but as I cannot wholly trust to the diligence of those inquiries, I will give you here the outlines of that establishment; which may possibly excite you to inform yourself of particulars, that you are more *à portée* to know than I am.

It was founded by Robert *de Sorbon*, in the year 1256, for sixteen poor scholars in divinity; four of each nation; of the university of which it made a part; since that it hath been much

extended and enriched, especially by the liberality and pride of
Cardinal Richelieu; who made it a magnificent building, for
six-and-thirty Doctors of that Society to live in; besides which,
there are six Professors and schools for divinity. This society
hath been long famous for theological knowledge, and exercita-
tions. There unintelligible points are debated with passion.
though they can never be determined by reason. Logical
subtleties set common sense at defiance; and mystical refinements disfigure and disguise the native beauty and simplicity of
true natural religion; wild imaginations form systems, which
weak minds adopt implicitly, and which sense and reason oppose in vain; their voice is not strong enough to be heard in
schools of divinity. Political views are by no means neglected
in those sacred places; and questions are agitated and decided
according to the degree of regard, or rather submission, which
the Sovereign is pleased to show the Church. Is the King a
slave to the Church, though a tyrant to the laity? the least
resistance to his will shall be declared damnable. But if he will
not acknowledge the superiority of their spiritual over his
temporal, nor even admit their *imperium in imperio*, which is
the least they will compound for, it becomes meritorious, not only
to resist, but to depose him. And I suppose, that the bold propositions in the Thesis you mention, are a return for the valuation
of *les biens du Clergé*.

I would advise you, by all means, to attend two or three of
their public disputations, in order to be informed both of the
manner and the substance of those scholastic exercises. Pray
remember to go to all such kind of things. Do not put it off,
as one is too apt to do things which one knows can be done every
day, or any day; for one afterwards repents extremely, when too
late, the not having done them.'

But there is another (so called) religious Society, of which the
minutest circumstance deserves attention, and furnishes great
matter for useful reflections. You easily guess that I mean the
society of *les R. R. P. P.** *Jesuites*, established but in the year
1540, by a Bull of Pope Paul III. Its progress, and I may say
its victories, were more rapid than those of the Romans; for
within the same century it governed all Europe; and in the

* *Les Révérends Pères.*

next it extended its influence over the whole world. Its founder was an abandoned profligate Spanish officer, Ignatius Loyola; who, in the year 1521, being wounded in the leg at the siege of Pampelona, went mad from the smart of his wound, the reproaches of his conscience, and his confinement, during which he read the Lives of the Saints. Consciousness of guilt, a fiery temper, and a wild imagination, the common ingredients of enthusiasm, made this madman devote himself to the particular service of the Virgin Mary ; whose knight-errant he declared himself, in the very same form in which the old knights-errant in romances used to declare themselves the knights and champions of certain beautiful and incomparable princesses, whom sometimes they had, but oftener had not, seen. For Dulcinea del Toboso was by no means the first Princess, whom her faithful and valorous knight had never seen in his life. The enthusiast went to the Holy Land, from whence he returned to Spain, where he began to learn Latin and philosophy at three-and-thirty years old, so that no doubt but he made a great progress in both. The better to carry on his mad and wicked designs, he chose four disciples, or rather apostles, all Spaniards, viz., Laynés, Salmeron, Bobadilla, and Rodriguez. He then composed the rules and constitutions of his Order; which, in the year 1547, was called the Order of Jesuits, from the church of Jesus in Rome, which was given them. Ignatius died in 1556, aged sixty-five, thirty-five years after his conversion, and sixteen years after the establishment of his society. He was canonized in the year 1609, and is doubtless now a saint in heaven.

If the religious and moral principles of the Society are to be detested, as they justly are, the wisdom of their political principles is as justly to be admired. Suspected, collectively as an Order, of the greatest crimes, and convicted of many, they have either escaped punishment, or triumphed after it; as in France, in the reign of Henry IV. They have, directly or indirectly, governed the consciences and councils of all the Catholic princes in Europe; they almost governed China in the reign of Cangghi; and they are now actually in possession of the Paraguay in America, pretending but paying no obedience to the Crown of Spain. As a collective body, they are detested even by the Catholics, not excepting the clergy, both secular and regular;

and yet, as individuals, they are loved, respected, and they govern wherever they are.

Two things, I believe, chiefly contribute to their success. The first, that passive, implicit, unlimited obedience to their General (who always resides at Rome) and to the Superiors of their several houses, appointed by him. This obedience is observed by them all, to a most astonishing degree; and I believe there is no one Society in the world of which so many individuals sacrifice their private interest to the general one of the Society itself. The second is, the education of youth, which they have in a manner engrossed; there they give the first, and the first are the lasting, impressions; those impressions are always calculated to be favourable to the Society. I have known many Catholics, educated by the Jesuits, who, though they detested the Society, from reason and knowledge, have always remained attached to it, from habit and prejudice. The Jesuits know, better than any set of people in the world, the importance of the art of pleasing, and study it more; they become all things to all men, in order to gain, not a few, but many. In Asia, Africa or America they become more than half Pagans, in order to convert the Pagans to be less than half Christians. In private families they begin by insinuating themselves as friends, they grow to be favourites, and they end *directors*. Their manners are not like those of any other Regulars in the world, but gentle, polite, and engaging. They are all carefully bred up to that particular destination to which they seem to have a natural turn; for which reason one sees most Jesuits excel in some particular thing. They even breed up some for martyrdom, in case of need, as a superior of a Jesuit seminary at Rome told Lord Bolingbroke: *Ed abbiamo anche martiri per il martirio, se bisogna.*

Inform yourself minutely of everything concerning this extraordinary establishment; go to their houses, get acquainted with individuals, hear some of them preach. The finest preacher I ever heard in my life is Père Neufville,* who, I believe, preaches

---

* Père Neufville, or more correctly Neuville, was born at Coutances in 1693, and died at St. Germain in 1774. His collected *Sermons*, *Oraisons Funèbres*, etc., were published two years afterwards, and their eloquence has called forth a high panegyric from La Harpe.—M.

still at Paris, and is so much in the best company, that you may easily get personally acquainted with him.

If you would know their *morale* read Pascal's *Lettres Provinciales*, in which it is very truly displayed from their own writings.

Upon the whole, this is certain, that a Society of which so little good is said, and so much ill believed, and that still not only subsists, but flourishes, must be a very able one. It is always mentioned as a proof of the superior abilities of Cardinal Richelieu, that, though hated by all the nation, and still more by his master, he kept his power in spite of both.

I would earnestly wish you to do every thing now, which I wish that I had done at your age, and did not do. Every country has its peculiarities, which one can be much better informed of during one's residence there, than by reading all the books in the world afterwards. While you are in Roman Catholic countries, inform yourself of all the forms and ceremonies of that tawdry * church ; see their convents both of men and women, know their several rules and orders, attend their most remarkable ceremonies ; have their terms of art explained to you, their *tierce, sexte, nones, matines, vépres, complies ;* their *bréviaires, rosaires, heures, chaplets, agnus, etc.,* things that many people talk of from habit, though few know the true meaning of any one of them. Converse with and study the characters of some of those incarcerated enthusiasts. Frequent some *parloirs,* and see the air and manners of those recluses, who are a distinct nation themselves, and like no other.

I dined yesterday with Mrs. Fitzgerald, her mother, and husband. He is an athletic Hibernian, handsome in his person, but excessively awkward and vulgar in his air and manner. She inquired much after you, and I thought with interest. I answered her as a *Mezzano* should do. *Et je prônai votre tendresse, vos soins, et vos soupirs.*

When you meet with any British returning to their own country, pray send me by them any little *brochûres, factums, théses, etc., qui font du bruit ou du plaisir à Paris.* Adieu, child.

* Gay and showy; *tawdry* had not quite its present signification in Chesterfield's time.

CLXXXV.

LONDON, *January* 23, O.S. 1752.

MY DEAR FRIEND,

Have you seen the new tragedy of *Varon*,* and what do you think of it? Let me know, for I am determined to form my taste upon yours. I hear that the situations and incidents are well brought on, and the catastrophe unexpected and surprising, but the verses bad. I suppose it is the subject of all the conversations at Paris, where both women and men are judges and critics of all such performances; such conversations, that both form and improve the taste and whet the judgment, are surely preferable to the conversations of our mixed companies here; which, if they happen to rise above bragg and whist, infallibly stop short of everything either pleasing or instructive. I take the reason of this to be, that (as women generally give the tone to the conversation) our English women are not near so well informed and cultivated as the French; besides that they are naturally more serious and silent.

I could wish there were a treaty made between the French and the English theatres, in which both parties should make considerable concessions. The English ought to give up their notorious violations of all the unities, and all their massacres, racks, dead bodies, and mangled carcases, which they so frequently exhibit upon their stage. The French should engage to have more action and less declamation; and not to cram and crowd things together to almost a degree of impossibility, from a too scrupulous adherence to the unities. The English should restrain the licentiousness of their poets, and the French enlarge the liberty of theirs; their poets are the greatest slaves in their country, and that is a bold word; ours are the most tumultuous subjects in England, and that is saying a good deal. Under such regulations one might hope to see a play in which one should not be lulled to sleep by the length of a monotonical declamation, nor frightened and shocked by the barbarity of the action. The unity of time extended occasionally to three or four days, and the unity of place broke into, as far as the same street, or some-

---

* In the *Dictionnaire des Anonymes par Barbier* the tragedy of *Varon* is said to have been written by the *Vicomte de Grave.*—M.

times the same town; both which, I will affirm, are as probable
as four-and-twenty hours and the same room.

More indulgence too, in my mind, should be shown, than the
French are willing to allow, to bright thoughts and to shining
images; for though, I confess, it is not very natural for a Hero
or a Princess to say fine things in all the violence of grief, love,
rage, etc., yet I can as well suppose that, as I can that they
should talk to themselves for half-an-hour, which they must
necessarily do or no tragedy could be carried on, unless they
had recourse to a much greater absurdity, the choruses of the
ancients. Tragedy is of a nature, that one must see it with a
degree of self-deception; we must lend ourselves a little to the
delusion; and I am very willing to carry that complaisance a
little farther than the French do.

Tragedy must be something bigger than life, or it would not
affect us. In nature, the most violent passions are silent; in
Tragedy they must speak, and speak with dignity too. Hence
the necessity of their being written in verse, and, unfortunately
for the French, from the weakness of their language, in rhymes.
And for the same reason, Cato, the Stoic, expiring at Utica,
rhymes masculine and feminine at Paris, and fetches his last
breath at London in most harmonious and correct blank verse.

It is quite otherwise with Comedy, which should be mere
common life, and not one jot bigger. Every character should
speak upon the stage, not only what it would utter in the situation there represented, but in the same manner in which it would
express it. For which reason I cannot allow rhymes in Comedy,
unless they were put into the mouth and came out of the mouth
of a mad poet. But it is impossible to deceive one's self enough
(nor is it the least necessary in Comedy) to suppose a dull rogue
of a usurer cheating, or *gros Jean* blundering in the finest rhymes
in the world.

As for Operas, they are essentially too absurd and extravagant
to mention; I look upon them as a magic scene, contrived to
please the eyes and the ears at the expense of the understanding;
and I consider singing, rhyming and chiming Heroes, and Princesses and Philosophers, as I do the hills, the trees, the birds,
and the beasts, who amicably joined in one common country
dance to the irresistible tune of Orpheus's lyre. Whenever I go

to an Opera, I leave my sense and reason at the door with my half-guinea, and deliver myself up to my eyes and my ears.

Thus I have made you my poetical confession; in which I have acknowledged as many sins against the established taste in both countries, as a frank heretic could have owned against the established Church in either; but I am now privileged by my age to taste and think for myself, and not to care what other people think of me in those respects; an advantage which youth, among its many advantages, has not. It must occasionally and outwardly conform, to a certain degree, to established tastes, fashions, and decisions. A young man may, with a becoming modesty, dissent, in private companies, from public opinions and prejudices; but he must not attack them with warmth, nor magisterially set up his own sentiments against them. Endeavour to hear and know all opinions; receive them with complaisance; form your own with coolness, and give in with modesty.

I have received a letter from Sir John Lambert, in which he requests me to use my interest to procure him the remittance of Mr. Spencer's * money, when he goes abroad; and also desires to know to whose account he is to place the postage of my letters. I do not trouble him with a letter in answer, since you can execute the commission. Pray make my compliments to him, and assure him that I will do all I can to procure him Mr. Spencer's business; but that his most effectual way will be by Messrs. Hoare, who are Mr. Spencer's cashiers; and who will undoubtedly have their choice whom they will give him his credit upon. As for the postage of the letters, your purse and mine being pretty near the same, do you pay it over and above your next draught.

Your relations, the Princes B(orghese), † will soon be with you at Paris; for they leave London this week; whenever you converse with them, I desire it may be in Italian; that language not being yet familiar enough to you.

* This was John Spencer, the only son of the Hon. John Spencer, son of the statesman, Charles, 3rd Earl of Sunderland by Anne, daughter and co-heiress of the Duke of Marlborough. His son was elected M.P. for Warwick; in 1761 he was created Viscount Spencer, and, in 1765, Earl Spencer. In 1755 he married a daughter of the Right Hon. Stephen Poyntz, and was great-grandfather of the present Earl, John Poyntz Spencer (b. 1835).

† See note to the letter of June 20, 1751.

By our printed papers, there seems to be a sort of compromise between the King and the Parliament, with regard to the affairs of the hospitals, by taking them out of the hands of the Archbishop of Paris,* and placing them in Monsieur d'Argenson's ; † if this be true, that compromise, as it is called, is clearly a victory on the side of the Court, and a defeat on the part of the Parliament; for if the Parliament had a right, they had it as much to the exclusion of Monsieur d'Argenson as of the Archbishop.

Adieu.

CLXXXVI.

LONDON, *February* 6, O.S. 1752.

MY DEAR FRIEND,

Your criticism of *Varon* is strictly just; but, in truth, severe. You French critics seek for a fault as eagerly as I do for a beauty; you consider things in the worst light, to show your skill, at the expense of your pleasure; I view them in the best, that I may have more pleasure, though at the expense of my judgment. *A trompeur trompeur et demi* ‡ is prettily said; and if you please, you may call *Varon, un Normand,* and *Sostrate, un Mançeau, qui vaut un Normand et demi;* and, considering the *dénouement,* in the light of trick upon trick, it would undoubtedly be below the dignity of the buskin, and fitter for the sock.

But let us see if we cannot bring off the author. The great question, upon which all turns, is to discover and ascertain who *Oleonice* really is. There are doubts concerning her *état;* how shall they be cleared? Had the truth been extorted from *Varon* (who alone knew), by the rack, it would have been a true tragical *dénouement.* But that would probably not have done with *Varon,* who is represented as a bold, determined, wicked, and at that time, desperate fellow; for he was in the hands of an enemy,

---

* Christophe de Beaumont, raised to that dignity in 1746, and famous in after-years for his opposition to the Court and his controversy with Rousseau.—M.

† Marc Pierre de Voyer, Comte d'Argenson, born in 1696, was at this period *Ministre de la Guerre.* It was he who, when the Abbé Desfontaines was apologising for his frequent publication of libels, and had added, *Il faut bien que je vive !*—drily replied *Je n'en vois pas la nécessité !*—M.

‡ 'To a deceiver be a deceiver-and-a-half'; you may over-reach one who wants to out-wit you

who he knew could not forgive him with common prudence or safety. The rack would therefore have extorted no truth from him; but he would have died enjoying the doubts of his enemies, and the confusion that must necessarily attend those doubts. A stratagem is therefore thought of, to discover what force and terror could not, and the stratagem such as no King or Minister would disdain, to get at an important discovery. If you call that stratagem *a trick*, you vilify it, and make it comical; but call that trick a *stratagem*, or a *measure*, and you dignify it up to tragedy; so frequently do ridicule or dignity turn upon one single word.

It is commonly said, and more particularly by Lord Shaftesbury,* that ridicule is the best test of truth; for that it will not stick where it is not just. I deny it. A truth learned in a certain light, and attacked in certain words, by men of wit and humour, may, and often does, become ridiculous, at least so far that the truth is only remembered and repeated for the sake of the ridicule. The overturn of Mary of Medicis into a river, where she was half drowned, would never have been remembered, if Madame de Verneuil,† who saw it, had not said *la Reine boit.* Pleasure or malignity often gives ridicule a weight, which it does not deserve. The versification, I must confess, is too much neglected, and too often bad; but, upon the whole, I read the play with pleasure.

If there is but a great deal of wit and character in your new comedy, I will readily compound for its having little or no plot. I chiefly mind dialogue and character in comedies. Let dull critics feed upon the carcases of plays; give me the taste and the dressing.

I am very glad you went to Versailles, to see the ceremony of creating the Prince de Condé,‡ *Chevalier de l'Ordre;* and I

---

* *Characteristics:* Dr. Johnson criticises this "foolish assertion" in his *Life of Akenside;* it was adopted by Akenside, and attacked by Warburton. See Chesterfield's Letter to his Godson, p. 656.

† Mary of Medicis was the wife of Henry IV., and Catherine Henriette d'Entragues, Marquise de Verneuil, was his mistress after the death of Gabrielle d'Estrées. She is frequently, but by no means favourably, mentioned in the *Mémoires de Sully.*

‡ Louis Joseph de Bourbon, grandfather of the ill-fated Duc d'Enghien: he was born in 1736, and died in 1818.

do not doubt but that, upon this occasion, you informed yourself thoroughly of the institution and rules of that Order. If you did, you were certainly told it was instituted by Henry III., immediately after his return, or rather his flight, from Poland; he took the hint of it at Venice; where he had seen the original manuscript of an Order of the *St. Esprit, ou droit désir*, which had been instituted in 1352, by Louis d'Anjou, King of Jerusalem and Sicily, and husband to Jane, Queen of Naples, Countess of Provence. This Order was under the protection of St. Nicholas de Bari, whose image hung to the collar. Henry III. found the Order of St. Michael prostituted and degraded, during the civil wars; he therefore joined it to his new Order of the St. Esprit, and gave them both together; for which reason every Knight of the St. Esprit is now called *Chevalier des Ordres du Roi*. The number of the Knights has been different, but is now fixed to *one hundred*, exclusive of the sovereign. There are many officers, who wear the ribbon of this Order, like the other Knights; and what is very singular is that these officers frequently sell their employments, but obtain leave to wear the blue ribbon still, though the purchasers of those offices wear it also.

As you will have been a great while in France, people will expect that you should be *au fait* of all these sort of things relative to that country. But the history of all the Orders of all countries is well worth your knowledge; the subject occurs often, and one should not be ignorant of it, for fear of some such accident as happened to a solid Dane at Paris, who, upon seeing *l'Ordre du St. Esprit*, said, *Nôtre St. Esprit chez nous c'est un Éléphant.* Almost all the princes in Germany have their Orders too, not dated, indeed, from any important events, or directed to any great object; but because they will have Orders, to show that they may; as some of them, who have the *jus cudendæ monetæ*, borrow ten shillings' worth of gold to coin a ducat. However, wherever you meet with them, inform yourself, and minute down a short account of them; they take in all the colours of Sir Isaac Newton's prisms. N.B. When you inquire about them, do not seem to laugh.

I thank you for *le Mandement de Monseigneur l'Archevêque*; it is very well drawn, and becoming an Archbishop. But pray do not lose sight of a much more important object, I mean the political disputes between the King and the Parliament, and the King and the Clergy; they seem both to be patching up; however, get the whole clue to them, as far as they have gone.

I received a letter yesterday from Madame Monconseil, who assures me you have gained ground *du côté des manières,* and that she looks upon you to be *plus qu'à moitié chemin.* I am very glad to hear this, because, if you are got above half way of your journey, surely you will finish it, and not faint in the course. Why do you think I have this affair so extremely at heart, and why do I repeat it so often? Is it for your sake, or for mine? You can immediately answer yourself that question; you certainly have, I cannot possibly have, any interest in it; if then you will allow me, as I believe you may, to be a judge of what is useful and necessary to you, you must, in consequence, be convinced of the infinite importance of a point which I take so much pains to inculcate.

I hear that the new Duke of Orléans * *a remercié Monsieur de Melfort,* and, I believe, *pas sans raison,* having had obligations to him; *mais il ne l'a pas remercié en mari poli,* but rather roughly. *Il faut que ce soit un bourru.* I am told, too, that people get bits of his father's rags, by way of relics; † I wish them joy; they will do them a great deal of good. See from hence what weaknesses human nature is capable of, and make allowances for such in all your plans and reasonings. Study the characters of the people you have to do with, and know what they are, instead of thinking them what they should be; address yourself generally to the senses, to the heart, and to the weaknesses of mankind, but very rarely to their reason.

Good night, or good morrow to you, according to the time you shall receive this letter from   Yours.

---

* Louis Philippe, Duc d'Orléans, born in 1725, and died in 1785. He was grandfather of Louis Philippe, King of the French, 1830–1848.

† Louis, Duc d'Orléans, born in 1703, was the son and successor of the Regent. His father's sudden death having struck his mind with religious awe, he passed the remainder of his days in the practice of austere devotion. During the last ten years of his life he had retired wholly to a cell in the *Abbaye de St. Geneviève.* He died February 4, 1752.—M.

CLXXXVII.

LONDON, *February* 14, O.S. 1752.

MY DEAR FRIEND,

In a month's time I believe I shall have the pleasure of sending you, and you will have the pleasure of reading, a work of Lord Bolingbroke's, in two volumes octavo, *Upon the Use of History*, in several Letters to Lord Hyde, then Lord Cornbury.* It is now put into the press. It is hard to determine whether this work will instruct or please most. The most material historical facts, from the great era of the treaty of Munster, are touched upon, accompanied by the most solid reflections, and adorned by all that elegancy of style which was peculiar to himself, and in which, if Cicero equals, he certainly does not exceed him, but every other writer falls short of him. I would advise you almost to get this book by heart. I think you have a turn to history, you love it, and have a memory to retain it; this book will teach you the proper use of it. Some people load their memories indiscriminately with historical facts, as others do their stomachs with food; and bring out the one, and bring up the other, entirely crude and undigested. You will find in Lord Bolingbroke's book an infallible specific against that epidemical complaint.

I remember a gentleman, who had read history in this thoughtless and undistinguishing manner, and who, having travelled, had gone through the Valteline. He told me that it was a miserable poor country, and therefore it was surely a great error in Cardinal Richelieu to make such a rout, and put France to so much expense about it. Had my friend read history as he ought to have done, he would have known that the great object of that great minister was to reduce the power of the house of Austria; and, in order to do that, to cut off as much as he could the communication between the several parts of their then extensive dominions; which reflections would have justified the Cardinal to him in the affair

---

* The name of this nobleman, the last descendant in the male line of the great Lord Clarendon, is enshrined not only in the prose of Bolingbroke but in the verse of Pope: "Disdain whatever Cornbury disdains!" He died before his father in 1753, and at the death of the latter, a few months afterwards, both the Earldom of Clarendon (1661) and that of Rochester (1682) which had centred in him became extinct.—M.

of the Valteline. But it was easier to him to remember facts than to combine and reflect.

One observation I hope you will make in reading history, for it is an obvious and a true one. It is: that more people have made great figures and great fortunes in Courts by their exterior accomplishments than by their interior qualifications. Their engaging address, the politeness of their manners, their air, their turn, has almost always paved the way for their superior abilities, if they have such, to exert themselves. They have been favourites before they have been ministers. In Courts, an universal gentleness and *douceur dans le manières* is most absolutely necessary; an offended fool, or a slighted *valet de chambre*, may very possibly do you more hurt at Court than ten men of merit can do you good.

Fools and low people are always jealous of their dignity, and never forget nor forgive what they reckon a slight. On the other hand, they take civility and a little attention as a favour, remember and acknowledge it; this, in my mind, is buying them cheap, and therefore they are worth buying. The Prince himself, who is rarely the shining genius of his Court, esteems you only by hearsay, but likes you by his senses, that is, from your air, your politeness, and your manner of addressing him, of which alone he is a judge. There is a Court garment, as well as a wedding garment, without which you will not be received. That garment is the *volto sciolto*, an imposing air, an elegant politeness, easy and engaging manners, universal attention, an insinuating gentleness, and all those *je ne sçais quoi* that compose the *graces*.

I am this moment disagreeably interrupted by a letter: not from you, as I expected, but from a friend of yours at Paris, who informs me that you have a fever, which confines you at home. Since you have a fever, I am glad you have prudence enough with it to stay at home, and take care of yourself; a little more prudence might probably have prevented it. Your blood is young, and consequently hot, and you naturally make a great deal, by your good stomach and good digestion; you should therefore necessarily attenuate and cool it, from time to time, by gentle purges, or by a very low diet, for two or three days together, if you would avoid fevers. Lord Bacon, who was a very great physician, in both senses of the word, has this aphorism in his Essay upon Health, *Nihil magis ad sanitatem tribuit quam crebræ et domesticæ purgationes.* By *domesticæ,* he means those simple uncompounded purgatives which everybody can administer to themselves—such as senna-tea, stewed prunes and senna, chewing a little rhubarb, or dissolving an ounce and a half of manna in fair water, with the juice of half a lemon to make it palatable. Such gentle and unconfining evacuations would certainly prevent those feverish attacks, to which everybody at your age is subject.

By the way, I do desire, and insist, that whenever, from any indisposition, you are not able to write to me upon the fixed days, that Christian shall ; and give me a *true* account how you are. I do not expect from him the Ciceronian epistolary style ; but I will content myself with the Swiss simplicity and truth.

I hope you extend your acquaintance at Paris, and frequent variety of companies—the only way of knowing the world. Every set of company differs in some particulars from another ; and a man of business must, in the course of his life, have to do with all sorts. It is a very great advantage to know the languages of the several countries one travels in ; and different companies may, in some degree, be considered as different countries. Each has its distinctive language, customs, and manners ; know them all, and you will wonder at none.

Adieu, child ! Take care of your health ; there are no pleasures without it.

CLXXXVIII.

London, *February* 20, O.S. 1752.

My dear Friend,

In all systems whatsoever, whether of religion, government, morals, etc., perfection is the object always proposed, though possibly unattainable—hitherto, at least, certainly unattained. However, those who aim carefully at the mark itself, will unquestionably come nearer to it than those who, from despair, negligence, or indolence, leave to chance the work of skill. The maxim holds equally true in common life ; those who aim at perfection will come infinitely nearer to it than those desponding or indolent spirits, who foolishly say to themselves—Nobody is perfect ; perfection is unattainable ; to attempt it is chimerical ; I

shall do as well as others; why then should I give myself trouble
to be what I never can, and what, according to the common course
of things, I need not be—*perfect?*

I am very sure that I need not point out to you the weakness
and the folly of this reasoning, if it deserves the name of reasoning. It would discourage, and put a stop to the exertion of any
one of our faculties. On the contrary, a man of sense and spirit
says to himself, Though the point of perfection may (considering
the imperfection of our nature) be unattainable, my care, my
endeavours, my attention, shall not be wanting to get as near it
as I can. I will approach it every day; possibly I may arrive at
it at last; at least, (what I am sure is in my own power) I will
not be distanced. Many fools (speaking of you) say to me, What,
would you have him perfect? I answer, Why not? What hurt
would it do him or me? Oh, but that is impossible, say they. I
reply, I am not sure of that; perfection in the abstract I admit
to be unattainable; but what is commonly called perfection in a
character, I maintain to be attainable, and not only that, but in
every man's power. He has, continue they, a good head, a good
heart, a good fund of knowledge, which will increase daily; what
would you have more? Why, I would have everything more that
can adorn and complete a character. Will it do his head, his
heart, or his knowledge, any harm, to have the utmost delicacy of
manners, the most shining advantages of air and address, the
most endearing attentions, and the most engaging graces? But
as he is, say they, he is loved wherever he is known. I am very
glad of it, say I; but I would have him be liked before he is
known, and loved afterwards. I would have him, by his first
abord and address, make people wish to know him, and inclined
to love him; he will save a great deal of time by it. Indeed,
reply they, you are too nice, to exact, and lay too much stress
upon things that are of very little consequence. Indeed, rejoin I,
you know very little of the nature of mankind, if you take those
things to be of little consequence; one cannot be too attentive to
them; it is they that always engage the heart, of which the
understanding is commonly the bubble. And I would much
rather that he erred in a point of grammar, of history, of philosophy, etc., than in a point of manners and address. But consider, he is very young, all this will come in time. I hope so;

but that time must be while he is young, or it will never be at all; the right *pli* must be taken young, or it will never be easy, nor seem natural. Come, come, say they (substituting, as is frequently done, assertion instead of argument) depend upon it he will do very well; and you have a great deal of reason to be satisfied with him. I hope and believe he will do well, but I would have him to do better than well. I am very well pleased with him, but I would be more, I would be proud of him. I would have him have lustre as well as weight. Did you ever know any body that re-united all these talents? Yes, I did; Lord Bolingbroke joined all the politeness, the manners, and the graces of a courtier, to the solidity of a statesman, and to the learning of a pedant. He was *omnis homo;* and pray what should hinder my boy from being so too, if he has, as I think he has, all the other qualifications that you allow him? Nothing can hinder him, but neglect of, or inattention to, those objects, which his own good sense must tell him are of infinite consequence to him, and which therefore I will not suppose him capable of either neglecting or despising.

This (to tell you the whole truth) is the result of a controversy that passed yesterday, between Lady Hervey and myself, upon your subject, and almost in the very words. I submit the decision of it to yourself; let your own good sense determine it, and make you act in consequence of that determination. The receipt to make this composition is short and infallible; here I give it you:

Take variety of the best company, wherever you are; be minutely attentive to every word and action; imitate respectively those whom you observe to be distinguished and considered for any one accomplishment; then mix all those several accomplishments together, and serve them up yourself to others.

I hope your fair, or rather your brown *American* is well. I hear that she makes very handsome presents, if she is not so herself. I am told there are people at Paris who expect from this secret connection to see in time a volume of letters superior to Madame de Graffigny's* Peruvian ones; I lay in my claim to one of the first copies.

* Frances d'Issembourg, born 1694, died 1758, was the wife of Hugues de Graffigny, chamberlain of the Duke of Lorraine, from whom she was separated on account of his brutality. She wrote the drama of *Cenie*, and *Lettres*

Francis's *Cenie* * has been acted twice with most universal
applause; to-night is his third night, and I am going to it. I
did not think it would have succeeded so well, considering how
long our British audiences have been accustomed to murder,
racks, and poison, in every tragedy; but it affected the heart so
much, that it triumphed over habit and prejudice. All the
women cried, and all the men were moved. The prologue,
which is a very good one, was made entirely by Garrick. The
epilogue is old Cibber's, but corrected, though not enough, by
Francis. He will get a great deal of money by it; and consequently be better able to lend you sixpence upon an emergency.

The Parliament of Paris, I find by the newspapers, has not
carried its point concerning the hospitals; and though the King
has given up the Archbishop, yet, as he has put them under the
management and direction *du Grand Conseil*, the Parliament is
equally out of the question. This will naturally put you upon
inquiring into the constitution of the *Grand Conseil*. You will,
doubtless, inform yourself, who it is composed of, what things
are *de son ressort*, whether or not there lies an appeal from thence
to any other place; and of all other particulars that may give you
a clear notion of this assembly. There are also three or four
other *Conseils* in France, of which you ought to know the constitution and the objects; I dare say you do know them already,
but if you do not, lose no time in informing yourself. These
things, as I have often told you, are best learned in various
French companies, but in no English ones; for none of our
countrymen trouble their heads about them. To use a very true
image, collect, like the bee, your store from every quarter. In
some companies (*parmi les fermiers généraux nommément*) you
may, by proper inquiries, get a general knowledge at least of *les
affaires de finances*. When you are with *des gens de robe*, suck

d'une Péruvienne, which first appeared, without her name, in 1747. She
was an associate of theAcademy of Florence, and received a pension from
the Court of Vienna.

* *Eugenia*, a translation, or imitation, of Madame de Graffigny's
Cenie. Philip Francis, son of the Dean of Lismore, and father of Sir
Philip Francis, is best known as the translator of Horace. He was
educated at Trinity College, Dublin; kept a school at Esher, where
Gibbon was one of his pupils; and died in 1773. See Letter of December
24, 1750, and Letter to Madame du Boccage of March 4, 1752.

them with regard to the constitution, and civil government, and *sic de cæteris.*

This shows you the advantage of keeping a great deal of different French company; an advantage much superior to any that you can possibly receive from loitering and sauntering away evenings in any English company at Paris, not even excepting Lord Albemarle's. Love of ease and fear of restraint (to both which I doubt you are, for a young fellow, too much addicted), may invite you among your countrymen; but pray withstand those mean temptations, *et prenez sur vous,* for the sake of being in those assemblies, which alone can inform your mind and improve your manners. You have not now many months to continue at Paris; make the most of them; get into every house there if you can; extend acquaintance, know everything and everybody there; that when you leave it for other places you may be *au fait,* and even able to explain whatever you may hear mentioned concerning it. Adieu!

CLXXXIX.

LONDON, *March* 2, O.S. 1752.

MY DEAR FRIEND,

Whereabouts are you in Ariosto? Or have you gone through that most ingenious contexture of truth and lies, of serious and extravagant, of knights-errant, magicians, and all that various matter, which he announces in the beginning of his poem:

> Le donne, i cavalier, l'arme, gli amori,
> Le cortesie, l'audaci imprese io canto.

I am by no means sure that Homer had superior invention, or excelled more in description, than Ariosto. What can be more seducing and voluptuous than the description of Alcina's person and palace? What more ingeniously extravagant than the search made in the moon for Orlando's lost wits, and the account of other people's that were found there? The whole is worth your attention, not only as an ingenious poem, but as the source of all modern tales, novels, fables, and romances, as Ovid's *Metamorphosis* was of the ancient ones; besides that, when you have read this work, nothing will be difficult to you in the Italian language. You will read Tasso's *Gierusalemme,* and the *Decame-*

rone di Boccaccio with great facility afterwards; and when you
have read these three authors, you will, in my opinion, have read
all the works of invention that are worth reading in that language;
though the Italians would be very angry at me for saying so.

A gentleman should know those which I call classical works,
in every language—such as Boileau, Corneille, Racine, Molière,
etc., in French; Milton, Dryden, Pope, Swift, etc., in English;
and the three authors above-mentioned in Italian. Whether you
have any such in German, I am not quite sure, nor, indeed, am
I inquisitive. These sort of books adorn the mind, improve the
fancy, are frequently alluded to by, and are often the subjects
of conversations of the best companies. As you have languages
to read, and memory to retain them, the knowledge of them is
very well worth the little pains it will cost you, and will enable
you to shine in company. It is not pedantic to quote and allude
to them, which it would be with regard to the ancients.

Among the many advantages which you have had in your
education, I do not consider your knowledge of several languages
as the least. You need not trust to translations; you can go to
the source; you can both converse and negotiate with people of
all nations, upon equal terms, which is by no means the case
of a man who converses or negotiates in a language which those
with whom he has to do know much better than himself. In
business, a great deal may depend upon the force and extent of
one word; and in conversation, a moderate thought may gain, or
a good one lose, by the propriety or impropriety, the elegancy
or inelegancy, of one single word. As, therefore, you now know
four modern languages well, I would have you study (and, by
the way, it will be very little trouble to you) to know them correctly, accurately, and delicately. Read some little books that
treat of them, and ask questions concerning their delicacies of
those who are able to answer you : as, for instance, should I say
in French, *la lettre que je vous ai* écrit, or *la lettre que je vous ai*
écrite? in which, I think, the French differ among themselves.
There is a short French grammar by the Port Royal, and another
by Père Buffier,* both which are worth your reading; as is also

---

* Claude Buffier was a Jesuit, and a contributor to the well-known
Journal de Trévoux. His French grammar appeared in 1709. Born 1661,
died 1737.

a little book called *les Synonimes François*. There are books of that kind upon the Italian language, into some of which I would advise you to dip. Possibly the German language may have something of the same sort; and since you already speak it, the more properly you speak it the better; one would, I think, as far as possible, do all one does correctly and elegantly. It is extremely engaging, to people of every nation, to meet with a foreigner who has taken pains enough to speak their language correctly; it flatters that local and national pride and prejudice, of which everybody has some share.

Francis's *Eugenia*, which I will send you, pleased most people of good taste here; the boxes were crowded till the sixth night, when the pit and gallery were totally deserted, and it was dropped. Distress, without death, was not sufficient to affect a true British audience, so long accustomed to daggers, racks, and bowls of poison; contrary to Horace's rule, they desire to see Medea murder her children upon the stage. The sentiments were too delicate to move them; and their hearts are to be taken by storm, not by parley.

Have you got the things which were taken from you at Calais restored?—and among them, the little packet which my sister gave you for Sir Charles Hotham? In this case, have you forwarded it to him? If you have not yet had an opportunity, you will have one soon, which I desire you will not omit; it is by Monsieur D'Aillon, whom you will see in a few days at Paris, in his way to Geneva, where Sir Charles now is, and will remain some time. Adieu!

CXC.

LONDON, *March* 5, O.S. 1752.

MY DEAR FRIEND,

As I have received no letter from you by the usual post, I am uneasy upon account of your health; for, had you been well, I am sure you would have written, according to your engagement and my requisition. You have not the least notion of any care of your health; but, though I would not have you be a valetudinarian, I must tell you, that the best and most robust health requires some degree of attention to preserve. Young fellows, thinking they have so much health and time before them,

are very apt to neglect or lavish both, and beggar themselves
before they are aware; whereas a prudent economy in both would
make them rich indeed; and, so far from breaking in upon their
pleasures, would improve, and almost perpetuate them. Be you
wiser; and, before it is too late, manage both with care and
frugality, and lay out neither, but upon good interest and
security.

I will now confine myself to the employment of your time,
which, though I have often touched upon formerly, is a subject
that, from its importance, will bear repetition. You have, it is
true, a great deal of time before you; but, in this period of your
life, one hour usefully employed may be worth more than four-
and-twenty hereafter; a minute is precious to you now, whole
days may possibly not be so forty years hence. Whatever time
you allow, or can snatch, for serious reading (I say snatch,
because company and a knowledge of the world is now your chief
object), employ it in the reading of some one book, and that a
good one, till you have finished it; and do not distract your
mind with various matters at the same time. In this light I
would recommend to you to read *tout de suite* Grotius * *de Jure
Belli et Pacis*, translated by Barbeyrac,† and Puffendorff's *Jus
Gentium*, translated by the same hand. For accidental quarters
of hours, read works of invention, wit, and humour, of the best,
and not of trivial authors, either ancient or modern.

Whatever business you have, do it the first moment you can;
never by halves, but finish it without interruption, if possible.
Business must not be sauntered and trifled with; and you must
not say to it, as Felix did to Paul, "at a more convenient season
I will speak to thee." The most convenient season for business
is the first; but study and business, in some measure, point out
their own times, to a man of sense; time is much oftener squan-
dered away in the wrong choice and improper methods of
amusement and pleasures.

Many people think that they are in pleasures, provided they
are neither in study nor in business. Nothing like it; they are
doing nothing, and might just as well be asleep. They contract

---

* Hugo Grotius was born at Delft in Holland in 1583, and died in 1645.

† Jean Barbeyrac, professor of law at Berne, translated Grotius and
Puffendorff's works into French. Born 1674, died 1747.

habitudes from laziness, and they only frequent those places where they are free from all restraints and attentions. Be upon your guard against this idle profusion of time; and let every place you go to be either the scene of quick and lively pleasures, or the school of your improvements; let every company you go into either gratify your senses, extend your knowledge, or refine your manners. Have some decent object of gallantry in view at some places; frequent others, where people of wit and taste assemble; get into others, where people of superior rank and dignity command respect and attention from the rest of the company; but pray frequent no neutral places, from mere idleness and indolence. Nothing forms a young man so much as being used to keep respectable and superior company, where a constant regard and attention is necessary. It is true, this is at first a disagreeable state of restraint; but it soon grows habitual, and consequently easy; and you are amply paid for it by the improvement you make, and the credit it gives you. What you said some time ago was very true, concerning le Palais Royal; to one of your age the situation is disagreeable enough; you cannot expect to be much taken notice of; but all that time you can take notice of others; observe their manners, decipher their characters, and insensibly you will become one of the company.

All this I went through myself, when I was of your age. I have sat hours in company, without being taken the least notice of; but then I took notice of them, and learned, in their company, how to behave myself better in the next, till by degrees I became part of the best companies myself. But I took great care not to lavish away my time in those companies where there were neither quick pleasures nor useful improvements to be expected.

Sloth, indolence, and mollesse are pernicious and unbecoming a young fellow; let them be your resource forty years hence at soonest. Determine, at all events, and however disagreeable it may be to you in some respects, and for some time, to keep the most distinguished and fashionable company of the place you are at, either for their rank, or for their learning, or le bel esprit et le goût. This gives you credentials to the best companies, whereever you go afterwards. Pray, therefore, no indolence, no laziness; but employ every minute of your life in active pleasures or useful employments. Address yourself to some woman of fashion and beauty, wherever you are, and try how far that will go. If the place be not secured beforehand and garrisoned, nine times in ten you will take it. By attentions and respect you may always get into the highest company; and by some admiration and applause, whether merited or not, you may be sure of being welcome among *les sçavants et les beaux esprits.* There are but these three sorts of company for a young fellow, there being neither pleasure nor profit in any other.

My uneasiness with regard to your health is this moment removed by your letter of the 8th, N.S. which, by what accident I do not know, I did not receive before.

I long to read Voltaire's *Rome Sauvée,* which, by the very faults that your *severe* critics find with it, I am sure I shall like; for I will at any time give up a good deal of regularity for a great deal of *brillant;* and for the *brillant* surely nobody is equal to Voltaire. Catiline's conspiracy is an unhappy subject for a tragedy; it is too single, and gives no opportunity to the poet to excite any of the tender passions; the whole is one intended act of horror. Crébillon was sensible of this defect; and, to create another interest, most absurdly made Catiline in love with Cicero's daughter, and her with him.

I am very glad you went to Versailles, and dined with Monsieur de St. Contest.* That is company to learn *les bonnes manières* in; and it seems you had *les bons morceaux* into the bargain. Though you were no part of the King of France's conversation with the foreign ministers, and probably not much entertained with it, do you think that it is not very useful to you to hear it, and to observe the turn and manners of people of that sort? It is extremely useful to know it well. The same in the next rank of people, such as Ministers of State, etc., in whose company, though you cannot yet, at your age, bear a part, and consequently be diverted, you will observe and learn what hereafter it may be necessary for you to act.

Tell Sir John Lambert that I have this day fixed Mr. Spencer's

---

* François Dominique, Marquis de St. Contest, born in 1701, had, in September, 1751, succeeded the Marquis de Puisieux as Minister for Foreign Affairs. Madame de Pompadour in truth governed absolutely under his name. He died in 1754.—M.

having his credit upon him; Mr. Hoare had also recommended him. I believe Mr. Spencer will set out next month for some place in France, but not Paris. I am sure he wants a great deal of France; for at present he is most entirely English; and you know very well what I think of that. And so we bid you heartily good night.

CXCI.*

* * * * * *

(*March*, 1752.)

A Chapter of the Garter is to be held at St. James's next Friday; in which Prince Edward, the Prince of Orange, the Earls of Lincoln, Winchelsea, and Cardigan, are to be elected Knights Companions of the Order of the Garter. Though solely nominated by the Crown, they are said to be elected; because there is a pretended election. All the Knights are summoned to attend the Sovereign at a Chapter, to be held on such a day, in order to elect so many new Knights into the vacant stalls of the deceased ones; accordingly they meet in the Council Chamber, where they all sit down according to their seniority, at a long table, where the Sovereign presides. There every Knight pretends to write a list of those for whom he intends to vote; and, in effect, writes down nine names, such as he thinks proper, taking care, however, to insert the names of those who are really to be elected; then the Bishop of Salisbury, who is always the Chancellor of the Order, goes round the table, and takes the paper of each Knight, pretends to look into them, and then declares the majority of votes to be for those persons who were nominated by the Crown. Upon this declaration, two of the old Knights go into the outward room, where the new ones are attending, and introduce them, one after another, according to their ranks. The new Knight kneels down before the King, who puts the riband about his neck: then he turns to the Prince of Wales, or, in his absence, to the oldest Knight, who puts the Garter about his leg. This is the ceremony of the Chapter; that of the Installation, which is always performed in St. George's

---

* This is only a fragment of a letter, and was formerly printed at the end of the Correspondence; but the date may be fixed from the fact that the Chapter of the Garter took place on the 13th March, 1752.

Chapel, at Windsor, completes the whole thing; for till then the new Knights cannot wear the Star, unless by a particular dispensation from the Sovereign, which is very seldom granted.

All ceremonies are in themselves very silly things; but yet, a man of the world should know them. They are the outworks of manners and decency, which would be too often broken in upon, if it were not for that defence, which keeps the enemy at a proper distance. It is for that reason that I always treat fools and coxcombs with great ceremony; true good breeding not being a sufficient barrier against them. The knowledge of the world teaches one to deal with different people differently, and according as characters and situations require. The *versatile ingenium* is a most essential point; and a man must be broke to it while he is young. Have it always in your thoughts, as I have you in mine.

P.S.—This moment I receive your letter of the 15th, N.S. with which I am very well pleased; it informs me, and, what I like still better, it shows me that you are informed.
Adieu.

CXCII.

LONDON, *March* 16, O.S. 1752.

My dear Friend,

How do you go on with the most useful and most necessary of all studies, the study of the world? Do you find that you gain knowledge? And does your daily experience at once extend and demonstrate your improvement? You will possibly ask me how you can judge of that yourself. I will tell you a sure way of knowing. Examine yourself, and see whether your notions of the world are changed, by experience, from what they were two years ago in theory; for that alone is one favourable symptom of improvement. At that age (I remember it in myself) every notion that one forms is erroneous; one has seen few models, and those none of the best, to form one's self upon. One thinks that everything is to be carried by spirit and vigour; that art is meanness, and that versatility and complaisance are the refuge of pusillanimity and weakness. This most mistaken opinion gives an indelicacy, a *brusquerie*, and a roughness to the manners. Fools, who can never be undeceived, retain them as long as they live; reflection, with a little experience, makes men of sense shake them off soon. When they come to be a little better acquainted with themselves, and with their own species, they discover that plain right reason is, nine times in ten, the fettered and shackled attendant of the triumph of the heart and passions; consequently they address themselves nine times in ten to the conqueror, not to the conquered; and conquerors, you know, must be applied to in the gentlest, the most engaging, and the most insinuating manner.

Have you found out that every woman is infallibly to be gained by every sort of flattery, and every man by one sort or other? Have you discovered what variety of little things affect the heart, and how surely they collectively gain it? If you have you have made some progress. I would try a man's knowledge of the world as I would a schoolboy's knowledge of Horace; not by making him construe *Mœcenas atavis edite regibus*, which he could do in the first form, but by examining him as to the delicacy and *curiosa felicitas* of that poet. A man requires very little knowledge and experience of the world, to understand glaring, high-coloured, and decided characters; they are but few, and they strike at first; but to distinguish the almost imperceptible shades, and the nice gradations of virtue and vice, sense and folly, strength and weakness (of which characters are commonly composed) demands some experience, great observation, and minute attention. In the same cases, most people do the same things, but with this material difference, upon which the success commonly turns.—A man who has studied the world knows when to time, and where to place them; he has analysed the characters he applies to, and adapted his address and his arguments to them; but a man of what is called plain good sense, who has only reasoned by himself, and not acted with mankind, mistimes, misplaces, runs precipitately and bluntly at the mark, and falls upon his nose in the way.

In the common manners of social life, every man of common sense has the rudiments, the A B C of civility; the means not to offend; and even wishes to please; and, if he has any real merit, will be received and tolerated in good company. But that is far from being enough; for though he may be received, he will never be desired; though he does not offend, he will never be loved; but, like some little, insignificant, neutral power,

surrounded by great ones, he will neither be feared nor courted
by any; but by turns invaded by all whenever it is their interest.
A most contemptible situation! Whereas, a man who has carefully attended to, and experienced the various workings of the
heart, and the artifices of the head; and who by one shade can
trace the progression of the whole colour; who can, at the
proper times, employ all the several means of persuading the
understanding, and engaging the heart; may and will have
enemies, but will and must have friends; he may be opposed,
but he will be supported too; his talents may excite the jealousy
of some, but his engaging hearts will make him beloved by many
more; he will be considerable, he will be considered.

Many different qualifications must conspire to form such a
man, and to make him at once respectable and amiable, and the
least must be joined to the greatest; the latter would be unavailing without the former; and the former would be futile and
frivolous without the latter. Learning is acquired by reading
books; but the much more necessary learning, the knowledge of
the world, is only to be acquired by reading men, and studying
all the various editions of them. Many words in every language
are generally thought to be synonymous; but those who study the
language attentively will find that there is no such thing; they
will discover some little difference, some distinction, between all
those words that are vulgarly called synonymous; one has always
more energy, extent, or delicacy, than another; it is the same
with men; all are in general, and yet no two in particular, exactly
alike. Those who have not accurately studied, perpetually mistake them; they do not discern the shades and gradations that
distinguish characters seemingly alike. Company, various com-
company, is the only school for this knowledge. You ought to
be by this time at least in the third form of that school, from
whence the rise to the uppermost is easy and quick; but then you
must have application and vivacity; and you must not only bear
with, but even seek, restraint in most companies, instead of stag-
nating in one or two only, where indolence and love of ease may
be indulged.

In the plan which I gave you in my last,* for your future

* That letter is missing; or else the plan was comprised in that part
of the previous letter which was lost.

motions, I forgot to tell you, that, if a King of the Romans should be chosen this year, you shall certainly be at that election; and as upon those occasions, all strangers are excluded from the place of the election, except such as belong to some Ambassador, I have already eventually secured you a place in the *suite* of the King's Electoral Ambassador, who will be sent upon that account to Frankfort, or wherever else the election may be. This will not only secure you a sight of the show, but a knowledge of the whole thing; which is likely to be a contested one, from the opposition of some of the electors and the protests of some of the princes of the empire. That election, if there is one, will, in my opinion, be a memorable era in the history of the empire; pens at least, if not swords, will be drawn; and ink, if not blood, will be plentifully shed, by the contending parties in that dispute.

During the fray, you may securely plunder, and add to your present stock of knowledge of the *jus publicum imperii.* The Court of France has, I am told, appointed le President Ogier,* a man of great abilities, to go immediately to Ratisbon, *pour y souffler la discorde.* It must be owned, that France has always profited skilfully of its having guaranteed the treaty of Munster; which has given it a constant pretence to thrust itself into the affairs of the empire. When France got Alsace yielded by treaty, it was very willing to have held it as a fief of the empire; but the empire was then wiser. Every power should be very careful, not to give the least pretence to a neighbouring power to meddle with the affairs of its interior. Sweden has already felt the effects of the Czarina's calling herself guarantee of its present form of government, in consequence of the treaty of Neustadt, confirmed afterwards by that of Abo; though, in truth, that guarantee was rather a provision against Russia's attempting to alter the then new-established form of government in Sweden, than any right given to Russia to hinder the Swedes from establishing what form of government they pleased. Read them both, if you can get them. Adieu.

* Le President Ogier became afterwards French Ambassador in Denmark, and was reprimanded by his Court for the part which he took in the Convention of Kloster-Seven.—See Sismondi, *Hist. des Français,* vol. xxix. p. 148.—M.

CXCIII.

LONDON, *April* 13, O.S. 1752.

MY DEAR FRIEND,

I receive this moment your letter of the 19th, N.S. with the enclosed pieces relative to the present dispute between the King and the Parliament. I shall return them by Lord Huntingdon, whom you will soon see at Paris, and who will likewise carry you the piece, which I forgot in making up the packet I sent you by the Spanish Ambassador. The representation of the Parliament is very well drawn, *suaviter in modo, fortiter in re.* They tell the king very respectfully, that in a certain case, *which they should think it criminal to suppose,* they would not obey him. This has a tendency to what we call here Revolution principles.

I do not know what the Lord's anointed, his viceregent upon earth, divinely appointed by him, and accountable to none but him for his actions, will either think or do, upon these symptoms of reason and good sense, which seem to be breaking out all over France; but this I foresee, that before the end of this century, the trade of both King and priest will not be half so good a one as it has been. Duclos, in his Reflections, has observed, and very truly, *qu'il y a un germe de raison qui commence à se développer en France.* A *développement* that must prove fatal to Regal and Papal pretensions. Prudence may, in many cases, recommend an occasional submission to either; but when that ignorance, upon which an implicit faith in both could only be founded, is once removed, God's viceregent, and Christ's vicar, will only be obeyed and believed, as far as what the one orders, and the other says, is conformable to reason and truth.

I am very glad (to use a vulgar expression) that *you make as if you* were not well, though you really are; I am sure it is the likeliest way to keep so. Pray leave off entirely your greasy, heavy pastry, fat creams, and indigestible dumplings; and then you need not confine yourself to white meats, which I do not take to be one jot wholesomer than beef, mutton, and partridge.

Voltaire sent me from Berlin his History *du Siècle de Louis XIV.* It came at a very proper time; Lord Bolingbroke had just taught me how History should be read; Voltaire shows me how it should be written. I am sensible that it will meet with almost as many critics as readers. Voltaire must be criticised; besides, every man's favourite is attacked; for every prejudice is exposed, and our prejudices are our mistresses; reason is at best our wife, very often heard indeed, but seldom minded. It is the history of the human understanding, written by a man of parts, for the use of men of parts. Weak minds will not like it, even though they do not understand it; which is commonly the measure of their admiration. Dull ones will want those minute and uninteresting details, with which most other histories are encumbered. He tells me all I want to know, and nothing more. His reflections are short, just, and produce others in his readers. Free from religious, philosophical, political, and national prejudices, beyond any historian I ever met with, he relates all those matters as truly and as impartially, as certain regards, which must always be to some degree observed, will allow him; for one sees plainly, that he often says much less than he would say, if he might. He has made me much better acquainted with the times of Louis XIV. than the innumerable volumes which I had read could do; and has suggested this reflection to me, which I had never made before—His vanity, not his knowledge, made him encourage all, and introduce many arts and sciences in his country. He opened in a manner the human understanding in France, and brought it to its utmost perfection; his age equalled in all, and greatly exceeded in many things (pardon me, pedants!) the Augustan. This was great and rapid; but still it might be done, by the encouragement, the applause, and the rewards of a vain, liberal, and magnificent Prince. What is much more surprising, is, that he stopped the operations of the human mind, just where he pleased; and seemed to say, "thus far shalt thou go, and no farther." For, a bigot to his religion, and jealous of his power, free and rational thoughts upon either never entered into a French head during his reign; and the greatest geniuses that ever any age produced, never entertained a doubt of the Divine right of Kings, or the infallibility of the Church. Poets, Orators, and Philosophers, ignorant of their natural rights, cherished their chains; and blind active faith triumphed, in those great minds, over silent and passive reason. The reverse of this seems now to be the case in France; reason opens itself; fancy and invention fade and decline.

I will send you a copy of this history by Lord Huntingdon, as I think it very probable that it is not allowed to be published and sold at Paris. Pray read it more than once, and with attention, particularly the second volume, which contains short, but very clear accounts of many very interesting things, which are talked of by everybody, though fairly understood by very few. There are two very puerile affectations, which I wish this book had been free from; the one is, the total subversion of all the old established French orthography; the other is, the not making use of any one capital letter throughout the whole book, except at the beginning of a paragraph. It offends my eyes to see rome, paris, france, cæsar, henry the 4th, etc., begin with small letters; and I do not conceive, that there can be any reason for doing it half so strong as the reason of long usage is to the contrary. This is an affectation below Voltaire; * whom, I am not ashamed to say, that I admire and delight in, as an author, equally in prose and in verse.

I had a letter a few days ago, from Monsieur du Boccage, in which he says, *Monsieur Stanhope s'est jetté dans la politique, et je crois qu'il y réussira;* you do very well, it is your destination; but remember, that to succeed in great things, one must first learn to please in little ones. Engaging manners and address must prepare the way for superior knowledge and abilities to act with effect. The late Duke of Marlborough's manners and address prevailed with the first King of Prussia to let his troops remain in the army of the Allies, when neither their representations, nor his own share in the common cause, could do it. The Duke of Marlborough had no new matter to urge to him, but had a manner which he could not, and did not, resist. Voltaire, among a thousand little delicate strokes of that kind, says of the Duke de la Feuillade,† *qu'il était l'homme le plus brillant et le plus aimable du Royaume, et quoique gendre du Ministre, il avoit pour lui la faveur publique.* Various little circumstances of that sort will often make a man of great real merit be hated, if he has not address and manners to make him be loved. Consider all your own circumstances seriously, and you will find, that, of all

* This affectation has been judiciously corrected in the subsequent editions.—M.

See Voltaire's *Siècle de Louis XIV.*, ch. xix

the arts, the art of pleasing is the most necessary for you to study and possess. A silly tyrant said, *oderint modo timeant;* a wise man would have said, *modo ament nihil timendum est mihi.* Judge from your own daily experience, of the efficacy of that pleasing *je ne sçais quoi,* when you feel, as you and everybody certainly does, that in men it is more engaging than knowledge, in women than beauty.

I long to see Lord and Lady —— (who are not yet arrived), because they have lately seen you; and I always fancy that I can fish out something new concerning you from those who have seen you last; not that I shall much rely upon their accounts, because I distrust the judgment of Lord and Lady —— in those matters about which I am most inquisitive. They have ruined their own son, by what they called and thought, loving him. They have made him believe that the world was made for him, not he for the world; and unless he stays abroad a great while, and falls into very good company, he will expect, what he will never find, the attentions and complaisance from others which he has hitherto been used to from Papa and Mamma. This, I fear, is too much the case of Mr. ——, who, I doubt, will be run through the body, and be near dying, before he knows how to live. However you may turn out, you can never make me any of these reproaches. I indulged no silly womanish fondness for you: instead of inflicting my tenderness upon you, I have taken all possible methods to make you deserve it; and thank God, you do; at least, I know but one article in which you are different from what I could wish you, and you very well know what that is. I want that I and all the world should like you as well as I love you. Adieu.

CXCIV.

LONDON, *April* 30, O.S. 1752.

MY DEAR FRIEND,

Avoir du monde is, in my opinion, a very just and happy expression for having address, manners, and for knowing how to behave properly in all companies; and it implies very truly, that a man that has not these accomplishments, is not of the world. Without them, the best parts are inefficient, civility is absurd, and freedom offensive. A learned parson, rusting in his cell at Oxford or Cambridge, will reason admirably well upon the nature of man; will profoundly analyse the head, the heart, the reason, the will, the passions, the senses, the sentiments, and all those subdivisions of we know not what; and yet, unfortunately, he knows nothing of man, for he has not lived with him, and is ignorant of all the various modes, habits, prejudices, and tastes, that always influence and often determine him. He views man as he does colours in Sir Isaac Newton's prism, where only the capital ones are seen; but an experienced dyer knows all their various shades and gradations, together with the result of their several mixtures. Few men are of one plain, decided colour; most are mixed, shaded, and blended; and vary as much, from different situations, as changeable silks do from different lights.

The man *qui a du monde* knows all this from his own experience and observation; the conceited cloister philosopher knows nothing of it from his own theory; his practice is absurd and improper, and he acts as awkwardly as a man would dance who had never seen others dance, nor learned of a dancing-master, but who had only studied the notes by which dances are now pricked down as well as tunes. Observe and imitate, then, the address, the arts, and the manners of those *qui ont du monde :* see by what methods they first make, and afterwards improve, impressions in their favour. Those impressions are much oftener owing to little causes than to intrinsic merit, which is less volatile, and has not so sudden an effect. Strong minds have undoubtedly an ascendant over weak ones, as Galigai Maréchale d'Ancre very justly observed, when, to the disgrace and reproach of those times, she was executed * for having governed Mary of Medicis by the arts of witchcraft and magic. But then ascendant is to be gained by degrees, and by those arts only which experience and the knowledge of the world teaches; for few are mean enough to be bullied, though most are weak enough to be bubbled. I have often seen people of superior, governed by people of much inferior, parts, without knowing or even suspecting that they were so governed. This can only happen when those people of inferior parts have more worldly dexterity and experience than those they govern. They see the weak and

* On the 8th of July, 1617.

unguarded part, and apply to it: they take it, and all the rest follows. Would you gain either men or women, and every man of sense desires to gain both, *il faut du monde*. You have had more opportunities than ever any man had, at your age, of acquiring *ce monde;* you have been in the best companies of most countries, at an age when others have hardly been in any company at all. You are master of all those languages which John Trott seldom speaks at all, and never well; consequently you need be a stranger nowhere. This is the way, and the only way, of having the *du monde;* but, if you have it not, and have still any coarse rusticity about you, may one not apply to you the *rusticus expectat* of Horace?

This knowledge of the world teaches us more particularly two things, both which are of infinite consequence, and to neither of which nature inclines us; I mean, the command of our temper, and of our countenance. A man who has no *monde* is inflamed with anger, or annihilated with shame, at every disagreeable incident; the one makes him act and talk like a madman, the other makes him look like a fool. But a man who has *du monde*, seems not to understand what he cannot or ought not to resent. If he makes a slip himself, he recovers it by his coolness, instead of plunging deeper by his confusion, like a stumbling horse. He is firm, but gentle; and practises that most excellent maxim, *suaviter in modo, fortiter in re*. The other is the *volto sciolto e pensieri stretti*. People, unused to the world, have babbling countenances; and are unskilful enough to show, what they have sense enough not to tell. In the course of the world, a man must very often put on an easy, frank countenance, upon very disagreeable occasions; he must seem pleased, when he is very much otherwise; he must be able to accost and receive with smiles, those whom he would much rather meet with swords. In Courts he must not turn himself inside out. All this may, nay must be done, without falsehood and treachery; for it must go no farther than politeness and manners, and must stop short of assurances and professions of simulated friendship. Good manners, to those one does not love, are no more a breach of truth, than " your humble servant," at the bottom of a challenge is; they are universally agreed upon, and understood to be things of course. They are necessary guards of the decency and

peace of society; they must only act defensively; and then not
with arms poisoned with perfidy. Truth, but not the whole
truth, must be the invariable principle of every man, who has
either religion, honour, or prudence. Those who violate it, may
be cunning, but they are not able. Lies and perfidy are the
refuge of fools and cowards. Adieu!

P. S. I must recommend to you again, to take your leave of
all your French acquaintance, in such a manner as may make
them regret your departure, and wish to see and welcome you at
Paris again; where you may possibly return before it is very
long. This must not be done in a cold, civil manner, but with
at least seeming warmth, sentiment, and concern. Acknowledge
the obligations you have to them, for the kindness they have
shown you during your stay at Paris; assure them that,
wherever you are, you shall remember them with gratitude;
wish for opportunities of giving them proofs of your *plus tendre
et respectueux souvenir*; beg of them, in case your good fortune
should carry you to any part of the world where you could be of
any the least use to them, that they would employ you without
reserve. Say all this, and a great deal more, emphatically and
pathetically; for you know *si vis me flere*——.* This can do
you no harm, if you never return to Paris; but if you do, as
probably you may, it will be of infinite use to you. Remember
too, not to omit going to every house, where you have ever been
once, to take leave, and recommend yourself to their remembrance. The reputation which you leave at one place, where
you have been, will circulate, and you will meet with it at twenty
places, where you are to go. That is a labour never quite lost.

This letter will show you, that the accident which happened to
me yesterday,† and of which Mr. Grevenkop gives you an
account, has had no bad consequences. My escape was a great
one.

---

* *Si vis me flere, dolendum est. Primum ipsi tibi.*
                  Horace, *De Arte Poetica.*

† A fall from his horse in Hyde Park.—See letter to Mr. Dayrolles of
May 19, 1752.

CXCV.

LONDON, *May* 11, O.S. 1752.

MY DEAR FRIEND,

I break my word by writing this letter; but I break it on the allowable side, by doing more than I promised. I have pleasure in writing to you; and you may possibly have some profit in reading what I write; either of the motives were sufficient for me, both I cannot withstand. By your last, I calculate that you will leave Paris this day se'nnight; upon that supposition, this letter may still find you there.

Colonel Perry arrived here two or three days ago, and sent me a book from you, *Cassandra* * abridged. I am sure it cannot be too much abridged. The spirit of that most voluminous work, fairly extracted, may be contained in the smallest *duodecimo*; and it is most astonishing that there ever could have been people idle enough to write or read such endless heaps of the same stuff. It was, however, the occupation of thousands in the last century; and is still the private, though disavowed, amusement of young girls, and sentimental ladies. A love-sick girl finds in the Captain with whom she is in love all the courage and all the graces of the tender and accomplished Oroondates; and many a grown-up sentimental lady talks delicate Clelia to the hero, whom she would engage to eternal love, or laments with her that love is not eternal.

> Ah! qu'il est doux d'aimer, si l'on aimoit toujours!
> Mais hélas! il n'est point d'éternelles amours.†

It is, however, very well to have read one of those extravagant

---

* *Cassandra*, a romance in ten volumes by Gautier de Costes, Seigneur de la Calprénède; he also wrote *Cleopatre* in twelve volumes. He died in 1663.

† Two lines from the *Clélie* of Mademoiselle de Scudery, which are ridiculed by Boileau in his ingenious dialogue, *Les Héros de Roman.* They are addressed by Lucretia to Brutus, and the reply of Brutus, which Boileau also quotes, is equally mawkish:

> Permettez moi d'aimer, merveille de nos jours,
> Vous verrez qu'on peut voir d'éternelles amours.

Well might the *Pluton* of Boileau's Dialogue exclaim: " Je ne sais tantôt plus où j'en suis. Lucrèce amoureuse! Lucrèce coquette! Et Brutus son gallant!"—M.

works (of all which La Calprénède's are the best), because it is well to be able to talk with some degree of knowledge upon all those subjects that other people talk sometimes upon; and I would by no means have anything that is known to others be totally unknown to you. It is a great advantage for any man to be able to talk or to hear, neither ignorantly nor absurdly, upon any subject; for I have known people, who have not said one word, hear ignorantly and absurdly; it has appeared in their inattentive and unmeaning faces. This, I think, is as little likely to happen to you as to anybody of your age; and if you will but add a versatility and easy conformity of manners, I know no company in which you are likely to be *de trop*.

This versatility is more particularly necessary for you at this time, now that you are going to so many different places; for though the manners and customs of the several Courts of Germany are in general the same, yet every one has its particular characteristic—some peculiarity or other, which distinguishes it from the next. This you should carefully attend to, and immediately adopt. Nothing flatters people more, nor makes strangers so welcome, as such an occasional conformity.

I do not mean by this that you should mimic the air and stiffness of every awkward German Court; no, by no means; but I mean that you should only cheerfully comply and fall in with certain local habits—such as ceremonies, diet, turn of conversation, etc. People who are lately come from Paris, and who have been a good while there, are generally suspected, and especially in Germany, of having a degree of contempt for every other place. Take great care that nothing of this kind appear, at least outwardly, in your behaviour; but commend whatever deserves any degree of commendation, without comparing it with what you may have left, much better, of the same kind at Paris. As, for instance, the German kitchen is, without doubt, execrable, and the French delicious; however, never commend the French kitchen at a German table, but eat of what you can find tolerable there, and commend it, without comparing it to anything better. I have known many British Yahoos, who, though while they were at Paris conformed to no one French custom, as soon as they got anywhere else, talked of nothing but what they did, saw, and eat at Paris.

The freedom of the French is not to be used indiscriminately at all the Courts in Germany, though their easiness may and ought; but that, too, at some places more than others. The Courts at Manheim and Bonn, I take to be a little more unbarbarised than some others; that of Mayence, an ecclesiastical one, as well as that of Treves (neither of which is much frequented by foreigners), retains, I conceive, a great deal of the Goth and Vandal still. There, more reserve and ceremony are necessary, and not a word of the French. At Berlin, you cannot be too French. Hanover, Brunswick, Cassel, etc., are of the mixed kind, *un peu décrottés, mais pas assez.*

Another thing which I most earnestly recommend to you, not only in Germany, but in every part of the world where you may ever be, is, not only real, but seeming attention to whomever you speak to, or to whoever speaks to you. There is nothing so brutally shocking, nor so little forgiven, as a seeming inattention to the person who is speaking to you; and I have known many a man knocked down for (in my opinion) a much slighter provocation than that shocking inattention which I mean. I have seen many people who, while you are speaking to them, instead of looking at, and attending to you, fix their eyes upon the ceiling, or some other part of the room, look out of the window, play with a dog, twirl their snuff-box, or pick their nose. Nothing discovers a little, futile, frivolous mind more than this, and nothing is so offensively ill-bred; it is an explicit declaration ou your part that every, the most trifling, object deserves your attention more than all that can be said by the person who is speaking to you. Judge of the sentiments of hatred and resentment which such treatment must excite in every breast where any degree of self-love dwells, and I am sure I never yet met with that breast where there was not a great deal. I repeat it again and again (for it is highly necessary for you to remember it) that sort of vanity and self-love is inseparable from human nature, whatever may be its rank or condition; even your footman will sooner forget and forgive a beating, than any manifest mark of slight and contempt. Be therefore, I beg of you, not only really, but seemingly and manifestly, attentive to whoever speaks to you; nay more, take their tone, and tune yourself to their unison. Be serious with the serious, gay with the gay, and trifle with the triflers. In assuming these various shapes, endeavour to make each of them seem to sit easy upon you, and even to appear to be your own natural one. This is the true and useful versatility, of which a thorough knowledge of the world at once teaches the utility, and the means of acquiring.

I am very sure, at least I hope, that you will never make use of a silly expression, which is the favourite expression, and the absurd excuse of all fools and blockheads. *I cannot do such a thing*—a thing by no means either morally or physically impossible. I *cannot* attend long together to the same thing, says one fool; that is, he is such a fool that he will not. I remember a very awkward fellow, who did not know what to do with his sword, and who always took it off before dinner, saying, that he could not possibly dine with his sword on; upon which I could not help telling him, that I really believed he could, without any probable danger either to himself or others. It is a shame and an absurdity for any man to say that he cannot do all those things which are commonly done by all the rest of mankind.

Another thing, that I must earnestly warn you against, is laziness; by which more people have lost the fruit of their travels, than, perhaps, by any other thing Pray be always in motion. Early in the morning go and see things; and the rest of the day go and see people. If you stay but a week at a place, and that an insignificant one, see, however, all that is to be seen there; know as many people, and get into as many houses, as ever you can

I recommend to you likewise, though probably you have thought of it yourself, to carry in your pocket a map of Germany, in which the post-roads are marked; and also some short book of travels through Germany. The former will help to imprint in your memory situations and distances; and the latter will point out many things for you to see, that might otherwise possibly escape you; and which, though they may in themselves be of little consequence, you would regret not having seen, after having been at the places where they were.

Thus warned and provided for your journey, God speed you; *Felix faustumque sit!* Adieu.

CXCVI.

LONDON, *May* 27, O.S. 1752.

MY DEAR FRIEND,

I send you the enclosed original,* from a friend of ours, with my own commentaries upon the text; a text which I have so often paraphrased, and commented upon already, that I believe I can hardly say anything new upon it; but, however, I cannot give it over till I am better convinced, than I yet am, that you feel all the utility, the importance, and the necessity of it; nay, not only feel, but practise it. Your panegyrist allows you, what most fathers would be more than satisfied with in a son, and chides me for not contenting myself with *l'essentiellement bon*; but I, who have been in no one respect like other fathers, cannot neither, like them, content myself with *l'essentiellement bon*; because I know that it will not do your business in the world, while you want *quelques couches de vernis*.

Few fathers care much for their sons, or, at least, most of them care more for their money; and, consequently, content themselves with giving them, at the cheapest rate, the common run of education; that is, a school till eighteen; the university till twenty; and a couple of years riding post through the several towns of Europe; impatient till their boobies come home to be married, and, as they call it, settled. Of those who really love their sons, few know how to do it. Some spoil them by fondling them while they are young, and then quarrel with them when they are grown up, for having been spoiled; some love them like mothers, and attend only to the bodily health and strength of the hopes of their family, solemnize his birthday, and rejoice, like the subjects of the Great Mogul, at the increase of his bulk;† while others, minding, as they think, only essentials, take pains and pleasure to see in their heir, all their favourite weaknesses and imperfections. I hope and believe that I have kept clear of all these errors, in the education which I have given you. No weaknesses of my own have warped it, no parsimony has starved it, no rigour has deformed it. Sound and extensive learning was the founda-

---

* That enclosure was not found amongst Mr. Stanhope's papers.

† This fact is derived from the description of the Mogul Court by Tavernier. (*Voyages,* vol. ii. p. 266–272, ed. 1679.)—M.

tion which I meant to lay; I have laid it; but that alone, I knew, would by no means be sufficient; the ornamental, the showish, the pleasing superstructure, was to be begun. In that view I threw you into the great world, entirely your own master, at an age when others either guzzle at the university, or are sent abroad in servitude to some awkward, pedantic, Scotch governor. This was to put you in the way, and the only way, of acquiring those manners, that address, and those graces, which exclusively distinguish people of fashion; and without which all moral virtues, and all acquired learning, are of no sort of use in Courts and *le beau monde*; on the contrary, I am not sure if they are not an hindrance. They are feared and disliked in those places, as too severe, if not smoothed and introduced by the *graces*; but of these graces, of this necessary *beau vernis*, it seems there are still *quelques couches qui manquent.*

Now, pray let me ask you, coolly and seriously, *pourquoi ces couches manquent-elles?* For you may as easily take them, as you may wear more or less powder in your hair, more or less lace upon your coat. I can, therefore, account for your wanting them, no other way in the world, than from your not being yet convinced of their full value. You have heard some English bucks say, "Damn these finical outlandish airs, give me a manly, resolute, manner. They make a rout with their graces, and talk like a parcel of dancing masters, and dress like a parcel of fops; one good Englishman will beat three of them." But let your own observation undeceive you of these prejudices. I will give you one instance only, instead of an hundred that I could give you, of a very shining fortune and figure, raised upon no other foundation whatsoever, than that of address, manners, and graces. Between you and me (for this example must go no farther), what do you think made our friend, Lord Albemarle, Colonel of a regiment of Guards, Governor of Virginia, Groom of the Stole, and Ambassador to Paris; amounting in all to £16,000 or £17,000 a year? Was it his birth? No; a Dutch gentleman only. Was it his estate? No; he had none. Was it his learning, his parts, his political abilities and application? You can answer these questions as easily, and as soon, as I can ask them. What was it then? Many people wondered, but I do not; for I know and will tell you. It was his air, his address, his manners, and his graces. He pleased, and by pleasing became a favourite; and by becoming a favourite he became all that he has been since.

Show me any one instance, where intrinsic worth and merit, unassisted by exterior accomplishments, have raised any man so high. You know the Duc de Richelieu, now *Maréchal, Cordon bleu, Gentilhomme de la Chambre*, twice Ambassador, etc. By what means? Not by the purity of his character, the depth of his knowledge, or any uncommon penetration and sagacity. Women alone formed and raised him. The Duchess of Burgundy* took a fancy to him, and had him before he was sixteen years old; this put him in fashion among the *beau monde*; and the late Regent's eldest daughter, now Madame de Modene,† took him next, and was near marrying him. . These early connections with women of the first distinction, gave . him those manners, graces, and address, which you see he has; and which, I can assure you, are all that he has; for, strip him of them, and he will be one of the poorest men in Europe.

Man or woman cannot resist an engaging exterior; it will please, it will make its way. You want, it seems, but *quelques couches*; for God's sake lose no time in getting them; and now you have gone so far, complete the work. Think of nothing else till that work is finished; unwearied application will bring about anything; and surely your application can never be so well employed as upon that object, which is absolutely necessary to facilitate all others. With your knowledge and parts, if adorned by manners and graces, what may you not hope one day to be? But without them, you will be in the situation of a man who should be very fleet of one leg, but very lame of the other. He could not run, the lame leg would check and clog the well one, which would be very near useless.

From my original plan for your education, I meant to make

---

* Marie Adélaide de Savoie, who died in 1712, within a few days of her husband and their eldest son. Her character is drawn by St. Simon at some length, and with much discrimination and skill. (*Mem.*, vol. x. p. 181.)—M.

† This princess, Charlotte Aglae, surnamed Mademoiselle de Valois, married, in 1720, Francis III. of the house of Este, Duke of Modena. Twenty years afterwards, the President De Brosses describes her as *fort grosse, assez haute en couleur, l'air majestueux et bon; en tout c'est toujours une belle femme.—Lettres sur l'Italie*, vol. ii. p. 459, ed. 1836.)—M.

you *un homme universel*; what depended upon me is executed,
the little that remains undone depends singly upon you. Do not
then disappoint, when you can so easily gratify me. It is your
own interest which I am pressing you to pursue, and it is the
only return that I desire for all the care and affection of—Yours.

CXCVII.

LONDON, *May* 31, O.S. 1752.

MY DEA FRIEND

The world is the book, and the only one to which, at present, I wou d nave vou apply yourself; and the thorough knowledge of it wil oe of more use to you, than all the books that
ever were read Lay aside the best book whenever you can go
into the best company; and depend upon it, you change for the
better. However, as the most tumultuous life, whether of business or pleasure, leaves some vacant moments every day, in
which a book is the refuge of a rational being, I mean now to
point out to you the method of employing those moments (which
will and ought to be but few) in the most advantageous manner.

Throw away none of your time upon those trivial futile books,
published by idle or necessitous authors, for the amusement of
idle and ignorant readers; such sort of books swarm and buzz
about one every day; flap them away, they have no sting. *Cer-
tum pete finem,* have some one object for those leisure moments,
and pursue that object invariably till you have attained it; and
then take some other. For instance, considering your destination, I would advise you to single out the most remarkable and
interesting eras of modern history, and confine all your reading
to that era. If you pitch upon the Treaty of Munster, (and that
is the proper period to begin with, in the course which I am now
recommending) do not interrupt it by dipping and deviating into
othe. books, unrelative to it; but consult only the most authentic
histories, letters, memoirs, and negotiations, relative to that great
transaction; reading and comparing them with all that caution
and distrust which Lord Bolingbroke recommends to you, in a
better manner and in better words than I can.* The next period,

* See Lord Bolingbroke's fourth Letter on the Study of History. He
warns us, that "History becomes very often a lying panegyric or a lying

worth your particular knowledge, is the Treaty of the Pyrenees; which was calculated to lay, and in effect did lay, the foundation of the succession of the House of Bourbon to the Crown of Spain. Pursue that in the same manner, singling, out of the millions of volumes written upon that occasion, the two or three most authentic ones; and particularly letters, which are the best authorities in matters of negotiation. Next come the Treaties of Nimeguen and Ryswick, postscripts in a manner to those of Munster and the Pyrenees. Those two transactions have had great light thrown upon thom by the publication of many authentic and original letters and pieces. The concessions made at the Treaty of Ryswick, by the then triumphant Louis the Fourteenth, astonished all those who viewed things only superficially; but, I should think, must have been easily accounted for by those who knew the state of the kingdom of Spain, as well as of the health of its king, Charles the Second, at that time.

The interval between the conclusion of the peace of Ryswick, and the breaking out of the great war in 1702, though a short, is a most interesting one. Every week of it almost produced some great event. Two Partition Treaties, the death of the King of Spain, his unexpected Will, and the acceptance of it by Louis the Fourteenth, in violation of the second treaty of partition, just signed and ratified by him; Philip the Fifth, quietly and cheerfully received in Spain, and acknowledged as King of it by most of those Powers who afterwards joined in an alliance to dethrone him. I cannot help making this observation upon that occasion. That character has often more to do in great transactions, than prudence and sound policy; for Louis the Fourteenth gratified his personal pride, by giving a Bourbon King to Spain, at the expense of the true interest of France; which would have acquired much more solid and permanent strength by the addition of Naples, Sicily, and Lorraine, upon the foot of the second Partition Treaty; and I think it was fortunate for Europe that he preferred the Will. It is true, he

satire; for different nations, or different parties in the same nation, belie one another without respect to truth, as they murder one another without regard to right. . . . But different religions have not been so barbarous to one another as sects of the same religion; and, in like manner, nation has had better quarter from nation than party from party."—M.

might hope to influence his grandson; but he could never expect that his Bourbon posterity in France should influence his Bourbon posterity in Spain; he knew too well how weak the ties of blood are among men, and how much weaker still they are among Princes.

The Memoirs of Count Harrach, and of Las Torres, give a good deal of light into the transactions of the Court of Spain, previous to the death of that weak King; and the letters of the Maréchal d'Harcourt, then the French Ambassador in Spain, of which I have authentic copies in manuscript, from the year 1698 to 1701, have cleared up that whole affair to me. I keep that book for you. It appears by those letters, that the imprudent conduct of the House of Austria, with regard to the King and Queen of Spain, and Madame Berlips, her favourite, together with the knowledge of the Partition Treaty, which incensed all Spain, were the true and only reasons of the Will in favour of the Duke of Anjou. Cardinal Portocarrero, nor any of the Grandees, were bribed by France, as was generally reported and believed at that time; which confirms Voltaire's anecdote upon that subject.* Then opens a new scene and a new century; Louis the Fourteenth's good fortune forsakes him, till the Duke of Marlborough and Prince Eugene make him amends for all the mischief they had done him, by making the Allies refuse the terms of peace offered by him at Gertruydenberg. How the disadvantageous peace of Utrecht was afterwards brought on, you have lately read; and you cannot inform yourself too minutely of all those circumstances, that treaty being the freshest source from whence the late transactions of Europe have flowed.

The alterations which have since happened, whether by wars or treaties, are so recent, that all the written accounts are to be helped out, proved, or contradicted, by the oral ones of almost every informed person, of a certain age or rank in life. For the facts, dates, and original pieces of this century, you will find them in Lamberti, till the year 1715, and after that time in Rousset's *Recueil*.

I do not mean that you should plod hours together in researches of this kind; no, you may employ your time more usefully; but

* *Siècle de Louis XIV.*, ch. xvi.; which contains a brief, but clear, and for the most part exact, account of these transactions.—M.

I mean, that you should make the most of the moments you do
employ, by method, and the pursuit of one single object at a
time; nor should I call it a digression from that object, if, when
you meet with clashing and jarring pretensions of different
Princes to the same thing, you had immediately recourse to other
books, in which those several pretensions were clearly stated; on
the contrary, that is the only way of remembering those contested rights and claims; for, were a man to read *tout de suite*,
Schwederus's Theatrum Pretensionum, he would only be confounded by the variety, and remember none of them; whereas,
by examining them occasionally, as they happen to occur, either
in the course of your historical reading, or as they are agitated
in your own times, you will retain them, by connecting them
with those historical facts which occasioned your inquiry. For
example, had you read, in the course of two or three folios of
Pretensions, those, among others, of the two Kings of England
and Prussia to Ost Frise, it is impossible that you should have
remembered them; but now that they are become the debated
object at the Diet at Ratisbon, and the topic of all political conversations, if you consult both books and persons concerning
them, and inform yourself thoroughly, you will never forget them
as long as you live. You will hear a great deal of them on one
side, at Hanover; and as much on the other side, afterwards, at
Berlin; hear both sides, and form your own opinion; but dispute with neither.

Letters from foreign Ministers to their Courts, and from their
Courts to them, are, if genuine, the best and most authentic
records you can read, as far as they go. Cardinal d'Ossat's,
President Jeannin's,* D'Estrades,† Sir William Temple's, will

---

* The President Jeannin, born in 1540, had attached himself to the
party of the League, but afterwards became one of the most able and upright Ministers of Henry IV., and was entrusted by that great monarch
with several important missions to the States-General in the years 1607,
1608, and 1609. His *Négociations* were first published in 1656, by his
grandson l'Abbé Castille.—M.

† Godefroi, Comte d'Estrades, a Maréchal of France, distinguished himself in the course of a long life (1607 to 1686) by his skilful negotiations
in various countries, especially in Germany and Holland. In 1709 his
Lettres et Mémoires appeared in five volumes; but a far more complete
edition, extending to nine volumes, followed in 1743.—M.

not only inform your mind, but form your style; which, in letters of business, should be very plain and simple, but at the same time exceedingly clear, correct and pure.

All that I have said may be reduced to these two or three plain principles: 1st. That you should now read very little, but converse a great deal; 2dly. To read no useless unprofitable books; and 3dly. That those which you do read may all tend to a certain object, and be relative to, and consequential to, each other. In this method, half-an-hour's reading every day will carry you a great way. People seldom know how to employ their time to the best advantage till they have too little left to employ; but if, at your age, in the beginning of life, people would but consider the value of it, and put every moment to interest, it is incredible what an additional fund of knowledge and pleasure such an economy would bring in. I look back with regret upon that large sum of time, which in my youth I lavished away idly, without either improvement or pleasure. Take warning betimes, and enjoy every moment; pleasures do not commonly last so long as life, and therefore should not be neglected; and the longest life is too short for knowledge, consequently every moment is precious.

I am surprised at having received no letter from you since you left Paris. I still direct this to Strasburg, as I did my two last. I shall direct my next to the post-house at Mayence, unless I receive, in the meantime, contrary instructions from you. Adieu! Remember *les attentions*; they must be your passports into good company.

CXCVIII.

LONDON, *June* 23, O.S. 1752.

MY DEAR FRIEND,

I direct this letter to Mayence, where I think it is likely to meet you, supposing, as I do, that you stayed three weeks at Manheim after the date of your last from thence; but should you have stayed longer at Manheim, to which I have no objection, it will wait for you at Mayence. Mayence will not, I believe, have charms to detain you above a week; so that I reckon you will be at Bonn at the end of July, N.S. There you may stay just as little or as long as you please, and then proceed to Hanover.

I had a letter by the last post from a relation of mine at Hanover, Mr. Stanhope Aspinwall,* who is in the Duke of Newcastle's office, and has lately been appointed the King's Minister to the Dey of Algiers; a post which, notwithstanding your views of foreign affairs, I believe you do not envy him. He tells me in that letter there are very good lodgings to be had at one Mrs. Meyers', the next door to the Duke of Newcastle's, which he offers to take for you. I have desired him to do it, in case Mrs. Meyers will wait for you till the latter end of August or the beginning of September, N.S., which I suppose is about the time when you will be at Hanover. You will find this Mr. Aspinwall of great use to you there. He will exert himself to the utmost to serve you; he has been twice or thrice at Hanover, and knows all the *allures* there; he is very well with the Duke of Newcastle,† and will puff you there. Moreover, if you have a mind to work as a volunteer in that *bureau*, he will assist and inform you; in short, he is a very honest, sensible, and informed man; *mais ne paye pas beaucoup de sa figure; il abuse même du privilége qu'ont les hommes d'être laids; et il ne sera pas en reste avec les lions et les leopards qu'il trouvera à Alger.*

As you are entirely master of the time when you will leave Bonn and go to Hanover, so are you master to stay at Hanover as long as you please, and to go from thence where you please, provided that at Christmas you are at Berlin for the beginning of the Carnival. This I would not have you say at Hanover, considering the mutual disposition of those two Courts; but, when anybody asks you where you are to go next, say that you propose rambling in Germany, at Brunswick, Cassel, etc., till the next spring, when you intend to be in Flanders, in your way to England. I take Berlin, at this time, to be the politest, the most shining, and the most useful Court in Europe for a young fellow to be at; and therefore I would upon no account not have you there, for at least a couple of months of the Carnival. If you are as well received, and pass your time as well, at Bonn, as

---

* Mr. Aspinwall's mother was a distant cousin of Lord Chesterfield; she was daughter of Charles Stanhope, Esq., who was a grandson of the first, and ancestor of the present, Earl.

† Thomas Holles, Duke of Newcastle, was at this period Secretary of State, and was attending the King as such on a visit to Hanover.—M.

I believe you will, I would advise you to remain there till about the 20th of August, N.S.; in four days more you will be at Hanover. As for your stay there, it must be shorter or longer, according to certain circumstances *which you know of:* * suppos- ing them at the best, then stay till within a week or ten days of the King's return to England; but supposing them at the worst, your stay must not be too short, for reasons which you also know: no resentment must either appear or be suspected; there- fore, at worst, I think you must remain there a month, and, at best, as long as ever you please. But I am convinced that all will turn out very well for you there. Everybody is engaged or inclined to help you; the Ministers, both English and German, the principal Ladies, and most of the foreign Ministers; so that I may apply to you *nullum numen abest, si sit prudentia.* Du Pesson will, I believe, be back there, from Turin, much about the time you get thither; pray be very attentive to him, and connect yourself with him as much as ever you can; for, besides that he is a very pretty and well-informed man, he is very much in fashion at Hanover, is personally very well with the King and certain Ladies; so that a visible intimacy and connection with him will do you credit and service.

Pray cultivate Monsieur Hop, the Dutch Minister, who has always been very much my friend, and will, I am sure, be yours. His manners, it is true, are not very engaging; he is rough, but he is sincere. It is very useful sometimes to see the things which one ought to avoid, as it is right to see very often those which one ought to imitate; and my friend Hop's manners will frequently point out to you what yours ought to be, by the rule of contraries.

Congreve points out a sort of critics, to whom he says that we are doubly obliged:

> Rules for good writing they with pains indite,
> Then show us what is bad, by what they write.

It is certain that Monsieur Hop, with the best heart in the world, and a thousand good qualities, has a thousand enemies, and hardly a friend, singly from the roughness of his manners.

---

* It was feared that some obstacle or objection might arise on account of Mr. Stanhope's illegitimate birth. This apprehension is frequently hinted at in the following correspondence, and was ere long verified at Brussels. See letter to Mr. Dayrolles of October 30, 1752.—M.

N.B. I heartily wish you could have staid long enough at Manheim to have been seriously and desperately in love with Madame de Taxis, who, I suppose, is a proud, insolent, fine lady, and who would consequently have expected attentions little short of adoration; nothing would do you more good than such a passion; and I live in hopes that somebody or other will be able to excite such a one in you; your hour may not yet be come, but it will come. Love has been not unaptly compared to the small-pox, which most people have sooner or later. Iphigenia had a wonderful effect upon Cimon; I wish some Hanoverian Iphigenia may try her skill upon you.

I recommend to you again, though I have already done it twice or thrice, to speak German, even affectedly, while you are at Hanover, which will show that you prefer that language, and be of more use to you there with *somebody* * than you can imagine. When you carry my letters to Monsieur Munchausen and Monsieur Schwiegeldt, address yourself to them in German; the latter speaks French very well, but the former extremely ill. Show great attention to Madame Munchausen's daughter, who is a great favourite; these little trifles please mothers, and sometimes fathers, extremely. Observe and you will find, almost universally, that the least things either please or displease most; because they necessarily imply either a very strong desire of obliging, or an unpardonable indifference about it. I will give you a ridiculous instance enough of this truth from my own experience. When I was Ambassador the first time in Holland, Comte de Wassenaer and his wife, people of the first rank and consideration, had a little boy of about three years old, of whom they were exceedingly fond; in order to make my court to them, I was so too, and used to take the child often upon my lap and play with him. One day his nose was very snotty, upon which I took out my handkerchief and wiped it for him. This raised a loud laugh, and they called me a very handy nurse; but the father and mother were so pleased with it, that to this day it is an anecdote in the family; and I never receive a letter from Comte Wassenaer, but he makes me the compliments *du morveux que j'ai mouché autrefois;* who, by the way, I am assured, is now the prettiest young fellow in Holland. Where one would gain people, remember that nothing is little. Adieu!

* King George the Second.

CXCIX.

LONDON, *June* 26, O.S. 1752.

MY DEAR FRIEND,

As I have reason to fear, from your last letter of the 18th, N.S., from Manheim, that all, or at least most of my letters to you since you left Paris have miscarried, I think it requisite, at all events, to repeat in this the necessary parts of those several letters, as far as they relate to your future motions.

I suppose that this will either find you, or be but a few days before you, at Bonn, where it is directed; and I suppose, too, that you have fixed your time for going from thence to Hanover. If things *turn out well at Hanover*, as in my opinion they will, *Chi stà bene non si muova*, stay there till a week or ten days before the King sets out for England; but, should *they turn out ill*, which I cannot imagine, stay however a month, that your departure may not seem a step of discontent or peevishness, the very suspicion of which is by all means to be avoided. Whenever you leave Hanover, be it sooner or later, where would you go? *Ella è Padrone*, and I will give you your choice. Would you pass the months of November and December at Brunswick, Cassel, etc.? Would you choose to go for a couple of months to Ratisbon, where you would be very well recommended to, and treated by, the King's Electoral Minister, the Baron de Böhr, and where you would improve your *jus publicum*? Or, would you rather go directly to Berlin, and stay there till the end of the Carnival? Two or three months at Berlin are, considering all circumstances, necessary for you; and the Carnival months are the best; *pour le reste décidez en dernier ressort, et sans appel comme d'abus*. Let me only know your decree when you have formed it. Your good or ill success at Hanover will have a very great influence upon your subsequent character, figure, and fortune in the world; therefore, I confess, that I am more anxious about it than ever bride was on her wedding-day, when wishes, hopes, fears, and doubts, tumultuously agitate, please, and terrify her. It is your first crisis; the character which you acquire there will, more or less, be that which will abide by you for the rest of your life.

You will be tried and judged there, not as a boy, but as a

man; and from that moment there is no appeal for character; it is fixed. To form that character advantageously, you have three objects particularly to attend to—your character, as a man of morality, truth, and honour; your knowledge in the objects of your destination, as a man of business; and your engaging and insinuating address, air, and manners, as a courtier; the sure and only steps to favour. Merit at Courts, without favour, will do little or nothing; favour, without merit, will do a great deal; but favour and merit together will do everything. Favour at Courts depends upon so many, such trifling, such unexpected, and unforeseen events, that a good Courtier must attend to every circumstance, however little, that either does or can happen; he must have no absences, no *distractions;* he must not say, "I did not mind it! who would have thought it?" He ought both to have minded and to have thought it. A chambermaid has sometimes caused revolutions in Courts, which have produced others in kingdoms. Were I to make my way to favour in a Court, I would neither wilfully, nor by negligence, give a dog or a cat there reason to dislike me. Two *pies griéches,* well instructed, you know, made the fortune of De Luines with Louis XIII. Every step a man makes at Court requires as much attention and circumspection as those which were made formerly between hot ploughshares, in the Ordeal, or fiery trials; which, in those times of ignorance and superstition, were looked upon as demonstrations of innocence or guilt. Direct your principal battery at Hanover at the Duke of Newcastle's; there are many very weak places in that citadel, where, with a very little skill, you cannot fail making a great impression. Ask for his orders in everything you do; talk Austrian and Antigallican to him; and, as soon as you are upon a foot of talking easily to him, tell him *en badinant,* that his skill and success in thirty or forty elections in England leave you no reason to doubt of his carrying his election for Frankfort, and that you look upon the Archduke * as his Member for the Empire. In his hours of festivity and compotation, drop that he puts you in mind of what Sir William Temple says of the Pensionary De Witt, who at that time governed half Europe—that he appeared at balls, assem-

* The Archduke Joseph, eldest son of Maria Theresa, and afterwards Emperor.

blies, and public places, as if he had nothing else to do, or to think of. When he talks to you upon foreign affairs, which he will often do, say that you really cannot presume to give any opinion of your own upon those matters, looking upon yourself, at present, only as a postscript to the *corps diplomatique ;* but that, if his Grace will be pleased to make you an additional volume to it, though but in *duodecimo,* you will do your best, that he shall neither be ashamed nor repent of it. He loves to have a favourite, and to open himself to that favourite ; he has now no such person with him ; the place is vacant, and if you have dexterity you may fill it. In one thing alone, do not humour him—I mean drinking ; for as I believe you have never yet been drunk, you do not yourself know how you can bear your wine, and what a little too much of it may make you do or say. You might possibly kick down all you had done before.

You do not love gaming, and I thank God for it ; but at Hanover I would have you show, and profess, a particular dislike to play, so as to decline it upon all occasions, unless where one may be wanted to make a fourth at whist or quadrille ; and then take care to declare it the result of your complaisance, not of your inclinations. Without such precaution, you may very possibly be suspected, though unjustly, of loving play, upon account of my former passion for it ; and such a suspicion would do you a great deal of hurt, especially with the King, who detests gaming. I must end this abruptly. God bless you !

CC.

MY DEAR FRIEND,

Versatility as a Courtier may be almost decisive to you hereafter ; that is, it may conduce to, or retard, your preferment in your own destination. The first reputation goes a great way ; and if you fix a good one at Hanover, it will operate also to your advantage in England. The trade of a Courtier is as much a trade as that of a shoemaker ; and he who applies himself the most will work the best ; the only difficulty is to distinguish (what I am sure you have sense enough to distinguish) between the right and proper qualifications and their kindred faults ; for there is but a line between every perfection and its neighbouring imperfection. As for example, you must be extremely well-bred and polite, but without the troublesome forms and stiffness of ceremony. You must be respectful and assenting, but without being servile and abject. You must be frank, but without indiscretion, and close without being costive. You must keep up dignity of character without the least pride of birth or rank. You must be gay within all the bounds of decency and respect; and grave without the affectation of wisdom, which does not become the age of twenty. You must be essentially secret without being dark and mysterious. You must be firm, and even bold, but with great seeming modesty.

With these qualifications, which, by the way, are all in your own power, I will answer for your success, not only at Hanover, but at any Court in Europe. And I am not sorry that you begin your apprenticeship at a little one; because you must be more circumspect, and more upon your guard there, than at a great one, where every little thing is not known nor reported.

When you write to me or to anybody else from thence, take care that your letters contain commendations of all you see and hear there; for they will most of them be opened and read; but as frequent courtiers will come from Hanover to England, you may sometimes write to me without reserve; and put your letters into a very little box, which you may send safely by some of them.

I must not omit mentioning to you, that at the Duke of Newcastle's table, where you will frequently dine, there is a great deal of drinking. Be upon your guard against it, both upon account of your health, which would not bear it, and of the consequences of your being flustered and heated with wine; it might engage you in scrapes and frolics, which the King (who is a very sober man himself) detests. On the other hand, you should not seem too grave and too wise to drink like the rest of the company; therefore use art; mix water with your wine; do not drink all that is in the glass; and if detected and pressed to drink more, do not cry out sobriety, but say that you have lately been out of order, that you are subject to inflammatory complaints, and that you must beg to be excused for the present. A young fellow ought to be wiser than he should seem to be; and an old fellow ought to seem wise, whether he really be so or not.

During your stay at Hanover, I would have you make two or three excursions to parts of that Electorate; the Hartz, where the silver mines are; Göttingen, for the university; Stade, for what commerce there is. You should also go to Zell. In short, see everything that is to be seen there, and inform yourself well of all the details of that country. Go to Hamburgh for three or four days, know the constitution of that little Hanseatic Republic, and inform yourself well of the nature of the King of Denmark's pretentions to it.

If all things turn out right for you at Hanover, I would have you make it your head-quarters till about a week or ten days before the King leaves it; and then go to Brunswick, which, though a little, is a very polite pretty Court. You may stay there a fortnight or three weeks, as you like it; and from thence go to Cassel, and there stay till you go to Berlin, where I would have you be by Christmas. At Hanover you will very easily get good letters of recommendation to Brunswick and to Cassel. You do not want any to Berlin; however, I will send you one for Voltaire.* *A propos* of Berlin; be very reserved and cautious, while at Hanover, as to that King and that country; both which are detested, because feared by everybody there, from his Majesty down to the meanest peasant; but however, they both extremely deserve your utmost attention; and you will see the arts and wisdom of government better in that country, now, than in any other in Europe. You must stay three months at Berlin, if you like it, as I believe you will; and after that I hope we shall meet here again.

Of all the places in the world (I repeat it once more) establish a good reputation at Hanover, *et faites vous valoir là, autant qu'il est possible, par le brillant, les manières, et les graces.* Indeed, it is of the greatest importance to you, and will make any future application to the King in your behalf very easy. He is more taken by those little things, than any man, or even woman, that I ever knew in my life; and I do not wonder at him. In short, exert to the utmost all your means and powers to please, and remember, that he who pleases the most will rise the soonest and the highest. Try but once the pleasure and advantage of

* That letter, which is dated August 27, 1752, will be found in the Miscellaneous Correspondence.

pleasing, and I will answer, that you will never more neglect the means.

I send you herewith two letters, the one to Monsieur Munchausen, the other to Monsieur Schwiegeldt, an old friend of mine, and a very sensible, knowing man. They will both, I am sure, be extremely civil to you, and carry you into the best company; and then it is your business to please that company. I never was more anxious about any period of your life, than I am about this your Hanover expedition, it being of so much more consequence to you than any other. If I hear from thence that you are liked and loved there for your air, your manners, and address, as well as esteemed for your knowledge, I shall be the happiest man in the world; judge then what I must be, if it happens otherwise. Adieu!

CCI.

LONDON, *July* 21, O.S. 1752.

My dear Friend,

By my calculation, this letter may probably arrive at Hanover three or four days before you; and as I am sure of its arriving there safe, it shall contain the most material points that I have mentioned in my several letters to you since you left Paris, as if you had received but few of them, which may very probably be the case.

As for your stay at Hanover, it must not *in all events* be less than a month; but if things turn out to *your satisfaction,* it may be just as long as you please. From thence you may go wherever you like; for I have so good an opinion of your judgment, that I think you will combine and weigh all circumstances, and choose the properest places. Would you saunter at some of the small Courts, as Brunswick, Cassel, etc., till the Carnival at Berlin? You are master. Would you pass a couple of months at Ratisbon, which might not be ill employed? *A la bonne heure.* Would you go to Brussels, stay a month or two there with Dayrolles, and from thence to Mr. Yorke at the Hague? With all my heart. Or, lastly, would you go to Copenhagen and Stockholm? *Ella è anche Padrone;* choose entirely for yourself, without any farther instructions from me; only let me know your determination in time, that I may settle your credit, in case you go to

places where at present you have none. Your object should be
to see the *mores multorum hominum et urbes;* begin and end it
where you please.

By what you have already seen of the German Courts, I am
sure you must have observed that they are much more nice and
scrupulous in points of ceremony, respect, and attention, than
the greater Courts of France and England. You will therefore,
I am persuaded, attend to the minutest circumstances of address
and behaviour, particularly during your stay at Hanover, which
(I will repeat it, though I have said it often to you already) is
the most important preliminary period of your whole life. Nobody in the world is more exact in all points of good-breeding
than the King, and it is the part of every man's character that he
informs himself of first. The least negligence, or the slightest
inattention, reported to him, may do you infinite prejudice, as
their contraries would service.

If Lord Albemarle (as I believe he did) trusted you with the
secret affairs of his department, let the Duke of Newcastle know
that he did so, which will be an inducement to him to trust you
too, and possibly to employ you in affairs of consequence. Tell
him that, though you are young, you know the importance of
secrecy in business, and can keep a secret; that I have always
inculcated this doctrine into you, and have, moreover, strictly
forbidden you ever to communicate, even to me, any matters of
a secret nature which you may happen to be trusted with in the
course of business.

As for business, I think I can trust you to yourself; but I wish
I could say as much for you with regard to those exterior accomplishments which are absolutely necessary to smooth and shorten
the way to it. Half the business is done when one has gained
the heart and the affections of those with whom one is to transact
it. Air and address must begin, manners and attention must
finish that work. I will let you into one secret concerning myself, which is, that I owe much more of the success which I have
had in the world to my manners, than to any superior degree of
merit or knowledge. I desired to please, and I neglected none
of the means. This, I can assure you, without any false modesty,
is the truth. You have more knowledge than I had at your age,
but then I had much more attention and good-breeding than you.

Call it vanity if you please, and possibly it was so; but my great object was to make every man I met with like me, and every woman love me. I often succeeded; but why? By taking great pains; for otherwise I never should; my figure by no means entitled me to it, and I had certainly an up-hill game; whereas your countenance would help you, if you made the most of it, and proscribed for ever the guilty, gloomy, and funereal part of it. Dress, address, and air, would become your best countenance, and make your little figure pass very well.

If you have time to read at Hanover, pray let the books you read be all relative to the history and constitution of that country, which I would have you know as correctly as any Hanoverian in the whole Electorate. Inform yourself of the powers of the States, and of the nature and extent of the several Judicatures; the particular articles of trade and commerce of Bremen, Harburg, and Stade; the details and value of the mines of the Hartz. Two or three short books will give you the outlines of all these things; and conversation, turned upon those subjects, will do the rest, and better than books can.

Remember of all things to speak nothing but German there; make it (to express myself pedantically) your vernacular language, and study to speak it with purity and elegancy, if it has any. This will not only make you perfect in it, but will please, and make your court there better than anything. *A propos* of languages; did you improve your Italian while you were at Paris, or did you forget it? Had you a master there, and what Italian books did you read with him? If you are master of Italian, I would have you afterwards, by the first convenient opportunity, learn Spanish, which you may very easily, and in a very little time do; you will then, in the course of your foreign business, never be obliged to employ, pay, or trust any translator, for any European language.

As I love to provide eventually for everything that can possibly happen, I will suppose the worst that can befal you at Hanover. In that case, I would have you go immediately to the Duke of Newcastle, and beg his Grace's advice, or rather orders, what you should do; adding, that his advice will always be orders to you. You will tell him, that though you are exceedingly mortified, you are much less so, than you should otherwise be, from the consideration, that, being utterly unknown to his Majesty, his objection could not be personal to you, and could only arise from circumstances, which it was not in your power either to prevent or remedy; that if his Grace thought, that your continuing any longer there would be disagreeable, you entreated him to tell you so; and that, upon the whole, you referred yourself entirely to him, whose orders you should most scrupulously obey. But this precaution, I dare say, is *ex abundanti*, and will prove unnecessary; however, it is always right to be prepared for all events, the worst as well as the best; it prevents hurry and surprise, two dangerous situations in business; for I know no one thing so useful, so necessary in all business, as great coolness, steadiness, and *sang froid*; they give an incredible advantage over whomever one has to do with.

I have received your letter of the 15th, N.S. from Mayence, where I find that you have diverted yourself much better than I expected. I am very well acquainted with Comte Cobentzel's * character, both of parts and business. He could have given you letters to Bonn, having formerly resided there himself. You will not be so agreeably *electrified*, where this letter will find you, as you were both at Manheim and Mayence; but I hope you may meet with a second German Mrs. Fitzgerald, who may make you forget the two former ones, and practise your German. Such transient passions will do you no harm; but, on the contrary, a great deal of good: they will refine your manners, and quicken your attention; they give a young fellow *du brillant*, and bring him into fashion; which last is a great article in setting out in the world.

I have wrote, above a month ago, to Lord Albemarle, to thank him for all his kindnesses to you; but pray, have you done as much? Those are the necessary attentions, which should never be omitted, especially in the beginning of life, when a character is to be established.

---

* Charles, Count Cobentzel, who was born in 1712, and died in 1770, was high in favour at the Court of Vienna, and faithfully served it in several important diplomatic missions. According to M. de Stassart "peu d'hommes d'état ont porté plus loin ces graces, ces agrémens et cet esprit qui font le charme de la société."—M. See Letter to Dayrolles, of September 21, 1753.

That ready wit which you so partially allow me, and so justly Sir Charles Williams, may create many admirers; but, take my word for it, it makes few friends. It shines and dazzles like the noon-day sun, but, like that too, is very apt to scorch; and therefore is always feared. The milder morning and evening light and heat of that planet soothe and calm our minds. Good sense, complaisance, gentleness of manners, attentions, and graces, are the only things that truly engage, and durably keep the heart at long run. Never seek for wit; if it presents itself, well and good; but even in that case, let your judgment interpose; and take care that it be not at the expense of any body. Pope says very truly,

> There are whom Heaven has blest with store of wit,
> Yet want as much again to govern it.

And in another place, I doubt with too much truth,

> For wit and judgment ever are at strife,
> Though meant each other's aid—like man and wife.*

The Germans are very seldom troubled with any extraordinary ebullitions or effervescences of wit, and it is not prudent to try it upon them; whoever does, *offendet solido*.

Remember to write me very minute accounts of all your transactions at Hanover, for they excite both my impatience and anxiety. Adieu.

CCII.

LONDON, *August* 4, O.S. 1752.

MY DEAR FRIEND,

I am extremely concerned at the return of your old asthmatic complaint, which your letter from Cassel of the 28th July, N.S. informs me of. I believe it is chiefly owing to your own negligence; for, notwithstanding the season of the year, and the heat and agitation of travelling, I dare swear you have not taken one single dose of gentle, cooling physic, since that which I made you take at Bath. I hope you are now better, and in better hands, I mean in Dr. Hugo's, at Hanover; he is certainly a very skilful physician, and therefore I desire that you will inform him most minutely of your own case, from your first attack in Carniola to this last at Marpurg; and not only follow his prescriptions

---

* *Essay on Criticism*, 82.

exactly at present, but take his directions, with regard to the regimen that he would have you observe, to prevent the returns of this complaint; and, in case of any returns, the immediate applications, whether external or internal, that he would have you make use of. Consider, it is very well worth your while to submit at present to any course of medicine or diet, to any restraint or confinement, for a time, in order to get rid, once for all, of so troublesome and painful a distemper; the returns of which would equally break in upon your business or your pleasures. Notwithstanding all this, which is plain sense and reason, I much fear, that, as soon as ever you are got out of your present distress, you will take no preventive care by a proper course of medicines and regimen; but, like most people of your age, think it impossible that you ever should be ill again. However, if you will not be wise for your own sake, I desire you will be so for mine, and most scrupulously observe Dr. Hugo's present and future directions.

Hanover, where I take it for granted you are, is at present the seat and centre of foreign negotiations; there are Ministers from almost every Court in Europe; and you have a fine opportunity of displaying with modesty, in conversation, your knowledge of the matters now in agitation. The chief I take to be the election of the King of the Romans, which, though I despair of, I heartily wish were brought about, for two reasons. The *first* is, that I think it may prevent a war upon the death of the present Emperor, who, though young and healthy, may possibly die, as young and healthy people often do; the *other* is the very reason that makes some Powers oppose it, and others dislike it who do not openly oppose it—I mean that it may tend to make the Imperial dignitary hereditary in the House of Austria, which I heartily wish, together with a very great increase of power in the Empire; till when Germany will never be anything near a match for France. Cardinal Richelieu showed his superior abilities in nothing more than in thinking no pains nor expense too great to break the power of the House of Austria in the Empire. Ferdinand had certainly made himself absolute, and the Empire consequently formidable to France, if that Cardinal had not piously adopted the Protestant cause, and put the Empire, by the treaty of Westphalia, in pretty much the same disjointed situation in which France itself was before Louis XI., when Princes of the Blood, at the head of provinces, and Dukes of Brittany, etc., always opposed, and often gave laws to the Crown.

Nothing but making the Empire hereditary in the House of Austria can give it that strength and efficiency which I wish it had, for the sake of the balance of power. For, while the Princes of the Empire are so independent of the Emperor, so divided among themselves, and so open to the corruption of the best bidders, it is ridiculous to expect that Germany ever will or can act as a compact and well-united body against France. But as this notion of mine would as little please *some of our friends,** as many of our enemies, I would not advise you, though you should be of the same opinion, to declare yourself too freely so. Could the Elector Palatine be satisfied, which I confess will be difficult, considering the nature of his pretensions, the tenaciousness and haughtiness of the Court of Vienna, and our inability to do, as we have too often done, their work for them; I say, if the Elector Palatine could be engaged to give his vote, I should think it would be right to proceed to the election with a clear majority of five votes, and leave the King of Prussia and the Elector of Cologne to protest and remonstrate as much as ever they please. The former is too wise, and the latter too weak, in every respect, to act in consequence of those protests. The distracted situation of France, with its ecclesiastical and Parliamentary quarrels— not to mention the illness, and possibly the death, of the Dauphin † —will make the King of Prussia, who certainly is no Frenchman in his heart, very cautious how he acts as one. The Elector of Saxony will be influenced by the King of Poland, who must be determined by Russia, considering his views upon Poland, which, by the bye, I hope he will never obtain; I mean, as to making that Crown hereditary in his family. As for his son's having it by the precarious tenure of election, by which his father now holds it, *à la bonne heure;* but should Poland have a good government under hereditary Kings, there would be a new devil raised in Europe, that I do not know who could lay. I am

---

* The King, as Elector of Hanover, and the Duke of Newcastle, as a skilful courtier.

† Louis the Dauphin died in 1765; his son, Louis XVI., born in 1754, succeeded to the throne in 1774.—M.

sure I would not raise him, though on my own side, for the present.

I do not know how I came to trouble my head so much about politics to-day, which has been so very free from them for some years. I suppose it was, because I knew that I was writing to the most consummate politician of this and his age. If I err, you will set me right; *si quid novisti rectius istis, candidus imperti*, etc.*

I am excessively impatient for your next letter, which I expect by the first post from Hanover, to remove my anxiety, as I hope it will, not only with regard to your health, but likewise to *other things.* In the meantime, in the language of a pedant, but with the tenderness of a parent, *jubeo te bene valere.*

Lady Chesterfield makes you many compliments, and is much concerned at your indisposition.

CCIII.

LONDON, *September* 19, 1752.

My dear Friend,

Since you have been at Hanover, your correspondence has been both unfrequent and laconic. You made indeed one great effort in folio on the 18th, with a postscript of the 22d of August, N.S. and since that, *vous avez ratté in quarto.* On the 31st August, N.S. you give me no informations of what I want chiefly to know; which is, what Dr. Hugo (whom I charged you to consult) said of your asthmatic complaint, and what he prescribed you to prevent the returns of it; and also what is the company you keep there; who has been kind and civil to you, and who not.

You say that you go constantly to the parade; and you do very well, for though you are not of that trade, yet military matters make so great a part both of conversation and negotiation, that it is very proper not to be ignorant of them. I hope you mind more than the mere exercise of the troops you see, and that you inform yourself at the same time of the more material details; such as their pay, and the difference of it when in and out of quarters; what is furnished them by the country when in quarters; and what is allowed them of ammunition, bread, etc.,

---

* Horace *Epistles*, I. vi., 67, 68.

when in the field; the number of men and officers in the several troops and companies, together with the non-commissioned officers, as *caporals, frey-caporals, anspessades*, serjeants, quarter-masters, etc.; the clothing, how frequent, how good, and how furnished; whether by the Colonel, as here in England, from what we call the *off-reckonings*, that is, deductions from the men's pay, or by Commissaries appointed by the Government for that purpose, as in France and Holland. By these inquiries you will be able to talk military with military men, who in every country in Europe, except England, make at least half of all the best companies.

Your attending the parades has also another good effect, which is, that it brings you of course acquainted with the officers, who, when of a certain rank and service, are generally very polite, well-bred people, *et du bon ton*. They have commonly seen a great deal of the world and of Courts; and nothing else can form a gentleman, let people say what they will of sense and learning, with both which a man may contrive to be a very disagreeable companion. I dare say there are very few Captains of foot who are not much better company than ever Descartes or Sir Isaac Newton were. I honour and respect such superior geniuses; but I desire to converse with people of this world, who bring into company their share, at least, of cheerfulness, good-breeding, and knowledge of mankind. In common life, one much oftener wants small money and silver than gold. Give me a man who has ready cash about him for present expenses; sixpences, shillings, half-crowns, and crowns, which circulate easily; but a man who has only an ingot of gold about him is much above common purposes, and his riches are not handy nor convenient. Have as much gold as you please in one pocket, but take care always to keep change in the other; for you will much oftener have occasion for a shilling than for a guinea. In this the French must be allowed to excel all people in the world; they have *un certain entregent, un enjouement, une aimable légèreté dans la conversation, une politesse aisée et naturelle, qui paroit ne leur rien couter*, which give society all its charms. I am sorry to add, but it is too true, that the English and the Dutch are the farthest from this of all the people in the world; I do by no means except even the Swiss.

Though you did not think proper to inform me, I know from other hands that you were to go to the Göhr * with a Comte Schullemburg, for eight or ten days only, to see the reviews. I know also, that you had a blister upon your arm, which did you a great deal of good : I know too you have contracted a great friendship with Lord Essex,† and that you two were inseparable at Hanover. All these things I would rather have known from you than from others ; and they are the sort of things that I am the most desirous of knowing, as they are more immediately relative to yourself.

I am very sorry for the Duchess of Newcastle's ‡ illness, full as much upon your as upon her account, as it has hindered you from being so much known to the Duke as I could have wished ; use and habit going a great way with him, as indeed they do with most people. I have known many people patronized, pushed up, and preferred by those who could have given no other reason for it than that they were used to them. We must never seek for motives by deep reasoning, but we must find them out by careful observation and attention ; no matter what they should be ; but the point is, what they are. Trace them up, step by step, from the character of the person. I have known *de par le monde*, as Brantôme says, great effects from causes too little ever to have been suspected. Some things must be known, and can never be guessed.

God knows where this letter will find you, or follow you ; not at Hanover, I suppose ; but wherever it does, may it find you in health and pleasure ! Adieu !

CCIV.

LONDON, *September* 22, 1752.

MY DEAR FRIEND,

The day after the date of my last, I received your letter of the 8th. I approve extremely of your intended progress, and

---

* A hunting-seat of the Electors of Hanover.

† William Anne Capel, succeeded his father as Earl of Essex in 1743. He married Frances, eldest daughter of Sir Charles Hanbury Williams. See Letter of March 4, 1758.

‡ Lady Harriet, eldest daughter and co-heir of Francis, Earl Godolphin, married in 1717, Thomas Holles, Duke of Newcastle, and died without issue in 1776.—M

am very glad that you go to the Göhr with Comte Schullemburg. I would have you see everything with your own eyes, and hear everything with your own ears, for I know, by very long experience, that it is very unsafe to trust to other people's. Vanity and interest cause many misrepresentations, and folly causes many more. Few people have parts enough to relate exactly and judiciously; and those who have, for some reason or other, never fail to sink or to add some circumstances.

The reception which you have met with at Hanover I look upon as an omen of your being well received everywhere else; for, to tell you the truth, it was the place that I distrusted the most in that particular. But there is a certain conduct, there are *certaines manières* that will, and must get the better of all difficulties of that kind. It is to acquire them that you still continue abroad, and go from Court to Court; they are personal, local, and temporal; they are modes which vary, and owe their existence to accidents, whim, and humour; all the sense and reason in the world would never point them out; nothing but experience, observation, and what is called knowledge of the world, can possibly teach them. For example, it is respectful to bow to the King of England; it is disrespectful to bow to the King of France; it is the rule to courtesy to the Emperor; and the prostration of the whole body is required by Eastern Monarchs. These are established ceremonies, and must be complied with; but why they were established, I defy sense and reason to tell us. It is the same among all ranks, where certain customs are received, and must necessarily be complied with, though by no means the result of sense and reason. As for instance, the very absurd, though almost universal custom of drinking people's healths. Can there be anything in the world less relative to any other man's health than my drinking a glass of wine? Common sense, certainly, never pointed it out, but yet common sense tells me I must conform to it. Good sense bids one be civil, and endeavour to please, though nothing but experience and observation can teach one the means, properly adapted to time, place, and persons. This knowledge is the true object of a gentleman's travelling, if he travels as he ought to do. By frequenting good company in every country, he himself becomes of every country; he is no longer an Englishman, a

Frenchman, or an Italian, but he is an European; he adopts, respectively, the best manners of every country, and is a Frenchman at Paris, an Italian at Rome, an Englishman at London.

This advantage, I must confess, very seldom accrues to my countrymen from their travelling, as they have neither the desire nor the means of getting into good company abroad; for, in the first place, they are confoundedly bashful, and in the next place, they either speak no foreign language at all, or, if they do, it is barbarously. You possess all the advantages that they want; you know the languages in perfection, and have constantly kept the best company in the places where you have been; so that you ought to be an European. Your canvas is solid and strong, your outlines are good; but remember, that you still want the beautiful colouring of Titian, and the delicate graceful touches of Guido. Now is your time to get them. There is, in all good company, a fashionable air, countenance, manner, and phraseology, which can only be acquired by being in good company, and very attentive to all that passes there. When you dine or sup at any well-bred man's house, observe carefully how he does the honours of his table to the different guests. Attend to the compliments of congratulation, or condolence, that you hear a well-bred man make to his superiors, to his equals, and to his inferiors; watch even his countenance and his tone of voice, for they all conspire in the main point of pleasing. There is a certain distinguishing diction of a man of fashion; he will not content himself with saying, like John Trott, to a new-married man, Sir, I wish you much joy; or to a man who has lost his son, Sir, I am sorry for your loss; and both with a countenance equally unmoved; but he will say in effect the same thing, in a more elegant and less trivial manner, and with a countenance adapted to the occasion. He will advance with warmth, vivacity, and a cheerful countenance to the new-married man, and embracing him, perhaps say to him, "If you do justice to my attachment to you, you will judge of the joy that I feel upon this occasion better than I can express it," etc. To the other in affliction he will advance slowly, with a grave composure of countenance, in a more deliberate manner, and, with a lower voice, perhaps say, " I hope you do me the justice to be convinced that I feel whatever you feel, and shall ever be affected where you are concerned."

Your *abord*, I must tell you, was too cold and uniform; I hope it is now mended. It should be respectfully open and cheerful with your superiors, warm and animated with your equals, hearty and free with your inferiors. There is a fashionable kind of *small talk*, that you should get; which, trifling as it is, is of use in mixed companies, and at table, especially in your foreign department; where it keeps off certain serious subjects, that might create disputes, or at least coldness for a time. Upon such occasions it is not amiss to know how to *parler cuisine*, and to be able to dissert upon the growth and flavour of wines. These, it is true, are very little things; but they are little things that occur very often, and therefore should be said *avec gentillesse et grace*. I am sure they must fall often in your way, pray take care to catch them. There is a certain language of conversation, a fashionable diction, of which every gentleman ought to be perfectly master, in whatever language he speaks. The French attend to it carefully, and with great reason; and their language, which is a language of phrases, helps them out exceedingly. That delicacy of diction is characteristical of a man of fashion and good company.

I could write folios upon this subject, and not exhaust it, but I think, and hope, that to you I need not. You have heard and seen enough, to be convinced of the truth and importance of what I have been so long inculcating into you upon these points. How happy am I, and how happy are you, my dear child, that these Titian tints, and Guido graces, are all that you want to complete my hopes and your own character! But then, on the other hand, what a drawback would it be to that happiness, if you should never acquire them! I remember, when I was of your age, though I had not near so good an education as you have, or seen a quarter so much of the world, I observed those masterly touches, and irresistible graces in others, and saw the necessity of acquiring them myself; but then an awkward *mauvaise honte*, of which I had brought a great deal with me from Cambridge, made me ashamed to attempt it, especially if any of my counntrymen and particular acquaintance were by. This was extremely absurd in me; for without attempting I

could never succeed. But at last, insensibly, by frequenting a
great deal of good company, and imitating those whom I saw
that everybody liked, I formed myself *tant bien que mal*. For
God's sake, let this last fine varnish, so necessary to give lustre
to the whole piece, be the sole and single object now of your
utmost attention. Berlin may contribute a great deal to it if you
please; there are all the ingredients that compose it.

A propos of Berlin; while you are there, take care to seem
ignorant of all political matters between the two Courts; such
as the affairs of Ostfrise, and Saxe Lawemburg, etc., and enter
into no conversations upon those points; however, be as well
at Court as you possibly can; live at it, and make one of it.
Should General Keith * offer you civilities, do not decline them;
but return them, however, without being *enfant de la maison
chez lui;* say *des choses flatteuses* of the Royal Family, and
especially of his Prussian Majesty, to those who are the most
like to repeat them. In short, make yourself well there, without
making yourself ill *somewhere else.* † Make compliments from
me to Algarotti, and converse with him in Italian.

I go next week to the Bath, for a deafness, which I have been
plagued with these four or five months; and which, I am assured,
that pumping my head will remove. This deafness, I own, has
tried my patience; as it has cut me off from society, at an age
when I had no pleasures but those left. In the meantime, I have,
by reading and writing, made my eyes supply the defect of my
ears. Madam H——, I suppose, entertained both yours alike;
however, I am very glad you were well with her; for she is a
good *Prôneuse*, and puffs are very useful to a young fellow at
his entrance into the world.

If you should meet with Lord Pembroke again, anywhere,
make him many compliments from me; and tell him, I should

---

* James Keith, brother of the exiled Earl Marischal of Scotland. He
afterwards attained the rank of Field-Marshal in the Prussian service,
and was killed at the battle of Hochkirchen, October 14, 1758.

† Great coldness, nay even aversion, prevailed at this period, between
the two monarchs, George and Frederick the Second. Only a year afterwards (September 21, 1753) we find the Duke of Newcastle write to Lord
Hardwicke as follows: "The King of Prussia is now avowedly the
principal, if not the sole support of the Pretender and of the Jacobite
cause."—M.

have written to him, but that I knew how troublesome an old correspondent must be to a young one. He is much commended in the accounts from Hanover.*

You will stay at Berlin just as long as you like it, and no longer; and from thence you are absolutely master of your own motions, either to the Hague, or to Brussels; but I think you had better go to the Hague first, because that from thence Brussels will be in your way to Calais, which is a much better passage to England, than from Helvoetsluys. The two Courts of the Hague and Brussels are worth your seeing; and you will see them both to advantage, by means of Colonel Yorke and Dayrolles. Adieu. Here is enough for some time.

CCV.

LONDON, *September* 26, 1752.

MY DEAR FRIEND,

As you chiefly employ, or rather wholly engross my thoughts, I see every day, with increasing pleasure, the fair prospect which you have before you. I had two views in your education; they draw nearer and nearer, and I have now very little reason to distrust your answering them fully. Those two were, Parliamentary and foreign affairs. In consequence of those views, I took care first, to give you a sufficient stock of sound learning, and next, an early knowledge of the world. Without making a figure in Parliament, no man can make any in this country; and eloquence alone enables a man to make a figure in Parliament, unless it be a very mean and contemptible one, which those make there who silently vote, and who do *pedibus ire in sententiam.* Foreign affairs, when skilfully managed, and supported by a Parliamentary reputation, lead to whatever is most considerable in this country. You have the languages necessary for that purpose, with a sufficient fund of historical and treaty knowledge; that is to say, you have the matter ready, and only want the manner. Your objects being thus fixed, I recommend

---

* Henry Herbert succeeded in 1751 his father as Earl of Pembroke. The favourable accounts from Hanover which Lord Chesterfield mentions, were far from being confirmed by his subsequent career, as may be seen more fully in Horace Walpole's Letters. (To Geo. Montague, February 22, 1762, etc.)—M.

to you to have them constantly in your thoughts, and to direct your reading, your actions, and your words, to those views. Most people think only *ex re natâ*, and few *ex professo :* I would have you do both, but begin with the latter.

I explain myself: Lay down certain principles, and reason and act consequentially from them. As for example: say to yourself, I will make a figure in Parliament, and in order to do that, I must not only speak, but speak very well. Speaking mere common sense will by no means do; and I must speak not only correctly but elegantly; and not only elegantly but eloquently. In order to this, I will first take pains to get an habitual, but unaffected purity, correctness, and elegancy of style in my common conversation; I will seek for the best words, and take care to reject improper, inexpressive, and vulgar ones. I will read the greatest masters of oratory, both ancient and modern, and I will read them singly in that view. I will study Demosthenes and Cicero, not to discover an old Athenian or Roman custom, nor to puzzle myself with the value of talents, mines, drachms, and sesterces, like the learned blockheads in *us ;* but to observe their choice of words, their harmony of diction, their method, their distribution, their *exordia,* to engage the favour and attention of their audience; and their perorations, to enforce what they have said, and to leave a strong impression upon the passions. Nor will I be pedant enough to neglect the moderns; for I will likewise study Atterbury, Dryden, Pope, and Bolingbroke; nay, I will read everything that I do read, in that intention, and never cease improving and refining my style upon the best models, till at last I become a model of eloquence myself, which, by care, it is in every man's power to be. If you set out upon this principle, and keep it constantly in your mind, every company you go into, and every book you read, will contribute to your improvement, either by showing you what to imitate, or what to avoid. Are you to give an account of anything to a mixed company ? or are you to endeavour to persuade either man or woman ? This principle, fixed in your mind, will make you carefully attend to the choice of your words, and to the clearness and harmony of your diction.

So much for your Parliamentary object; now to the foreign one.

Lay down first those principles which are absolutely necessary to form a skilful and successful negotiation, and form yourself accordingly. What are they? First, the clear historical knowledge of past transactions of that kind. That you have pretty well already, and will have daily more and more; for, in consequence of that principle, you will read history, memoirs, anecdotes, etc., in that view chiefly. The other necessary talents for negotiation are—the great art of pleasing, and engaging the affection and confidence, not only of those with whom you are to cooperate, but even of those whom you are to oppose: to conceal your own thoughts and views, and to discover other people's: to engage other people's confidence, by a seeming cheerful frankness and openness, without going a step too far: to get the personal favour of the King, Prince, Ministers, or Mistress, of the court to which you are sent: to gain the absolute command over your temper and your countenance, that no heat may provoke you to say, nor no change of countenance betray, what should be a secret. To familiarise and domesticate yourself in the houses of the most considerable people of the place, so as to be received there rather as a friend to the family than as a foreigner. Having these principles constantly in your thoughts, everything you do and everything you say, will some way or other tend to your main view: and common conversation will gradually fit you for it. You will get a habit of checking any rising heat; you will be upon your guard against any indiscreet expression; you will by degrees get the command of your countenance, so as not to change it upon any the most sudden accident: and you will, above all things, labour to acquire the great art of pleasing, without which nothing is to be done.

Company is, in truth, a constant state of negotiation; and if you attend to it in that view, will qualify you for any. By the same means that you make a friend, guard against an enemy, or gain a mistress, you will make an advantageous treaty, baffle those who counteract you, and gain the Court you are sent to. Make this use of all the company you keep, and your very pleasures will make you a successful negotiator. Please all who are worth pleasing; offend none. Keep your own secret, and get out other people's. Keep your own temper, and artfully warm other people's. Counterwork your rivals with diligence and dexterity, but at the same time with the utmost personal civility to them; and be firm without heat. Messieurs D'Avaux and Servien* did no more than this. I must make one observation, in confirmation of this assertion; which is, that the most eminent negotiators have always been the politest and best-bred men in company; even what the women call the *prettiest men.* For God's sake, never lose view of these two your capital objects; bend everything to them, try everything by their rules, and calculate everything for their purposes. What is peculiar to these two objects, is, that they require nothing but what one's own vanity, interest, and pleasure would make one do independently of them. If a man were never to be in business, and always to lead a private life, would he not desire to please and to persuade? so that in your two destinations, your fortune and figure luckily conspire with your vanity and your pleasures. Nay more; a foreign minister, I will maintain it, can never be a good man of business if he is not an agreeable man of pleasure too. Half his business is done by the help of his pleasures; his views are carried on, and perhaps best, and most unsuspectedly, at balls, suppers, assemblies, and parties of pleasure; by intrigues with women, and connections insensibly formed with men, at those unguarded hours of amusement.

These objects now draw very near you, and you have no time to lose in preparing yourself to meet them. You will be in Parliament almost as soon as your age will allow, and I believe you will have a foreign department still sooner, and that will be earlier than ever anybody had one. If you set out well at one-and-twenty, what may you not reasonably hope to be at one-and-forty? All that I could wish you. Adieu!

CCVI.

LONDON, *September* 29, 1752.

My DEAR FRIEND,

There is nothing so necessary, but at the same time there is nothing more difficult (I know it by experience) for you young

---

* Abel Servien, born at Grenoble in 1593, highly distinguished himself in several negotiations, and was during three years the colleague of Comte D'Avaux at the Congress of Munster.—M.

fellows, than to know how to behave yourselves prudently towards
those whom you do not like. Your passions are warm, and your
heads are light; you hate all those who oppose your views,
either of ambition or love; and a rival, in either, is almost a
synonymous term for an enemy. Whenever you meet such a
man, you are awkwardly cold to him, at best; but often rude, and
always desirous to give him some indirect slap. This is unreasonable; for one man has as good a right to pursue an employment, or a mistress, as another; but it is, into the bargain,
extremely imprudent; because you commonly defeat your own
purpose by it, and while you are contending with each other, a
third often prevails. I grant you, that the situation is irksome;
a man cannot help thinking as he thinks, nor feeling what he
feels; and it is a very tender and sore point to be thwarted and
counterworked in one's pursuits at Court, or with a mistress; but
prudence and abilities must check the effects, though they cannot remove the cause. Both the pretenders make themselves
disagreeable to their mistress, when they spoil the company by
their pouting, or their sparring; whereas, if one of them has
command enough over himself (whatever he may feel inwardly)
to be cheerful, gay, and easily and unaffectedly civil to the other,
as if there were no manner of competition between them, the
lady will certainly like him the best, and his rival will be ten
times more humbled and discouraged; for he will look upon such
a behaviour as a proof of the triumph and security of his rival;
he will grow outrageous with the lady, and the warmth of his
reproaches will probably bring on a quarrel between them. It
is the same in business; where he who can command his temper
and his countenance the best, will always have an infinite advantage over the other. This is what the French call *un procédé
honnête et galant,* to *pique* yourself upon showing particular civilities to a man, to whom lesser minds would in the same case
show dislike, or perhaps rudeness. I will give you an instance
of this in my own case; and pray remember it, whenever you
come to be, as I hope you will, in a like situation.

When I went to the Hague, in 1744,* it was to engage the

* According to the present style of computation, Lord Chesterfield
should have said 1745. But until the passing of his own Act, in 1751, the
Civil, Ecclesiastical, and Legal year was reckoned as commencing only on

Dutch to come roundly into the war, and to stipulate their quotas of troops, etc.; your acquaintance, the Abbé de la Ville, was there on the part of France, to endeavour to hinder them from coming into the war at all. I was informed, and very sorry to hear it, that he had abilities, temper, and industry. We could not visit, our two masters being at war; but the first time I met him at a third place, I got somebody to present me to him; and I told him, that though we were to be national enemies, I flattered myself we might be, however, personal friends; with a good deal more of the same kind, which he returned in full as polite a manner. Two days afterwards I went, early in the morning, to solicit the deputies of Amsterdam, where I found l'Abbé de la Ville,* who had been beforehand with me; upon which I addressed myself to the Deputies, and said, smilingly, *Je suis bien fâché, Messieurs, de trouver mon ennemi avec vous; je le connois déjà assez pour le craindre; la partie n'est pas égale, mais je me fie à vos propres intérêts contre les talens de mon ennemi; et au moins si je n'ai pas eu le premier mot j'aurai le dernier aujourd'hui.* They smiled; the Abbé was pleased with the compliment, and the manner of it, stayed about a quarter of an hour, and then left me to my Deputies, with whom I continued upon the same tone, though in a very serious manner, and told them that I was only come to state their own true interests to them, plainly and simply, without any of those arts, which it was very necessary for my friend to make use of to deceive them. I carried my point, and continued my *procédé* with the Abbé; and by this easy and polite commerce with him, at third places, I often found means to fish out from him whereabouts he was.

Remember, there are but two *procédés* in the world for a gentleman and a man of parts; either extreme politeness or knocking down. If a man, notoriously and designedly insults and affronts you, knock him down; but if he only injures you, your best revenge is to be extremely civil to him in your outward behaviour, though at the same time you counterwork him, and return him the compliment, perhaps with interest. This is not perfidy nor dissimulation; it would be so, if you were at the same

the 25th of March.—See Sir Harris Nicholas's valuable Chronology of History, p. 38, ed. 1833.—M.

* See Letter of 7 April, 1751.

time, to make professions of esteem and friendship to this man, which I by no means recommend, but, on the contrary, abhor. All acts of civility are, by common consent, understood to be no more than a conformity to custom, for the quiet and conveniency of society, the *agrémens* of which are not to be disturbed by private dislikes and jealousies. Only women and little minds pout and spar for the entertainment of the company, that always laughs at, and never pities them. For my own part, though I would by no means give up any point to a competitor, yet I would pique myself upon showing him rather more civility than to another man. In the first place, this *procédé* infallibly makes all *les rieurs* of your side, which is a considerable party; and in the next place, it certainly pleases the object of the competition, be it either man or woman; who never fail to say, upon such occasion, that *they must own you have behaved yourself very handsomely in the whole affair.* The world judges from the appearances of things, and not from the reality, which few are able, and still fewer are inclined, to fathom; and a man who will take care always to be in the right in those things, may afford to be sometimes a little in the wrong in more essential ones; there is a willingness, a desire to excuse him. With nine people in ten, good-breeding passes for goodnature, and they take attentions for good offices. At courts there will be always coldnesses, dislikes, jealousies, and hatred, the harvest being but small in proportion to the number of labourers; but then, as they arise often, they die soon, unless they are perpetuated by the manner in which they have been carried on, more than by the matter which occasioned them. The turns and vicissitudes of courts frequently make friends of enemies and enemies of friends; you must labour, therefore, to acquire that great and uncommon talent, of hating with good-breeding, and loving with prudence; to make no quarrel irreconcilable, by silly and unnecessary indications of anger; and no friendship dangerous in case it breaks, by a wanton, indiscreet, and unreserved confidence.

Few (especially young) people know how to love, or how to hate; their love is an unbounded weakness, fatal to the person they love; their hate is a hot, rash, and imprudent violence, always fatal to themselves. Nineteen fathers in twenty, and every mother who had loved you half as well as I do, would have ruined you; whereas I always made you feel the weight of my authority, that you might one day know the force of my love. Now, I both hope and believe, my advice will have the same weight with you from choice, that my authority had from necessity. My advice is just eight-and-thirty years older than your own, and consequently, I believe you think, rather better. As for your tender and pleasurable passions, manage them yourself; but let me have the direction of all the others. Your ambition, your figure, and your fortune, will, for some time at least, be rather safer in my keeping than in your own. Adieu!

CCVII.

BATH, *October* 4, 1752.

MY DEAR FRIEND,

I consider you now at the court of Augustus,* where, if ever the desire of pleasing animated you, it must make you exert all the means of doing it. You will see there, full as well, I dare say, as Horace did at Rome, how States are defended by arms, adorned by manners, and improved by laws. Nay, you have an Horace there, as well as an Augustus; I need not name Voltaire, *qui nil molitur inepte*, as Horace himself said of another poet. I have lately read over all his works that are published, though I had read them more than once before. I was induced to this by his *Siècle de Louis XIV.*, which I have yet read but four times. In reading over all his works, with more attention I suppose than before, my former admiration of him is, I own, turned into astonishment. There is no one kind of writing in which he has not excelled. You are so severe a classic, that I question whether you will allow me to call his *Henriade* an epic poem, for want of the proper number of gods, devils, witches, and other absurdities. requisite for the machinery; which machinery is (it seems) necessary to constitute the *Epopée*. But whether you do or not, I will declare (though possibly to my own shame) that I never read any epic poem with near so much pleasure. I am grown old, and have possibly lost a great deal of that fire which formerly made me love fire in others at any rate, and however attended with smoke; but now I must have all sense, and cannot for the sake of five righteous lines forgive a thousand absurd ones.

* Frederick the Second.

In this disposition of mind, judge whether I can read all Homer through *tout de suite*. I admire his beauties; but, to tell you the truth, when he slumbers I sleep. Virgil, I confess, is all sense, and therefore I like him better than his model; but he is often languid, especially in his five or six last books, during which I am obliged to take a good deal of snuff. Besides, I profess myself an ally of Turnus's against the pious Æneas, who, like many *soi disant* pious people, does the most flagrant injustice and violence, in order to execute what they impudently call the will of Heaven. But what will you say, when I tell you truly, that I cannot possibly read our countryman, Milton, through? I acknowledge him to have some most sublime passages, some prodigious flashes of light; but then you must acknowledge, that light is often followed by *darkness visible*, to use his own expression. Besides, not having the honour to be acquainted with any of the parties in his poem, except the man and the woman, the characters and speeches of a dozen or two of angels, and of as many devils, are as much above my reach as my entertainment. Keep this secret for me; for if it should be known, I should be abused by every tasteless pedant, and every solid divine, in England.

Whatever I have said to the disadvantage of these three Poems, holds much stronger against Tasso's *Gierusalemme;* it is true, he has very fine and glaring rays of poetry; but then they are only meteors, they dazzle, then disappear, and are succeeded by false thoughts, poor *concetti*, and absurd impossibilities; witness the Fish and the Parrot; extravagances unworthy of an heroic poem, and would much better have become Ariosto, who professes *le coglionerie.*

I have never read the *Lusiad* of Camoens, except in a prose translation, consequently I have never read it at all, so shall say nothing of it; but the *Henriade* is all sense from the beginning to the end, often adorned by the justest and liveliest reflections, the most beautiful descriptions, the noblest images, and the sublimest sentiments; not to mention the harmony of the verse, in which Voltaire undoubtedly exceeds all the French poets. Should you insist upon an exception in favour of Racine, I must insist, on my part, that he at least equals him. What hero ever interested more than Henry IV., who, according to the rules of

Epic poetry, carries on one great and long action, and succeeds in it at last ? What description ever excited more horror than those, first of the massacre, and then of the famine, at Paris ? Was love ever painted with more truth and *morbidezza* than in the ninth book ? Not better, in my mind, even in the fourth of Virgil. Upon the whole, with all your classical rigour, if you will but suppose *St. Louis* a god, a devil, or a witch, and that he appears in person and not in a dream, the *Henriade* will be an Epic poem, according to the strictest statute laws of the *Epopée;* but in my court of equity it is one as it is.

I could expatiate as much upon all his different works, but that I should exceed the bounds of a letter, and run into a dissertation. How delightful is his History of that Northern brute, the King of Sweden ! * for I cannot call him a man; and I should be sorry to have him pass for a hero, out of regard to those true heroes, such as Julius Cæsar, Titus, Trajan, and the present King of Prussia; who cultivated and encouraged arts and sciences; whose animal courage was accompanied by the tender and social sentiments of humanity; and who had more pleasure in improving than in destroying their fellow creatures. What can be more touching or more interesting, what more nobly thought or more happily expressed, than all his dramatic pieces ? What can be more clear and rational than all his philosophical letters ? and what ever was so graceful and gentle as all his little poetical trifles ? You are fortunately *à portée* of verifying, by your knowledge of the man, all that I have said of his works.

Monsieur de Maupertuis (whom I hope you will get acquainted with) is, what one rarely meets with, deep in philosophy and mathematics, and yet *honnête et aimable homme;* Algarotti is young Fontenelle. Such men must necessarily give you the desire of pleasing them; and if you can frequent them, their acquaintance will furnish you the means of pleasing everybody else.

A propos of pleasing; your pleasing Mrs. Fitzgerald is expected here in two or three days; I will do all that I can for you with her. I think you carried on the romance to the third or

* Charles the Twelfth. Voltaire's Life of that monarch first appeared in 1731.

fourth volume; I will continue it to the eleventh; but as to the
twelfth and last, you must come and conclude it yourself. *Non
sum qualis eram.*

Good-night to you, child! for I am going to bed, just at the
hour at which I suppose you are beginning to live, at Berlin.

CCVIII.

BATH, *November* 16, 1752.

MY DEAR FRIEND,

Vanity, or to call it by a gentler name, the desire of admiration and applause, is perhaps the most universal principle of
human actions. I do not say that it is the best; and I will own
that it is sometimes the cause of both foolish and criminal effects.
But it is so much oftener the principle of right things, that,
though they ought to have a better, yet, considering human
nature, that principle is to be encouraged and cherished in consideration of its effects. Where that desire is wanting, we are
apt to be indifferent, listless, indolent, and inert; we do not exert
our powers, and we appear to be as much below ourselves as the
vainest man living can desire to appear above what he really is.

As I have made you my confessor, and do not scruple to confess even my weaknesses to you, I will fairly own that I had that
vanity, that weakness, if it be one, to a prodigious degree; and
what is more, I confess it without repentance; nay, I am glad I
had it; since, if I have had the good fortune to please in the
world, it is to that powerful and active principle that I owe it. I
began the world, not with a bare desire, but with an insatiable
thirst, a rage of popularity, applause, and admiration. If this
made me do some silly things, on one hand, it made me, on the
other hand, do almost all the right things that I did; it made
me attentive and civil to the women I disliked, and to the men I
despised, in hopes of the applause of both; though I neither
desired, nor would I have accepted, the favours of the one, nor
the friendship of the other. I always dressed, looked, and talked
my best, and, I own, was overjoyed whenever I perceived that by
all three, or by any one of them, the company was pleased with
me. To men, I talked whatever I thought would give them the
best opinion of my parts and learning, and to women, what I was
sure would please them—flattery, gallantry, and love.

And, moreover, I will own to you, under the secrecy of confession, that my vanity has very often made me take great pains to make many a woman in love with me, if I could, for whose person I would not have given a pinch of snuff. In company with men, I always endeavoured to out-shine, or, at least if possible, to equal, the most shining man in it. This desire elicited whatever powers I had to gratify it; and where I could not perhaps shine in the first, enabled me, at least, to shine in a second or third sphere. By these means I soon grew in fashion; and when a man is once in fashion all he does is right. It was infinite pleasure to me, to find my own fashion and popularity. I was sent for to all parties of pleasure, both of men or women, where, in some measure, I gave the tone. This gave me the reputation of having had some women of condition; and that reputation, whether true or false, really got me others. With the men I was a Proteus, and assumed every shape in order to please them all: among the gay I was the gayest, among the grave the gravest; and I never omitted the least attentions of good breeding, or the least offices of friendship, that could either please, or attach them to me, and accordingly I was soon connected with all the men of any fashion or figure in town.

To this principle of vanity, which philosophers call a mean one, and which I do not, I owe great part of the figure which I have 'made in life. I wish you had as much, but I fear you have too little of it; and you seem to have a degree of laziness and listlessness about you, that makes you indifferent as to general applause. This is not in character at your age, and would be barely pardonable in an elderly and philosophical man. It is a vulgar, ordinary saying, but it is a very true one, that one should always put the best foot foremost. One should please, shine, and dazzle, wherever it is possible. At Paris, I am sure you must observe *que chacun se fait valoir autant qu'il est possible;* and La Bruyere observes, very justly, *qu'on ne vaut dans ce monde que ce qu'on veut valoir;* wherever applause is in question, you will never see a French man, nor woman, remiss or negligent. Observe the eternal attentions and politeness that all people have there for one another. *Ce n'est pas pour leurs beaux yeux, au moins.* No, but for their own sakes—for commendations and applause. Let me then recommend this principle of vanity to you; act upon it *meo periculo;* I promise you it will turn to your account. Practise all the arts that ever coquette did, to please; be alert and indefatigable in making every man admire, and every woman in love with you. I can tell you, too, that nothing will carry you higher in the world.

I have had no letter from you since your arrival at Paris, though you must have been long enough there to have written me two or three. In about ten or twelve days I propose leaving this place, and going to London. I have found considerable benefit by my stay here, but not all that I want. Make my compliments to Lord Albemarle.

CCIX.

BATH, *November* 28, 1752.

MY DEAR FRIEND,

Since my last to you, I have read Madame Maintenon's Letters ;* I am sure they are genuine, and they both entertained and informed me. They have brought me acquainted with the character of that able and artful lady; whom I am convinced that I now know much better than her *directeur* the Abbé de Fenelon (afterwards Archbishop of Cambray) did, when he wrote her 185th letter; and I know him the better too for that letter. The Abbé, though brimful of the divine love, had a great mind to be first Minister and Cardinal, in order, *no doubt,* to have an opportunity of doing the more good. His being *directeur* at that time to Madame Maintenon, seemed to be a good step towards those views. She put herself upon him for a saint, and he was weak enough to believe it; he, on the other hand, would have put himself upon her for a saint too, which I dare say she did not believe; but both of them knew that it was necessary for them to appear saints to Louis XIV., who they were very sure was a bigot. It is to be presumed, nay, indeed, it is plain by that 185th letter, that Madame Maintenon had hinted to her *directeur* some scruples of conscience, with relation to her commerce with the King; and which I humbly apprehend to have been only some scruples of prudence, at once to flatter the bigot character and increase the desires of the King.

* The letters of Madame de Maintenon, as collected by La Beaumelle, were first published at Nancy in 1752.—M.

The pious Abbé, frightened out of his wits, lest the King should impute to the *directeur* any scruples or difficulties which he might meet with on the part of the lady, writes her the above-mentioned letter; in which he not only bids her not to teaze the King by advice and exhortations, but to have the utmost submission to his will; and, that she might not mistake the nature of that submission, he tells her it is the same that Sarah had for Abraham; to which submission Isaac perhaps was owing. No bawd could have written a more seducing letter to an innocent country girl than the *directeur* did to his *penitente*, who, I dare say, had no occasion for his good advice. Those who would justify the good *directeur*, alias the pimp, in this affair, must not attempt to do it by saying that the King and Madame Maintenon were at that time privately married; that the *directeur* knew it; and that this was the meaning of his *enigme*. That is absolutely impossible; for that private marriage must have removed all scruples between the parties; nay, could not have been contracted upon any other principle, since it was kept private, and consequently prevented no public scandal. It is therefore extremely evident, that Madame Maintenon could not be married to the King at the time when she scrupled granting, and when the *directeur* advised her to grant, those favours with so much submission granted to Abraham; and what the *directeur* is pleased to call *le mystère de Dieu*, was most evidently a state of concubinage. The letters are very well worth your reading; they throw light upon many things of those times.

I have just received a letter from Sir William Stanhope, from Lyons; in which he tells me that he saw you at Paris, that he thinks you a little grown, but that you do not make the most of it, for that you stoop still; *d'ailleurs* his letter was a panegyric of you.

The young Comte de Schullemburg, the Chambellan whom you knew at Hanover, is come over with the King, *et fait aussi vos éloges*.

Though, as I told you in my last, I have done buying pictures, by way of *virtù*, yet there are some portraits of remarkable people that would tempt me. For instance, if you could by chance pick up at Paris, at a reasonable price and undoubted originals (whether heads, half-lengths, or whole-lengths, no matter) of

Cardinals Richelieu, Mazarin, and Retz, Monsieur de Turenne, le grand Prince de Condé, Mesdames de Montespan, de Fontanges, de Montbazon, de Sévigné, de Maintenon, de Chevreuse, de Longueville, d'Olonne, etc., I should be tempted to purchase them. I am sensible that they can only be met with by great accident, at family sales and auctions, so I only mention the affair to you eventually.

I do not understand, or else I do not remember, what affair you mean in your last letter; which you think will come to nothing, and for which you say I had once a mind that you should take the road again. Explain it to me.

I shall go to town in four or five days, and carry back with me a little more hearing than I brought; but yet not half enough for common use. One wants ready pocket money much oftener than one wants great sums; and, to use a very odd expression, I want to hear at sight. I love every-day senses, every-day wit and entertainment; a man who is only good on holidays is good for very little. Adieu!

CCX.

London, New-Year's-Day, 1753.

My dear Friend,

It is now above a fortnight since I have received a letter from you. I hope, however, that you are well, but engrossed by the business of Lord Albemarle's *bureau* in the mornings, and by business of a genteeler nature in the evenings; for I willingly give up my own satisfaction to your improvement, either in business or manners.

Here have been lately imported from Paris two gentlemen, who I find, were much acquainted with you there; Comte Sinzendorf, and Monsieur Clairaut, the Academician.* The former is a very pretty man, well-bred, and with a great deal of useful knowledge; for those two things are very consistent. I examined him about you, thinking him a competent judge. He told me, *que vous parliez l'Allemand comme un Allemand ; que vous sçaviez*

---

* Alexis Claude Clairaut, born at Paris in 1713, obtained a high reputation by his mathematical attainments. He was one of the Academicians who travelled to Lapland in order to measure a degree of the meridian, and thus determine the figure of the earth.

*le droit public de l'empire parfaitement bien ; que vous aviez le
goût sur, et des connoissances fort étendues.*   I told him, that I
knew all this very well, but that I wanted to know whether you
had *l'air, les manières, les attentions, enfin le brillant d'un honnête
homme ;* his answer was, *Mais oui en vérité c'est fort bien.* This,
you see, is but cold, in comparison of what I do wish, and of
what you ought to wish.   Your friend Clairaut interposed, and
said, *Mais je vous assure qu'il est fort poli ;* to which I answered,
*Je le crois bien, vis-a-vis des Lapons vos amis ; je vous recuse pour
juge, jusqu'à ce que vous ayez été délaponné, au moins dix ans,
parmi les honnêtes gens.*   These testimonies in your favour are
such as perhaps you are satisfied with, and think sufficient ; but
I am not ; they are only the cold depositions of disinterested and
unconcerned witnesses, upon a strict examination.   When upon
a trial, a man calls witnesses to his character, and those witnesses
only say, that they never heard, nor do not know any ill of him ;
it intimates at best a neutral aud insignificant, though innocent
character.   Now I want, and you ought to endeavour, that *les
agrémens, les graces, les attentions*, etc., should be a distinguished
part of your character, and specified of you by people unasked.
I wish to hear people say of you, *Ah, qu'il est aimable !   Quelles
manières, quelles graces, quel art de plaire !* Nature, thank God,
has given you all the powers necessary ; and if she has not yet,
I hope in God she will give you the will of exerting them.

  I have lately read, with great pleasure, Voltaire's two little
Histories of *les Croisades,* and *l'Esprit Humain ;* which I recommend to your persual, if you have not already read them.   They
are bound up with a most poor performance, called *Micromégas,*
which is said to be Voltaire's too ; but I cannot believe it, it is
so very unworthy of him ;* it consists only of thoughts stolen
from Swift, but miserably mangled and disfigured.   But his
History of the *Croisades* shows, in a very short and strong light,
the most immoral and wicked scheme, that was ever contrived
by knaves, and executed by madmen and fools, against humanity.
There is a strange, but never-failing relation, between honest
madmen and skilful knaves ; and whenever one meets with

  * It was, however, written by Voltaire, and is comprised in all complete editions of his works. The idea is derived from *Gulliver's Travels.*

collected numbers of the former, one may be very sure that they are secretly directed by the latter. The Popes who have generally been both the ablest and the greatest knaves in Europe, wanted all the power and money of the East; for they had all that was in Europe already. The times and the minds favoured their design, for they were dark and uninformed; and Peter the Hermit, at once a knave and a madman, was a fine Papal tool for so wild and wicked an undertaking. I wish we had good histories of every part of Europe, and indeed of the world, written upon the plan of Voltaire's *de l'Esprit Humain;* for I own I am provoked at the contempt which most historians show for humanity in general; one would think by them that the whole human species consisted but of about a hundred and fifty people, called and dignified (commonly very undeservedly too) by the titles of Emperors, Kings, Popes, Generals, and ministers.

I have never seen in any of the newspapers any mention of the affairs of the Cevennes,* or Grenoble, which you gave me an account of some time ago; and the Duke de Mirepoix† pretends, at least, to know nothing of either. Were they false reports, or does the French Court choose to stifle them? I hope that they are both true, because I am very willing that the cares of the French government should be employed and confined to themselves.

Your friend, the Electress Palatine,‡ has sent me six wild boars' head, and other *pièces de sa chasse,* in return for the fans, which she approved of extremely. This present was signified to me by one Mr. Harold, who wrote me a letter in very indifferent English; I suppose he is a Dane who has been in England.

Mr. Harte came to town yesterday, and dined with me to-day.

---

* Lord Chesterfield here alludes to the renewal of persecution against the Protestants in the Cevennes. In 1752, François Bénezet, one of their preachers, was executed at Montpellier, and died, says Sismondi, *chantant le psaume* 51, *et offrant sa vie à Dieu avec un visage serein.* The same historian adds, that whenever prisoners were taken from this poor "hill-folk," *les hommes furent condamnés aux galères à vie; les femmes à la prison perpétuelle* . . . *maintesfois les soldats tirèrent sur ces troupes désarmées et fugitives, et le champ de la prière fut souvent convert de morts ou de blessés.* (*Hist. des Francais,* vol. xxix. p. 46.) —M.

† The French Ambassador in London.

‡ Mary Elizabeth, born 1721, and consort of Charles Theodore, Elector Palatine. Or, perhaps, the Dowager Electress, Eleonora Philippina of Hesse Rheinfeld.—M.

We talked you over; and I assure you, that though a parson, and no member *du beau monde,* he thinks all the most shining accomplishments of it full as necessary for you as I do. His expression was, *That is all that he wants; but if he wants that, considering his situation and destination, he might as well want everything else.*

This is the day when people reciprocally offer and receive the kindest and warmest wishes, though in general without meaning them on one side, or believing them on the other.   They are formed by the head, in compliance with custom, though disavowed by the heart, in consequence of nature. His wishes upon this occasion are the best, that are the best turned; you do not, I am sure, doubt the truth of mine, and therefore I will express them with a Quaker-like simplicity. May this new year be a very new one indeed to you; may you put off the old, and put on the new man! but I mean the outward, not the inward man. With this alteration, I might justly sum up all my wishes for you in these words: Dii tibi dent annos, de te nam cætera sumes! *

This minute I receive your letter of the 26th past, which gives me a very disagreeable reason for your late silence. By the symptoms which you mention of your illness, I both hope and believe that it was wholly owing to your own want of care. You are rather inclined to be fat, you have naturally a good stomach, and you eat at the best tables; which must of course make you plethoric; and, upon my word, you will be very subject to these accidents, if you will not from time to time, when you find yourself full, heated, or your head aching, take some little easy preventive purge, that would not confine you; such as chewing a little rhubarb when you go to bed at night, or some senna tea in the morning. You do very well to live extremely low, for some time; and I could wish, though I do not expect it, that you would take one gentle vomit; for those giddinesses, and swimmings in the head, always proceed from some foulness of the stomach.   However, upon the whole, I am very glad that your old complaint has not mixed itself with this, which I am fully convinced arises singly from your own negligence.   Adieu!

I am sorry for Monsieur Kurzé,† upon his sister's account.

---

* Ovid, *Epistles from Pontus,* ii. 1, 53, quoted before in Letter of Dec. 26, 1749.

† A brother, probably, of Madame de Mouconseil.—M.

CCXI.

LONDON, *January* 15, 1753.

MY DEAR FRIEND,

I never think my time so well employed, as when I think it employed to your advantage. You have long had the greatest share of it; you now engross it. The moment is now decisive; the piece is now going to be exhibited to the public; the mere outlines, and the general colouring, are not sufficient to attract the eyes, and to secure applause; but the last finishing, artful, and delicate strokes, are necessary. Skilful judges will discern, and acknowledge their merit; the ignorant will, without knowing why, feel their power. In that view, I have thrown together, for your use, the enclosed maxims, or, to speak more properly, observations on men and things; for I have no merit as to the invention; I am no system-monger; and, instead of giving way to my imagination, I have only consulted my memory; and my conclusions are all drawn from facts, not fancy.

Most maxim-mongers have preferred the prettiness to the justness of a thought, and the turn to the truth; but I have refused myself to everything that my own experience did not justify and confirm. I wish you would consider them seriously, and separately, and recur to them again *pro re natâ* in similar cases. Young men are as apt to think themselves wise enough, as drunken men are to think themselves sober enough. They look upon spirit to be a much better thing than experience; which they call coldness. They are but half mistaken; for though spirit, without experience, is dangerous, experience, without spirit, is languid and defective. Their union, which is very rare, is perfection; you may join them, if you please, for all my experience is at your service, and I do not desire one grain of your spirit in return. Use them both; and let them reciprocally animate and check each other. I mean here, by the spirit of youth, only the vivacity and presumption of youth; which hinder them from seeing the difficulties or dangers of an undertaking; but I do not mean what the silly vulgar call spirit, by which they are captious, jealous of their rank, suspicious of being undervalued, and tart (as they call it) in their repartees, upon the slightest occasions. This is an evil and a very silly spirit which should be driven out and transferred to a herd of swine. This is not the spirit of a man of fashion, who has kept good company.

People of an ordinary low education, when they happen to fall into good company, imagine themselves the only object of its attention; if the company whispers, it is, to be sure, concerning them; if they laugh, it is at them, and if anything ambiguous, and by the most forced interpretation can be applied to them, happens to be said, they are convinced that it was meant at them; upon which they grow out of countenance first, and then angry. This mistake is very well ridiculed in the "Stratagem,"* where Scrub says, "*I am sure they talked of me, for they laughed consumedly.*" A well-bred man seldom thinks, but never seems to think, himself slighted, undervalued, or laughed at in company, unless where it is so plainly marked out, that his honour obliges him to resent it in a proper manner; *mais les honnêtes gens ne se boudent jamais.* I will admit, that it is very difficult to command one's-self enough to behave with ease, frankness, and good-breeding towards those, who one knows dislike, slight, and injure one as far as they can without personal consequences; but I assert, that it is absolutely necessary to do it; you must embrace the man you hate, if you cannot be justified in knocking him down; for otherwise you avow the injury, which you cannot revenge. A prudent cuckold (and there are many such at Paris) pockets his horns, when he cannot gore with them; and will not add to the triumph of his maker, by only butting with them ineffectually.

A seeming ignorance is very often a most necessary part of worldly knowledge. It is, for instance, commonly advisable to seem ignorant of what people offer to tell you; and, when they say, Have you not heard of such a thing? to answer, No, and to let them go on, though you know it already. Some have a pleasure in telling it, because they think that they tell it well; others have a pride in it, as being the sagacious discoverers; and many have a vanity in showing that they have been, though very undeservedly, trusted; all these would be disappointed, and consequently displeased, if you said, Yes. Seem always ignorant (unless to one most intimate friend) of all matters of private scandal and defamation, though you should hear them a thousand times; for

* The *Beaux Stratagem*, by Farquhar. Act ii. 1.

the parties affected always look upon the receiver to be almost as bad as the thief; and whenever they become the topic of conversation, seem to be a sceptic, though you are really a serious believer; and always take the extenuating part.

But all this seeming ignorance should be joined to thorough and extensive private informations; and, indeed, it is the best method of procuring them; for most people have such a vanity, in showing a superiority over others, though but for a moment, and in the merest trifles, that they will tell you what they should not, rather than not show that they can tell what you did not know; besides that, such seeming ignorance will make you pass for incurious, and consequently undesigning. However, fish for facts, and take pains to be well informed of everything that passes; but fish judiciously, and not always, nor indeed often, in the shape of direct questions; which always put people upon their guard, and, often repeated, grow tiresome. But sometimes take the things that you would know for granted; upon which somebody will, kindly and officiously, set you right; sometimes say, that you have heard so and so; and at other times seem to know more than you do, in order to know all that you want; but avoid direct questioning as much as you can. All these necessary arts of the world require constant attention, presence of mind, and coolness. Achilles, though invulnerable, never went to battle but completely armed. Courts are to be the theatres of your wars, where you should be always as completely armed, and even with the addition of a heel-piece. The least inattention, the least *distraction*, may prove fatal. I would fain see you what pedants call *omnis homo*, and what Pope much better calls *all-accomplished;* you have the means in your power, add the will, and you may bring it about. The vulgar have a coarse saying, of *spoiling a hog for a halfpenny worth of tar;* prevent the application, by providing the tar; it is very easily to be had, in comparison with what you have already got.

The fine Mrs. Pitt, who, it seems, saw you often at Paris, speaking of you the other day, said, in French, for she speaks little English,— . . .* Whether it is that you did not pay the homage due to her beauty, or that it did not strike you as it does others, I cannot determine; but I hope she had some other

---

* What Mrs. Pitt said is not given in previous editions.

reason than truth for saying it. I will suppose that you did not care a pin for her; but, however, she surely deserved a degree of propitiatory adoration from you, which I am afraid you neglected. Had I been in your case, I should have endeavoured, at least, to have supplanted Mr. Mackay in his office of nocturnal reader to her. I played at cards, two days ago, with your friend Mrs. Fitzgerald, and her most sublime mother, Mrs. Seagrave; they both inquired after you; and Mrs. Fitzgerald said, she hoped you went on with your dancing; I said Yes, and that you assured me, you had made such considerable improvements in it, that you had now learned to stand still, and even upright. Your *virtuosa*, la Signora Vestri, sang here the other day, with great applause; I presume you are intimately acquainted with her merit. Good night to you, whoever you pass it with.

I have this moment received a packet, sealed with your seal, though not directed by your hand, for Lady Hervey. No letter from you! Are you not well?

MAXIMS:

ENCLOSED IN LETTER OF JANUARY 15, 1753.

A proper secrecy is the only mystery of able men : mystery the only secrecy of weak and cunning ones.

A man who tells nothing, or who tells all, will equally have nothing told him.

If a fool knows a secret, he tells it because he is a fool; if a knave knows one, he tells it wherever it is his interest to tell it. But women and young men are very apt to tell what secrets they know, from the vanity of having been trusted. Trust none of these whenever you can help it.

Inattention to the present business, be it what it will; the doing one thing and thinking at the same time of another, or the attempting to do two things at once, are the never-failing signs of a little frivolous mind.

A man who cannot command his temper, his attention, and his countenance, should not think of being a man of business. The weakest man in the world can avail himself of the passion of the wisest. The inattentive man cannot know the business, and consequently cannot do it. And he who cannot command his countenance, may e'en as well tell his thoughts as show them.

Distrust all those who love you extremely upon a very slight acquaintance, and without any visible reason. Be upon your guard, too, against those who confess as their weaknesses all the cardinal virtues.

In your friendships and in your enmities let your confidence and your hostilities have certain bounds : make not the former dangerous, nor the latter irreconcileable. There are strange vicissitudes in business !

Smooth your way to the head through the heart. The way of reason is a good one ; but it is commonly something longer, and perhaps not so sure.

Spirit is now a very fashionable word : to act with spirit, to speak with spirit, means only to act rashly and to talk indiscreetly. An able man shows his spirit by gentle words and resolute actions ; he is neither hot nor timid.

When a man of sense happens to be in that disagreeable situation, in which he is obliged to ask himself more than once, *What shall I do?* he will answer himself, Nothing. When his reason points out to him no good way, or at least no one way less bad than another, he will stop short and wait for light. A little busy mind runs on at all events, must be doing, and, like a blind horse, fears no dangers because he sees none. *Il faut sçavoir s'ennuyer*.

Patience is a most necessary qualification for business ; many a man would rather you heard his story than granted his request. One must seem to hear the unreasonable demands of the petulant unmoved, and the tedious details of the dull untired. That is the least price that a man must pay for a high station.

It is always right to detect a fraud, and to perceive a folly ; but it is often very wrong to expose either. A man of business should always have his eyes open, but must often seem to have them shut.

In Courts, nobody should be below your management and attention : the links that form the Court-chain are innumerable and inconceivable. You must hear with patience the dull grievances of a Gentleman Usher, or a Page of the Back-stairs; who, very probably, lies with some near relation of the favourite maid, of the favourite mistress, of the favourite Minister, or perhaps of the King himself; and who, consequently, may do you more dark and indirect good or harm than the first man of quality.

One good patron at Court may be sufficient, provided you have no personal enemies; and, in order to have none, you must sacrifice (as the Indians do to the Devil) most of your passions and much of your time to the numberless evil beings that infest it; in order to prevent and avert the mischiefs they can do you.

A young man, be his merit what it will, can never raise himself; but must, like the ivy round the oak, twine himself round some man of great power and interest. You must belong to a Minister some time before anybody will belong to you. And an inviolable fidelity to that Minister, even in his disgrace, will be meritorious, and recommend you to the next. Ministers love a personal, much more than a party attachment.

As Kings are begotten and born like other men, it is to be presumed that they are of the human species; and perhaps, had they the same education, they might prove like other men. But, flattered from their cradles, their hearts are corrupted and their heads are turned, so that they seem to be a species by themselves. No King ever said to himself, *Homo sum, nihil humani a me alienum puto.*

Flattery cannot be too strong for them; drunk with it from their infancy, like old drinkers they require drams.

They prefer a personal attachment to a public service, and reward it better. They are vain and weak enough to look upon it as a free-will offering to their merit, and not as a burnt-sacrifice to their power.

If you would be a favourite of your King, address yourself to his weaknesses. An application to his reason will seldom prove very successful.

In Courts, bashfulness and timidity are as prejudicial on one hand, as impudence and rashness are on the other. A steady assurance and a cool intrepidity, with an exterior modesty, are the true and necessary medium.

Never apply for what you see very little probability of obtaining; for you will, by asking improper and unattainable things, accustom the Ministers to refuse you so often, that they will find it easy to refuse you the properest and most reasonable ones. It is a common, but a most mistaken rule at Court, to ask for everything in order to get something: you do get something by it, it is true, but that something is refusals and ridicule.

There is a Court jargon, a chit-chat, a small talk, which turns singly upon trifles; and which, in a great many words, says little or nothing. It stands fools instead of what they cannot say, and men of sense instead of what they should not say. It is the proper language of levees, drawing-rooms, and antechambers: it is necessary to know it.

Whatever a man is at Court, he must be genteel and wellbred; that cloak covers as many follies as that of charity does sins. I knew a man of great quality, and in a great station at Court, considered and respected, whose highest character was that he was humbly proud and genteelly dull.

It is hard to say which is the greatest fool; he who tells the whole truth, or he who tells no truth at all. Character is as necessary in business as in trade. No man can deceive often in either.

At Court, people embrace without acquaintance, serve one another without friendship, and injure one another without hatred. Interest, not sentiment, is the growth of that soil.

A difference of opinion, though in the merest trifles, alienates little minds, especially of high rank. It is full as easy to commend as to blame a great man's cook, or his tailor: it is shorter too; and the objects are no more worth disputing about than the people are worth disputing with. It is impossible to inform, but very easy to displease them.

A cheerful, easy countenance and behaviour, are very useful at Court; they make fools think you a good-natured man; and they make designing men think you an undesigning one.

There are some occasions in which a man must tell half his secret, in order to conceal the rest; but there is seldom one in which a man should tell it all. Great skill is necessary to know how far to go, and where to stop.

Ceremony is necessary in Courts, as the outwork and defence of manners.

Flattery, though a base coin, is the necessary pocket-money at Court; where, by custom and consent, it has obtained such a currency, that it is no longer a fraudulent, but a legal payment.

If a minister refuses you a reasonable request, and either slights or injures you; if you have not the power to gratify your resentment, have the wisdom to conceal and dissemble it. Seeming good-humour on your part may prevent rancour on his, and perhaps bring things right again; but if you have the power to hurt, hint modestly, that if provoked, you may possibly have the will too. Fear, when real and well-founded, is perhaps a more prevailing motive at Courts than love.

At Court, many more people can hurt than can help you; please the former, but engage the latter.

Awkwardness is a more real disadvantage than it is generally thought to be; it often occasions ridicule, it always lessens dignity.

A man's own good-breeding is his best security against other people's ill-manners.

Good-breeding carries along with it a dignity, that is respected by the most petulant. Ill-breeding invites and authorises the familiarity of the most timid. No man ever said a pert thing to the Duke of Marlborough. No man ever said a civil one (though many a flattering one) to Sir Robert Walpole.

When the old clipped money was called in for a new coinage in King William's time, to prevent the like for the future, they stamped on the edges of the crown-pieces these words: *et Decus et Tutamen*. That is exactly the case of good breeding.

Knowledge may give weight, but accomplishments only give lustre; and many more people see than weigh.

Most arts require long study and application; but the most useful art of all, that of pleasing, requires only the desire.

It is to be presumed, that a man of common sense who does not desire to please, desires nothing at all; since he must know that he cannot obtain anything without it.

A skilful negotiator will most carefully distinguish between the little and the great objects of his business, and will be as frank and open in the former, as he will be secret and pertinacious in the latter.

He will, by his manners and address, endeavour, at least, to make his public adversaries his personal friends. He will flatter and engage the man, while he counterworks the minister; and he will never alienate people's minds from him, by wrangling for points, either absolutely unattainable, or not worth attaining. He will make even a merit of giving up what he could not or would not carry, and sell a trifle for a thousand times its value.

A foreign minister who is concerned in great affairs, must necessarily have spies in his pay; but he must not too easily credit their informations, which are never exactly true, often. very false. His best spies will always be those whom he does not pay, but whom he has engaged in his service by his dexterity and address, and who think themselves nothing less than spies.

There is a certain jargon, which in French I should call *un persifflage d'affaires*, that a foreign minister ought to be perfectly master of, and may use very advantageously at great entertainments, in mixed companies, and in all occasions when he must speak, and should say nothing. Well turned and well spoken, it seems to mean something, though in truth it means nothing. It is a kind of political *badinage*, which prevents or removes a thousand difficulties to which a foreign minister is exposed in mixed conversations.

If ever the *volto sciolto*, and the *pensieri stretti* are necessary, they are so in these affairs. A grave, dark, reserved, and mysterious air, has *fœnum in cornu*. An even, easy, unembarrassed one invites confidence, and leaves no room for guesses and conjectures.

Both simulation and dissimulation are absolutely necessary for a foreign minister, and yet they must stop short of falsehood and perfidy; that middle point is the difficult one; there ability consists. He must often seem pleased when he is vexed, and grave when he is pleased; but he must never say either; that would be falsehood, an indelible stain to character.

A foreign minister should be a most exact economist; an expense proportioned to his appointments and fortune is necessary; but, on the other hand, debt is inevitable ruin to him. It sinks him into disgrace at the Court where he resides, and into the most servile and abject dependence on the Court that sent him. As he cannot resent ill-usage, he is sure to have enough of it.

The Duc de Sully observes very justly, in his Memoirs, that nothing contributed more to his rise than that prudent economy which he had observed from his youth, and by which he had always a sum of money beforehand, in case of emergencies.

It is very difficult to fix the particular point of economy; the best error of the two is on the parsimonious side. That may be corrected, the other cannot.

The reputation of generosity is to be purchased pretty cheap; it does not depend so much upon a man's general expense, as it does upon his giving handsomely where it is proper to give at all. A man, for instance, who should give a servant four shillings, would pass for covetous, while he who gave him a crown would be reckoned generous; so that the difference of those two opposite characters turns upon one shilling. A man's character in that particular depends a great deal upon the report of his own servants; a mere trifle above common wages makes their report favourable.

Take care always to form your establishment so much within your income, as to leave a sufficient fund for unexpected contingencies, and a prudent liberality. There is hardly a year in any man's life in which a small sum of ready money may not be employed to great advantage.*

CCXII.

LONDON, May 27, 1753.

MY DEAR FRIEND,

I have this day been tired, jaded, nay tormented, by the company of a most worthy, sensible, and learned man, a near relation of mine, who dined and passed the evening with me. This seems a paradox, but is a plain truth; he has no knowledge of the world, no manners, no address; far from talking without book, as is commonly said of people who talk sillily, he only talks by book; which, in general conversation, is ten times worse. He has formed in his own closet, from books, certain systems of everything, argues tenaciously upon those principles, and is both surprised and angry at whatever deviates from them. His theories are good, but unfortunately are all impracticable. Why? Because he has only read and not conversed. He is acquainted with books and an absolute stranger to men. Labouring with his matter, he is delivered of it with pangs; he hesitates, stops

* Upon the back of the original was written, in Mr. Stanhope's hand, "Excellent Maxims, but more calculated for the meridian of France or Spain than of England."

in his utterance, and always expresses himself inelegantly. His
actions are all ungraceful; so that, with all his merit and knowledge, I would rather converse six hours with the most frivolous
tittle-tattle woman, who knew something of the world, than with
him.

The preposterous notions of a systematical man, who does not
know the world, tire the patience of a man who does. It would
be endless to correct his mistakes, nor would he take it kindly;
for he has considered everything deliberately, and is very sure
that he is in the right. Impropriety is a characteristic, and a
never-failing one, of these people. Regardless, because ignorant, of customs and manners, they violate them every moment.
They often shock, though they never mean to offend; never
attending either to the general character, or the particular distinguishing circumstances of the people to whom, or before
whom, they talk; whereas the knowledge of the world teaches
one, that the very same things which are exceedingly right and
proper in one company, time, and place, are exceedingly absurd
in others. In short, a man who has great knowledge from
experience and observation, of the characters, customs, and manners of mankind, is a being as different from and as superior to a
man of mere book and systematical knowledge, as a well-managed
horse is to an ass. Study, therefore, cultivate and frequent men
and women; not only in their outward, and consequently
guarded, but in their interior, domestic, and consequently less
disguised characters and manners.

Take your notions of things as by observation and experience
you find they really are, and not as you read that they are or
should be; for they never are quite what they should be. For
this purpose, do not content yourself with general and common
acquaintance; but, wherever you can, establish yourself, with a
kind of domestic familiarity, in good houses. For instance, go
again to Orli for two or three days, and so at two or three
reprises. Go and stay two or three days at a time at Versailles,
and improve and extend the acquaintance you have there. Be at
home at St. Cloud; and whenever any private person of fashion
invites you to pass a few days at his country-house, accept of the
invitation. This will necessarily give you a versatility of mind,
and a facility to adopt various manners and customs; for every-

body desires to please those in whose house they are; and people
are only to be pleased in their own way. Nothing is more engaging than a cheerful and easy conformity to people's particular
manners, habits, and even weaknesses; nothing (to use a vulgar
expression) should come amiss to a young fellow. He should be,
for good purposes, what Alcibiades was commonly for bad ones,
a Proteus, assuming with ease, and wearing with cheerfulness,
any shape. Heat, cold, luxury, abstinence, gravity, gaiety,
ceremony, easiness, learning, trifling, business, and pleasure, are
modes which he should be able to take, lay aside, or change
occasionally, with as much ease as he would take or lay aside his
hat. All this is only to be acquired by use and knowledge of the
world, by keeping a great deal of company, analysing every
character, and insinuating yourself into the familiarity of various
acquaintance. A right, a generous ambition to make a figure in
the world, necessarily gives the desire of pleasing; the desire of
pleasing points out, to a great degree, the means of doing it;
and the art of pleasing is, in truth, the art of rising, of distinguishing one's-self, of making a figure and a fortune in the world.
But without pleasing, without the Graces, as I have told you a
thousand times, *ogni fatca è vana.*

You are now but nineteen, an age at which most of your
countrymen are illiberally getting drunk in port at the University.
You have greatly got the start of them in learning; and, if you
can equally get the start of them in the knowledge and manners
of the world, you may be very sure of outrunning them in Court
and Parliament, as you set out so much earlier than they. They
generally begin but to see the world at one-and-twenty; you will
by that age have seen all Europe. They set out upon their
travels unlicked cubs, and in their travels they only lick one
another, for they seldom go into any other company. They know
nothing but the English world, and the worst part of that too,
and generally very little of any but the English language; and
they come home at three or four-and-twenty refined and polished
(as is said in one of Congreve's plays) like Dutch skippers from a
whale-fishing.

The care which has been taken of you, and (to do you justice)
the care you have taken of yourself, has left you, at the age of
nineteen only, nothing to acquire but the knowledge of the

world, manners, address, and those exterior accomplishments. But they are great and necessary acquisitions, to those who have sense enough to know their true value; and your getting them before you are one-and-twenty, and before you enter upon the active and shining scenes of life, will give you such an advantage over your contemporaries, that they cannot overtake you; they must be distanced. You may probably be placed about a young Prince, who will probably be a young King. There all the various arts of pleasing, the engaging address, the versatility of manners, the *brillant*, the Graces, will outweigh and yet outrun all solid knowledge and unpolished merit. Oil yourself, therefore, and be both supple and shining for that race, if you would be first or early at the goal. Ladies will most probably too have something to say there; and those who are best with them will probably be best somewhere else. Labour this great point, my dear child, indefatigably; attend to the very smallest parts, the minutest graces, the most trifling circumstances, that can possibly concur in forming the shining character of a complete Gentleman, *un galant homme, un homme de Cour,* a man of business and pleasure; *estimé des hommes, recherché des femmes, aimé de tout le monde.* In this view, observe the shining part of every man of fashion who is liked and esteemed; attend to, and imitate that particular accomplishment for which you hear him chiefly celebrated and distinguished; then collect those various parts, and make yourself a Mosaic of the whole. No one body possesses everything, and almost everybody possesses some one thing worthy of imitation; only choose your models well; and, in order to do so, choose by your ear more than by your eye. The best model is always that which is most universally allowed to be the best, though in strictness it may possibly not be so. We must take most things as they are, we cannot make them what we would, nor often what they should be; and, where moral duties are not concerned, it is more prudent to follow than to attempt to lead. Adieu!

CCXIII.

BATH, *October* 3, 1753.

MY DEAR FRIEND,

You have set out well at the Hague; you are in love with
Madame Munter, which I am very glad of; you are in the fine
company there, and I hope one of it; for it is not enough, at
your age, to be merely in good company; but you should, by
your address and attentions, make that good company think you
one of them. There is a tribute due to beauty, even independently of further views; which tribute, I hope, you paid with
alacrity to Madame Munter and Madame Degenfeldt; depend
upon it they expected it, and were offended in proportion as that
tribute seemed either unwillingly or scantily paid.

I believe my friend Kreuningen * admits nobody now to his
table, for fear of their communicating the plague to him, or at
least the bite of a mad dog. Pray profit of the *entrées libres* that
the French Ambassador has given you; frequent him, and *speak*
to him. I think you will not do amiss to call upon Mr. Burrish,
at Aix la Chapelle, since it is so little out of your way; and you
will do still better, if you would, which I know you will not,
drink those waters, for five or six days only, to scour your
stomach and bowels a little; I am sure it would do you a great
deal of good. Mr. Burrish can, doubtless, give you the best letters to Munich; and he will naturally give you some to Comte
Preysing, or Comte Sinsheim, and such sort of grave people; but
I could wish that you would ask him for some to young fellows
of pleasure, or fashionable coquettes, that you may be *dans
l'honnête débauche de Munich*. *A propos* of your future motions;
I leave you in a great measure the master of them, so shall only
suggest my thoughts to you upon that subject.

You have three Electoral Courts in view, Bonn, Munich, and
Manheim. I would advise you to see two of them rather cur-
sorily, and fix your tabernacle at the third, whichever that may
be, for a considerable time. For instance, should you choose (as
I fancy you will) to make Manheim the place of your residence,
stay only ten or twelve days at Bonn, and as long at Munich, and

* Baron de Kreuingen, one of Lord Chesterfield's principal friends at
the Hague.—See his letter to him of July 7, 1752.

then go and fix at Manheim; and so *vice versâ*, if you should like Bonn or Munich better than you think you would Manheim, make that the place of your residence, and only visit the other two. It is certain that no man can be much pleased himself, or please others much, in any place where he is only a bird of passage for eight or ten days; neither party thinking it worth while to make an acquaintance, still less to form any connection, for so short a time; but when months are the case, a man may domesticate himself pretty well; and very soon not be looked upon as a stranger. This is the real utility of travelling, when, by contracting a familiarity at any place, you get into the inside of it, and see it in its undress. This is the only way of knowing the customs, the manners, and all the little characteristical peculiarities that distinguish one place from another; but then this familiarity is not to be brought about by cold, formal visits of half an hour; no, you must show a willingness, a desire, an impatience, of forming connections, *il faut s'y prêter, et y mettre du liant, du désir de plaire.* Whatever you do approve, you must be lavish in your praises of; and you must learn to commend what you do not approve of, if it is approved of there. You are not much given to praise, I know; but it is because you do not yet know how extremely people are engaged by a seeming sanction to their own opinions, prejudices, and weaknesses, even in the merest trifles.

Our self-love is mortified, when we think our opinions, and even our tastes, customs, and dresses, either arraigned or condemned; as, on the contrary, it is tickled and flattered by approbation. I will give you a remarkable instance of this kind. The famous Earl of Shaftesbury, in the flagitious reign of Charles the Second, while he was Chancellor, had a mind to be a favourite as well as a Minister of the King; in order, therefore, to please His Majesty, whose prevailing passion was women, my Lord kept one, whom he had no occasion for and made no manner of use of. The King soon heard of it, and asked him if it was true; he owned it was; but that, though he kept that one woman, he had several others besides, for he loved variety. A few days afterwards, the King, at his public levée, saw Lord Shaftesbury at some distance, and said in the circle, " One would not think that that little weak man is the greatest —— in England; but I can assure you that he is." Upon Lord Shaftesbury's coming into the circle, there was a general smile ; the King said, "This is concerning you, my Lord." "Me, Sir !" answered the Chancellor, with some surprise. "Yes, you," answered the King; "for I had just said, that you were the greatest ———— in England. Is it not true ?" "Of a *subject*, Sir," replied Lord Shaftesbury, "perhaps I am."

It is the same in everything ; we think a difference of opinion, of conduct, of manners, a tacit reproach, at least, upon our own ; we must therefore use ourselves to a ready conformity to whatever is neither criminal nor dishonourable. Whoever differs from any general custom, is supposed both to think, and proclaim himself wiser than the rest of the world; which the rest of the world cannot bear, especially in a young man. A young fellow is always forgiven, and often applauded, when he carries a fashion to an excess ; but never if he stops short of it. The first is ascribed to youth and fire ; but the latter is imputed to an affectation of singularity, or superiority. At your age, one is allowed to *outrer* fashion, dress, vivacity, gallantry, &c., but by no means to be behind hand in any one of them. And one may apply to youth in this case, *Si non errasset, fecerat ille minùs.* Adieu !

CCXIV.

BATH, *October* 19, 1753.

MY DEAR FRIEND,

Of all the various ingredients that compose the useful and necessary art of pleasing, no one is so effectual and engaging as that gentleness, that *douceur* of countenance and manners, to which you are no stranger, though (God knows why) a sworn enemy. Other people take great pains to conceal or disguise their natural imperfections ; some by the make of their clothes, and other arts, endeavour to conceal the defects of their shape ; women who unfortunately have natural bad complexions lay on good ones; and both men and women, upon whom unkind nature has inflicted a surliness and ferocity of countenance, do at least all they can, though often without success, to soften and mitigate it; they affect *douceur*, and aim at smiles, though often in the attempt, like the Devil in Milton, they *grin horrible*

*a ghastly smile.** But you are the only person I ever knew,
in the whole course of my life, who not only disdain, but absolutely reject and disguise a great advantage that nature has
kindly granted. You easily guess I mean *countenance;* for she
has given you a very pleasing one; but you beg to be excused, you will not accept it; on the contrary, take singular
pains to put on the most *funeste*, forbidding, and unpleasing one,
that can possibly be imagined. This one would think impossible;
but you know it to be true. If you imagine that it gives you a
manly, thoughtful, and decisive air, as some, though very few of
your countrymen do, you are most exceedingly mistaken; for it
is at best the air of a German corporal, part of whose exercise is
to look fierce, and to *blasemeer-op.*

You will say, perhaps, What, am I always to be studying my
countenance, in order to wear this *douceur?* I answer, No, do it
but for a fortnight, and you will never have occasion to think of it
more. Take but half the pains to recover the countenance that
nature gave you, that you must have taken to disguise and deform it as you have, and the business will be done. Accustom
your eyes to a certain softness, of which they are very capable,
and your face to smiles, which become it more than most faces
I know. Give all your motions, too, an air of *douceur*, which is
directly the reverse of their present celerity and rapidity. I wish
you would adopt a little of *l'air du couvent* (you very well know
what I mean) to a certain degree; it has something extremely
engaging; there is a mixture of benevolence, affection, and
unction in it; it is frequently really sincere, but is almost always
thought so, and consequently pleasing. Will you call this
trouble? It will not be half an hour's trouble to you in a week's
time. But suppose it be, pray tell me, why did you give yourself the trouble of learning to dance so well as you do? It is
neither a religious, moral, or civil duty. You must own, that
you did it then singly to please, and you were in the right on't.
Why do you wear your fine clothes, and curl your hair? Both
are troublesome; lank locks, and plain flimsy rags, are much
easier. This, then, you also do in order to please, and you do
very right. But then, for God's sake, reason and act consequentially; and endeavour to please in other things too, still

* *Paradise Lost.* ii. 846.

more essential, and without which the trouble you have taken in those is wholly thrown away.

You show your dancing, perhaps, six times a year, at most; but you show your countenance, and your common motions every day, and all day. Which, then, I appeal to yourself, ought you to think of the most, and care to render easy, graceful, and engaging? *Douceur* of countenance and gesture can alone make them so. You are by no means ill-natured; and would you then most unjustly be reckoned so? Yet your common countenance intimates, and would make anybody, who did not know you, believe it. *A propos* of this, I must tell you what was said the other day to a fine lady whom you know, who is very good-natured, in truth, but whose common countenance implies ill-nature, even to brutality. It was Miss Hamilton, Lady Murray's* niece, whom you have seen, both at Blackheath and at Lady Hervey's. Lady Murray was saying to me, that you had a very engaging countenance, when you had a mind to it, but that you had not always that mind; upon which Miss Hamilton said, that she liked your countenance best, when it was as glum as her own. Why then, replied Lady Murray, you two should marry; for, while you both wear your worst countenances, nobody else will venture upon either of you; and they call her now Mrs. Stanhope!

To complete this *douceur* of countenance and motions, which I so earnestly recommend to you, you should carry it also to your expressions and manner of thinking; *mettez y toujours de l'affectueux et de l'onction;* take the gentle, the favourable, the indulgent side of most questions. I own, that the manly and sublime John Trott, your countryman, seldom does; but, to show his spirit and decision, takes the rough and harsh side, which he generally adorns with an oath, to seem more formidable. This he only thinks fine; for, to do John justice, he is commonly as good-natured as anybody. These are among the many little things which you have not, and I have lived long enough in the world to know of what infinite consequence they are in the course

---

* This lady appears to have been the daughter of John Hamilton, Esq., and wife of Sir Patrick Murray, Bart., of Ochtertyre. One of their grandsons was General Sir George Murray, Master-General of the Ordnance.—M.

of life. Reason then, I repeat it again, within yourself *conse-quentially ;* and let not the pains you have taken, and still take, to please in some things, be *à pure perte*, by your negligence of, and inattention to, others, of much less trouble, and much more consequence.

I have been of late much engaged, or rather bewildered, in Oriental history, particularly that of the Jews, since the destruction of their temple, and their dispersion by Titus; but the confusion and uncertainty of the whole, and the monstrous extravagances and falsehoods of the greatest part of it, disgusted me extremely. Their Thalmud, their Mischna, their Targums, and other traditions and writings of their Rabbins and Doctors, who were most of them Cabalists, are really more extravagant and absurd, if possible, than all that you have read in Comte de Gabalis ; and, indeed, most of his stuff is taken from them. Take this sample of their nonsense, which is transmitted in the writings of one of their most considerable Rabbins. "One Abas Saul, a man of ten feet high, was digging a grave, and happened to find the eye of Goliath, in which he thought proper to bury himself; and so he did, all but his head, which the giant's eye was unfortunately not quite deep enough to receive." This, I assure you, is the most modest lie of ten thousand.

I have also read the Turkish History, which, excepting the religious part, is not fabulous, though very possibly not true. For the Turks, having no notion of letters, and being even by their religion forbid the use of them, except for reading and transcribing the Koran, they have no historians of their own, nor any authentic records or memorials for other historians to work upon ; so that what histories we have of that country, are written by foreigners ; as Platina, Sir Paul Rycaut, Prince Cantemir, &c., or else snatches only of particular and short periods, by some who happened to reside there at those times ; such as Busbequius, whom I have just finished. I like him, as far as he goes, much the best of any of them ; but then his account is, properly, only an account of his own embassy, from the Emperor Charles the Fifth to Solyman the Magnificent. However, there he gives, episodically, the best account I know of the customs and manners of the Turks, and of the nature of that government, which is a most extraordinary one. For, despotic as it always seems, and sometimes is, it is in truth a military republic, and the real power resides in the Janissaries; who sometimes order their Sultan to strangle his Vizir, and sometimes the Vizir to depose or strangle his Sultan, according as they happen to be angry at the one or the other. I own, I am glad that the capital strangler should, in his turn, be *strangle-able*, and now and then strangled; for I know of no brute so fierce, nor criminal so guilty, as the creature called a Sovereign, whether King, Sultan, or Sophy, who thinks himself, either by divine or human right, vested with an absolute power of destroying his fellow-creatures; or who, without enquiring into his right, lawlessly exerts that power. The most excusable of all those human monsters are the Turks, whose religion teaches them inevitable fatalism.

A propos of the Turks; my Loyola, I pretend, is superior to your Sultan. Perhaps you think this impossible, and wonder who this Loyola is. Know then, that I have had a *Barbet* brought me from France, so exactly like Sultan, that he has been mistaken for him several times; only his snout is shorter, and his ears longer than Sultan's. He has also the acquired knowledge of Sultan; and I am apt to think that he studied under the same master at Paris. His habit, and his white band, show him to be an ecclesiastic; and his begging, which he does very earnestly, proves him to be of a Mendicant order; which, added to his flattery and insinuation, make him supposed to be a Jesuit, and have acquired him the name of Loyola. . . .

I do not yet hear one jot the better for all my bathings and pumpings, though I have been here already full half my time. I consequently go very little into company, being very little fit for any. I hope you keep company enough for us both; you will get more by that than I shall by all my reading. I read singly to amuse myself, and fill up my time, of which I have too much; but you have two much better reasons for going into company, Pleasure and Profit. May you find a great deal of both, in a great deal of company! Adieu.

CCXV.

LONDON, *November 20*, 1753.

MY DEAR FRIEND,—

Two mails are now due from Holland, so that I have no letter from you to acknowledge; but that, you know by long experience, does not hinder my writing to you; I always receive your letters with pleasure; but I mean, and endeavour, that you should receive mine with some profit, preferring always your advantage to my own pleasure.

If you find yourself well settled and naturalized at Manheim, stay there for some time, and do not leave a certain for an uncertain good; but if you think you shall be as well, or better established at Munich, go there as soon as you please; and if disappointed, you can always return to Manheim. I mentioned, in a former letter, your passing the Carnival at Berlin, which, I think, may be both useful and pleasing to you; however, do as you will; but let me know what you resolve. That King and and that country have, and will have, so great a share in the affairs of Europe, that they are well worth being thoroughly known.

Whether, where you are now, or ever may be hereafter, you speak French, German, or English most, I earnestly recommend to you a particular attention to the propriety and elegancy of your style; employ the best works you can find in the language, avoid *cacophony*, and make your periods as harmonious as you can. I need not, I am sure, tell you, what you must often have felt how much the elegancy of diction adorns the best thoughts, and palliates the worst. In the House of Commons, it is almost everything: and indeed, in every assembly, whether public or private. Words, which are the dress of thoughts, deserve, surely, more care than clothes, which are only the dress of the person, and which, however, ought to have their share of attention. If you attend to your style, in any one language, it will give you an habit of attending to it in every other; and if once you speak either French or German very elegantly, you will afterwards speak much the better English for it. I repeat it to you again, for at least the thousandth time; exert your whole attention now in acquiring the ornamental parts of character. People know very little of the world, and talk nonsense, when they talk of plainness and solidity unadorned, they will do in nothing; mankind has been long out of a state of nature, and the golden age of native simplicity will never return. Whether for the better or the worse, no matter; but we are refined; and plain manners, plain dress, and plain diction, would as little do in life, as acorns, herbage, and the water of the neighbouring spring, would do at table. Some people are just come, who interrupt me in the middle of my sermon; so good night.

CCXVI.

LONDON, November 26, 1753.

MY DEAR FRIEND,

Fine doings at Manheim! If one may give credit to the weekly histories of Monsieur Roderigue, the finest writer among the moderns, not only *des chasses brillantes et nombreuses, des opéras où les acteurs se surpassent les jours de Saints de LL. AA. EE.** *Sérénissimes, célébrés en grand gala;* but, to crown the whole, Monsieur Zuchmantel is happily arrived, and Monsieur Wartensleben hourly expected. I hope that you are *pars magna* of all these delights; though, as Noll Bluff says, in the *Old Batchelor,* "that rascally Gazatteer takes no more notice of you, than if you were not in the land of the living." I should think, that he might at least have taken notice, that in those rejoicings you appeared with a rejoicing and not a gloomy countenance; and you distinguished yourself, in that numerous and shining company, by your air, dress, address, and attentions. If this was the case, as I will both hope and suppose that it was, I will, if you require it, have him written to, to do you justice in his next *supplément.* Seriously, I am very glad, that you are whirled in that *tourbillon* of pleasures; they smooth, polish, and rub off rough corners; perhaps, too, you have some particular *collision,* which is still more effectual.

Schannat's History of the Palatinate was, I find, written originally in German, in which language, I suppose, it is that you have read it; but, as I must humbly content myself with the French translation, Vaillant has sent for it for me, from Holland, so that I have not yet read it. While you are in the

* Leurs Altesses Electorales.

Palatinate, you do very well to read everything relative to it; you will do still better if you make that reading the foundation of your inquiries into the more minute circumstances and anecdotes of that country, whenever you are in company with informed and knowing people. .

The Ministers here, intimidated by the absurd and groundless clamours of the mob, have, very weakly, in my mind, repealed, this session, the bill which they had passed the last, for rendering Jews capable of being naturalized, by subsequent Acts of Parliament. The clamourers triumph, and will, doubtless, make farther demands; which, if not granted, this piece of complaisance will soon be forgotten. Nothing is truer in politics, than this reflection of the Cardinal de Retz, *Que le peuple craint toujours quand on ne le craint pas;* and, consequently, they grow unreasonable and insolent, when they find that they are feared. Wise and honest governors will never, if they can help it, give the people just cause to complain; but then, on the other hand, they will firmly withstand groundless clamour. Besides that, this noise against the Jew bill proceeds from that narrow mob-spirit of *intoleration* in religious, and inhospitality in civil matters; both which all wise governments should oppose.

The confusion in France increases daily, as, no doubt, you are informed where you are. There is an answer of the Clergy's to the remonstrances of the Parliament, lately published; which was sent me by the last post from France, and which I would have sent you, enclosed in this, were it not too bulky. Very probably you may see it at Manheim, from the French Minister; it is very well worth your reading, being most artfully and plausibly written, though founded upon false principles; the *jus divinum* of the Clergy, and, consequently, their supremacy in all matters of faith and doctrine, are asserted; both which I absolutely deny. Were those two points allowed the Clergy of any country whatsoever, they must necessarily govern that country absolutely; everything being, directly or indirectly, relative to faith or doctrine; and whoever is supposed to have the power of saving and damning souls to all eternity (which power the Clergy pretend to), will be much more considered, and better obeyed, than any civil power, that forms no pretensions beyond this world. Whereas, in truth, the Clergy in every country are, like all other subjects, dependent upon the supreme legislative power; and are appointed by that power, under whatever restrictions and limitations it pleases, to keep up decency and decorum in the Church, just as constables are to keep peace in the parish. This Fra Paolo has clearly proved, even upon their own principles of the Old and New Testament, in his book *de Beneficiis,* which I recommend to you to read with attention; it is short. Adieu!

CCXVII.

LONDON, *December* 25, 1753.

MY DEAR FRIEND,

Yesterday again I received two letters at once from you, the one of the 7th, the other of the 15th, from Manheim.

You never had in your life so good a reason for not writing, either to me or to anybody else, as your sore finger lately furnished you. I believe it was painful, and I am glad it is cured; but a sore finger, however painful, is a much lesser evil than laziness of either body or mind, and attended by fewer ill consequences.

I am very glad to hear that you were distinguished at the Court of Manheim from the rest of your countrymen and fellow-travellers; it is a sign that you had better manners and address than they; for take it for granted, the best-bred people will always be the best received wherever they go. Good manners are the settled medium of social, as *specie* is of commercial life; returns are equally expected for both; and people will no more advance their civility to a Bear than their money to a Bankrupt. I really both hope and believe that the German Courts will do you a great deal of good; their ceremony and restraint being the proper correctives and antidotes for your negligence and inattention. I believe they would not greatly relish your weltering in your own laziness, and an easy chair, nor take it very kindly if, when they spoke to you, or you to them, you looked another way, as much as to say ——. As they give so they require attention; and, by the way, take this maxim for an undoubted truth: That no young man can possibly improve in any company for which he has not respect enough to be under some degree of restraint.

I dare not trust to Meyssonier's report of his Rhenish, his Burgundy not having answered either his account or my expectations. I doubt, as a wine-merchant, he is the *perfidus caupo*, whatever he may be as a banker. I shall therefore venture upon none of his wine; but delay making my provision of old hock till I go abroad myself next spring; as I told you in the utmost secrecy in my last,* that I intend to do; and then, probably, I may taste some that I like, and go upon sure ground. There is commonly very good both at Aix-la-Chapelle and Liege; where I formerly got some excellent, which I carried with me to Spa, where I drank no other wine.

As my letters to you frequently miscarry, I will repeat in this that part of my last which related to your future motions. Whenever you shall be tired of Berlin, go to Dresden, where Sir Charles Williams will be, who will receive you with open arms. He dined with me to-day, and sets out for Dresden in about six weeks. He spoke of you with great kindness, and impatience to see you again. He will trust and employ you in business (and he is now in the whole secret of importance) till we fix our place to meet in; which probably will be Spa.

Wherever you are, inform yourself minutely of, and attend particularly to, the affairs of France; they grow serious, and, in my opinion, will grow more and more so every day. The King is despised, and I do not wonder at it; but he has brought it about to be hated at the same time, which seldom happens to the same man. His Ministers are known to be as disunited as incapable; he hesitates between the Church and the Parliaments, like the ass in the fable, that starved between two hampers of hay; too much in love with his mistress to part with her, and too much afraid for his soul to enjoy her; jealous of the Parliaments who would support his authority; and a devoted bigot to the Church that would destroy it.

The people are poor, consequently discontented; those who have religion are divided in their notions of it; which is saying that they hate one another. The Clergy never do forgive; much less will they forgive the Parliament; the Parliament never will forgive them. The Army must, without doubt, take, in their own minds at least, different parts in all these disputes, which,

* That letter is missing.—M.

upon occasion, would break out. Armies, though always the
supporters and tools of absolute power for the time being, are
always the destroyers of it too; by frequently changing the hands
in which they think proper to lodge it. This was the case of the
Prætorian bands, who deposed and murdered the monsters they
had raised to oppress mankind. The Janissaries in Turkey,
and the regiments of Guards in Russia, do the same now. The
French nation reasons freely, which they never did before, upon
matters of religion and government, and begin to be *spregiudi-
cati;* the officers do so too; in short, all the symptoms which I
have ever met with in history, previous to great changes and
revolutions in Government, now exist, and daily increase in
France. I am glad of it; the rest of Europe will be the quieter,
and have time to recover.

England, I am sure, wants rest; for it wants men and money;
the Republic of the United Provinces wants both still more; the
other Powers cannot well dance, when neither France nor the
Maritime Powers can, as they used to do, pay the piper. The
first squabble in Europe that I foresee will be about the Crown
of Poland, should the present King die; and therefore I wish
his Majesty a long life and a merry Christmas. So much for
foreign politics; *à propos* of them, pray take care, while you are
in those parts of Germany, to inform yourself correctly of all the
details, discussions, and agreements which the several wars, con-
fiscations, bans, and treaties, occasioned between the Bavarian
and Palatine Electorates; they are interesting and curious.

I shall not, upon the occasion of the approaching New Year,
repeat to you the wishes which I continue to form for you; you
know them all already; and you know that it is absolutely in
your own power to satisfy most of them. Among many other
wishes, this is my most earnest one: That you would open the
New Year with a most solemn and devout sacrifice to the Graces;
who never reject those that supplicate them with fervour; without
them, let me tell you, that your friend, Dame Fortune, will stand
you in little stead; may they all be your friends! Adieu!

CCXVIII.

LONDON, *January* 15, 1754.

MY DEAR FRIEND,

I have this moment received your letter of the 26th past, from Munich. Since you are got so well out of the distress and dangers of your journey from Manheim, I am glad that you were in them,

> Condisce i diletti
> Memoria di pene,
> Ne sà che sia bene
> Chi mal non soffri.

They were but little samples of the much greater distress and dangers which you must expect to meet with in your great, and I hope long journey through life. In some part of it flowers are scattered with profusion, the road is smooth, and the prospect pleasant; but in others (and I fear the greater number) the road is rugged, beset with thorns and briars, and cut by torrents. Gather the flowers in your way; but at the same time guard against the briars that are either mixed with them, or that most certainly succeed them.

I thank you for your wild boar, who, now he is dead, I assure him *se laissera bien manger malgré qu'il en ait;* though I am not sure that I should have had that personal valour which so successfully distinguished you in single combat with him, which made him bite the dust like Homer's heroes, and, to conclude my period sublimely, put him into that *pickle* from which I propose eating him. At the same time that I applaud your valour, I must do justice to your modesty, which candidly admits that you were not overmatched, and that your adversary was of about your own age and size. A *Marcassin,* being under a year old, would have been below your indignation. *Bête de compagnie,* being under two years old, was still, in my opinion, below your glory; but I guess that your enemy was *un Ragot,* that is, from two to three years old; an age and size which, between man and boar, answer pretty well to yours.

If accidents of bad roads or waters do not retain you at Munich, I do not fancy that pleasure will; and I rather believe you will seek for, and find them at the Carnival at Berlin; in which supposition I eventually direct this letter to your banker

there. While you are at Berlin (I earnestly recommend it to
you again and again) pray *care* to see, hear, know, and mind,
every thing there. *The ablest Prince in Europe* is surely an
object that deserves attention; and the least thing that he does,
like the smallest sketches of the greatest painters, has its value,
and a considerable one too.

Read with care the *Code Frédéric*, and inform yourself of the
good effects of it in those parts of his dominions where it has
taken place, and where it has banished the former chicanes,
quirks, and quibbles of the old law. Do not think any detail
too minute or trifling for your inquiry and observation. I wish
that you could find one hour's leisure every day, to read some
good Italian author, and to converse in that language with our
worthy friend Signor Angelo Cori; it would both refresh and
improve your Italian, which, of the many languages you know,
I take to be that in which you are the least perfect; but of
which, too, you already know enough to make yourself master of,
with very little trouble, whenever you please.

Live, dwell, and grow at the several Courts there; use them
so much to your face, that they may not look upon you as a
stranger. Observe, and take their tone, even to their affectations and follies; for such there are, and perhaps should be, at
all Courts. Stay, in all events, at Berlin, till I inform you of
Sir Charles Williams's arrival at Dresden; where, I suppose,
you would not care to be before him, and where you may go as
soon after him as ever you please. Your time there will neither
be unprofitably nor disagreeably spent; he will introduce you
into all the best company, though he can introduce you to none
so good as his own. He has of late applied himself very
seriously to foreign affairs, especially those of Saxony and
Poland; he knows them perfectly well, and will tell you what
he knows. He always expresses, and I have good reason to
believe very sincerely, great kindness and affection for you.

The works of the late Lord Bolingbroke are just published,
and have plunged me into philosophical studies; which hitherto
I have not been much used to, or delighted with, convinced of
the futility of those researches; but I have read his Philosophical Essay upon the extent of human knowledge, which, by the
way, makes two large quartos and a half. He there shows very

clearly, and with most splendid eloquence, what the human mind can and cannot do; that our understandings are wisely calculated for our place in this planet, and for the link which we form in the universal chain of things; but that they are by no means capable of that degree of knowledge which our curiosity makes us search after, and which our vanity makes us often believe we arrive at. I shall not recommend to you the reading of that work. But, when you return hither, I shall recommend to your frequent and diligent perusal all his tracts that are relative to our history and constitution; upon which he throws lights and scatters graces which no other writer has ever done.

Reading, which was always a pleasure to me, in the time even of my greatest dissipation, is now become my only refuge; and, I fear, I indulge it too much, at the expense of my eyes. But what can I do? I must do something; I cannot bear absolute idleness: my ears grow every day more useless to me, my eyes, consequently, more necessary. I will not hoard them like a miser, but will rather risk the loss than not enjoy the use of them.

Pray let me know all the particulars, not only of your reception at Munich, but also at Berlin; at the latter, I believe, it will be a good one; for his Prussian Majesty knows that I have long been *an admirer and respecter of his great and various talents.* Adieu.

CCXIX.

LONDON, *February* 1, 1754.

MY DEAR FRIEND,

I received yesterday yours of the 12th from Munich, in consequence of which I direct this to you there, though I directed my three last to Berlin, where, I suppose, you will find them at your arrival. Since you are not only domesticated, but *niché* at Munich, you are much in the right to stay there. It is not by seeing places that one knows them, but by familiar and daily conversations with the people of fashion. I would not care to be in the place of that prodigy of beauty whom you are to drive *dans la course de Traineaux;* and I am apt to think you are much more likely to break her bones than she is, though ever so cruel, to break your heart. Nay, I am not sure but that,

according to all the rules of gallantry, you are obliged to overturn her on purpose: in the first place, for the chance of . . . ;
in the next, for the sake of the contrition and concern which it
would give you an opportunity of showing; and lastly, upon
account of all the *gentillesses et épigrammes*, which it would
naturally suggest. Voiture has made several stanzas upon an
accident of that kind, which happened to a lady of his acquaintance. There is a great deal of wit in them, rather too much;
for, according to the taste of those times, they are full of what
the Italians call *concetti spiritosissimi*; the Spaniards, *agudeze*;
and we, affectation and quaintness. I hope you have endeavoured
to suit your *Traineau* to the character of the fair one whom it is
to contain. If she is of an irascible, impetuous disposition (as
fine women can sometimes be) you will, doubtless, place her in
the body of a lion, a tiger, a dragon, or some tremendous beast
of prey and fury; if she is a sublime and stately beauty, which I
think more probable (for unquestionably she is *hoch gebohrne*)
you will, I suppose, provide a magnificent swan or proud peacock
for her reception; but if she is all tenderness and softness, you
have, to be sure, taken care amorous doves and wanton sparrows
should seem to flutter round her. Proper mottos, I take it for
granted, that you have eventually prepared; but if not, you may
find a great many ready-made ones, in *Les entretiens d'Ariste et
d'Eugène, sur les devises*, written by Père Bouhours, and worth
your reading at any time. I will not say to you, upon this occasion, like the father in Ovid, *Parce puer stimulis et fortius utere
loris*. On the contrary, drive on briskly; it is not the chariot of
the sun that you drive, but you carry the sun in your chariot;
consequently, the faster it goes, the less it will be likely either to
scorch or consume. This is Spanish enough, I am sure.

If this finds you still at Munich, pray make many compliments
from me to Mr. Burrish, to whom I am very much obliged for all
his kindness to you: it is true, that while I had power I endeavoured to serve him; but it is as true too, that I served many
others more, who have neither returned nor remembered those
services.

I have been very ill this last fortnight of your old Carniolian
complaint,* the *arthritis vaga;* luckily, it did not fall upon my

* See Letter of June 6, 1751.

breast, but seized on my right arm; there it fixed its seat of empire; but, as in all tyrannical governments, the remotest parts felt their share of its severity. Last post I was not able to hold a pen long enough to write to you, and therefore desired Mr. Grevenkop to do it for me; but that letter was directed to Berlin. My pain is now much abated, though I have still some fine remains of it in my shoulder, where, I fear, it will teaze me a great while. I must be careful to take Horace's advice, and consider well, *Quid valeant humeri quid ferre recusent.*

Lady Chesterfield bids me make you her compliments, and assure you, that the music will be much more welcome to her with you, than without you.

In some of my last letters, which were directed to, and will, I suppose, wait for you at Berlin, I complimented you, and with justice, upon your great improvement of late in the epistolary way, both with regard to the style and the turn of your letters. Your four or five last to me have been very good ones, and one that you wrote to Mr. Harte, upon the New Year, was so pretty a one, and he was so much and so justly pleased with it, that he sent it to me from Windsor, the instant he had read it. This talent (and a most necessary one it is in the course of life) is to be acquired by resolving, and taking pains, to acquire it; and, indeed, so is every talent except poetry, which is, undoubtedly, a gift. Think therefore, night and day, of the turn, the purity, the correctness, the perspicuity, and the elegancy of whatever you speak or write; take my word for it your labour will not be in vain, but greatly rewarded by the harvest of praise and success which it will bring you. Delicacy of turn, and elegancy of style, are ornaments as necessary to common sense, as attentions, address, and fashionable manners, are to common civility; both may subsist without them, but then, without being of the least use to the owner. The figure of a man is exactly the same, in dirty rags, or in the finest and best-chosen clothes; but in which of the two he is the most likely to please, and to be received in good company, I leave you to determine.

Both my arm and my paper hint to me, to bid you good-night.

CCXX.

LONDON, *February* 12, 1754.

MY DEAR FRIEND,

I take my aim, and let off this letter at you, at Berlin; I should be sorry it missed you, because I believe you will read it with as much pleasure as I write it. It is to inform you, that, after some difficulties and dangers, your seat in the new Parliament is at last absolutely secured, and that without opposition, or the least necessity of your personal trouble or appearance. This success, I must further inform you, is, in a great degree, owing to Mr. Eliot's friendship to us both; for he brings you in with himself, at his surest borough.* As it was impossible to act with more zeal and friendship than Mr. Eliot has acted in this whole affair, I desire that you will, by the very next post, write him a letter of thanks; warm and young thanks, not old and cold ones. You may enclose it in yours to me, and I will send it to him, for he is now in Cornwall.

Thus, sure of being a Senator, I dare say you do not propose to be one of the *pedarii senatores et pedibus ire in sententiam;* for, as the House of Commons is the theatre where you must make your fortune and figure in the world, you must resolve to be an actor, and not a *persona muta*, which is just equivalent to a candle-snuffer upon other theatres. Whoever does not shine there is obscure, insignificant, and contemptible; and you cannot conceive how easy it is, for a man of half your sense and knowledge, to shine there if he pleases.

The receipt to make a speaker, and an applauded one too, is short and easy. Take of common sense *quantum sufficit*, add a little application to the rules and orders of the House, throw obvious thoughts in a new light, and make up the whole with a large quantity of purity, correctness, and elegancy of style. Take it for granted, that by far the greatest part of mankind do neither analyse nor search to the bottom; they are incapable of penetrating deeper than the surface. All have senses to be gratified, very few have reason to be applied to. Graceful utter-

* This arrangement was in its details slightly altered. At the General Election in the spring of 1754, Mr. Eliot was returned for St. Germain's, and Mr. Stanhope for Liskeard.— M.

ance and action please their eyes, elegant diction tickles their ears; but strong reason would be thrown away upon them. I am not only persuaded by theory, but convinced by my experience, that (supposing a certain degree of common sense) what is called a good speaker, is as much a mechanic as a good shoemaker; and that the two trades are equally to be learned by the same degree of application. Therefore, for God's sake, let this trade be the principal object of your thoughts; never lose sight of it.

Attend minutely to your style, whatever language you speak or write in; seek for the best words, and think of the best turns. Whenever you doubt of the propriety or elegancy of any word, search the dictionary, or some good author for it, or inquire of somebody, who is master of that language; and in a little time, propriety and elegancy of diction will become so habitual to you, that they will cost you no more trouble. As I have laid this down to be mechanical, and attainable by whoever will take the necessary pains, there will be no great vanity in my saying, that I saw the importance of the object so early, and attended to it so young, that it would now cost me more trouble to speak or write ungrammatically, vulgarly, and inelegantly, than ever it did to avoid doing so. The late Lord Bolingbroke, without the least trouble, talked all day long full as elegantly as he wrote. Why? Not by a peculiar gift from heaven; but, as he has often told me himself, by an early and constant attention to his style. The present Solicitor - General, Murray,* has less law than many lawyers, but has more practice than any; merely upon account of his eloquence, of which he has a never-failing stream.

I remember, so long ago as when I was at Cambridge, whenever I read pieces of eloquence (and indeed they were my chief study) whether ancient or modern, I used to write down the shining passages, and then translate them, as well and as elegantly as ever I could; if Latin or French, into English; if English, into French. This, which I practised for some years, not only improved and formed my style, but imprinted in my mind and memory the best thoughts of the best authors. The trouble was little, but the advantage I have experienced was great. While you are abroad, you can neither have time nor opportunity to read pieces of English, or Parliamentary elo-

* See Letter of Feb. 11, 1751.

quence, as I hope you will carefully do when you return; but, in the meantime, whenever pieces of French eloquence come in your way, such as the speeches of persons received into the Academy, *oraisons funèbres*, representations of the several Parliaments to the King, etc., read them in that view, in that spirit; observe the harmony, the turn and elegancy of the style; examine in what you think it might have been better; and consider in what, had you written it yourself, you might have done worse. Compare the different manners of expressing the same thoughts, in different authors; and observe how differently the same things appear in different dresses. Vulgar, coarse, and ill-chosen words, will deform and degrade the best thoughts, as much as rags and dirt will the best figure. In short, you now know your object; pursue it steadily, and have no digressions that are not relative to, and connected with, the main action. Your success in Parliament will effectually remove all *other objections;* either a foreign or a domestic destination will no longer be refused you, if you make your way to it through Westminster.

I think I may now say, that I am quite recovered of my late illness, strength and spirits excepted, which are not yet restored. Aix-la-Chapelle and Spa will, I believe, answer all my purposes.

I long to hear an account of your reception at Berlin, which I fancy will be a most gracious one. Adieu.

CCXXI.

LONDON, *February* 15, 1754.

MY DEAR FRIEND,

I can now with great truth apply your own motto to you, *Nullum numen abest, si sit prudentia.* You are sure of being, as early as your age will permit, a Member of that House which is the only road to figure and fortune in this country. Those indeed who are bred up to, and distinguish themselves in, particular professions, as the army, the navy, and the law, may by their own merit raise themselves to a certain degree; but you may observe too, that they never get to the top, without the assistance of Parliamentary talents and influence. The means of distinguishing yourself in Parliament are, as I told you in my last, much more easily attained than I believe you imagine

Close attendance to the business of the House will soon give you the Parliamentary *routine;* and strict attention to your style will soon make you, not only a speaker, but a good one. The vulgar look upon a man who is reckoned a fine speaker, as a pheno-menon, a supernatural being, and endowed with some peculiar gift of Heaven; they stare at him, if he walks in the Park, and cry, *that is he.* You will, I am sure, view him in a juster light, and *nullâ formidine.* You will consider him only as a man of good sense, who adorns common thoughts with the graces of elocution, and the elegancy of style. The miracle will then cease; and you will be convinced, that with the same application and attention, to the same objects, you may most certainly equal, and perhaps surpass, this prodigy.

Sir William Yonge, with not a quarter of your parts, and not a thousandth part of your knowledge, has, by a glibness of tongue singly,* raised himself successively to the best employ-ments of the kingdom; he has been Lord of the Admiralty, Lord of the Treasury, Secretary at War, and is now Vice-Treasurer of Ireland; and all this, with a most sullied, not to say blasted character. Represent the thing to yourself, as it really is, easily attainable, and you will find it so. Have but ambition enough passionately to desire the object, and spirit enough to use the means, and I will be answerable for your success. When I was younger than you are, I resolved within myself that I would in all events be a speaker in Parliament, and a good one too, if I could. I consequently never lost sight of that object, and never neglected any of the means that I thought led to it. I succeeded to a certain degree, and I assure you with great ease, and with-out superior talents.

Young people are very apt to overrate both men and things, from not being enough acquainted with them. In proportion as you come to know them better, you will value them less. You will find that reason, which always ought to direct mankind, seldom does; but that passions and weaknesses commonly usurp its seat, and rule in its stead. You will find that the ablest have

---

* So great was Sir William's "glibness of tongue," that his very fluency has been urged as his reproach; and Pope has coupled him with Bubb Dodington in one sarcastic line: "The flowers of Bubo, and the flow of Yonge!"—*Epilogue to Satires* i., 68.

their weak sides too, and are only comparatively able, with regard to the still weaker herd; having fewer weaknesses themselves they are able to avail themselves of the innumerable ones
of the generality of mankind; being more masters of themselves,
they become more easily masters of others.   They address themselves to their weaknesses, their senses, their passions, never to
their reason, and consequently seldom fail of success.   But then
analyse those great, those governing, and, as the vulgar imagine,
those perfect characters; and you will find the great Brutus a
thief in Macedonia, the great Cardinal de Richelieu a jealous
poetaster, and the great Duke of Marlborough a miser.   Till you
come to know mankind by your own experience, I know nothing
nor no man that can, in the meantime, bring you so well acquainted with them as le Duc de la Rochefoucalt; his little book
of maxims, which I would advise you to look into, for some
moments at least, every day of your life, is, I fear, too like, and
too exact a picture of human nature.   I own it seems to degrade
it, but yet my experience does not convince me that it degrades
it unjustly.

Now to bring all this home to my first point: all these considerations should not only invite you to attempt to make a figure
in Parliament, but encourage you to hope that you shall succeed.
To govern mankind, one must not overrate them; and to please
an audience, as a speaker, one must not overvalue it.   When I
first came into the House of Commons, I respected that assembly
as a venerable one, and felt a certain awe upon me; but upon
better acquaintance that awe soon vanished, and I discovered,
that of the five hundred and sixty, not above thirty could understand reason, and that all the rest were *peuple ;* that those thirty
only required plain common sense, dressed up in good language;
and that all the others only required flowing and harmonious
periods, whether they conveyed any meaning or not; having
ears to hear, but not sense enough to judge.   These considerations made me speak with little concern the first time, with less
the second, and with none at all the third.   I gave myself no
farther trouble about anything except my elocution and my
style; presuming, without much vanity, that I had common
sense sufficient not to talk nonsense.   Fix these three truths
strongly in your mind: first, that it is absolutely necessary for

you to speak in Parliament; secondly, that it only requires a
little human attention, and no supernatural gifts; and thirdly,
that you have all the reason in the world to think that you shall
speak well. When we meet, this shall be the principal subject
of our conversations; and if you will follow my advice, I will
answer for your success.

Now from great things to little ones; the transition is to me
easy, because nothing seems little to me that can be of any use
to you. I hope you take great care of your mouth and teeth,
and that you clean them well every morning with a sponge and
tepid water, with a few drops of arquebusade water dropped into
it, besides washing your mouth carefully after every meal. I do
insist upon your never using those sticks, or any hard substance
whatsoever, which always rub away the gums, and destroy the
varnish of the teeth. I speak this from woeful experience; for
my negligence of my teeth, when I was younger than you are,
made them bad; and afterwards my desire to have them look
better, made me use sticks, irons, etc., which totally destroyed
them; so that I have not now above six or seven left. I lost
one this morning, which suggested this advice to you.

I have received the tremendous wild boar which your still more
tremendous arm slew in the immense deserts of the Palatinate;
but have not yet tasted of it, as it is hitherto above my low
regimen. The late King of Prussia, whenever he killed any
number of wild boars, used to oblige the Jews to buy them, at a
high price, though they could eat none of them; so they defrayed
the expense of his hunting. His son has juster rules of government, as the *Code Frédéric* plainly shows.

I hope that by this time you are as well *ancré* at Berlin as you
were at Munich; but if not, you are sure of being so at Dresden.
Adieu!

CCXXII.

LONDON, *February* 26, 1754.

MY DEAR FRIEND,

I have received your letters of the 4th from Munich, and of
the 11th from Ratisbon; but I have not received that of the 31st
of January, to which you refer in the former. It is to this negligence and uncertainty of the post, that you owe your accidents

between Munich and Ratisbon; for, had you received my letters
regularly, you would have received one from me, before you left
Munich, in which I advised you to stay, since you were so well
there. But at all events, you were in the wrong to set out from
Munich in such weather and such roads; since you could never
imagine that I had set my heart so much upon your going to
Berlin, as to venture your being buried in the snow for it. Upon
the whole, considering all, you are very well off. You do very
well, in my mind, to return to Munich, or, at least, to keep within
the circle of Munich, Ratisbon, and Manheim, till the weather
and the roads are good; stay at each or any of those places as
long as ever you please; for I am extremely indifferent about
your going to Berlin.

   As to our meeting, I will tell you my plan, and you may form
your own accordingly. I propose setting out from hence the last
week in April, then drinking the Aix-la-Chapelle waters for a
week, and from thence being at Spa about the 15th of May,
where I shall stay two months at most, and then returning
straight to England. As I both hope and believe that there will
be no mortal at Spa during my residence there, the fashionable
season not beginning till the middle of July, I would by no
means have you come there at first, to be locked up with me and
some few *Capucins*, for two months, in that miserable hole; but
I would advise you to stay where you like best, till about the
first week in July, and then to come and pick me up at Spa, or
meet me upon the road at Liege or Brussels. As for the intermediate time, should you be weary of Manheim and Munich, you
may, if you please, go to Dresden to Sir Charles Williams, who
will be there before that time; or you may come for a month or
six weeks to the Hague; or, in short, go or stay wherever you
like best. So much for your motions.

   As you have sent for all the letters directed to you at Berlin,
you will receive from thence volumes of mine, among which you
will easily perceive that some were calculated for a supposed
perusal previous to your opening them. I will not repeat anything contained in them, excepting, that I desire you will send
me a warm and cordial letter of thanks for Mr. Elliot; who has,
in the most friendly manner imaginable, fixed you at his own
borough of Liskeard, where you will be elected, jointly with him,

without the least opposition or difficulty. I will forward that letter to him into Cornwall, where he now is.

Now, that you are to be soon a man of business, I heartily wish you would immediately begin to be a man of method; nothing contributing more to facilitate and despatch business, than method and order. Have order and method in your accounts, in your reading, in the allotment of your time; in short, in everything. You cannot conceive how much time you will save by it, nor how much better everything you do will be done. The Duke of Marlborough * did by no means spend, but he slatterned himself into that immense debt, which is not yet near paid off. The hurry and confusion of the Duke of Newcastle do not proceed from his business, but from his want of method in it. Sir Robert Walpole, who had ten times the business to do, was never seen in a hurry, because he always did it with method.

The head of a man who has business and no method nor order, is properly that *rudis indigestaque moles quam dixere chaos*. As you must be conscious that you are extremely negligent and slatternly, I hope you will resolve not to be so for the future. Prevail with yourself, only to observe good method and order for one fortnight; and I will venture to assure you, that you will never neglect them afterwards, you will find such conveniency and advantage arising from them. Method is the great advantage that lawyers have over other people, in speaking in Parliament; for, as they must necessarily observe it in their pleadings in the Courts of Justice, it becomes habitual to them everywhere else. Without making you a compliment, I can tell you with pleasure, that order, method, and more activity of mind, are all that you want, to make, some day or other, a considerable figure in business. You have more useful knowledge, more discernment of characters, and much more discretion, than is common at your age; much more, I am sure, than I had at that age. Experience you cannot yet have, and therefore trust in the mean time to mine. I am an old traveller; am well acquainted with all the bye as well as the great roads; I cannot misguide you from ignorance, and you are very sure I shall not from design.

* Charles Spencer, fourth Earl of Sunderland, succeeded, in 1733, as heir in the female line to the Dukedom of Marlborough. At his death, in 1758, he had attained high military rank, and even perhaps military reputation.—M.

I can assure you, that you will have no opportunity of subscribing yourself, my Excellency's etc.*　Retirement and quiet were my choice some years ago, while I had all my senses, and health and spirits enough to carry on business; but now I have lost my hearing, and find my constitution declining daily, they are become my necessary and only refuge.　I know myself (no common piece of knowledge, let me tell you), I know what I can, what I cannot, and consequently what I ought to do.　I ought not, and therefore will not, return to business, when I am much less fit for it than I was when I quitted it.　Still less will I go to Ireland, where, from my deafness and infirmities, I must necessarily make a different figure from that which I once made there.　My pride would be too much mortified by that difference.　The two important senses of seeing and hearing should not only be good, but quick, in business; and the business of a Lord-Lieutenant of Ireland (if he will do it himself) requires both those senses in the highest perfection.　It was the Duke of Dorset's not doing the business himself, but giving it up to favourites, that has occasioned all this confusion in Ireland; and it was my doing the whole myself, without either Favourite, Minister, or Mistress, that made my administration so smooth and quiet.　I remember, when I named the late Mr. Liddel † for my Secretary, everybody was much surprised at it; and some of my friends represented to me, that he was no man of business, but only a very genteel, pretty young fellow; I assured them, and with truth, that that

---

* This passage shows that some overture was made, or expected to be made, to Lord Chesterfield to resume the Lord-Lieutenancy of Ireland. Already, in 1750, he had refused the offer of a high Cabinet office, the Presidency of the Council. "Lord Chesterfield has declined it," writes Horace Walpole; "for he says he cannot hear causes as he is grown deaf." (To Sir H. Mann, December 19, 1750.) A subsequent letter from Walpole shows that Lord Chesterfield gave another reason for his refusal; "he said he would not be President, because he would not be between two fires"—meaning the Pelham brothers. He added: ' The two brothers are like Arbuthnot's Lindamira and Indamora; the latter was a peaceable tractable gentlewoman, but her sister was always quarrelling and kicking; and as they grew together there was no parting them!'" (Walpole to Mann, December 22, 1750.) On Lord Chesterfield's refusal, the office was conferred upon Lord Granville.—M.

† Richard Liddel, Esq., member of Parliament for Bossiney, in Cornwall. He died in June, 1746.—M.

was the very reason why I chose him; for that I was resolved to do all the business myself, and without even the suspicion of having a Minister; which the Lord-Lieutenant's Secretary, if he is a man of business, is always supposed, and commonly with reason, to be.

Moreover, I look upon myself now to be *emeritus* in business, in which I have been near forty years together; I give it up to you; apply yourself to it, as I have done, for forty years, and then I consent to your leaving it for a philosophical retirement, among your friends and your books. Statesmen and beauties are very rarely sensible of the gradations of their decay; and, too sanguinely hoping to shine on in their meridian, often set with contempt and ridicule. I retired in time, *uti conviva satur;* or, as Pope says, still better, *" Ere tittering youth shall shove you from the stage."* My only remaining ambition is to be the councillor and minister of your rising ambition. Let me see my own youth revived in you; let me be your Mentor, and with your parts and knowledge, I promise you, you shall go far. You must bring, on your part, activity and attention, and I will point out to you the proper objects for them. I own, I fear but one thing for you, and that is what one has generally the least reason to fear from one of your age; I mean your laziness; which, if you indulge, will make you stagnate in a contemptible obscurity all your life. It will hinder you from doing anything that will deserve to be written, or from writing anything that may deserve to be read; and yet one or other of these two objects should be at least aimed at by every rational being.

I look upon indolence as a sort of *suicide;* for the man is effectually destroyed, though the appetites of the brute may survive. Business by no means forbids pleasures; on the contrary, they reciprocally season each other; and I will venture to affirm, that no man enjoys either in perfection, that does not join both. They whet the desire for each other. Use yourself, therefore, in time, to be alert and diligent in your little concerns; never procrastinate, never put off till to-morrow, what you can do to-day; and never do two things at a time; pursue your object, be it what it will, steadily and indefatigably; and let any difficulties (if surmountable) rather animate than slacken your endeavours. Perseverance has surprising effects.

I wish you would use yourself to translate, every day, only three or four lines, from any book, in any language, into the correctest and most elegant English that you can think of; you cannot imagine how it will insensibly form your style, and give you an habitual elegancy; it would not take you up a quarter of an hour in a day. This letter is so long, that it will hardly leave you that quarter of an hour, the day you receive it. So good-night.

CCXXIII.
MAXIMS OF CARDINAL DE RETZ.

1. Il y a souvent de la folie à conjurer; mais il n'y a rien de pareil pour faire les gens sages dans la suite: au moins pour quelque tems. Comme le péril dans ces sortes d'affaires dure même après les occasions, l'on est prudent et circonspect dans les momens qui les suivent.

2. Un esprit médiocre, et susceptible par conséquent d'injustes défiances, est de tous les caractères celui qui est le plus opposé à un bon chef de parti; dont la qualité la plus souvent et la plus indispensablement nécessaire, est de supprimer en beaucoup d'occasions, et de cacher en toutes, les soupçons même les plus légitimes.

3. Rien n'anime et n'appuye plus un mouvement, que le ridicule de celui contre lequel on le fait.

4. Le secret n'est pas si rare qu'on le croit, entre des gens qui sont accoutumés à se mêler des grandes affaires.

5. Descendre jusqu'aux petits est le plus sûr moyen de s'égaler aux grands.

6. La mode qui a du pouvoir en toutes choses, ne l'a si sensible-ment en aucune, qu'à être bien ou mal à la Cour; il y a des tems où la disgrace est une manière de feu qui purifie toutes les mauvaises qualités, et qui illumine toutes les bonnes; il y a des tems où il ne sied pas bien à un honnête homme d'être disgracié.

7. La souffrance aux personnes d'un grand rang, tient lieu d'une grande vertu.

8. Il y a une espèce de galimatias que la pratique fait con-noître quelquefois, mais que la spéculation ne fait jamais en-tendre.

9. Toutes les Puissances ne peuvent rien contre la réputation d'un homme qui se la conserve dans son Corps.

10. On est aussi souvent dupe par la défiance que par la confiance.

11. L'extrémité du mal n'est jamais à son période, que quand ceux qui commandent ont perdu la honte ; parce que c'est justement le moment dans lequel ceux qui obéissent perdent le respect ; et c'est dans ce même moment que l'on revient de la léthargie : mais par des convulsions.

12. Il y a un voile qui doit toujours couvrir tout ce que l'on peut dire, et tout ce que l'on peut croire, du Droit des Peuples et de celui des Rois, qui ne s'accordent jamais si bien ensemble que dans le silence.

13. Il y a des conjonctures dans lesquelles on ne peut plus faire que des fautes ; mais la fortune ne met jamais les hommes dans cet état, qui est de tous le plus malheureux, et personne n'y tombe que ceux qui s'y précipitent par leur faute.

14. Il sied plus mal à un Ministre de dire des sottises, que d'en faire.

15. Les avis que l'on donne à un Ministre passent pour des crimes, toutes les fois qu'on ne le lui est point agréable.

16. Auprès des Princes, il est aussi dangereux, et presqu'aussi criminel, de pouvoir, le bien que de vouloir le mal.

17. Il est bien plus naturel à la peur de consulter que de decider.

18. Cette circonstance paroit ridicule ; mais elle est fondée. A Paris, dans les émotions populaires, les plus échauffés ne veulent pas, ce qu'ils appellent, *se désheurer.*

19. La flexibilité est de toutes les qualités la plus nécessaire pour le maniement des grandes affaires.

20. On a plus de peine dans les partis, de vivre avec ceux qui en sont, que d'agir contre ceux qui y sont opposés.

21. Les plus grands dangers ont leurs charmes, pour peu que l'on apperçoive de gloire dans la perspective des mauvais succès ; les médiocres dangers n'ont que des horreurs, quand la perte de la réputation est attachée à la mauvaise fortune.

22. Les extrêmes sont toujours fâcheux. Mais ce sont des moyens sages quand ils sont nécessaires : ce qu'ils ont de consolant c'est qu'ils ne sont jamais médiocres, et qu'ils sont décisifs quand ils sont bons.

23. Il y a des conjonctures où la prudence même ordonne de ne consulter que le chapitre des accidens.

24. Il n'y a rien dans le monde qui n'ait son moment décisif; et le chef d'œuvre de la bonne conduite, est de connoître et de prendre ce moment.

25. L'abomination joint au ridicule fait le plus dangereux et le plus irremediable de tous les composés.

26. Les gens foibles ne plient jamais quand ils le doivent.

27. Rien ne touche et n'émeut tant les peuples, et même les Compagnies, qui tiennent beaucoup du peuple, que la variété des spectacles.

28. Les exemples du passé touchent sans comparaison plus les hommes, que ceux de leur siècle; nous nous accoutumons à tout ce que nous voyons; et peut-être que le Consulat du Cheval de Caligula ne nous auroit pas tant surpris, que nous nous l'imaginons.

29. Les hommes foibles se laissent aller ordinairement au plus grand bruit.

30. Il ne faut jamais contester ce qu'on ne croit pas pouvoir obtenir.

31. Le moment où l'on reçoit les plus heureuses nouvelles, est justement celui où il faut redoubler son attention pour les petites.

32. Le pouvoir dans les peuples est fâcheux, en ce qu'il nous rend responsables de ce qu'ils font malgré nous.

33. L'une des plus grandes incommodités des guerres civiles, est, qu'il faut encore plus d'application à ce que l'on ne doit pas dire à ses amis, qu'à ce que l'on doit faire contre ses ennemis.

34. Il n'y a point de qualité qui dépare tant un grand homme, que de n'être pas juste à prendre le moment décisif de la réputation. L'on ne le manque presque jamais que pour mieux prendre celui de la fortune; c'est en quoi l'on se trompe, pour l'ordinaire, doublement.

35. La vue la plus commune dans les imprudences c'est celle que l'on a de la possibilité des resources.

36. Toute Compagnie est peuple; ainsi tout y dépend des instans.

37. Tout ce qui paroit hazardeux, et qui pourtant ne l'est pas, est presque toujours sage.

38. Les gens irrésolus prennent toujours, avec facilité, les ouvertures qui les mènent à deux chemins, et qui par conséquent ne les pressent pas d'opter.

39. Il n'y a point de petits pas dans les grandes affaires.

40. Il y a des tems où certaines gens ont toujours raison.

41. Rien ne persuade tant les gens qui ont peu de sens que ce qu'ils n'entendent pas.

42. Il n'est pas sage de faire, dans les factions, où l'on n'est que sur la défensive, ce qui n'est pas pressé. Mais l'inquiétude des subalternes est la chose la plus incommode dans ces rencontres ; ils croyent que dès qu'on n'agit pas, on est perdu.

43. Les chefs dans les factions n'en sont les maîtres, qu'autant qu'ils sçavent prévenir ou appaiser les murmures.

44. Quand la frayeur est venue à un certain point, elle produit les mêmes effets que la témérité.

45. Il est aussi nécessaire de choisir les mots dans les grandes affaires, qu'il est superflu de les choisir dans les petites.

46. Rien n'est plus rare ni plus difficile aux Ministres qu'un certain ménagement dans le calme qui suit immédiatement les grandes tempêtes, parceque la flatterie y redouble, et que la défiance n'y est pas éteinte.

47. Il ne faut pas nous choquer si fort des fautes des ceux qui sont nos amis, que nous en donnions de l'avantage à ceux contre lesquels nous agissons.

48. Le talent d'insinuer est plus utile que celui de persuader, parceque l'on peut insinuer à tout le monde, et que l'on ne persuade presque jamais personne.

49. Dans les matières qui ne sont pas favorables par elles-mêmes, tout changement qui n'est pas nécessaire est pernicieux, parce-qu'il est odieux.

50. Il faut faire voir à ceux qui ne sont naturellement foibles toutes sortes d'abîmes : parceque c'est le vrai moyen de les obliger de se jetter dans le premier chemin qu'on leur ouvre.

51. L'on doit hazarder le possible toutes les fois que l'on se sent en état de profiter même du manquement de succés.

52. Les hommes irrésolus se déterminent difficilement pour les moyens, quoique même ils soient déterminés pour la fin.

53. C'est presque jen sûr avec les hommes fourbes, de leur faire croire que l'on veut tromper ceux que l'on veut servir.

54. L'un des plus grands embarras que l'on ait avec les Princes, c'est que l'on est souvent obligé, par la considération de leur propre service, de leur donner des conseils dont on ne peut pas leur dire les véritables raisons.

55. Quand on se trouve obligé de faire un discours que l'on prévoit ne devoir pas agréer, l'on ne peut lui donner trop d'apparence de sincérité : parceque c'est l'unique moyen de l'adoucir.

56. On ne doit jamais se jouer avec la faveur : on ne la peut trop embrasser quand elle est véritable ; on ne la peut trop éloigner quand elle est fausse.

57. Il y a de l'inconvénient á s'engager sur des suppositions de ce que l'on croit impossible ; et pourtant il n'y a rien de si commun.

58. La plûpart des hommes examinent moins les raisons de ce qu'on leur propose contre leur sentiment, que celles qui peuvent obliger celui qui les propose de s'en servir.

59. Tout ce qui est vuide dans les tems de faction et d'intrigue passe pour mystérieux dans les esprits de ceux qui ne sont pas accoutumés aux grandes affairs.

60. Il n'est jamais permis à un inférieur de s'égaler en paroles à celui à qui il doit du respect, quoiqu'il s'y égale dans l'action.

61. Tout homme que la fortune seule, par quelque accident, a fait homme public, devient presque toujours avec un peu de tems un particulier ridicule.

62. La plus grande imperfection des hommes est la complaisance, qu'ils trouvent, à se persuader que les autres ne se point exempts des défauts qu'ils se reconnoissent à eux mêmes.

63. Il n'y a que l'expérience qui puisse apprendre aux hommes à ne pas preférér ce qui les pique dans le prêsent à ce qui les doit toucher bien plus essentiellement dans l'avenir.

64. Il faut s'appliquer, avec soin, dans les grandes affaires encore plus que dans les autres, à se défendre du goût qu'on trouve pour la plaisanterie.

65. On ne peut assez peser les moindres mots dans les grandes affaires.

66. Il n'y a que la continuation du bonheur qui fixe la plûpart des amitiés.

67. Quiconque assemble le peuple, l'emeut.

I have taken the trouble of extracting and collecting for your use, the foregoing political Maxims of the Cardinal de Retz, in his *Memoirs*. They are not aphorisms of his invention, but the true and just observations of his own experience in the course of great business. My own experience attests the truth of them all. Read them over with attention as here above, and then read with the same attention, and *tout de suite*, the *Memoirs;* where you will find the facts and characters from whence those observations are drawn, or to which they are applied ; and they will reciprocally help to fix each other in your mind. I hardly know any book so necessary for a young man to read and remember. You will there find how great business is really carried on ; very differently from what people, who have never been concerned in it, imagine. You will there see what Courts and Courtiers really are, and observe that they are neither so good as they should be, nor so bad as they are thought by most people. The Court poet, and the sullen cloistered pedant, are equally mistaken in their notions, or at least in the accounts they give us of them. You will observe the coolness in general, the perfidy in some cases, and the truth in a very few, of Court friendships. This will teach you the prudence of a general distrust ; and the imprudence of making no exception to that rule upon good and tried grounds. You will see the utility of good-breeding towards one's greatest enemies ; and the high imprudence and folly of either insulting or injurious expressions. You will find in the Cardinal's own character, a strange, but by no means an uncommon mixture, of high and low, good and bad, parts and indiscretion. In the character of Monsieur le Duc d'Orleans, you may observe the model of weakness, irresolution, and fear, though with very good parts. In short, you will, in every page of that book, see that strange inconsistent creature, Man, just as he is. If you would know that period of history (and it is well worth knowing) correctly, after you have read the Cardinal's *Memoirs*, you should read those of Joly, and of Madame de Motteville; both which throw great light upon the first. By all those accounts put together, it appears that Anne of Austria (with great submission to a crowned head do I say it) was a b——. She had spirit and courage without parts, devotion without common morality, and lewdness without tenderness either to justify or to dignify it. Her two sons were no more Louis the Thirteenth's than they were mine; and, if Buckingham had staid a little longer, she would probably have had another by him.

Cardinal Mazarin was a great knave, but no great man; much more cunning than able; scandalously false, and dirtily greedy. As for his enemy, Cardinal de Retz, I can truly call him a man of great parts, but I cannot call him a great man. He never was so much so as in his retirement. The ladies had then a great, and have always had some share in State affairs in France; the spring and the streams of their politics have always been, and always will be, the interest of their present lover, or their resentment against a discarded and perfidious one. Money is their great object, of which they are extremely greedy, if it coincides with their arrangement with the lover for the time being; but true glory and public good never enter into their heads. They are always governed by the man they love, and they always govern the man who loves them. He or she who loves the most is always governed by him or her who loves the least. Madame de Montbazon governed Monsieur de Beaufort, who was fond of her; whereas she was only proud of his rank and popularity. The *Drudi* for the time being always governed Madame and Mademoiselle de Chevreuse, and steered their politics. Madame de Longueville governed her brother the Prince de Conti, who was in love with her; but Marsillac, with whom she was in love, governed her. In all female politics, the head is certainly not the part that takes the lead; the true and secret spring lies lower and deeper. La Palatine, whom the Cardinal celebrates as the ablest and most sensible woman he ever met with, and who seems to have acted more systematically and consequentially than any of them, starts aside, however, and deviates from her plan whenever the interests or the inclinations of La Vieuville, her lover, required it. I will add (though with great submission to a late friend of yours at Paris) that no woman ever yet either reasoned or acted long together consequentially; but some little thing, some love, some resentment, some present momentary interest, some supposed slight or some humour, always breaks in upon, and oversets their most prudent resolutions and schemes.

AXIOMS IN TRADE.

(DRAWN UP BY LORD CHESTERFIELD FOR HIS SON.)

To sell, upon the whole, more than you buy.

To buy your materials as cheap, and to sell your manufactures as dear as you can.

To ease the manufactures, as much as possible, of all taxes and burthens.

To lay small or no duties upon your own manufactures exported, and to lay high duties upon all foreign manufactures imported.

To lay small or no duties upon foreign materials that are necessary for your own manufactures; but to lay very high duties upon, or rather totally prohibit, the exportation of such of your own materials as are necessary for the manufacture of other countries, as wool, fuller's earth, etc.

To keep the interest of money low, that people may place their money in trade.

Not to imagine (as people commonly do) that it is either prudent or possible to prohibit the exportation of your gold or silver, whether coined or uncoined. For, if the balance of trade be against you, that is, if you buy more than you sell, you must necessarily make up that difference in money; and your bullion, or your coin, which are in effect the same thing, must and will be exported in spite of all laws. But if you sell more than you buy, then foreigners must do the same by you, and make up their deficiency in bullion or coin. Gold and silver are but merchandise, as well as cloth or linen; and that nation that buys the least and sells the most, must always have the most money.

A free trade is always carried on with more advantage to the public than an exclusive one by a company. But the particular circumstances of some trades may sometimes require a joint stock and exclusive privileges.

All monopolies are destructive to trade.

To get as much as possible, the advantages of manufacturing and freight.

To contrive to undersell other nations in foreign markets.

SOME ACCOUNT OF THE GOVERNMENT OF THE REPUBLIC OF THE SEVEN UNITED PROVINCES.

The following account of the Dutch Republic was drawn up by Lord Chesterfield, at the Hague. It was found among Mr. Philip Stanhope's papers, and had, no doubt, been sent to him for his instruction. The Notes were added by Lord Chesterfield at a latter date than the text, probably in 1761, on the death of the Prince of Orange, as appears by his mention of H. R. H. the *Gouvernante.*—M.

The Government of the Republic of the Seven United Provinces is thought by many to be Democratical; but it is merely Aristocratical :* the people not having the least share in it, either themselves, or by representatives of their own choosing; they have nothing to do but to pay and grumble.

The Sovereign Power is commonly thought to be in the States General, *as they are called,* residing at the Hague. It is no such thing; they are only limited Deputies, obliged to consult their Constituents upon every point of any importance that occurs. It is very true, that the Sovereign Power is lodged in the States General; but who are those States General? Not those who are commonly called so; but the Senate, Council, or *Vrootschaps,* call it what you will, of every town, in every Province that sends Deputies to the Provincial States of the said Province. These *Vrootschaps* are in truth the States General; but, were they to assemble, they would amount, for aught I know, to two or three thousand ; it is, therefore, for convenience and despatch of business, that every Province sends Deputies to the Hague, who are constantly assembled there; who are commonly called the States General ; and in whom many people falsely imagine that the Sovereign Power is lodged. These Deputies are chosen by the *Vrootschaps ;* but their powers are extremely circumscribed ; and they consent to nothing,† without writing, or returning themselves, to their several

* The Members of the Senate, or *Vrootschaps,* were originally elected by the Burghers, in a general, and often a tumultuous assembly; but now for near two hundred years, the *Vrootschaps* found means to persuade the people that these elections were troublesome and dangerous; and kindly took upon themselves to elect their own Members, upon vacancies, and to keep their own body full, without troubling the people with an election; it was then that the Aristocracy was established.

† When the Deputies of the States signed the Triple Alliance with Sir William Temple, in two or three days' time, and without consulting their Principals, (however Sir William Temple values himself upon it,) in reality

constituent towns, for instructions in that particular case. They are authorised to concur in matters of order; that is, to continue things in the common, current, ordinary train; but for the least innovation, the least step out of the ordinary course, new instructions must be given, either to deliberate or to conclude.

Many people are ignorant enough to take the Province of Holland, singly, for the Republic of the Seven United Provinces; and when they mean to speak of the Republic, they say *Holland* * will, or will not, do such a thing; but most people are ignorant enough to imagine, that the Province of Holland has a

they only signed *sub spe rati*. The act was not valid; and, had it not been ratified by the several Constituents of the several Provinces, it had been as *non avenu*. The Deputies, who signed that treaty *sub spe rati*, knew well enough that, considering the nature of the treaty, and the then situation of affairs, they should not only be avowed, but approved of, by their Masters the States.

* When the Province of Holland has once taken an important resolution of Peace, or War, or Accession to any treaty, it is very probable that the other Provinces will come into that measure, but by no means certain; it is often a great while first; and then the little Provinces know that the Province of Holland has their concurrence much at heart, they will often annex conditions to it; as the little towns in Holland frequently do, when the great ones want their concurrence. As for instance, when I was soliciting the accession of the Republic to the Treaty of Vienna, in 1731, which the Pensionary Comte Sinzendorf, and I, had made secretly at the Hague; all the towns in Holland came pretty readily into it, except the little town of Briel; whose Deputies frankly declared, that they would not give their consent, till *Major Such-a-one*, a very honest gentleman of their town, was promoted to the rank of Lieutenant-Colonel, and that, as soon as that was done, they would agree, for they approved of the treaty. This was accordingly done in two or three days, and then they agreed. This is a strong instance of the absurdity of the unanimity required, and of the use that is often made of it. However, should one, or even two of the lesser Provinces, who contribute little, and often pay less, to the public charge, obstinately and frivolously, or perhaps corruptly, persist in opposing a measure which Holland and the other more considerable Provinces thought necessary, and had agreed to, they would send a Deputation to those opposing Provinces, to reason with, and persuade them to concur; but, if this would not do, they would, as they have done in many instances, conclude without them. The same thing is done in the Provincial States of the respective Provinces; where if one or two of the least considerable towns pertinaciously oppose a necessary measure, they conclude without them. But as this is absolutely unconstitutional, it is avoided as much as possible, and a complete unanimity procured, if it can be, by such little concessions as that which I have mentioned to the Briel Major.

legal, a constitutional power over the other six; whereas, by the Act of Union, the little Province of *Groningen* is as much Sovereign as the Province of Holland. The Seven Provinces are seven distinct Sovereignties, confederated together in one Republic; no one having any superiority over, or dependance upon any other; nay, in point of precedence, Holland is but the second, Gueldres being the first. It is very natural to suppose, and it is very true in fact, that Holland, from its superiority of strength and riches, and paying 58 per cent., should have great weight and influence in the other six provinces; but power it has none.

The unanimity, which is constitutionally requisite for every act of each Town, and each Province, separately, and then for every act of the Seven collectively, is something so absurd, and so impracticable in government, that one is astonished that even the form of it has been tolerated so long; for the substance is not strictly observed. And five Provinces will often conclude, though two dissent, provided that Holland and Zealand are two of the five; as fourteen or fifteen of the principal towns of Holland will conclude an affair, notwithstanding the opposition of four or five of the lesser. I cannot help conjecturing that William, the first Prince of Orange, called the *Taciturn*, the ablest man, without dispute, of the age he lived in, not excepting even the Admiral Coligny,* and who had the modelling of the Republic as he pleased; I conjecture, I say, that the Prince of Orange would never have suffered such an absurdity to have crippled that government which he was at the head of, if he had not thought it useful to himself and his family. He covered the greatest ambition with the greatest modesty, and declined the insignificant, outward signs, as much as he desired the solid substance of power; might he not therefore think, that this absurd, though requisite unanimity, made a Stadtholder absolutely necessary to render the government practicable? In which case he was very sure the Stadtholder would always be taken out of his family; and he minded things, not names. The

---

* I am persuaded, that, had the *Taciturn* been in the place of the Admiral Coligny, he would never have been prevailed upon to have come to Paris, and to have put himself into the power of those two monsters of perfidy and cruelty, Catherine of Medicis and Charles the Ninth. His prudent escape from Flanders is a proof of it; when he rather chose to be *Prince sans terre* than *Prince s····· tête*

Pensionary * thinks this conjecture probable; and, as we were talking confidentially upon the subject, we both agreed that this monstrous and impracticable unanimity, required by the constitution, was alone sufficient to bring about a Stadtholder in spite of all the measures of the Republican party to prevent it. He confessed to me, that, upon his being made Pensionary, he entered into solemn engagements not to contribute, directly nor indirectly, to any change of the present form of government, and that he would scrupulously observe these engagements; but that he foresaw the defects in their form of government, and the abuses crept into every part of it, would infallibly produce a Stadtholder,† tumultuously imposed upon the Republic by an insurrection of the populace, as in the case of King William. I told him that, in my opinion, if that were to happen a second time, the Stadtholder so made would be their King.‡ He said he believed so too, and that he had urged all this to the most considerable Members of the Government, and the most jealous Republicans. That he had even formed a plan, which he had laid before them, as the only possible one to prevent this impending danger. That a Stadtholder was originally the chief spring upon which their government turned; and that, if they

---

* Monsieur Slingelandt, the ablest Minister, and the honestest man I ever knew. I may justly call him my Friend, my Master, and my Guide; for I was then quite new in business: he instructed me, he loved, he trusted me.

† It has since appeared that he judged very rightly.

‡ And so he ought to be now, even for the sake and preservation of the Seven Provinces. The necessary principle of a Republic, *Virtue*, subsists no longer there. The great riches of private people (though the public is poor) have long ago extinguished that principle, and destroyed the equality necessary to a Commonwealth. A Commonwealth is unquestionably, upon paper, the most rational and equitable form of government; but it is as unquestionably impracticable, in all countries where riches have introduced luxury, and a great inequality of conditions. It will only do in those countries that poverty keeps virtuous. In England, it would very soon grow a tyrannical Aristocracy; soon afterwards, an Oligarchy; and soon after that, an absolute Monarchy; from the same causes that Denmark, in the last century, became so,—the intolerable oppression of the bulk of the people, from those whom they looked upon as their equals. If the young Stadtholder has abilities, he will, when he grows up, get all the powers of a limited Monarchy, such as England, no matter under what name; and if he is really wise, he will desire no more; if the people are wise, they will give it him.

would have no Stadtholder, they must substitute a *succedaneum*. That one part of that *succedaneum* must be to abolish the unanimity required by the present form of government, and which only a Stadtholder could render practicable by his influence. That the abuses which were crept into the military part of the government must be corrected, or that they alone, if they were suffered to go on, would make a Stadtholder; in order that the army and the navy, which the public paid for, might be of some use, which at present they were not. That he had laid these and many other considerations of the like nature before them, in the hopes of one of these two things: either to prevail with them to make a Stadtholder unnecessary, by a just reformation of the abuses of the government, and substituting a majority, or at most two-thirds, to the absurd and impracticable unanimity now requisite; or, if they would not come into these preventive regulations, that they would treat amicably with the Prince of Orange and give him the *Stadtholderate*, under strict limitations, and with effectual provisions for their liberty. But they would listen to neither of these expedients: the first affected the private interests of most of the considerable people of the Republic, whose power and profit arose from those abuses; and the second was too contrary to the violent passions and prejudices of Messrs. d'Obdam, Booteslaer, Hallewyn, and other Heads of the high Republican party. Upon this I said to the Pensionary, that he had fully proved to me, not only that there would, but that there ought to be, a Stadtholder. He replied, "There will most certainly be one, and you are young enough to live to see it. I hope I shall be out of the way first; but if I am not out of the world at that time, I will be out of my place, and pass the poor remainder of my life in quiet. I only pray that our new Master, whenever we have him, may be gently given us. My friend, the Greffier,* thinks a Stadtholder absolutely necessary to save the Republic, and so do I as much as he, if they will not accept of

---

* The Greffier Fagel, who had been *Greffier*, that is, Secretary of State, above fifty years. He had the deepest knowledge of business, and the soundest judgment, of any man I ever knew in my life; but he had not that quick, that intuitive sagacity, which the Pensionary Slingelandt had. He has often owned to me, that he thought things were gone too far for any other remedy than a Stadtholder.

the other expedient; but we are in very different situations; he is under no engagements to the contrary, and I am." He then asked me, in confidence, whether I had any instructions to promote the Prince of Orange's views and interest. I told him truly I had not; but that, however, I would do it, as far as ever I could, quietly and privately. That he himself had convinced me, that it was for the interest of the Republic, which I honoured and wished well to: and also that it would be a much more efficient ally to England, under that form of government. "I must own," replied he, "that at present we have neither strength, secrecy, nor despatch." I said that I knew but too well, by my own experience; and I added (laughing) that I looked upon him as the Prince of Orange's greatest enemy; and upon that Prince's violent and impetuous enemies * to be his best friends; for that,

* These hot-headed Republicans pushed things with the unjustest acrimony against the Prince of Orange. They denied him his rank in the army; and they kept him out of the possession of the Marquisat of Tervere and Flessingen, which were his own patrimony; and by these means gave him the merit with the people, of being unjustly oppressed. Had he been an abler man himself, or better advised by others, he might have availed himself much more solidly than he did, of the affection, or rather the fury, of the people, in his favour, when they tumultuously made him Stadtholder; but he did not know the value and importance of those warm moments, in which he might have fixed and clinched his power. Dazzled with the show and trappings of power, he did not enough attend to the substance. He attempted a thing impossible, which was, to please everybody; he heard everybody, began everything, and finished nothing. When the people, in their fury, made him Stadtholder, they desired nothing better than totally to dissolve the Republican form of government. He should have let them. The tumultuous love of the populace must be seized and enjoyed in its first transports; there is no hoarding of it to use upon occasions; it will not keep. The most considerable people of the former government would gladly have compounded for their lives, and would have thought themselves very well off in the castle of Louvestein; where one of the Prince of Orange's predecessors sent some of their ancestors, in times much less favourable. An affected moderation made him lose that moment. The government is now in a disjointed, loose state. Her R.H. the Gouvernante has not power enough to do much good; and yet she has more power than authority. Peace and economy, both public and domestic, should, therefore, be the sole objects of her politics, during the minority of her son. The Public is almost a bankrupt; and her son's private fortune extremely incumbered. She has sense and ambition; but it is, still, the sense and ambition of a woman; that is *inconsequential.* What remains to be done, requires a firm, manly, and vigorous mind.

if his (the Pensionary's) plan were to take place, the Prince would have very little hopes.   He interrupted me here, with saying, *Ne craignez rein, Milord, de ce côté là; mon plan blesse trop l'intérêt particulier, pour être reçu à présent que l'amour du public n'existe plus.*   I thought this conversation too remarkable not to write down the heads of it when I came home.

The Republic has hardly any Navy at all; the single fund for the Marine being the small duties upon exports and imports; which duties are not half collected, by the connivance of the Magistrates themselves, who are interested in smuggling, so that the Republic has now no other title but courtesy to the name of a Maritime Power.   Their trade decreases daily, and their national debt increases.   I have good reason to believe that it amounts to at least fifty millions sterling.

The decrease of their herring-fishery, from what it appears by Monsieur De Witt's Memoirs of Holland in his time, is incredible; and will be much greater now we are at last wise enough to take our own herrings upon our own coasts.

They do not now get by freight one quarter of what they used to get; they were the general sea-carriers of all Europe.   The Act of Navigation passed in Cromwell's time, and afterwards confirmed in Charles the Second's, gave the first blow to that branch of profit; and now we carry more than they do.   Their only profitable remaining branches of commerce are, their trade to the East Indies, where they have engrossed the spices; and their illicit trade in America from Surinam, St. Eustatia, Curaçoa, etc.

Their woollen and silk manufactures bear not the least comparison with ours, neither in quantity, quality, nor exportation.

Their *police* is still excellent, and is now the only remains of that prudence, vigilance, and good discipline, which formerly made them esteemed, respected, and courted.

AN ACCOUNT OF THE TEUTONIC ORDER.

(DRAWN UP BY LORD CHESTERFIELD FOR HIS SON, AND ENCLOSED IN HIS LETTER OF AUGUST 2, 1748.)

In the ages of ignorance, which is always the mother of super-stition, it was thought not only just, but meritorious, to propagate religion by fire and sword, and to take away the lives and pro-perties of unbelievers. This enthusiasm produced the several Croisadoes in the eleventh, twelfth, and following centuries ; the object of which was to recover the Holy Land out of the hands of the Infidels, who, by the way, were the lawful possessors. Many honest enthusiasts engaged in these Croisadoes, from a mis-taken principle of religion, and from the pardons granted by the Popes for all the sins of these pious adventurers ; but many more knaves adopted these holy wars in hopes of conquest and plunder.

After Godfrey of Bouillon, at the head of these knaves and fools, had taken Jerusalem, in the year 1099, Christians of various nations remained in that city ; among the rest, one good honest German, that took particular care of his countrymen who came hither in pilgrimages. He built a house for their reception, and an hospital dedicated to the Virgin. This little establish-ment soon became a great one by the enthusiasm of many considerable people who engaged in it, in order to drive the Saracens out of the Holy Land. This society then began to take its first form ; and its members were called Marian Teutonic Knights : Marian, from their chapel, sacred to the Virgin Mary,—Teutonic, from the German, or Teuton, who was the author of it,—and Knights, from the wars which they were to carry on against the Infidels.

These Knights behaved themselves so bravely at first, that Duke Frederic of Suabia, who was general of the German army, in the Holy Land, sent, in the year 1191, to the Emperor Henry VI. and Pope Celestin III. to desire that this brave and charitable fraternity might be incorporated into a regular Order of Knight-hood ; which was accordingly done, and rules and a particular habit was given them. Forty Knights, all of noble families, were at first created by the King of Jerusalem, and other princes then in the army. The first Grand Master of this Order was Henry Wallpott, of a noble family upon the Rhine. This Order soon began to operate in Europe, drove all the Pagans out of Prussia, and took possession of it. Soon after, they got Livonia and Courland, and invaded even Russia, where they introduced the Christian religion. In 1510, they elected Albert, Marquis of Brandenburg, for their Grand Master, who, turning Protestant soon afterwards, took Prussia from the Order, and kept it for himself with the consent of Sigismund, King of Poland, of whom it was to hold. He then quitted his Grand Mastership, and made himself Hereditary Duke of that country, which is thence called Ducal Prussia.

This Order now consists of twelve provinces: viz. Alsatia, Austria, Coblentz and Etsch, which are the four under the Prussian jurisdiction; Franconia, Hesse, Biessen, Westphalia, Lorrain, Thuringia, Saxony, and Utrecht, which eight are of the German jurisdiction. The Dutch now possess all that the Order had in Utrecht. Every one of these provinces have their particular *Commanderies;* and the most ancient of these *Commandeurs* is called the *Commandeur Provincial.* These twelve *Commandeurs* are all subordinate to the Grand Master of Germany as their chief, and have the right of electing the Grand Master. The Elector of Cologne is at present *Grand Maitre.*

This Order, founded by mistaken Christian zeal upon the Antichristian principles of violence and persecution, soon grew strong by the weakness and ignorance of the times, acquired unjustly great possessions, of which they justly lost the greatest part by their ambition and cruelty, which made them feared and hated by all their neighbours.

LORD CHESTERFIELD'S LETTERS TO HIS GODSON ON THE ART OF PLEASING.

This series of fourteen Letters was addressed by Lord Chesterfield to Philip Stanhope, his godson and distant kinsman, who became his heir and successor to the Earldom. They were first published in the *Edinburgh Magazine and Review*, Feb. to May, 1774, probably from copies made by Dr. Dodd; they were reprinted in a Dublin edition of the Letters to his Son, in 1776; in the supplementary quarto volume to Maty's edition of Chesterfield's Works, by B. W., of the Inner Temple; and in Lord Mahon's edition of 1845. In all these several obvious errors—mistakes of the copyist or printers—occur, but have here been corrected. In Lord Carnarvon's *Lord Chesterfield's Letters to his Godson*, they are reprinted from the originals, but apparently with some inaccuracies.

I.

Bath, *Oct.* 31, 1765.

My dear little Boy,

Our correspondence has hitherto been very desultory and various. My letters have had little or no relation to each other, and I endeavoured to suit them to your age and passion for variety. I considered you as a child, and trifled with you accordingly; and, though I cannot yet look upon you as a man, I shall consider you as being capable of some serious reflections. You are now above half a man, for before your present age is doubled you will be quite a man : therefore, *Paulo majora canamus.*

You already know your religious and moral duties, which, indeed are exceedingly simple and plain; the former consist in fearing and loving your Creator, and in observing His laws, which He has written in every man's heart, and which your conscience will always remind you of, if you give it but a fair hearing; the latter, I mean your moral duties, are fully contained in these few words, *Do as you would be done by.* Your classical knowledge, others more able than myself will instruct you in. There remains, therefore, nothing in which I can be useful to you, except to communicate to your youth and inexperience what a long observation and knowledge of the world enables me to give you.

I shall then, for the future, write you a series of letters, which I desire you will read twice over, and keep by you, upon the *duty,* the *utility,* and the *means* of pleasing—that is, of being what the

French call *aimable;* an art which, it must be owned, they
possess almost exclusively; they have studied it the most, and
they practise it the best. I shall, therefore, often borrow their
expressions in the former letters, as answering my ideas better
than any I can find in my own language.

Remember this, and fix it in your mind, that whoever is not
aimable, is in truth *nobody at all* with regard to the general intercourse of life; his learning is pedantry, and even his virtues
have no lustre. Perhaps my subject may oblige me to say things.
above your present *forte;* but, in proportion as your understanding opens and extends itself, you will understand them; and
then *hæc olim meminisse juvabit.*

I presume you will not expect elegancy, or even accuracy, in
letters of this kind, which I write singly for your use. I give
you my matter just as it occurs to me. May it be useful to you,
for I do not mean it for public perusal.

P.S. If you were in this place, it would quite turn your little
head; here would be so much of your dear variety, that you
would think rather less, if possible, than most of the company
who saunter away their whole time and do nothing.

II.

BATH, *Nov.* 7, 1765.

MY DEAR LITTLE BOY,

The desire of being pleased is universal; the desire of
pleasing should be so too; it is included in that great and fundamental principle of morality, of doing to others what one wishes
they should do to us. There are, indeed, some moral duties of a
much higher nature, but none of a more amiable; and I do not
hesitate to place it at the head of what Cicero calls the *leniores
virtutes.*

The benevolent and feeling heart performs this duty with
pleasure, and in a manner that gives it at the same time; but
the great, the rich, the powerful, too often bestow their favours
upon their inferiors in the manner they bestow their scraps
upon their dogs, so as neither to oblige man nor dogs. It is no
wonder if favours, benefits, and even charities thus bestowed un-
graciously, should be as coldly and faintly acknowledged. Gratitude is a burden upon our imperfect nature, and we are but

too willing to ease ourselves of it, or at least to lighten it as much as we can.

The *manner*, therefore, of conferring favours or benefits, is, as to pleasing, almost as important as the matter itself. Take care, then, never to throw away the obligations, which perhaps you may have it in your power to confer upon others by an air of insolent protection, or by a cold and comfortless manner, which stifles them in their birth. Humanity inclines, religion requires, and our moral duties oblige us, as far as we are able, to relieve the distresses and miseries of our fellow-creatures; but this is not all, for a true heartfelt benevolence and tenderness will prompt us to contribute what we can to their ease, their amusement, and their pleasure, as far as innocently we may. Let us, then, not only scatter benefits, but even strew flowers for our fellow-travellers, in the rugged ways of this wretched world!

There are some, and but too many in this country particularly, who, without the least visible taint of ill-nature or malevolence, seem to be totally indifferent, and do not show the least desire to please; as, on the other hand, they never designedly offend. Whether this proceeds from a lazy, negligent, and listless disposition, from a gloomy and melancholy nature, from ill-health and low spirits, or from a secret and sullen pride, arising from the consciousness of their boasted liberty and independency, is hard to determine, considering the various movements of the human heart, and the wonderful errors of the human mind; but, be the cause what it will, that neutrality, which is the effect of it, makes these people, as neutralities do, despicable, and mere blanks in society. They would surely be roused from their indifference, if they would seriously consider the infinite *utility of pleasing*, which I shall do in my next.

III.

BATH, *Nov.* 13, 1765.

My DEAR LITTLE BOY,

As the *utility* of pleasing seems to be almost a self-evident proposition, I shall rather hint it to you than dwell upon it. The person who manifests a constant desire to please, places his, perhaps, small stock of merit at great interest. When vast returns, then, must real merit, when thus adorned, necessarily bring in? A prudent usurer would with transport place his last shilling at such interest, and upon so solid a security.

The man who is amiable will make almost as many friends as he does acquaintances; I mean in the current acceptation of the word, but not such sentimental friends as Pylades or Orestes, Nisus and Euryalus, etc.; but he will make people in general wish him well, and inclined to serve him in anything not inconsistent with their own interest.

Civility is the essential article towards pleasing, and is the result of good-nature and of good-sense; but good breeding is the decoration, the lustre of civility, and only to be acquired by a minute attention to, and experience of, good company. A good-natured ploughman or fox-hunter may be intentionally as civil as the politest courtier, but their manner often degrades and vilifies their matter; whereas, in good breeding, the *manner* always adorns and dignifies the *matter* to such a degree that I have often known it give currency to base coin. We may truly say, in this case, *materiem superat opus.*

Civility is often attended by a ceremoniousness, which good breeding corrects, but will not quite abolish. A certain degree of ceremony is a necessary outwork of manners, as well as of religion; it keeps the forward and petulant at a proper distance, and is a very small restraint to the sensible and to the well-bred part of the world. We find, in the *Tale of a Tub,* that Peter had too much pomp and ceremony, Jack too little; but Martin's conduct seems to be a good rule for both worship and manners, and good-sense and good-breeding pursue this true medium. In my next, I shall consider the *means* of pleasing.

P.S. I am very sorry I can send you no venison this year, but I have no doe venison this time, the season has been so unfavourable. You must celebrate your natal day this year without it, which you will do best by reflecting that you are now ten years old, and that you have no time to lose in trifling childish dissipation. You must apply now or never.

IV.

BATH, *Nov.* 20, 1765.

MY DEAR LITTLE BOY,

The means of pleasing vary according to time, place, and persons; but the general rule is the trite one: Endeavour to please, and you will infallibly please to a certain degree; constantly show a desire to please, and you will engage people's self-love in your interest—a most powerful advocate. This, as indeed almost everything else, depends on attention, or more properly *les attentions*. Be, therefore, minutely attentive to the circumstances of time, place, and person, or you may happen to offend where you intend to please; for people, in what touches themselves, make no allowances for slips or inadvertencies.

To be *distrait* in company is unpardonable, and implies a contempt for it, and is not less ridiculous than offensive. There is little difference between a dead man and a *distrait*; what difference there is, is entirely to the advantage of the former, whose insensibility everybody sees is not voluntary. Some people, most absurdly, affect distraction, as thinking that it implies deep thought and superior wisdom; but they are greatly mistaken, for everybody knows that, if natural, it is a great weakness of the mind, and an egregious folly affected. A wise man, instead of not using the senses which he has, would wish them all to be multiplied, in order to see and hear, at once, whatever is said or done in company.

Be you, then, attentive to the most trifling thing that passes where you are; have, as the vulgar phrase is, your eyes and your ears always about you. It is a very foolish thought a very common saying, "I really did not mind it," or, "I was thinking of quite another thing at that time." The proper answer to such ingenious excuses, and which admits of no reply, is, Why did you not mind it—you was present when it was said or done? Oh! but you may say, you was thinking of quite another thing; if so, why was you not in quite another place proper for that important other thing, which you say you was thinking of? But you will say, perhaps, that the company was so silly that it did not deserve your attention. That, I am sure, is the saying of a silly man; for a man of sense knows that there is no company so silly, that some use may not be made of by attention.

You should have (and it is to be had, if you please) a versatility of attention, which you may instantaneously apply to different objects and persons as they occur. Remember, that without these *attentions* you will never be fit to live in good company, nor indeed any company at all, and the best thing you can do, will be to turn *Chartreux*. When you present yourself, or are presented for the first time in company, study to make the first impression you give of yourself as advantageous as possible. This you can only do, at first, by what solid people commonly call trifles, which are *air*, *dress*, and *address*. Here invoke the assistance of the Graces. Even that silly article of dress is no trifle upon these occasions.

Never be the first nor the last in the fashion. Wear as fine clothes as men of your rank commonly do, and rather better than worse; and when you are well-dressed once a day, do not seem to know that you have any clothes on at all, but let your motions be as easy as they could be in your night-gown. A fop values himself upon his dress, but a man of sense will not neglect it in his youth at least. The greatest fop I ever saw, was at the same time the greatest sloven, for it is an affected singularity of dress, be it of what sort it will, that constitutes a fop, and everybody will prefer an over-dressed fop to a slovenly one. Let your address, when you first come into any company, be modest, but without the least bashfulness or sheepishness—steady, without impudence, and unembarrassed, as if you were alone in your own room. This is a difficult point to hit, and therefore deserves great attention; nothing but a long usage of the world, and in the best company, can possibly give it.

A young man without knowledge of the world, when he first goes into a fashionable company, where most are his superiors, is commonly either annihilated by *mauvaise honte*, or, if he rouses and lashes himself up to what he only thinks a modest assurance, he runs into impudence and absurdity, and consequently offends instead of pleasing. Have always, as much as you can, that *air de douceur*, which never fails to make favourable impressions, provided it be equally free from an insipid smile or a pert smirk.

V.

BATH, *Nov.* 25, 1765.

MY DEAR LITTLE BOY,—

Carefully avoid an argumentative and disputative turn, which too many people have, and some even value themselves upon, in company; and, when your opinion differs from others, maintain it only with modesty, calmness, and gentleness; but never be eager, loud, or clamorous; and, when you find your antagonist beginning to grow warm, put an end to the dispute by some genteel *badinage* : for, take it for granted, if the two best friends in the world dispute with eagerness, upon the most trifling subject imaginable, they will, for the time, find a momentary alienation from each other. Disputes upon any subject are a sort of trial of the understanding, and must end in the mortification of one or other of the disputants. On the other hand, I am far from meaning that you should give an universal assent to all that you hear said in company; such an assent would be mean, and in some cases criminal; but blame with indulgence, and correct with *douceur*.

It is impossible for a man of sense not to have a contempt for fools, and for a man of honour not to have an abhorrence of knaves; but you must gain upon yourself, so as not to discover either in their full extent. They are, I fear, too great a majority to contend with; and their number makes them formidable, though not respectable. They commonly hang together, for the mutual use they make of each other. Show them a reserved civility, and let them not exist with regard to you. Do not play off the fool, as is too commonly done by would-be wits, nor shock the knave unnecessarily, but have as little as possible to do with either; and remember always, that whoever contracts a friendship with a knave or a fool, has something bad to do or to conceal. A young man, especially at his first entering into the world, is generally judged of by the company he keeps—and it is a very fair way of judging; and though you will not at first be able to make your way, perhaps, into the best company, it is always in your power to avoid bad. It may be, that you will ask me how I define *good* and *bad* company? and I will do it as well as I can, for it is of the greatest importance to know the difference.

Good company consists of a number of people of a certain fashion (I do not mean birth), of whom the majority are reckoned to be people of sense, and of decent characters—in short, of those who are allowed universally to be, and are called, good company. It is possible, nay probable, that a fool or two may sneak, or a knave or two intrude into such company; the former, in hopes of getting the reputation of a little common sense, and the latter, that of some common honesty. But, *ubi plura nitent*, like Horace, you must not be offended *paucis maculis*.

Bad company is, whatever is not generally allowed to be good company; but there are several gradations in this, as well as in the other; and it will be impossible for you, in the common course of life, not to fall sometimes into bad company; but get out of it as soon and as well as you can. There are some companies so blasted and scandalous, that to have been with them twice would hurt your character, both as to virtue and parts; such is the company of bullies, sharpers, jockies, and low debauchees either in wine or women, not to mention fools. On the other hand, do not, while young, declaim and preach against them like a Capuchin. You are not called upon to be a repairer of wrongs, or a reformer of manners. Let your own be pure, and leave others to the contempt or indignation they deserve.

There is a third sort of company, which, without being scandalous, is vilifying and degrading. I mean, what is called *low* company, which young men of birth and fashion, at their first appearance in the world, are too apt to like, from a degree of bashfulness, *mauvaise honte*, and laziness, which is not easily rubbed off. If you sink into this sort of company but for one year, you will never emerge from it, but remain as obscure and insignificant as they are themselves. Vanity is also a great inducement to keep low company; for a man of quality is sure to be the first man in it, and to be admired and flattered, though, perhaps, the greatest fool in it. Do not think I mean, by low company, people of no birth; for birth goes for nothing with me, nor, I hope, with you; but I mean, by low company, obscure, insignificant people, unknown and unseen in the polite part of the world, and distinguished by no one particular merit or talent, unless, perhaps, by soaking and sotting out their evenings; for drinking is generally the dull and indecent occupation of such company.

There is another sort of company which I wish you to avoid in general, though now and then (but seldom) there may be no harm in seeing it. I mean the company of wags, witlings, buffoons, mimics, and merry fellows, who are all of them commonly the dullest fellows in the world with the strongest animal spirits. If from mere curiosity you go into such company, do not wear in it a severe, philosophical face of contempt of their illiberal mirth, but content yourself with acting a very inferior part in it; contract no familiarity with any of the performers, which would give them claims upon you that you could not with decency either satisfy or reject. Call none of them by their Christian names, as Jack, Frank, etc., but use rather a more ceremonious civility with them than with your equals, for nothing keeps forward and petulant puppies at a proper distance so effectually as a little ceremony.

VI.

BATH, *Dec.* 4, 1765.

MY DEAR LITTLE BOY,

Bad company is much more easily defined than good; what is bad must strike everybody at first sight; folly, knavery, and profligacy can never be mistaken for wit, honour, and decency. Bad company have *fœnum in cornu, longe fuge;* but in good, there are several gradations from good to the best; merely good, is rather free from objections than deserving of praise. Aim at the best; but what is the best? I take it to be those societies of men or women, or a mixture of both, where great politeness, good-breeding, and decency, though, perhaps, not always virtue, prevail.

Women of fashion and character—I do not mean absolutely unblemished—are a necessary ingredient in the composition of good company; the *attention* which they require, and which is always paid them by well-bred men, keeps up politeness, and gives a habit of good-breeding; whereas men, when they live together without the lenitive of women in company, are apt to grow careless, negligent, and rough among one another. In company, every woman is every man's superior, and must be addressed with respect—nay more, with flattery—and you need not fear making it too strong. Such flattery is not mean on your part, nor pernicious to them, for it can never give them a greater opinion of their beauty or their sense than they had before; therefore, make the dose strong—it will be greedily swallowed.

Women stamp the character, fashionable or unfashionable, of all young men at their first appearance in the world. Bribe them with minute attentions, good-breeding, and flattery. I have often known their proclamation give a value and currency to base coin enough, and, consequently, it will add a lustre to the truest sterling. Women, though otherwise called sensible, have all of them, more or less, weaknesses, singularities, whims and humours, especially vanity; study attentively all their failings, gratify them as far as you can—nay, flatter them, and sacrifice your own little humours to them. Young men are too apt to show a dislike, not to say an aversion and contempt, for ugly and old women, which is both impolitic and injudicious; for there is a respectful politeness due to the whole sex. Besides, the ugly and the old, having the least to do themselves, are jealous of being despised, and never forgive it; and I could suppose cases, in which you would desire their friendship, or at least their neutrality. Let it be a rule with you never to show that contempt which very often you will have, and with reason, for a human creature, for it will never be forgiven. An injury is sooner pardoned than an insult.

VII.

BATH, Dec. 12, 1765.

MY DEAR LITTLE BOY,

If you have not command enough over yourself to conquer your humours, as I hope you will, and as I am sure every rational creature may have, never go into company while the fit of ill-humour is upon you. Instead of companies diverting you in those moments, you will displease, and probably shock them, and you will part worse friends than you met; but whenever you find in yourself a disposition to sullenness, contradiction, or testiness, it will be in vain to seek for a cure abroad. Stay at home, let your humour ferment and work itself off. Cheerfulness and good-humour are, of all qualifications, the most amiable in company; for, though they do not necessarily imply good-nature and good-breeding, they act them, at least, very well; and that is all that is required in mixed company.

I have, indeed, known some very ill-natured people, who were very good-humoured in company; but I never knew anybody generally ill-humoured in company, who was not essentially ill-natured. Where there is no malevolence in the heart, there is always a cheerfulness and ease in the countenance and manners. By good-humour and cheerfulness, I am far from meaning noisy mirth and loud peals of laughter, which are the distinguishing characteristics of the vulgar and of the ill-bred, whose mirth is a kind of storm. Observe it, the vulgar often laugh, but never smile; whereas, well-bred people often smile, but seldom laugh. A witty thing never excited laughter; it pleases only the mind, and never distorts the countenance. A glaring absurdity, a blunder, a silly accident, and those things that are generally called comical, may excite a laugh, though never a loud nor a long one, among well-bred people.

Sudden passion is called short-lived madness; it is a madness indeed, but the fits of it return so often in choleric people, that it may well be called a continual madness. Should you happen to be of this unfortunate disposition, which God forbid, make it your constant study to subdue, or, at least, to check it. When you find your choler rising, resolve neither to speak to nor answer the person who excites it; but stay till you find it subsiding, and then speak deliberately. I have known many people, who, by the rapidity of their speech, have run away with themselves into a passion. I will mention to you a trifling, and perhaps, you will think, a ridiculous receipt towards checking the excess of passion, of which I think that I have experienced the utility myself. Do everything in minuet-time; speak, think, and move always in that measure—equally free from the dulness of slow, or the hurry or huddle of quick, time. This movement will, moreover, allow you some moments to think forwards, and the Graces to accompany what you say or do; for they are never represented as either running or dozing. Observe a man in a passion, see his eyes glaring, his face inflamed, his limbs trembling, and his tongue stammering and faltering with rage, and then ask yourself calmly, whether upon any account you would be that human wild-beast. Such creatures are hated and dreaded in all companies, where they are let loose, as people do not choose to be exposed to the disagreeable necessity of either knocking down those brutes, or being knocked down by them. Do you, on the contrary, endeavour to be cool and steady upon all occasions; the advantages of such a steady calmness are innumerable, and would be too tedious to relate. It may be acquired by care and reflection; if it could not, that reason which distinguishes man from brutes, would be given us to very little purpose. As a proof of this, I never saw, nor scarcely ever heard of, a

Quaker in a passion. In truth, there is in that sect a decorum, and decency, and an amiable simplicity, that I know in no other.

Having mentioned the Graces in this letter, I cannot end it without recommending to you, most earnestly, the advice of the wisest of the ancients, to sacrifice to them devoutly and daily. When they are propitious, they adorn everything, and engage everybody. But, are they to be acquired? Yes, to a certain degree, by attention, observation, and assiduous worship. Nature, I admit, must first have made you capable of adopting them, and then observation and imitation will make them in time your own.

There are Graces of the mind, as well as of the body; the former giving an engaging turn to the thoughts and the expressions; the latter to the motions, attitudes, and address. No man, perhaps, ever possessed them all; he would be too happy that did; but, if you will attentively observe those graceful and engaging manners which please you most in other people, you may easily correct what will please others in you, and engage the *majority* of the Graces on your side; ensure the casting vote and be returned *aimable*. There are people whom the *Précieuse* of Moliere very justly, though very affectedly calls, *les antipodes des Graces*. If these unhappy people are formed by Nature invincibly *maussades* and awkward, they are to be pitied, rather than blamed or ridiculed. But Nature has disinherited few people to that degree.

VIII.

BATH, *Dec.* 18, 1765.

MY DEAR LITTLE BOY,

If God gives you wit, which I am not sure that I wish you, unless He gives you at the same time, at least an equal portion of judgment to keep it in good order, wear it like your sword in the scabbard, and do not brandish it to the terror of the whole company. If you have real wit, it will flow spontaneously, and you need not aim at it; for, in that case, the rule of the Gospel is reversed, and it will prove—seek, and you shall *not* find. Wit is so shining a quality that everybody admires it; most people aim at it, all people fear it, and few love it unless in themselves. A man must have a good share of wit himself to endure a great share in another. When wit exerts itself in satire, it is a most malignant distemper. Wit, it is true, may be shown in satire;

but satire does not constitute wit, as many imagine. A man of real wit will find a thousand better ocasions of showing it.

Abstain, therefore, most carefully from satire, which, though it fall on no particular person in company, and momentarily, from the malignancy of the human heart, pleases all, yet, upon reflection, it frightens all too. Every one thinks it may be his turn next, and will hate you for what he finds you could say of him, more than be obliged to you for what you do not say. Fear and hatred are next-door neighbours. The more wit you have, the more good-nature and politeness you must show, to induce people to pardon your superiority ; for that is no easy matter. Learn to shrink yourself to the size of the company you are in. Take their tone, whatever it may be, and excel in it if you can ; but never pretend to give the tone. A free conversation will no more bear a Dictator, than a free Government will.

The character of a man of wit is a shining one that every man would have, if he could, though it is often attended with some inconveniences ; the dullest Alderman ever aims at it, cracks his dull joke, and thinks, or at least hopes, that it is wit ; but the denomination of *a wit* is always formidable, and very often ridiculous. These *titular wits* have commonly much less wit than petulance and presumption ; they are at best the *rieurs de leur quartier,* in which narrow sphere they are at once feared and admired.

You will perhaps ask me, and justly, how, considering the delusion of self-love and vanity, from which no man living is absolutely free, how you shall know whether you have wit or not. To which the best answer I can give you is, not to trust to the voice of your own judgment, for it will deceive you, nor to your ears, which will always greedily receive flattery, if you are worth being flattered ; but trust only to your eyes, and read in the countenance of good company their approbation or dislike of what you say. Observe, carefully, too, whether you are sought for, solicited, and in a manner pressed into good company. But even all this will not absolutely ascertain your wit ; therefore do not, upon this encouragement, flash your wit in people's faces *à ricochets,* in the shape of *bon mots,* epigrams, small repartees.

Appear to have rather less than more wit than you really have. A wise man will live as much within his wit as his income. Content yourself with good sense and reason, which at the long-run are ever sure to please everybody who has either; if wit comes into the bargain, welcome it, but never invite it. Bear this truth always in your mind, that you may be admired for your wit, if you have any; but that nothing but good sense and good qualities can make you be loved; they are substantial, every day's wear. Wit is for *les jours de gala*, where people go chiefly to be stared at.

P.S. I received your last letter, which is very well written. I shall see you next week, and bring you some pretty things from hence; because I am told you are a very good boy, and have learned very well.

IX.

BATH, *Dec.* 28, 1765.

MY DEAR LITTLE BOY,

There is a species of minor wit, which is much used and much more abused; I mean raillery. It is a most mischievous and dangerous weapon, when in unskilful or clumsy hands; and it is much safer to let it quite alone than to play with it; and yet almost everybody does play with it, though they see daily the quarrels and heart-burnings that it occasions. In truth, it implies a supposed superiority in the *railleur* to the *raillé*, which no man likes even the suspicion of, in his own case, though it may divert him in other people's.

An innocent *raillerie* is often inoffensively begun, but very seldom inoffensively ended; for that depends upon the *raillé* who, if he cannot defend himself, will grow brutal; and, if he can, very possibly his *railleur*, baffled, becomes so. It is a sort of trial of wit, in which no man can bear to have his inferiority made appear.

The character of a *railleur* is more generally feared and more heartily hated than any one I know in the world. The injustice of a bad man is sooner forgiven than the insult of a witty one; the former only hurts one's liberty and property, but the latter hurts and mortifies that secret pride which no human breast is free from. I will allow that there is a sort of raillery which may not only be inoffensive, but even flattering, as when, by a genteel irony, you accuse people of those imperfections which they are most notoriously free from, and consequently insinuate that they possess the contrary virtues. You _nay safely call Aristides a knave, or a very handsome woman an ugly one. Take care, however, that neither the man's character, nor the lady's beauty, be in the least doubtful. But this sort of raillery requires a very light and steady hand to administer it. A little too strong, it may be mistaken into an offence; and a little too smooth, it may be thought a sneer, which is a most odious thing.

There is another sort—I will not call it wit, but merriment and buffoonery—which is *mimicry*. The most successful mimic in the world is always the most absurd fellow; and an ape is infinitely his superior. His profession is to imitate and ridicule those natural defects and deformities for which no man is in the least accountable, and in the imitation of which he makes himself for the time as disagreeable and shocking as those he mimics. But I will say no more of those creatures who only amuse the lowest rabble of mankind.

There is another sort of human animals, called wags, whose profession is to make the company laugh immoderately, and who always succeed, provided the company consist of fools; but who are greatly disappointed in finding that they can never alter a muscle in the face of a man of sense. This is a most contemptible character, and never esteemed even by those who are silly enough to be diverted by them.

Be content for yourself with sound good sense, and good manners, and let wit be thrown into the bargain where it is proper and inoffensive. Good sense will make you be esteemed, good manners, beloved, and wit gives a lustre to both. In whatever company you happen to be, whatever pleasures you are engaged in, though perhaps not of a very laudable kind, take care to preserve a great personal dignity; I do not in the least mean a pride of birth and rank—that would be too silly; but I mean a dignity of character. Let your moral character of honesty and honour be unblemished, and even unsuspected. I have known some people dignify even their vices—first, by never boasting of them, and next, by not practising them in an illiberal and indecent manner. . . . If they loved drinking too well, they did not practise that beastly vice in beastly companies, but with those whose good humour in some degree seemed to excuse it, though nothing can justify it. When you see a drunken man, as probably you will see many, study him with attention, and ask yourself soberly, whether you would upon any account be that beast, that disgrace to human reason. The Lacedæmonians very wisely make their slaves drunk, to deter their children from being so; and with good effect, for nobody ever heard of a Lacedœmonian drunk.

X.

BATH, *Jan.* 2, 1766.

My DEAR LITTLE Boy,

If there is a lawful and proper object of raillery, it seems to be a coxcomb, as an usurper of the common rights of mankind. But here some precautions are necessary. Some wit, and great presumption, constitute a coxcomb, for a true coxcomb must have parts. The most consummate coxcomb I ever knew was a man of the most wit, but whose wit, bloated with presumption, made him too big for any company, where he always usurped the seat of empire, and crowded out common sense.

Raillery seems to be a proper rod for these offenders; but great caution and skill are necessary in the use of it, or you may happen to catch a Tártar as they call it, and then the laughter will be against you. The best way with these people is to let them quite alone, and give them rope enough.

On the other hand, there are many, and perhaps more who suffer from their timidity and *mauvaise honte,* which sink them infinitely below their level. Timidity is generally taken for stupidity, which for the most part it is not, but proceeds from a want of education in good company. Mr. Addison was the most timid and awkward man in good company I ever saw; and no wonder, for he had been wholly cloistered up in the cells of Oxford till he was five-and-twenty years old. La Bruyère says, and there is a great deal of truth in it, *Qu'on ne vaut dans ce monde que ce que l'on veut valoir;* for, in this respect, mankind show great indulgence, and value people at pretty near the price they set on themselves, if it be not exorbitant.

I could wish you to have a cool intrepid assurance with great seeming modesty; never *demonté,* and never forward. Very awkward timid people, who have not been used to keep good company, are either ridiculously bashful or absurdly impudent. I have known many a man, impudent from shamefacedness, endeavouring to act a reasonable assurance, and lashing himself to what he imagined to a proper and easy behaviour. A very timid bashful man is annihilated in good company, especially of his superiors; he does not know what he says or does; and is in a ridiculous agitation both of body and mind. Avoid both extremes, and endeavour to possess yourself with coolness and steadiness; speak to the King with full as little concern though with more respect, as you would to your equals. This is the distinguishing characteristic of a gentleman and a man of the world.

The way to acquire this most necessary behaviour is, as I have told you before, to keep company, whatever difficulty it may cost you at first, with your superiors and with women of fashion, instead of taking refuge, as too many young people do, in low or bad company, in order to avoid the restraint of good-breeding. It is, I confess, a very difficult, not to say an impossible thing, for a young man, at his first appearance in the world, and unused to the ways and manners of it, not to be disconcerted and embarrassed when he first enters what is called the best company. He sees that they stare at him, and it they happen to laugh, he is sure that they laugh at him. This awkwardness is not to be blamed, as it often proceeds from audable causes, from a modest diffidence of himself, and a consciousness ot not yet knowing the modes and manners o good company. But let him persevere with a becoming modesty and he will find that all people of good-nature and good-breeding will assist and help him out, instead of laughing at him; and then a very little usage of the world, and an attentive observation, will soon bring him a proper knowledge of it.

It is the characteristic of low and bad company, which commonly consists of wags and witlings, to laugh and disconcert, and, as they call it, bamboozle a young fellow of ingenuous modesty. You will tell me, perhaps, that, to do all this, one must have a good share of vanity; I grant it; but the great point is, *Ne quid nimis:* for I fear Monsieur de la Rochefoucault's maxim is too true, *Que la vertu n'iroit pas loin, si la vanité ne lui tenoit pas compagnie.* A man who despairs of pleasing will never please; u man that is sure that he shall always please wherever he goes, is a coxcomb; but the man who hopes and endeavours to please, and believes that he may, will most infallibly please.

XI.

BATH, *Jan.* 10, 1766.

MY DEAR LITTLE BOY,

I know that you are generous and benevolent in your nature; but that, though the principal point, is not quite enough; you must seem so too. I do not mean ostentatiously; but do not be ashamed, as many young fellows are, of owning the laudable sentiments of good-nature and humanity which you really feel. I have known many young men who desired to be reckoned men of spirit, affect a hardness and unfeelingness, which in reality they never had; their conversation is in the decisive and menacing tone; they are for breaking bones, throwing people out of windows, cutting off ears, etc.; and all these fine declarations they ratify with horrid and silly oaths—all this to be thought men of spirit. Astonishing error this! which necessarily reduces them to this dilemma: if they really mean what they say, they are brutes; and if they do not, they are fools for saying it. This, however, is a common character among young men. Carefully avoid this contagion, and content yourself with being calmly and mildly resolute and steady, when you are thoroughly convinced you are in the right; for this is true spirit. What is commonly called in the world a man or a woman of spirit, are the two most detestable and most dangerous animals that inhabit it. They are wrong-headed, captious, jealous, offended without reason, and offending with as little. The man of spirit has immediate recourse to his sword, and the woman of spirit to her tongue; and it is hard to say which of the two is the most mischievous weapon. It is too usual a thing in many companies, to take the tone of scandal and defamation; some gratify their malice, and others think they show their wit by it; but I hope you will never adopt this tone. On the contrary, do you always take the favourable side of the question; and, without any offensive and flat contradiction, seem to doubt, and represent the uncertainty of reports, where private malice is at least very apt to mingle itself. This candid and temperate behaviour will please the whole uncandid company, though a sort of gentle contradiction to their unfavourable insinuations, as it makes them hope they may in their turns find an advocate in you.

There is another kind of offensiveness often used in company; which is, to throw out hints and insinuations, only applicable to, and felt by, one or two persons in the company, who are consequently both embarrassed and angry, and the more so, as they are unwilling to show that they apply those hints to themselves. Have a watch over yourself, never to say anything that either the whole company, or any one person in it can reasonably or probably take ill; and remember the French saying, *Qu'il ne faut pas parler de corde dans la maison d'un pendu.* Good-nature universally charms, even those who have none; and, it is impossible to be *aimable* without both the reality and the appearances of it.

XII.

BATH, *Jan.* 14, 1766.

MY DEAR LITTLE BOY

The egotism is the most usual and favourite figure of most people's rhetoric, which I hope you will never adopt, but, on the contrary, most scrupulously avoid. Nothing is more disagreeable or irksome to the company than to hear a man either praising or condemning himself, for 'both proceed from the same motive, vanity. I would allow no man to speak of himself, unless in a court of justice, in his own defence, or as a witness. Shall a man speak in his own praise? No; the hero of his own little tale always puzzles and disgusts the company, who do not know what to say or how to look. Shall he blame himself? No; vanity is as much the motive of his condemnation as of his panegyric.

I have known many people take shame to themselves, and, with a modest contrition, confess themselves guilty of most of the cardinal virtues. They have such a weakness in their nature, that they cannot help being too much moved with the misfortunes and miseries of their fellow-creatures, which they feel perhaps more, but, at least, as much as they do their own. Their generosity, they are sensible, is imprudence; for they are apt to carry it too far, from the weak, the irresistible beneficence of their nature. They are possibly too jealous of their honour, too irascible when they think it is touched; and this proceeds from their unhappy warm constitution, which makes them too sensible upon that point—and so on of all the virtues possibly. A poor trick, and a wretched instance of human vanity, and what defeats its own purpose. Do you be sure never to speak *of* yourself, *for* yourself, nor *against* yourself; but let your character speak for you. Whatever that says will be believed; but whatever you say of it will not, and will only make you odious or ridiculous.

Be constantly on your guard against the various snares and effects of vanity and self-love; it is impossible to extinguish them; they are, without exception, in every human breast; and, in the present state of nature, it is very right it should be so; but endeavour to keep them within due bounds, which is very possible. In this case, dissimulation is almost meritorious, and the seeming modesty of the hero or the patriot adorns their other virtues. I use the word *seeming* for their valets de chambre know better.

Vanity is the more odious and shocking to everybody, because everybody, without exception, has vanity; and two vanities can never love one another, any more than, according to the vulgar saying, two of a trade can. If you desire to please men and women, address yourself to their passions and weaknesses. Gain their hearts, and then let their reason do its worst against you.

XIII.

BATH, *Jan.* 21, 1766.

MY DEAR LITTLE BOY,

I have more than once recommended to you, in the course of our correspondence, attention; but I shall frequently recur to that subject, which is as inexhaustible as it is important. Attend carefully, in the first place, to human nature in general, which is pretty much the same in all human creatures, and varies chiefly by modes, habits, education, and example. Analyse, and, if I may use the expression, anatomize it; study your own, and that will lead you to know other people's; carefully observe the words, the looks, and gestures of the whole company you are in, and retain all their little singularities, humours, tastes, affections, and antipathies; which will enable you to please or avoid them occasionally as your judgment may direct you.

I will give you the most trifling instance of this that can be imagined, and yet will be sure to please. If you invite anybody to dinner, you should take care to provide those things which you have observed them to like more particularly, and not to have those things which you know they have an antipathy to. These trifling things go a great way in the Art of Pleasing, and the more so, from being so trifling, that they are flattering proofs of your regard for those persons. These things are what the French call *des attentions*; which, to do them justice, they study and practise more than any people in Europe.

Attend to, and look at whoever speaks to you, and never seem *distrait* or *rêveur*, as if you did not hear them at all; for nothing is more contemptuous, and consequently more shocking. It is true, you will by this means often be obliged to attend to things not worth anybody's attention; but it is a necessary sacrifice to be made to good manners in society. A minute attention is also necessary to time, place, and character; a *bon mot* in one company is not so in another, but, on the contrary, may prove offensive. Never joke with those whom you observe to be at the time pensive and grave; and, on the other hand, do not preach and moralize in a company full of mirth and gaiety. Many people come into company full of what they intend to say in it themselves, without the least regard to others; and thus charged up to the muzzle are resolved to let it off at any rate. I knew a man who had a story about a gun, which he thought a good one and that he told it very well. He tried all means in the world to turn the conversation upon guns; but, if he failed in his attempt, he started in his chair, and said he heard a gun fired; but when the company assured him they heard no such thing, he answered, perhaps then I was mistaken; but, however, since we are talking of guns,—and then told his story, to the great indignation of the company.

Become, as far as with innocence and honour you can, all things to all men, and you will gain a great many. Have *des prevenances* too, and say or do what you judge beforehand will be most agreeable to them, without their hinting at or expecting it. It would be endless to specify the numberless opportunities a man has of pleasing, if he will but make use of them; your own good sense will suggest them to you, and your good-nature, and even your interest, will induce you to practise

them. Great attention is to be had to times and seasons; for
example, at meals talk often, but never long at a time; for the
frivolous bustle of servants, and often the more frivolous conversation of the guests, which chiefly turns upon kitchen-stuff,
and cellar-stuff, will not bear any long reasonings or relations.
Meals are and were always reckoned the moments of relaxation
of the mind, and sacred to easy mirth and social cheerfulness.
Conform to this custom, and furnish your quota of good-humour;
but be not induced by example to the frequent excess of gluttony
or intemperance; the former inevitably produces dulness, the
latter madness.

Observe the *à propos* in everything you say or do. In conversing with those who are much your superiors, however easy
and familiar you may and ought to be with them, preserve the
respect that is due to them. Converse with your equals with an
easy familiarity, and at the same time with great civility and decency. But too much familiarity, according to the old saying,
often breeds contempt, and sometimes quarrels. I know nothing
more difficult in common behaviour than to fix due bounds to
familiarity; too little implies an unsociable formality, too much
destroys friendly and social intercourse. The best rule I can
give you to manage familiarity is, never to be more familiar with
anybody than you would be willing and even glad that he
should be with you. On the other hand, avoid that uncomfortable reserve and coldness which is generally the shield of
cunning, or the protection of dulness. The Italian maxim is a
wise one, *il volto sciolto, i pensieri stretti;* that is, let your
countenance be open and your thoughts be close. To your inferiors you should use a hearty benevolence in your words and
actions, instead of a refined politeness, which would be apt to
make them suspect that you rather laughed at them. For example,
your civility to a mere country gentleman must be in a very
different way to what you would use to a man of the world;
your reception of him should seem hearty, and rather coarse, to
relieve him from the embarrassment of his own *mauvaise honte.*

Have attention even in the company of fools; for, though they
are fools, they may, perhaps, drop or repeat something worth
your knowing, and which you may profit by. Never talk your
best in the company of fools; for they would not understand

you, and would perhaps suspect that you jeered them, as they commonly call it; but talk only the plainest common sense to them, and very gravely, for there is no jesting nor *badinage* with them. Upon the whole, with attention, and *les attentions*, you will be sure to please; without them, you will be sure to offend.

XIV.

[*Undated.*]

My dear little Boy,

Carefully avoid all affectation either of body or of mind. It is a very true and a very trite observation that no man is ridiculous for being what he really is, but for affecting to be what he is not. No man is awkward by nature, but by affecting to be genteel. I have known many a man of common sense pass generally for a fool, because he affected a degree of wit that God had denied him. A ploughman is by no means awkward in the exercise of his trade, but would be exceedingly ridiculous if he attempted the air and graces of a man of fashion. You learned to dance, but it was not for the sake of dancing; it was to bring your air and motions back to what they would naturally have been, if they had had fair play, and had not been warped in your youth by bad examples, and awkward imitations of other boys.

Nature may be cultivated and improved, both as to the body and the mind; but it is not to be extinguished by art; and all endeavours of that kind are absurd, and an inexpressible fund for ridicule. Your body and mind must be at ease, to be agreeable; but affectation is a particular restraint, under which no man can be genteel in his carriage, or pleasing in his conversation. Do you think your motions would be easy or graceful, if you wore the clothes of another man much slenderer or taller than yourself? Certainly not; it is the same thing with the mind, if you affect a character that does not fit you, and that nature never intended for you. But do not mistake, and think that it follows from hence, that you should exhibit your whole character to the public, because it is your natural one. No; many things must be suppressed, and many things concealed, in the best character. Never force nature; but it is by no means necessary to show it all.

Here discretion must come to your assistance, that sure and safe guide through life; discretion, that necessary companion to reason, and the useful *garde-fou*, if I may use the expression, to wit and imagination. Discretion points out the *à propos*, the *decorum*, the *ne quid nimis*, and will carry a man with moderate parts further than the most shining parts would without it. It is another word for judgment, though not quite synonymous to it. Judgment is not upon all occasions required, but discretion always is. Never affect nor assume a particular character; for it will never fit you, but will probably give you a ridicule; leave it to your conduct, your virtues, your morals, and your manners, to give you one. Discretion will teach you to have particular attention to your *mœurs*, which we have no one word in our language to express exactly. *Morals* are too much, *manners* too little. Decency comes the nearest to it, though rather short of it. Cicero's word *decorum* is properly the thing; and I see no reason why that expressive word should not be adopted and naturalized in our language; I have never scrupled using it in that sense.

A propos of words. Study your own language more carefully than most people do; get a habit of speaking it with propriety and elegance; for nothing is more disagreeable than to hear a gentleman talk the barbarisms, the solecisms, and the vulgarisms of porters. Avoid, on the other hand, a stiff and formal accuracy, especially what the women call hard words, when plain ones as expressive are at hand. The French make it their study *bien narrer*, but are apt *narrer trop*, and with too affected an elegancy.

The three commonest topics of conversation are religion, politics, and news. All people think they understand the two first perfectly, though they never studied either; and are therefore very apt to talk both dogmatically and ignorantly, consequently with warmth. But religion is by no means a proper subject of conversation in a mixed company; it should only be treated among a very few people of learning, for mutual instruction. It is too awful and respectable a subject to become a familiar one. Therefore never mingle yourself in it any further, than to express an universal toleration and indulgence to all errors in it, if conscientiously entertained; for, every man has as good a right to think as he does, as you have to to think as you do; nay, in truth, he cannot help it.

As for politics, they are still more universally understood; and, as every one thinks his private interest more or less concerned in them, nobody hesitates to pronounce decisively upon them, not even the ladies, the copiousness of whose eloquence is more to be admired than the conclusiveness of their logic.

It will be impossible for you to avoid engaging in these conversations, for there are hardly any others; but take care to do it coolly, and with great good-humour; and whenever you find that the company begin to be heated, and noisy for the good of their country, be only a patient hearer, unless you can interpose by some agreeable *badinage,* and restore good-humour to the company. And here I cannot help observing to you, that nothing is more useful either to put off or to parry disagreeable and puzzling affairs, than a good-humoured and genteel *badinage;* I have found it so by long experience. But this *badinage* must not be carried to *mauvaise plaisanterie;* it must be light, without being frivolous; sensible, without being sententious; and, in short, have that *je ne sçais quoi* which everybody feels, and nobody can describe.

I shall now for a time suspend the course of these Letters; but as the subject is inexhaustible, I shall occasionally resume it. In the meantime, believe, that a man, who does not generally please is nobody; and that a constant endeavour to please, will infallibly please to a certain degree at least.

LORD CHESTERFIELD'S LETTER * TO HIS GODSON AND HEIR.

(TO BE DELIVERED AFTER HIS OWN DEATH.)

Extracts.

MY DEAR BOY,

You will have received by my will solid proofs of my esteem and affection. This paper is not a will, and only conveys to you my most earnest requests, for your good alone, which requests, from your gratitude for my past care, from your good heart, and your good sense, I persuade myself, you will observe as punctually as if you were obliged by law to do so. They are not the dictates of a peevish, sour old fellow, who affects to give good rules, when he can no longer give bad examples, but the advice of an indulgent and tender friend (I had almost said parent), and the result of the long experience of one *hackneyed in the ways of life,* and calculated only to assist and guide your unexperienced youth.

You will probably come to my title and estate too soon, and at an age at which you will be much less fit to conduct yourself with discretion than you were at ten years old. This I know is a very unwelcome truth to a sprightly young fellow, and will hardly be believed by him, but it is nevertheless a truth, and a truth which I most sincerely wish, though I cannot reasonably hope, that you may be firmly convinced of. At that critical period of life, the dangerous passions are busy, impetuous, and stifle all reflection, the spirits high, the examples in general bad. It is a state of continual ebriety for six or seven years at least, and frequently attended by fatal and permanent consequences, both to body and mind. Believe yourself then to be drunk, and as drunken men, when reeling, catch hold of the next thing in their way to support them, do you, my dear boy, hold by the rails of my experience. I hope they will hinder you from falling, though perhaps not from staggering a little sometimes.

* First printed in *Letters from a Celebrated Nobleman to his Heir* (London and Brighthelmstone, 1783).

As to your religious and moral obligations I shall say nothing, because I know that you are thoroughly informed of them, and hope that you will scrupulously observe them, for if you do not you can neither be happy here nor hereafter.

I suppose you of the age of one-and-twenty, and just returned from your travels much fuller of fire than reflection; the first impressions you give of yourself, at your first entrance upon the great stage of life in your own country, are of infinite consequence, and to a great degree decisive of your future character. You will be tried first by the grand jury of Middlesex, and if they find a Bill against you, you must not expect a very favourable verdict from the many petty juries who will try you again in Westminster.

Do not set up a tawdry, flaunting equipage, nor affect a grave one: let it be the equipage of a sensible young fellow, and not the gaudy one of a thoughtless young heir; a frivolous éclat and profusion will lower you in the opinion of the sober and sensible part of mankind. Never wear over-fine clothes; be as fine as your age and rank require, but do not distinguish yourself by any uncommon magnificence or singularity of dress. Follow the example of Martin, and equally avoid that of Peter or Jack.* Do not think of shining by any one trifling circumstance, but shine in the aggregate, by the union of great and good qualities, joined to the amiable accomplishments of manners, air and address.

At your first appearance in town, make as many acquaintances as you please, and the more the better, but for some time contract no friendships. Stay a little and inform yourself of the characters of those young fellows with whom you must necessarily live more or less, but connect yourself intimately with none but such whose moral characters are unblemished. For it is a true saying *tell me who you live with and I will tell you what you are;* and it is equally true, that, when a man of sense makes a friend of a knave or a fool he must have something bad to do, or to conceal. A good character will be soiled at least by frequent contact with a bad one.

Do not be seduced by the fashionable word *spirit.* A man of spirit in the usual acceptation of that word is, in truth, a creature

* In Swift's *Tale of a Tub.*

of strong and warm animal life with a weak understanding; passionate, wrong-headed, captious, jealous of his mistaken honour, and suspecting intended affronts, and, which is worse, willing to fight in support of his wrong head. Shun this kind of company, and content yourself with a cold, steady firmness and resolution. By the way, a woman of spirit is *mutatis mutandis*, the duplicate of this man of spirit; a scold and a vixen.

I shall say little to you against gaming, for my example cries aloud to you DO NOT GAME. Gaming is rather a rage than a passion; it will break in upon all your rational pleasures, and perhaps with some stain upon your character, if you should happen to win; for whoever plays deep must necessarily lose his money or his character. I have lost great sums at play, and am sorry I lost them, but I should now be much more sorry if I had won as much. As it is, I can only be accused of folly, to which I plead guilty. But as in the common intercourse of the world you will often be obliged to play at social games, observe strictly this rule: Never sit down to play with men only, but let there always be a woman or two of the party, and then the loss or the gain cannot be considerable.

Do not be in haste to marry, but look about you first, for the affair is important. There are but two objects in marriage, love or money. If you marry for love, you will certainly have some very happy days, and probably many very uneasy ones, if for money, you will have no happy days and probably no uneasy ones; in this latter case let the woman at least be such a one that you can live decently and amicably with, otherwise it is a robbery; in either case, let her be of an unblemished and unsuspected character, and of a rank not indecently below your own.

You will doubtless soon after your return to England be a Member of one of the two Houses of Parliament; there you must take pains to distinguish yourself as a speaker. The task is not very hard if you have common sense, as I think you have, and a great deal more. The *Pedarii Senatores*, who were known only by their feet, and not by their heads, were always the objects of general contempt. If on your first, second or third attempt to speak, you should fail, or even stop short, from that trepidation and concern, which every modest man feels upon those occasions, do not be discouraged, but persevere; it will do at last. Where there is a certain fund of parts and knowledge, speaking is but a knack, which cannot fail of being acquired by frequent use. I must however add this caution, never write down your speeches beforehand; if you do you may perhaps be a good declaimer, but will never be a debater. Prepare and digest your matter well in your own thoughts, and *Verba non invita sequantur.* But if you can properly introduce into your speech a shining declamatory period or two which the audience may carry home with them, like the favourite song of an opera, it will have a good effect. The late Lord Bolingbroke had accustomed himself so much to a florid eloquence even in his common conversation (which anybody with care may do) that his real *extempore* speeches seemed to be studied. Lord Mansfield was, in my opinion, the next to him in undeviating eloquence, but Mr. Pitt carried with him, unpremeditated, the strength of thunder, and the splendour of lightning. The best matter in the world if ill-dressed and ungracefully spoken, can never please. Conviction or conversion are equally out of the question in both Houses, but he will come the nearest to them who pleases the most. In that, as in everything else, sacrifice to the Graces. Be very modest in your *exordium*, and as strong as you can be in your *peroratio.*

I can hardly bring myself to caution you against drinking, because I am persuaded that I am writing to a rational creature, a gentleman, and not to a swine. However, that you may not be insensibly drawn into that beastly custom of even sober drinking and sipping, as the sots call it, I advise you to be of no club whatsoever. The object of all clubs is either drinking or gaming, but commonly both. A sitting member of a drinking club is not indeed always drunk, perhaps seldom quite so, but he is certainly never quite sober, and is *beclareted* next morning with the guzzle of the preceding evening. A member of a gaming club should be a cheat, or he will soon be a beggar.

You will and you ought to be in some employment at Court.* It is the best school for manners, and whatever ignorant people may think or say of it, no more the seat of vice than a village is;

* In 1798 he was appointed Master of the Horse.

human nature is the same everywhere, the modes only are different. In the village they are coarse; in the Court they are polite; like the different clothes in the two several places, frieze in the one, and velvet in the other.

Be neither a servile courtier nor a noisy patriot; custom, that governs the world instead of reason, authorizes a certain latitude in political matters not always consistent with the strictest morality, but in all events remember *servare modum, finemque tueri.*

Be not only tender and jealous of your moral, but of your political, character. In your political warfare, you will necessarily make yourself enemies, but make them only your political and temporary, not personal, enemies. Pursue your own principles with steadiness, but without personal reflection or acrimony, and behave yourself to those who differ from you with all the politeness and good humour of a gentleman, for in the frequent jumble of political atoms, the hostile and the amicable ones often change places.

In business be as able as you can, but do not be cunning; cunning is the dark sanctuary of incapacity. Every man can be cunning if he pleases, by simulation, dissimulation, and in short by lying. But that character is universally despised and detested, and justly too; no truly great man was ever cunning. Preserve a dignity of character by your virtue and veracity. You are by no means obliged to tell all that you know and think, but you are obliged by all the most sacred ties of morality and prudence, never to say anything contrary to what you know or think to be true. Be master of your countenance, and let not every fool who runs read it. One of the fundamental rules, and almost the only honest one of Italian politics, is *Volto sciolto e pensieri stretti,* an open countenance and close thoughts.

Never be proud of your rank or birth, but be as proud as you please of your character. Nothing is so contrary to true dignity as the former kind of pride. You are, it is true, of a noble family, but whether of a very ancient one or not I neither know nor care, nor need you, and I dare say there are twenty fools in the House of Lords who could out-descend you in pedigree. That sort of stately pride is the standing jest of all people who can make one; but dignity of character is universally respected.

Acquire and preserve that most carefully. Should you be unfortunate enough to have vices, you may, to a certain degree, even dignify them by a strict observance of decorum; at least they will lose something of their natural turpitude.

Carefully avoid every singularity that may give a handle to ridicule, for ridicule (with submission to Lord Shaftesbury),* though not founded upon truth, will stick for some time, and if thrown by a skilful hand perhaps for ever. Be wiser and better than your contemporaries, but seem to take the world as it is, and men as they are, for you are too young to be a *censor morum*; you would be an object of ridicule. Act contrary to many Churchmen, practise virtue, but do not preach it whilst you are young.

If you should ever fill a great station at Court, take care above all things to keep your hands clean and pure from the infamous vice of corruption, a vice so infamous that it degrades even the other vices that may accompany it. Accept no present whatever; let your character in that respect be transparent and without the least speck, for as avarice is the vilest and dirtiest vice in private, corruption is so in public life. I call corruption the taking of a sixpence more than the just and known salary of your employment, under any pretence whatsoever. Use what power and credit you may have at Court in the service of merit rather than of kindred, and not to get pensions and reversions for yourself or your family, for I call that also, what it really is, scandalous pollution, though of late it has been so frequent that it has almost lost its name.

Never run in debt, for it is neither honest nor prudent, but on the contrary, live so far within your annual income as to leave yourself room sufficient for acts of generosity and charity. Give nobly to indigent merit, and do not refuse your charity even to those who have no merit but their misery. Voltaire expresses my thought much better than I can myself:

> " *Repandez vos bienfaits avec magnificence,*
> *Même aux moins vertueux ne les refusez pas,*
> *Ne vous informez pas de leur reconnoissance:*
> *Il est grand, il est beau, de faire des ingrats.*"

* Referring to his saying that " ridicule is the best test of truth." See Letter of Feb. 6, 1752, and note.

Such expense will do you more honour, and give you more pleasure, than the idle profusion of a modish and *erudite* luxury.

These few sheets will be delivered to you by Dr. Dodd at your return from your travels, probably long after I shall be dead; read them with deliberation and reflection, as the tender and last testimonies of my affection for you. They are not the severe and discouraging dictates of an old parent, but the friendly and practicable advice of a sincere friend, who remembers that he has been young himself and knows the indulgence that is due to youth and inexperience. Yes, I have been young, and a great deal too young. Idle dissipation and innumerable indiscretions, which I am now heartily ashamed and repent of, characterized my youth. But if my advice can make you wiser and better than I was at your age, I hope it may be some little atonement.

God bless you !   CHESTERFIELD.

POLITICAL AND MISCELLANEOUS,
1712–1772.

POLITICAL AND MISCELLANEOUS, 1712–1772.

I.

A M. JOUNEAU.*

TRIN. HALL, CAMBRIDGE, *ce* 22 *Août*, 1712.

MONSIEUR,

J'AI eu un sensible plaisir en lisant la lettre, que vous avez eu la bonté de m'écrire ; il me sembloit que vous me parliez vous même, et que j'étois dans la compagnie de l'homme du monde que j'estime le plus, et à qui je souhaite le plus ardemment de pouvoir faire plaisir. J'y aurois répondu plûtôt, n'eut été que j'ai passé cette semaine chez l'Evêque d'Ely,† qui demeure à quinze milles d'ici. J'ai, dans ce peu de tems, vu plus de la campagne que je n'avois vu auparavant dans toute ma vie, et qui ici-autour est très agréable.

Je continue bien ferme dans mes études, qui ne sont encore que le Latin et le Grec, à cause que la foire, qui va venir en dix jours, les auroit interrompues, mais après que ce divertissement sera fini, je dois commencer le droit civil, la philosophie, et un peu de mathématiques ; mais pour l'anatomie, je ne la pourrai point apprendre ; car, quoiqu'il y ait eu un pauvre pendu, le chirurgien, qui avoit coutume de faire ces opérations, n'en a point

---

* M. Jouneau was one of the French Protestants whom the Revocation of the Edict of Nantes, in 1685, drove from their native country. He became Minister of a French congregation in Berwick Street, Soho. Lord Chesterfield was put under his care by his grandmother, Lady Halifax, and received from him his first instruction in languages and history.—Maty.

† Dr. John Moore (translated from Norwich) was Bishop of Ely from 1707 to 1713.—M.

voulu faire cette fois, parceque c'étoit un homme, et alors il dit que les écoliers ne veulent point venir.

Je trouve ce collège, dans lequel je suis, infiniment le meilleur de toute l'université, car c'est le plus petit, et il est rempli d'avocats, qui ont été dans le monde, et qui savent vivre. Nous n'avons qu'un ministre, qui est aussi le seul ivrogne du collège. Quoiqu'on en dise, il y a fort peu de débauche dans cette université, et surtout parmi les gens de condition ; car il faudroit avoir un goût de portefaix ou de crocheteur, pour la pouvoir souffrir ici.

Il me semble que nous sommes fort mal dans nos affaires, mais, ne pouvant les empêcher, je ne me mêle guère de politique : seulement je me fais un plaisir d'aller voir quelquefois au café les batailles rangées qui s'y donnent, entre les héros de chaque côté, avec une bravoure inconcevable, et qui ne se terminent qu'après l'entière défaite de quelques tasses de thé des deux côtés.

Je crains de vous avoir déjà trop ennuyé ; au moins de peur de le faire, il est bien tems de vous dire que je suis, etc.

II.

A M. JOUNEAU.

Ce 21 *Septembre* [1712].

MONSIEUR,

JE n'ai pas voulu perdre la première occasion de vous envoyer cette bagatelle, ce que j'aurois honte de faire, si je ne vous assurois en même tems, que je voudrois bien que ce fût dix fois autant. Je vins en ville hier au soir, pour quelques jours, et j'espère qu'il ne se passera pas longtems avant que j'aye le plaisir de vous voir. Je suis, etc.

III.

A M. JOUNEAU.

Ce 12 *Octobre,* 1712.

MONSIEUR,

LES divertissemens de Newmarket, où je fus trois ou quatre jours, m'ont empêché de vous écrire sitôt que j'avois intention ; outre que j'ai été dans un embarras furieux en changeant de chambres. J'espère que me voici accommodé pour le tems que je demeurerai ici.

C'est à cette heure, Monsieur, que j'ai bien des affaires sur les bras, car j'employe plus d'une heure par jour au droit civil, et tout autant à la philosophie; et la semaine qui vient, l'aveugle * commencera ses leçons de mathématiques; de sorte que me voici bien occupé. Croiriez-vous bien aussi que je lis Lucien et Xenophon en Grec ? ce qui m'est rendu assez aisé, car je ne m'embarrasse point d'apprendre toutes les règles de la grammaire: mais l'homme qui est avec moi, et qui est une grammaire vivante,† me les enseigne en lisant. Je me reserve du tems pour jouer à la paume, car je souhaite aussi bien le *corpus sanum* que le *mens sana*; il me semble que l'un ne vaut guères sans l'autre.

Depuis mon arrivée ici, j'ai reçu la lettre que vous envoyâtes à Oxford, quelqu'un l'ayant changé pour Cambridge; et je trouve votre mémoire (dont vous vous plaignez tant) excellente, car elle est, à quelques petits mots près, justement la même que l'autre que vous envoyâtes après, mais que je n'eus pas pour cela moins de plaisir en lisant.

Decies repetita placebit—

ce qui est la devise qu'un ministre ici (qui épousa l'autre jour une très jolie fille) mit dans la bague de noce.

Ecrivez moi donc souvent, Monsieur, je vous en prie, quand vous n'aurez rien autre chose à faire, et vous obligerez infiniment, Monsieur, votre, etc.

IV.

A M. JOUNEAU.

Ce Jeudi Saint [1713].

JE vous demande mille pardons, Monsieur, de n'avoir pas plûtôt rendu réponse à votre dernière lettre, mais il y a quelque

---

* Nicholas Saunderson, an eminent mathematician, was born in 1682, at Thurlston, in Yorkshire. When twelve months old he lost his sight from smallpox; he showed such a taste for mathematics that his friends sent him to Cambridge, where he became Lucasian Professor, and delivered lectures on mathematics to crowded audiences. He died in 1739.

† The Rev. Dr. Crow, who was Lord Chesterfield's private tutor, and who afterwards became one of the Chaplains of King George the Second. "When Lord Chesterfield was at the university he used to study in his apartment without stirring from it till six o'clock in the evening." (Maty's *Memoirs.*)

tems que j'ai été fort occupé à l'anatomie, outre mes exercices ordinaires, ou bien j'aurois été en ville avant ce tems ici.

Je ne m'étonne guères de l'honneteté que votre fils, avec les enfans de Sir George Byng,* trouva de la part des François. En vérité ils nous en doivent de reste, et c'est une pauvre recompense pour tout ce que nous leur avons donné.†

Je suis fort obligé à Mr. Chasseloup du bien qu'il dit de moi, et ce n'est pas pour lui rendre la pareille, que je vous dis que c'est un fort joli garçon.

Il ne faut pas que vous attendiez des nouvelles d'ici, de sorte que je finirai, en vous assurant que je ne manquerai pas de faire ce que vous me demandez, quand je serai à Londres, ce qui sera en peu de temps, et que cependant je suis, etc.

V.

TO THE HON. GEORGE BERKELEY.‡

TRIN. HALL, CAMBRIDGE, *June* 25, O.S. [1713].

MY DEAR GEORGE,

I would have written to you before I received your last letter, but I found by your first that you were so expeditious in moving from place to place that I thought my former directions would not serve. You do not know what you ask when you would have me write long letters; you would quickly be a weary on it, should I obey you: what a number of insignificant trifles must I put together to fill up this sheet of paper, and how tiresome would it be to you to have a true and faithful history of Midsummer fair, which is our present diversion? But since you will—faith, you shall have enough on it; but I give you free leave to throw this letter by as soon as ever you are tired on it.

I came down from London a week ago, which place afforded me little diversion. Plays and operas were left off, and I fell short of the pleasure I proposed to myself from the French Am-

* M. Jouneau's son had been bred a physician, and travelled with Sir George Byng's sons.—M.

† By the Peace of Utrecht.—M.

‡ George Berkeley was youngest son of the second Earl Berkeley. In 1735 he married Henrietta Hobart, Dowager Countess of Suffolk—another friend and correspondent of Lord Chesterfield.—M.

bassador's * masquerades; for our good Queen, thinking them
encouragements to vice, discountenanced them so much, that he,
out of complaisance, gave them over.

But now to come to Cambridge: I must first tell you that I
have not yet seen Miss Neville, but it will not be long first, for
her sagacious rather is at London; so, if the daughter and the
greyhound be not locked up, I will take this opportunity of a
tête-à-tête.

*   *   *   *   *
*   *   *   *   *

Jack Cowper is more and more in love every day, passes three
parts in four of his life with the nymph, and is gay or sad just
as it pleases her Ladyship to frown or smile. Our old stupid
Heads † would not let us nave a public *commencement*, to the great
disappointment of all our young folks, whether male or female.

Your departure, dear George, has been very unsuccessful to
us, for as soon as you went away we immediately lost the name
of the Witty Club, and I am afraid we shall soon dwindle into
no club at all, for Extou Sayer is gone to London, and George
Stanley goes this week; the *Bonny* goes in a fortnight into
Staffordshire; so do but think what a poor solitary remnant we
shall be. Prithee comfort us as often as you can with a letter,
which we will retail at proper times, as our own wit, to retrieve
as much of our character as we can. None of our Cambridge
verses ‡ are worth sending you; a great many of them are
egregiously silly; mine are some of the prettiest in the book;
the *Bonny* made them for me; we are now burlesquing them as
fast as ever we can. ‿ rejoice much that your nut-brown girl
afforded you such good sport; I should be glad to be with you
to partake of those innocent amusements to which you dedicate
your *horas subsecivas ;* but pray set one or two of them apart
sometimes, to oblige with a letter, my dear George,

                                    Thy most sincere friend.

* The Duke d'Aumont.
† The Heads of Houses. See Gray's satirical lines " On the Heads of
Houses " (new Aldine edition, p. 92).
‡ The "Cambridge Verses " were a collection of short poems on the
Peace of Utrecht. It is not known to whom Lord Chesterfield alludes as
Bonny, nor has the Editor of the Suffolk Letters been able to trace with
certainty the other persons mentioned in this letter.—M.

VI.

TO THE HON. GEORGE BERKELEY.

HAGUE, *May* 29, 1714.

MY DEAR GEORGE,

I hope you will pardon me for not having thanked you for the favour of your letter (which I received at Antwerp) till now; I hope you will not impute it to indifference or forgetfulness in one that always loves and remembers you. But the truth is, that at Antwerp the Duke and Duchess * were so civil to me that I had not time to be so to anybody else, for I was with them from morning to night all the while I stayed there. The Duke and the Duchess inquired extremely after their friend, as they called you, and commanded me the first time I writ to you to assure you of their good wishes.

This place is now extremely pleasant and entertaining; I wish I could describe it so to you as to tempt you to take a little journey, and make it more so: I have power to tell you that there is a large room in a certain house very much at your service, where I am sure you might pass two or three months this summer much cheaper, and I believe more agreeably, than at London. Pray send me some news from London; and whatever I can pick up here I shall inform you of, though it is but a poor return.   I am, etc.

VII.

À M. JOUNEAU.

A LA HAYE, *ce* 10 *Août*, N.S. [1714].

MONSIEUR,

Je vous aurois plûtôt remercié de la lettre que vous avez eu la bonté de m'écrire, si des petits voyages que j'ai faits depuis peu pour voir les endroits à l'entour d'ici, comme Amsterdam, Leyde, Utrecht, etc., ne m'en eussent empêché. C'est avec justice que vous me reprochez de ne vous avoir pas écrit, selon ma promesse, et j'avoue qu'il y avoit de la paresse dans mon

---

* The Duke and Duchess of Marlborough, who, in 1712, had deemed it prudent to withdraw from England, and had fixed their residence at Antwerp.—M.

fait ; car, quoique je ne souhaitasse rien davantage que de vous témoigner l'estime et le respect que j'ai pour vous, toutefois je remettois de jour en jour et le plaisir et la peine de vous écrire.

Pour la description des villes de Flandres, que vous me demandez, je crois qu'il seroit assez inutile de vous l'envoyer, car vous la savez déjà mieux que moi, par des personnes qui en ont pu mieux juger ; et, pour des réflexions, je n'en ai pu faire aucune, car vous savez qu'elles doivent être faites plûtôt sur les personnes que sur les choses ; et, comme je ne faisois que passer, je n'ai pas eu le tems d'y faire aucune connoissance ; mais, quand même j'en eusse fait, je ne sais si j'aurois eu la hardiesse de vous les communiquer. Je connois trop bien votre jugement et le mien.

Le séjour que j'ai fait ici m'a été fort agréable, car cet endroit est tout-à-fait charmant dans l'été, et la compagnie y est fort bonne, à cause du grand nombre d'étrangers qui y demeurent ; car, pour les gens du pays, il est certain qu'ils ne sont pas du commerce le plus rafiné : ce sont d'assez bonnes gens, mais qui ne se mêlent pas de la conversation.

La semaine qui vient, je pars pour un endroit qu'on m'assure ne sera pas moins divertissant, je veux dire Turin, où je resterai jusqu'au Carnaval ; puis j'irai à Venise, de-là à Rome, etc.* Quand vous voudrez bien me faire le plaisir de m'écrire (ce que j'espère vous voudrez bien souvent), vous n'avez qu'à envoyer vos lettres chez Milady Halifax, qui me les fera recevoir ; et moi de mon côté, je ne manquerai pas de vous en remercier, et de vous assurer avec combien de sincérité et respect je suis, etc.

Je vous prie de faire mes complimens
  à Madame votre femme.

VIII.

À M. JOUNEAU.

PARIS, *Dec.* 7 [1714].

MONSIEUR,

Je suis fort fâché de n'avoir pas reçu votre lettre, dont vous me parlez dans celle que je reçus hier de votre part, d'autant plus

---

* This project was laid aside on the events which followed the death of Queen Anne.—M.

que je crois que vous m'y donniez quelque occasion de vous faire plaisir, ce que je chercherai toujours avec empressement. Je suis bien aise que Milady Halifax ait fait ce qu'elle a pu en votre faveur. Vous me reprochez (et pas sans quelque raison) de ne vous avoir pas écrit depuis mon arrivée à Paris. J'avoue ma faute, je m'en repens, et vous verrez la sincérité de mon repentir, par la quantité de lettres dont je vous accablerai dans la suite. Vous me demanderez quartier, mais vous aurez beau faire; je vous punirai de n'avoir pas connu votre premier bonheur.

Il y avoit trop peu de tems que j'étois sorti de l'Angleterre pour souhaiter d'y retourner à quelque prix que ce fût; autrement j'aurois bien voulu y avoir été à l'arrivée du Roi, pour prendre part à la joie qu'on en devoit avoir. Si je n'avois point d'autre raison, la seule tristesse que témoignent les François, et les Anglois de la suite du Prétendant, sur la mort de la Reine, seroit capable de m'en consoler. Mais quand je vois combien loin les choses étoient déjà avancées en faveur du Prétendant et du Papisme, et que nous étions à deux doigts de l'esclavage, je compte absolument pour le plus grand bonheur qui soit jamais arrivé à l'Angleterre, la mort de cette femme, qui, si elle eût vécu encore trois mois, alloit sans doute établir sa religion, et par conséquent la tyrannie, et nous auroit laissé, après sa mort, pour Roi, un bâtard, tout aussi sot qu'elle, et qui, comme elle, auroit été mené par le nez par une bande de scélérats. La déclaration du Prétendant, et mille autres choses, sont des preuves convaincantes du dessein qu'avaient ces conjurés du ministère, de le faire entrer.

Si vous voulez que je vous dise franchement mes sentimens de la France, il faut que vous me permettiez de vous considérer comme Anglois, et alors je vous dirai, que hormis Versailles, il n'y a rien ici que nous n'ayons de plus beau et de meilleur en Angleterre. Je ne vous dirai pas mes sentimens des François, parceque je suis fort souvent pris pour un, et plus d'un François, m'a fait le plus grand compliment qu'ils croyent pouvoir faire à personne, qui est, " Monsieur, vous êtes tout comme nous." Je vous dirai seulement, que je suis insolent; que je parle beaucoup, bien haut, et d'un ton de maître; que je chante et que je danse en marchant; et, enfin, que je fais une dépense furieuse en poudre, plumets, gands blancs, etc.

J'écrirai à Mr. Morris qu'il vous donne la moitié de cette bagatelle ; et pour le reste, j'aurai l'honneur de vous le donner moi-même en très peu de tems.

Je suis, Monsieur, etc.

IX.

TO G. BUBB (DODINGTON), ESQ.*

August 20, 1716.

DEAR SIR,

We have both had the luck we could have wished for, for I have had the happiness to receive your letters, and find by them that you have escaped the trouble of mine.

Your last gave me some hopes of seeing you here this winter, but I am since informed that I must be some time longer without that satisfaction. How far your public spirit may prevail I can't tell, and make you prefer your country's service to any other consideration ; but, setting that motive aside, I believe you would not be unwilling to see London again, nor like it the worse for coming from Madrid ; the gravity and reservedness of the one may be very good preparation towards tasting the other.

If you have a great turn to politics, you will find here ample matter for the exercise of that talent. Never were more specu-lations and to less purpose than now ; for the mystery of State is become, like that of Godliness, ineffable and incomprehensible, and has likewise the same good luck of being thought the finer for not being understood.

As for the gay part of the town, you would find it much more flourishing than you left it. Balls, assemblies, and masquerades have taken place of dull formal visiting days, and the women are become much more agreeable trifles than they were designed.

I can't omit telling you that puns are extremely in vogue and the license very great ; the variation of three or four letters in a word breaks no squares, insomuch that an indifferent punster may make a very good figure in the best companies.

I am, dear Sir, etc.

* George Bubb, who took the name of Dodington, and who, in 1761, obtained the title of Lord Melcombe, was at this time envoy in Spain. His celebrated "Diary," published in 1784, is a record of his own political profligacy. He died in 1762.

X.

TO ———*

PARIS, *June* 27.

DEAR SIR,

I remember when I left England I threatened you that I would write to you, and you promised you would write to me; and it has happened, as it generally does in the world, that the threats are performed and the promises broke. It would sincerely have been a very great satisfaction to me, to have heard from you, though I know you have so much other business that I scarce expected it. You may possibly now have some idle time upon your hands since the recess of the Parliament and the King's journey.† If you have, I can assure you you cannot bestow any part on't upon one that will be more obliged to you for it than myself. I must congratulate you upon the great addition of strength you have acquired by the late change, and must own you are a liberal rewarder of true penitents; but still remember a line in *Othello*,‡ "Look to her, Moor; she has deceived her father and may thee!"

I cannot help mentioning to you now what I spoke to you of in England, and desiring to know whether you have taken any step in it yet. I own, the more I think of it, the more I wish it may be thought either proper or practicable; it being in my mind the only way of my coming into any business, and leaving an idle life that I am grown weary of. I leave entirely to you, as the best judge, what methods to take in it, and rely so much upon your friendship, that I am convinced you will not omit any that may promote it. I should only be glad to know whether you think there is any probability of success, that I may regulate my conduct in the next Sessions accordingly. For as, of the one side, I should be very willing to engage in debate and the business of the House, as well as I am able, which, though I

---

* This letter is among Archdeacon Coxe's copies at the British Museum, vol. lxxii. p. 119. It has no address nor date of year, but was in all probability addressed to some one in office, or at Court, and dated in 1720, just after the Ministers had been joined by Walpole and Townshend.—M.

† To Hanover.   ‡ Quoted inaccurately from Act iii. Sc. 3, 206.

should do very indifferently, I could not do worse than the present possessor, so, of the other side, to enter the lists and get a broken head merely as a volunteer would be childish and impertinent. I must remind you that I am very far from expecting that a remove should be made in my favour, for I would desire nothing more than a promise when such vacancy should happen. If you think of anything more that is proper to be done of my side, you will give me your directions. I am in the mean time with the greatest truth, etc.

When you do me the favour to write, pray send your letter in some of Sir Robert Sutton's * pacquets, for those that are sent by the post generally miscarry.

XI.

TO MRS. HOWARD'S † LAP-DOG.‡

BATH, *September* 5.

DEAR MARQUISE,

I received with a great deal of pleasure the account of your happy delivery, and (as I judge by the brevity and conciseness) from some fair hand of your acquaintance.

I always thought epistolary correspondence the properest with those of your species, which makes me glad of this opportunity to congratulate you upon this occasion at a distance, where I cannot have your answer by word of mouth. I have no rules to give you for your conduct in the month but to avoid all noise as much as possible, and therefore I would only recommend to you the company of that laconic lady § who sent me that very short relation of your labour, unless you find some few others (which possibly you may) of equal taciturnity.

I beg of you not to be at all concerned at any insinuations that

---

* The British Ambassador at Paris.

† Henrietta, eldest daughter of Sir Henry Hobart, Bart., married, about 1708, the Hon. Charles Howard, who, by the death of his nephews and two elder brothers, succeeded in 1731 to the earldom of Suffolk. Lady Suffolk is well known by the favour of George the Second, and the friendship of men of letters.—M.

‡ "This is a reply, written, when Lord Chesterfield was very young, to a letter addressed to him in the name of Mrs. Howard's lap-dog, announcing her *accouchement*." Note to Suffolk Papers.

§ Mrs. Howard.

may be thrown out, that your issue does not bear that resemblance to the father which it ought.   Many salvos might be found out for it, if necessary; but it is very long since any wise mother has been very uneasy, or any prudent husband too inquisitive, as to affairs of that kind.   The great tenderness I hear you have shown towards your little nursery, is never enough to be commended; and as it may be an example for many parents to follow, and others to blush at, so ought it to be said to your honour, that you use your dogs like children, while they use their children like dogs.   But alas! the care you have hitherto taken relates only to their bodies.   The great concern is still to come; I mean the forming of their minds.   As to which, I look upon it as their peculiar advantage, and your happiness (notwithstanding what some grave authors assert to the contrary), that they are to have their education in a Court, a Court that ——; but, as I have the honour to be one of it,* I must not give it its due commendations.   As example is better than precept, you will there have an opportunity to set before their eyes examples of all kinds.   It is impossible but that, among the number of ladies you daily converse with, you may point out to your two female little ones some virtues to imitate, and many faults to avoid; above all, show them the inconveniences of a snappish and snarling disposition, especially in their sex; and, if you can produce examples, it would not be amiss neither to caution them against over-discretion, which you may enforce by assuring them, that, had you been over-nice, they had not been at all, and you had died a maid.

As for your issue male, they will likewise reap very great and glorious advantages from example; for, were you only to set

---

* Lord Chesterfield, as Lord Stanhope of Shelford, was at this period one of the Gentlemen of the Bedchamber to the Prince of Wales, and had followed his Royal Highness into Opposition.   Great efforts were made by the Court to reclaim him, the title of Duke being offered for his father. But this temptation could not induce the young nobleman to forsake either his attachments or his principles.   "He thought, likewise, that the younger sons of a Duke ought to have larger fortunes than either his brothers or his children were likely to have.   The old Earl of Chesterfield, though shy of the Court, was less indifferent to its trappings.   He expressed his displeasure at his son's refusal, and perhaps was happy in having a new excuse to justify his ill-treatment of him."—Maty's *Memoirs*.

before them the nine Lords,* you may make them very accomplished puppies; but you may with very good success take a greater latitude, and borrow very useful hints from several others of the family. While they are little you cannot do better than let them play with the secretary; † but, when they come to dog's estate, bid them imitate, and, if possible, emulate, the magnanimity and fortitude of Herbert ‡ and Belhaven,§ that they may one day be justly promoted to the dignity of house dogs. In short, that your progeny may in time be both the ornaments and the guardians of the Lodge,‖ is the hearty and sincere wish of,

Yours, etc.

XII.

TO THE HON. MRS. HOWARD.

THE PEAK, June 30, 1725.

MADAM,

I think I have acquired a sort of a right of troubling you with a letter every time I go into the country; I am sure, at least, I have a temptation to do it, which I cannot resist—that is, your usual goodness in letting me afterwards have one from you.

After assuring you of my respects, which no place can alter, I am more at a loss what to say from hence, than I should have been from any other part, either of this world or the next; for, were I to give you a true description of this place, I should lie under the imputation that travellers generally do. I will only tell you, by way of specimen, that the inhabitants here are as utter strangers to the sun as they are to shoes and stockings; and were it, by some strange revolution in nature, once to shine

---

* Of the Prince's Bedchamber.—M.

† Probably Mr. Molyneux, Secretary to the Prince.—M.

‡ Henry, afterwards ninth Earl of Pembroke, was a Lord of the Bedchamber to George the Second, both as Prince of Wales and as King. He had a great taste for the arts, and in the words of Horace Walpole "the soul of Inigo Jones, who had been patronized by his ancestors, seemed still to hover over its favourite Wilton." He died in January 1751, and in the following September his widow was married again to N. L. Barnard, Esq., a Major of Dragoons.—M.

§ John, fourth Lord Belhaven.—M.

‖ Richmond Lodge.—M.

upon them, the unusual light would certainly blind them, in case the heat did not suddenly kill them. It is called the Peak; and you have heard that the Devil is reported to have some possessions in it, which I certainly believe. For, had I been a Papist (as, thank God, I am not), I should have thought myself in purgatory; but, being a good Protestant, I was obliged most orthodoxly to conclude myself to be in Hell. But, reflecting, since, how little good company I meet with *here*, and how much I might expect to find *there*, together with the consideration of my excessive poverty, I begin to believe I am in Scotland, where, like the rest of that nation, I only stay till I am master of half-a-crown to get out of it.

But, after all this, I ought in justice, and indeed, to *give the Devil his due*, to inform you of the satisfactions I meet with here.

In the first place, the waters, that my father came here to drink, have done him a great deal of good, and, I hope, have confirmed his health for a considerable time. In the next place, I have my two brothers, who make it their whole business to entertain me. They never suffer me to be alone, thinking me inclined to melancholy. Then, having heard that I love music, they spare no pains to please me that way; the eldest performing tolerably ill upon a broken hautboy, and the youngest something worse upon a cracked flute. As I would be civil in my turn too, I beg of them not to give themselves so much trouble upon my account, being apprehensive that the great expense of breath may impair their lungs; but all to no purpose, for they assure me they will venture anything to divert me, and so play the more.

Besides these domestic amusements, I have likewise my recreations abroad, both pleasant and profitable; for I have won three half-crowns of the curate at a horse-race, and six shillings of Gaffer Foxeley at a cock-match. But whether this success may not one day or other prove to my cost, by drawing me into gaming, I cannot answer.

I am afraid I have, like most memoir writers, troubled you too long with the account of my own life; but you will easily excuse me, for the sake of that agreeable variety you will find in it. So, wishing you all imaginable success at Trey-ace, Commerce, or whatever else may be the prevailing diversion at the Lodge, I am, with the greatest truth and respect, Yours, etc.

P.S. I must beg of you, if his Royal Highness should be ever so good as to mention me, that you will present my most profound duty and respect to him, when you find it not improper. I hope their three* Highnesses are well.

XIII.

TO THE HON. MRS. HOWARD.

BRETBY,† *Oct.* 23, 1725.

MADAM,

You have so often indulged me in troubling you with my applications, and the satisfaction I have in being particularly obliged to you is so great, that I fear I do not enough consider the trouble I may give you ; however, I must venture once more upon this occasion, and beg the favour of you to make my excuse to the Prince for not paying my duty to him upon his birthday,‡ as I ought to do.

I hope his Royal Highness will do me the justice to believe that it is neither a negligence of my duty, nor a want of inclination to pay it, but an almost indispensable necessity, that hinders me from coming to town ; for ever since my father had his fits (which were such and so many as I believe no other body ever survived) he has continued entirely senseless ; § in which condition it is impossible for me, upon many accounts besides filial piety, to leave him. How long he will continue so, I cannot tell ; but this I am sure of, that if it be much longer I shall be the maddest of the two : this place being the seat of horror and despair, where no creatures but ravens, screech-owls, and birds

* The Prince of Wales's three children: Frederick, William, and Augusta.—M.

† Bretby Park, in Derbyshire, the seat of the Earls of Chesterfield. It is remarkable that, in this whole collection, only this letter and the following are dated from it ; and even these two are filled with complaints of being there!—M.

‡ October 30, O.S.

§ His father Philip, third Earl of Chesterfield, survived for three months, and died January 27, 1726.

of ill-omen, seem willingly to dwell; for as for the very few human faces that I behold, they look, like myself, rather condemned than inclined to stay here.

Were I given to romances, I should think myself detained by enchantments in the castle of some inexorable magician, which I am sure Don Quixote often did upon much slighter grounds; or were I inclined to a religious melancholy, I should fancy myself in Hell: but not having the happiness of being yet quite out of my senses, I fancy—what is worse than either—that I am just where I am, in the old mansion-seat of the family, and that, too, not my own.

I ask a thousand pardons for giving you all this trouble; but at the same time beg you will believe that it is impossible to be more sensible of the many obligations I have to you than I am; which I should not be entirely unworthy of, could there be any merit in being, with the greatest respect and sincerity, etc.

XIV.

TO THE HON. MRS. HOWARD.

BRETBY, *Nov.* 18, 1725.

MADAM,

When you did me the honour of writing to me, I believe you could not expect to escape being troubled with my thanks for it, though my satisfaction was very much lessened by finding that your illness prevented my having that honour sooner. I hope you are now perfectly recovered; and I may venture to assure you, that among the numbers of people that (I dare say) interest themselves in your health, none can do it more sincerely than I do.

I am glad to find you do justice to my filial piety. I own I think it surpasses that of Æneas; for when he took such care of his father he was turned of fourscore, and not likely to trouble him long; but you may observe that he prudently disposed of his wife, who being much younger, was consequently more likely to stick by him; which makes me shrewdly suspect that had his father been of the same age as mine, he would not have been quite so well looked after. I hope, like him, I shall be at last rewarded with a Lavinia, or at least a Dido, which possibly may be full as well.

I am afraid you are too much in the right when you tell me I am in purgatory; for souls always stay there till they go to Heaven, which I doubt will be my case; whereas I should be very glad of baiting a considerable time at London in my way to it. I am, with the greatest truth and respect, etc.

XV.

TO THE HON. MRS. HOWARD.

HAGUE,* *May* 18, N.S. [1728].

MADAM,

Among the many privileges I enjoy here, I exercise none with so much pleasure as I do that which you granted me of writing to you, in order to put you sometimes in mind of a very humble servant, too insignificant to be remembered by any thing but his importunity.

Could I imagine that you had the goodness to interest yourself in the least in what concerns me here, I could yet give you but a very indifferent account of myself hitherto, the little time I have passed here having been wholly employed in ceremonies as disagreeable to receive as to relate; the only satisfaction that I have yet had has been to find, that the people here, being convinced that I am determined to please them as much as I am able, are equally resolved in return to please me as much as possible, and I cannot express the civilities I have met with from all sorts of people. Notwithstanding which, as far as I can judge, neither my acquaintances nor my pleasures here will make me forget, or even hinder me from regretting, those I left at London. My great comfort is, that I have all the reason in the world to believe that my stay here will be highly beneficial both to my body and my soul; here being few temptations, and still fewer opportunities to sin, as you will find by the short but true account I will give you of myself.

* The death of George the First, in 1727, opened to the new Earl of Chesterfield the path of honours and employments. He was appointed Ambassador to Holland, and set out for his destination on the 23rd of April, 1728.—M.

My morning is entirely taken up in doing the King's business very ill, and my own still worse; this lasts till I sit down to dinner with fourteen or fifteen people, where the conversation is cheerful enough, being animated by the *patronazza*, and other loyal healths.   The evening, which begins at five o'clock, is wholly sacred to pleasures; as, for instance, the Forault* till six; then either a very bad French play, or a *reprize* at quadrille with three ladies, the youngest upwards of fifty, at which, with a very ill run, one may lose, besides one's time, three florins; this lasts till ten o'clock, at which time I come home, reflecting with satisfaction on the innocent amusements of a well spent day that leave no sting behind them, and go to bed at eleven, with the testimony of a good conscience.   In this serenity of mind I pity you who are forced to endure the tumultuous pleasures of London.   I considered you particularly last Tuesday, suffering the heat and disorders of the masquerade, supported by the Duchess of Richmond† of one side, and Miss Fitzwilliam‡ of the other, all three weary and wanting to be gone; upon which I own I pitied you so much that I wished myself there, only to help you out of the crowd.

After all this, to speak seriously, I am very far from disliking this place; I have business enough one part of the day to make me relish the amusements of the other part, and even to make them seem pleasures; and if anything can comfort one for the absence of those one loves or esteems, it is meeting with the good will of those one is obliged to be with, which very fortunately, though undeservedly, is my case.   There is, besides, one pleasure that I may have here, and that I own I am sanguine enough to expect, which will make me amends for the want of many others, which is, if you will have the goodness to let me 'know sometimes that you are well, and that you have not quite forgot that perfect esteem and respect with which I am,

Yours, etc.,

* Or according to the Dutch spelling, *Voorhout*; a public walk, said to have been laid out and planted by the Emperor Charles V.

† Sarah, daughter and co-heir of William, first Earl Cadogan. Among Lord Chesterfield's light pieces of poetry, is one in celebration of her beauty, beginning " What do scholars and bards and astronomers wise."

‡ The Hon. Mary Fitzwilliam, afterwards Countess of Pembroke.

XVI.

TO THE HON. MRS. HOWARD.

HAGUE, *July* 13, 1728.

MADAM,

The part which you do me the honour to say you took, both in my illness and my recovery, is too obliging for me to omit the very first opportunity of making you my acknowledgments for it; it has reconciled me to my own illness, for having caused such a declaration, and has added (if possible) to my concern for yours, for having hindered me from receiving it sooner.

To show you how desirous I am to contribute as much as I can to your perfect recovery, if you can find means to give me that offending head and that provoking face you complain so much of, I will most willingly send you mine in return by the first courier; and though you say they are of no use to the present owner, I assure you they would be of singular use to me. The head should do my master's business, and the face should do my own, and I would find employment enough for them both, not to give them time to ache.

I find you wrong both my head and my heart extremely, when you think I can blame Lord Finch for his late exploit; * so far from it, that I envy him the glorious opportunity he has procured himself of sacrificing all to love. He has showed the lady the strength of his passion by offering her an estate while he thought he had one; she may now convince him of the strength of hers, by taking him without it; and I shall only blame them both if they do not think five hundred pounds a year a great deal more than enough, where there is such a fund of mutual love to subsist upon. I never heard of the happiest couple in Arcadia, or Arabia the blessed, that had half so good an income.

I am afraid your time hangs a good deal upon your hands at

---

* Daniel, Lord Finch, afterwards Earl of Winchelsea and Nottingham, had, much against his father's wishes, contracted an engagement with Lady Fanny Fielding, whom he married accordingly next year. Mrs. Howard writes to Mr. Gay, June 15, 1728 :—" By what I have heard, Lord Nottingham has not only disinherited Lord Finch, in case he marries Lady Fanny Fielding, but has drawn the deed in such a manner (which he drew with his own hand) that when he dies, the profits of the estates are to be paid in to trustees, till either Lady Fanny is dead or married, or Lord Finch is married."—M.

Richmond, by my being so frequently the subject of your conversations; which I do not flatter myself can be owing to any
thing but a great want of something else to do, and I doubt it
would be my interest to wish you had some better employment,
for I fear I often come off but scurvily. However, since I have
put on the new man, I own I should not be sorry to assist, invisibly,
at those conversations, to hear how the old one is treated. I
shall be extremely obliged to you if you will, when it is finished,
send me the anatomy and dissection of my late self, which I have
been long so desirous to see that I had some thoughts of taking
the opportunity of my late illness to have it given out that I was
dead, and dead for the love of ——. Upon which I should have
seen my own epitaph, elegy, life and character, etc. by Curll,*
with many other particulars, which no man alive can hear of
himself till he is dead. Some would have been astonished that
I died for love, who might possibly have called my tenderness in
question while alive; others would have wondered how it could
be for love of that person, upon whose account they never in the
least suspected me—which would indirectly be commending my
discretion; in short, various and curious would the accounts
have been that I should have had of my deceased self; but I was
hindered from executing this design by my chaplain,† who is
indeed a very good man, and who told me that mocking was
catching, and death not a thing to be played with.

This place, though empty in comparison of what it is in the
winter, is not yet without its recreations. I played at blind
man's buff till past three this morning; we have music in the
Wood; parties out of town; besides the constant amusements of
quadrille and scandal, which flourish and abound. We have even
attempted two or three balls, but with very moderate success;
the ladies here being a little apt to quarrel with one another,
insomuch, that before you can dance down three couple, it is
highly probable that two of them are sat down in a huff. Upon
these occasions I show the circumspection of a minister, and
observe a strict neutrality; by which means I have hitherto
escaped being engaged in a war.

---

* The piratical bookseller by whom the surreptitious edition of Pope's
Letters was published, in 1727.

† Mr. Chenevix, afterwards Bishop of Waterford. See Letter of Feb.
15, 1740, and note.

I condole with Miss Meadows * for her disappointment in not having the gout; and I congratulate Miss Fitzwilliam whenever she returns from grass at Ampthill; I respect Lord Herbert and Fop,† not without a due mixture of fear of both.   I hope to hear soon of my Lord's having quarrelled with Pem ‡ upon his marrying some necessitous beauty for love; his lordship having given pregnant instances of all heroic virtues but love.

I do not know whether you will forgive this long and tedious letter; if you do, I beg you will let me know it soon; and if you do not, pray let me hear it before it is long.   For if you believe (as I am persuaded you do) that part of my thoughts at least are generally in England, you will do me the justice to believe too, that the greater share of them attend you, and consequently that nothing can be more welcome to that part of them that remains here than any marks of your friendship and remembrance.

I am with the utmost truth and respect, etc.

May I beg you to make my compliments to every body? Herbert ought to write to me.

XVII.

TO THE HON. MRS. HOWARD.

HAGUE, *August* 13, 1728.

MADAM,

I know I ought in good breeding to make you a great many apologies for the trouble I am going to give you; but as I think they generally rather increase than excuse the trouble, you will give me leave to proceed directly to my business in the plain Dutch way, without any preamble.

I have bought some china here (which was brought by the last East India ships that came in) of a very particular sort; its greatest merit is being entirely new; which in my mind may be almost as well as being undoubtedly old; and I have got all there was of it, which amounts to no more than a service for tea and chocolate, with a basin and ewer.   They are of metal, ena-

* The eldest of the maids of honour.—M.
† Lord Herbert's lap-dog.—M.
‡ Thomas, eighth Earl of Pembroke.—M.

melled inside and out with china of all colours. As I know the Queen loves china, I fancy she would like these; but it would not become me to take the liberty of offering them to her Majesty; but if you think she would like them, I must beg you will be so good as to take the whole affair upon yourself, and manage it so that I may not seem impertinent. Were they not mere baubles, I could not presume to offer them to her Majesty at all; and as they are such, I am ashamed of doing it. However, if notwithstanding these difficulties, you command me to send them, I desire you will at the same time let me know when and to whom I must direct them.

The occurrences of this place, as I have had the honour of telling you before, are not interesting enough to inform you of; but as one thing has lately happened, in which I have been a principal actor, and have acquired some degree of reputation, I must trouble you with an account of it. You must know then, that last Sunday I treated the people here with an English christening, in my chapel, of a Black-a-Moor boy that I have; having had him first instructed fully in the Christian faith by my chaplain, and examined by myself. The behaviour of the young Christian was decent and exemplary, and he renounced his *likeness*** with great devotion, to the infinite edification of a very numerous audience of both sexes. Though I have by these means got the reputation of a very good Christian; yet the more thrifty and frugal people here call my parts and economy a good deal in question for having put it out of my power ever to sell him.

The next remarkable thing here is, that I am at present over head and ears in mortar, and that I am building a room of fifty feet long, and thirty-four broad. Whether these are the right proportions or no, I must submit to you and Lord Herbert, who I hope will both be so good as to give me your sentiments upon it. It will, I am sure, have five great faults, which are five great windows, each of them big enough to admit intolerable light. However, such as it is, it will be handselled upon his Majesty's birthday next; at which time, if you will do me the honour to come there, and bring your own company, you will be extremely welcome. I believe you will think me extremely silly for building my tabernacle here; therefore I must tell you, in my own

* That is *the Devil.*

justification, that I had not one large room in my house before, either to eat, dance, or pray in, and that the building of this will cost me less than removing to another house would have done.

As I see in the news that the Duchess of Kent* is dead, I take it for granted the match between his Grace† and Miss Fitzwilliam is as good as concluded by this time. He will, without doubt, have a mind to perpetuate his title and estate; and I know nobody better able to contribute to so desirable an end than she; only I hope she will take care, both for his sake, her own, and that of so ancient a family, that the continuation of his family shall not be at the same time the continuation of his species.

Lady Albemarle ‡ and Lady Sophia are expected back here in about six weeks; at which time too, Lady Cadogan § and the Duchess of Richmond will return here from Spa; so that we shall have a sort of English assembly, which I believe will be at least as lively as the Dutch ones. Madame Creuning is at present at the top of the *beau-monde* here; and Mr. Creuning affords me a good deal of his company, as he promised me in England he would.

I should ask a great many pardons for having troubled you so long; but as you know I used to be accused in England (and I doubt pretty justly) of having a need for such a proportion of *talk* in a day, that is now changed into a need of such a proportion of *writing* in a day; and business falling short to-day, you are unfortunately afflicted with that share of writing which I could not so properly dispose of to the Secretary's Office. If this reason will not induce you to forgive me, I have a better, and a very true one; which is, the pleasure I always have in

* Jemima Crewe, Duchess of Kent.

† "Henry Grey, only Duke of Kent of that family, married in 1729 Lady Sophia Bentinck. He died in 1740. Lord Chesterfield's supposition of a match between him and Miss Fitzwilliam was a mere pleasantry." Note to the Suffolk Letters.

‡ Isabella Gravemoor, a Dutch lady, married in 1701 the first Earl of Albemarle, who left her a widow in 1718. Lady Sophia, born in 1711, was their only daughter.—M.

§ Margaretta Cecilia Munter, a Dutch lady, widow of the first Earl Cadogan, and mother of the Duchess of Richmond.—M.

every opportunity of assuring you of the very great consideration and respect with which I have the honour to be, etc.

If I can be of any use to you here, especially in an Indian-house * way, I hope you will command me.

XVIII.

TO LORD TOWNSHEND,

SECRETARY OF STATE.

Private.

HAGUE, *August* 31, N.S., 1728.

MY LORD,

I cannot omit returning your Lordship my thanks for the honour of your letter *apart*, of the 13th August, O.S. It gave me the utmost satisfaction to see the very friendly manner in which your Lordship not only forgave, but even approved, the liberty I had taken, and flatters me with the continuance of your friendship and protection, which I shall always be equally solicitous to deserve and proud to obtain. It is upon this friendship that I rely when I venture to make, and persuade myself your Lordship will (at least) pardon, the following request. By the death of the Duke of York † there are now two Garters vacant, that probably will not long remain so, and your Lordship knows by the former applications I have troubled you with on that score, how desirous and ambitious I am of that honour. Your Lordship knows too, that, though it is at all times a mark of honour and his Majesty's favour, yet it can never be of so much (or indeed of any real) use to me, as now, that I have the honour to be in the station I am in. In the first place, the thing itself is much more considered abroad than in England; in the second place, such a mark of favour is much more necessary for those who have the honour of being employed abroad, than for those who have the advantage of being at home; and I am sure every

---

* " The shops in which curiosities of furniture and apparel were sold in London used to be so called, from the predominance of Indian articles." Note to Suffolk Letters.

† Ernest Augustus, a brother of George the First, was Bishop of Osnabruck and Duke of York and Albany. He died unmarried, August 14, 1728.—M.

body will agree that I can never have it so advantageously for
myself, (especially in this country) as at a time when it must be
known to be entirely owing to your Lordship's friendship and
recommendation. It may possibly be owning a great weakness
when I confess to your Lordship that I would rather have this
one mark of his Majesty's and your favour than any one other
thing that your Lordship can recommend to, or the King dispose
of; but at the same time I hope it may in some measure excuse
the great earnestness with which I beg leave to recommend this
request to your protection, which, if it is possible any thing can,
will add to the obligations I already have to your Lordship, and
to the very great respect with which I have the honour to be,
etc.

XIX.

TO THE HON. MRS. HOWARD.

HAGUE, *October* 21, 1728.

MADAM,

I hope I need not tell you, with how much satisfaction I
received the honour of your last letter; I had heard of your
illness from other hands, and I could not hear of your recovery
so agreeably as from your own. I cannot help being very angry
at your head for having given us both so much pain; were it like
many heads I am acquainted with, I could easier forgive it; but
since I am sure it knows how to behave itself better if it pleases,
I confess I think this wilful misbehaviour is unpardonable. I
have known some ladies' heads very troublesome to others, but
at the same time very easy to themselves; yours is just the reverse, and only uses *you* ill. But however, as I would do justice
to every body's head, and especially to yours, I do not know
whether something may not be said in its defence; your head
plainly perceives that you are the only person in the world that
does not value it, and so, from a resentment that I cannot say is
entirely unjust, you are the only person in the world it uses ill.
However angry you may be at it, pray commit it no more to the
care of Mr. Cheselden,* whose ignorance has appeared to be

* One of the most famous surgeons and oculists of his day. He was
author of " The Anatomy of the Human Body," and " On the High Opera-

very gross in both cases; it is plain he does not know a head from a heart; for in my dissection he took one for the other. Those thick coats he mentions were upon my head; for as for a heart, it can very well be attested that there was none to be found; and, moreover, the place where it should have been was so dried up, that it was believed the heart had been lost for some years.

I am extremely sensible of the great honour the Queen does me in accepting of the china I took the liberty to offer. I have sent it this day by a sloop, directed as you commanded, and under the care of Mr. Chardin, who goes to England. Her Majesty need not apprehend being bribed by me; she is only to be bribed by merit, a bribe which it is not in my power to offer.

I must inform you that there is an extreme fine Chinese bed, window curtains, chairs, etc., to be sold for between £70 and £80. If you should have a mind to it for Marble Hill, and can find any way of getting it over, I will with a great deal of pleasure obey your commands.

As it may possibly be thought extraordinary that I give no entertainment here upon his Majesty's coronation day, I must beg the favour of you, when you have an opportunity, to let drop in a proper place, that my house is yet so full of workmen, that I have not a room to dine in; I hope to make amends upon the birth-day. I am sure all I can do will not express the duty and gratitude I feel, not only for past marks of his Majesty's goodness, but for late assurances of fresh ones.

I hope the Chapter* at Windsor has had the desired effect as to Miss Fitzwilliam, though, with submission, I think she judged it wrong to put her hopes upon that day; for upon those occasions the performers expect to be admired themselves, and have not time to admire others. Methinks I see her, like a second Princess of Cleves,† suiting her knots and apparel to the colours

---

tion for the Stone." He was born in 1688, and died in 1752. Pope's line records him:

        "I'll do what Mead and Cheselden advise."

  * Of the Garter.

  † The heroine of Madame de la Fayette's novel, "The Princess of Cleves." Madame de la Fayette was also the authoress of "Zaide," and "Memoirs of the Court of France." She died in 1633.

of her much-loved Duke, but happier in being free from the prior but cruel engagements to a Prince of Cleves.

I am very sorry that Lord Herbert has been convinced by experience that herbs and water are not preservatives against a fever; if his friendship for Fop could prevail with him to follow his example at dinner and supper, I believe it would be better for him. The Duchess of Richmond, who arrived here last week, makes you a great many compliments; she is extremely well, and grown fat.

I would make you a great many excuses, if I knew how, for troubling you so long; but for want of them I must only beg you will forgive the tediousness, in favour of the esteem and respect of

Yours, etc.

,   XX.

TO LORD TOWNSHEND.

Private.

HAGUE, November 30, N.S., 1728.

MY LORD,

I trouble your Lordship with this letter *apart*, to inform you of the contents of a letter the Pensionary * received about a week ago from General Keppell, and which he communicated to me in the utmost confidence. Mr. Keppell tells him that the Queen of Prussia, upon receiving the Queen of England's letter (of which your Lordship sent me a copy), was in such joy, that she immediately communicated it to him, together with all the steps that had been taken in that affair; that she had told him she was persuaded it would not only bring back the King to a right way of thinking, but even make him continue firm in it. He adds the greatest commendations imaginable of that Princess, and speaks of the match as a thing that he expects will be attended with the best consequences.†

---

* Simon Van Slingelandt, Pensionary of Holland, and one of the ablest statesmen of his day. See Lord Chesterfield's character of him, in his "Account of the Government of the Republic of the Seven United Provinces."

† These hints refer to the project of a marriage between Frederick Prince of Wales, and the Princess Royal of Prussia, afterwards Margra-

After having talked over this affair with the Pensionary, he asked me whether what he had seen in the newspapers was true, that the Prince of Orange was to have one of the vacant Garters. I told him I knew nothing of it, but that I thought it seemed natural enough, considering the regard the King had for that name and family, and that there had hardly ever been a Prince of Orange without it. He said that was very true, if people would but consider it rightly, but that he doubted they would draw other consequences from it, which might have an ill effect; that his coming here (which by the way is put off till Christmas, upon the account of the ill news of his Governor*) had already given an alarm which would be very much increased, if it were accompanied with that mark of the King's favour and distinction; that in the present situation of this Republic he did not know which was the most dangerous, to have a Stadtholder or not; that if the Stadtholder had not power sufficient to reform the abuses the Republic groaned under, he would be useless, and that if he had he might commit as many of his own. He concluded with saying that this was not a time to determine either way. Notwithstanding the confidence I live in with the Pensionary, I have always avoided any conversation with him upon the affair of the Stadtholder; being firmly convinced that he will be against one while there is any possibility of carrying on the Government without one; † and he had never spoke to me so much on that subject as in this conversation; however, I avoided entering into it upon this occasion by saying that I was not enough informed of the nature of this Government to be able to judge whether a Stadtholder would prove advantageous or prejudicial to it, but that I was persuaded if the Prince of Orange had the Garter it was without any further view, and only as a mark of the consideration the King had for him and his family.

After this I went to M. de Linden and told him part of the conversation that had passed between the Pensionary and myself

---

vine of Bareith. A full account of this curious transaction is given by the lady herself in the first volume of her Memoirs.—M.

* Monsieur Du Parc. The Prince of Orange was at this time only seventeen years of age.—M.

† See Lord Chesterfield's further remarks and reports of conversations on this point; p. 621.

about the Prince's having the Garter, and asked his opinion upon it. He said he thought it highly improper that the Prince should have it, till other things were ready to go along with it; that he was sure it would give an unnecessary alarm, which might prove prejudicial to some things which are now secretly transacting in favour of that Prince here; and which I will inform your lordship of more fully hereafter.

M. de Linden is the only person here to whom I ever speak upon this subject; he is both an honest and an able man, has the same fondness for the Prince that he could have were he his own son; and as he has the utmost confidence in me, and informs me of every step that is taken in that Prince's affairs, I can with great safety open myself to him whenever occasion shall require it.

I hope your Lordship will do me the justice to believe that I have no view of my own in submitting these considerations to your judgment. I shall neither have the Garter the more nor the less, the sooner nor the later, for the Prince of Orange's having it or not; but I thought myself obliged for his sake to lay this matter before Lordship, that you may act in it as you think proper. I own I have his interest a good deal at heart, and hope not to be altogether useless to him during my stay here.

Your Lordship will give me leave to take this oppportunity of recommending myself again to your friendship and protection in an affair which I believe is yet pretty remote, but which probably will happen, which is this: If when the match shall be agreed upon between Prince Frederick and the Princess Royal of Prussia, an Ambassador is to be sent to Berlin upon that extraordinary occasion, that your Lordship will be so good as to recommend me to his Majesty's consideration upon that account, for which I ask no extraordinaries nor additional allowance; so that it will be a considerable saving to the King. I would not be mistaken and be thought to desire to quit this place, but as I take it for granted such a commission would be very short, it would require very little absence from hence.

After so long a letter I will not trouble your Lordship with any professions of my gratitude for the past marks of your friendship, nor of my endeavours to deserve the continuance of it; I will only assure you that it is impossible to be with greater truth and respect

Your Lordship's, etc.

XXI.

TO LORD TOWNSHEND.

Very private.

HAGUE, *December* 14, N.S., 1728.

MY LORD,

I cannot express how sensible I am of His Majesty's great goodness and the confidence he is pleased to show he has in me, by not only entrusting me with, but even employing me in, an affair of such secrecy and importance as that contained in your Lordship's very private letter of the 29th November, O.S., which I have just now received.* I wish I were as able as I am desirous to execute his Majesty's commands to his satisfaction; but, sensible of my own inabilities, I must beg that his Majesty's indulgence will in favour of my known zeal for his service, excuse what may be wanting on my part, in the means of pursuing it.

I must more particularly beg your Lordship to solicit his Majesty's indulgence towards me upon this occasion, since I take the liberty of delaying to obey his Majesty's commands till I have first laid before your Lordship my reasons for so doing; and till I have received further instructions upon them.

I must inform your Lordship then, in the first place, that I believe it is possible that some things might be communicated to the Pensionary in confidence, which he would not tell the Greffier; † but I am firmly persuaded there is no one thing in the world that could be communicated to the Greffier that he would not immediately tell the Pensionary; and therefore I

---

* This affair was a project of marriage, and an overture to be made towards it, between the Prince of Orange, and Anne, Princess Royal of England. In 1734 the desired alliance took place.—M.

† The post of *Greffier* in the Dutch Republic may be compared to that of Secretary of State in other countries. It was at this period most ably filled by M. Fagel, "who," says Lord Chesterfield, "had the deepest knowledge of business and the soundest judgment of any man I ever knew in my life. See p. 622.

submit it to your Lordship whether such a distinguished confidence in the one would not very much exasperate the other, when he should come to know it, which he certainly would immediately. The Pensionary is extremely averse to the thoughts of that match already, and I doubt this would make him much more so. In talking to me some time ago upon that subject, he told me he would much rather see the match made between Don Carlos and the Arch-Duchess,* than between the Princess Royal and the Prince of Orange. I must observe to your Lordship too, that the sentiments of the Pensionary and Greffier upon the affair of the Stadtholder are extremely changed since your Lordship has seen them; when they inclined to a Stadtholder, Mr. Slingelandt was then but Treasurer, and was opposed and thwarted by the then Pensionary in almost everything; but now that Mr. Slingelandt is Pensionary, and Messrs. Vander Haym and Teinhoven (both relations and creatures of the Greffier's) Treasurer and Secretary of State, the Pensionary and Greffier have the whole management of affairs in their own hands, and think they may lose, but cannot get, by a Stadtholder, and consequently, while they can possibly carry on affairs without one, will in my opinion, be as much against one, as any two people in the Republic. Should this opinion of mine be true, as I have a good deal of reason to believe it is, if I had communicated this affair to the Greffier, I am persuaded he would have given me no answer till he had first consulted the Pensionary upon it; and I am equally persuaded that they would both have done their utmost endeavours to prevent it; that match being considered by everybody, and with reason, as the sure forerunner of the Stadtholdership.

Your Lordship will now give me leave to acquaint you with what passed a month ago between M. de Linden and myself, in conversation upon this subject. I asked M. de Linden when he thought there was any prospect of the Prince of Orange's being Stadtholder of the Province of Holland? He told me certainly not of two years at soonest; that it could not be attempted till he had taken his place in the Council of State as Stadtholder of Gueldres, which he could not do till next September, not being

---

* Don Carlos, son of the King of Spain, by his second marriage, and the Archduchess Maria Theresa, heiress of the Austrian monarchy.—M.

of age for that Province till then. I then asked him, whether in case a marriage that had been talked of for that Prince should take place, it would promote or obstruct his arriving at that dignity? He said it would certainly promote it; and indeed I think it is pretty clear that it will, from the dread that all the Anti-Stadtholder party have of that match; which would undoubtedly give spirit and vigour to all the Prince's friends, and extremely deject the opposite party. He told me afterwards in the utmost secrecy, that there was now a design carrying on of getting that Prince chosen Stadtholder of another Province; which would give him a majority of the Seven Provinces, and extremely facilitate his election in this; that the stroke was to be struck in March next; but that the whole depended upon the secrecy of the affair, and upon a little money properly distributed. Upon which I gave him some hopes, but no promises, that they might meet with some assistance from England as to the last particular. By all that I have been able to observe here, and I have omitted no opportunity of informing myself upon that subject, I think there is no reason to doubt but that that Prince will inevitably be one day Stadtholder of this Province; but how soon, I believe it is impossible for anybody to guess. The Army are nine in ten for him, and the common people unanimously so; his greatest enemies are the town of Amsterdam and the chief Burgomasters of the other towns, whose oppressions, rapines and extortions are now grown so flagrant and grievous, and daily increase so much, that they must, before it is very long, reduce the honest and thinking part of the Republic to fly to a Stadtholder as the only remedy. Or should that fail, the common people themselves, who groan under the oppressions and abuses of the magistrates, will by a general insurrection, impose one upon them. I know that a person in the Government has written to Sir Matthew Decker * to acquaint him, that should any steps be taken in favour of the Prince of Orange, that the town of Amsterdam, together with the Nobles and eleven other towns of this Province, would immediately declare the Prince of Nassau-Seigen Stadtholder; and possibly Sir Matthew may have acquainted your Lordship with this; but you need have no appre-

* An eminent merchant in London. See the Suffolk Letters, vol. ii. p. 293.—M.

hensions of it, for I know it to be a poor artifice of Mr. Buys to deter the Prince of Orange's party from stirring in his favour, and it was wrote into England in the same view.

After having said all this, I don't know whether I may take the liberty of offering most humbly my poor opinion upon this affair; but I am persuaded that however erroneous it may be, your Lordship will at least do me the justice to believe it meant for his Majesty's service.

I should think therefore that if his Majesty is determined to give the Princess Royal to the Prince of Orange, it had better be communicated jointly to the Pensionary and Greffier, as a thing determined, than proposed to them as a thing doubtful; for upon the supposition I go upon, that they will both be extremely averse to it, they will be less offended if it be done without, than against, their consent. I submit it likewise to your Lordship, whether anything of the Stadtholdership should be mentioned to them or no; for I am sure it will startle them extremely, and whether it is mentioned or no, it will undoubtedly be sooner or later the necessary consequence of the match.

I ask a thousand pardons for presuming to communicate my poor thoughts upon this subject, and still more for not immediately executing his Majesty's orders; but I thought it my duty in an affair of this very great importance, to suggest to your Lordship's consideration everything that could occur to me; hoping that the little delay of this messenger's going and coming can be of no great consequence. I am sure it is impossible for anybody to have anything more at heart than I have the success of this affair, and however mistaken I may be now, I am sure of being set right by his Majesty's further orders, which I shall have from your Lordship by the return of this messenger.*

I am, with the greatest truth.

---

* The conduct of Lord Chesterfield in this delicate transaction was in all respects satisfactory to his Court. "I received this morning," writes Lord Townshend, in reply, on December 6, O.S., 1728, "your Excellency's very private and very instructive despatch of the 14th instant, N.S., which I immediately laid before the King, who read it with great attention and approbation, and has commanded me to let you know, that for the reasons you give, he entirely approves of your conduct in not communicating to the Greffier what you had orders to say to him."—M.

XXII.

TO LORD TOWNSHEND.

Private.

THE HAGUE, *January* 11, N.S., 1729.

MY LORD,

Last week a poor Frenchman of a good character, whose trade is writing and copying, brought me the inclosed papers, and gave me the following account of them. A gentleman, well dressed, and whom, by his speaking French very well, he takes to be a Frenchman, came to him on Tuesday was sevennight, in the afternoon, and bid him with all possible despatch copy the paper No. 1, and that he would call again for it in an hour; the fellow, finding there was some mystery in it, took two copies, and kept one for himself. The man came back at the time appointed, gave the copyer a florin, and took away his letter in great haste, enjoining secrecy. When he was gone the copyer endeavoured to decipher the letter, which he easily did, the letters being only transposed, No. 2.*

I immediately sent an agent to Rotterdam, to inquire who this John Cromwell might be. He informed me that he could hear of

A LA HAYE, ce 28 *Decembre*, 1728.

* MON CHER AMI,

Depuis huit jours que je suis arrivé ici de Bruxelles j'ai reçu deux lettres, l'une de Paris et l'autre de Soissons, par lesquelles on me confirme comme il n'y a rien de plus vrai qu'on a proposé au Roi de faire ensorte que Gibraltar fut surpris par les Espagnols en lui donnant une grosse somme d'argent, ceux-ci, ne voulant rien conclure sans la restitution de cette place, et que le Roi a tenu plusieurs conseils sécrets sur cette affaire là. Cela me fait ressouvenir de plusieurs coups de langues qui m'ont été donnés à Soissons par le Maître d'Hotel de Monsieur de Bournonville; un jour il me dit que Gibraltar avoit coûté bien du monde aux Espagnols pendant le siège, mais qu'on sauroit bien trouver le sécret de le ravoir sans qu'il en coûta tant; exhortez nos bons amis des Communes à veiller sur cette affaire, et ne perdez pas du temps. Car cette place est trop importante à la nation, et tous ceux qui donneroient un pareil conseil au Roi mériteroient un châtiment exemplaire. Les billets seront bientôt imprimés, il y en a huit mille en trois langues. Le Capitaine Jean Cromvel m'a promis à Rotterdam de les passer et de les faire porter en toute sûreté chez le Sieur Jourdain suivant votre mémoire, mais il m'a demandé dix guinées; je suis sur mon départ pour Middelbourg, les affaires régleront mon retour, mais je ne crois pas de vous voir, avant la fin de

no such body as John Cromwell, but that there was one John Cranwell, Captain of a sloop, who went from thence for England about ten days ago, and who, I suppose, is the same person, the mistake between Cromwell and Cranwell being natural for a foreigner to make in an English name. The papers intended to be dispersed, I imagine, are concerning Gibraltar. This is all I have been able to find out of this affair, notwithstanding the most diligent inquiries I have been able to make. If your Lordship thinks it deserves any attention, you will easily find out this John Cranwell in the river, who will be able to inform your Lordship who that Jourdain mentioned in the paper is.

The Prince of Orange's coming here is put off for a fortnight longer, upon account of the illness of his governor, Mons. Du Parc, who is really very ill; but as the Prince's enemies here have given out that this is only a feigned illness, and that the Prince dared not come, Monsieur de Linden and I have agreed that he shall come at all events in a fortnight; thinking it may be of ill consequence to let anybody suppose the least timidity on his part, or on the part of those who direct him.

General Keppell informed me, in confidence, that Monsieur Reichembach, the Prussian Agent at London, writes very impertinent and malicious accounts to his own Court, of that of England : of this your Lordship may find means to be better informed.

I am, with the greatest truth, etc.

XXIII.

TO LORD TOWNSHEND.

Private.

HAGUE, February 15, N.S., 1729.

MY LORD,

I received on Saturday, the honour of your Lordship's very secret letter of the 28th Jan., with the inclosed letter from Prince

Février; mes compliments je vous prie à tous nos bons amis sans oublier ma chère belle-sœur. Adieu, mon ami, je suis à mon ordinaire tout à vous.

P.S. J'ai été voir à Amsterdam le marchand qui livra les armes au Sieur Jourdain il y a deux années, mais il ne veut pas les donner au même prix; je verrai ailleurs.

Eugene to Count Kinski, which I communicated in confidence to the Pensionary and Greffier, who desired me to return your Lordship their thanks for that communication.

Lady Portland * being sent for so suddenly into England, has raised various speculations here, and the more, because it happens unluckily, just at the time that the Prince of Orange is to come, who will be here next Thursday. I must upon this occasion take the liberty of suggesting to your Lordship, that although I am thoroughly convinced of Lady Portland's zeal and attachment for the Princess Royal, and of her good intentions for the Prince of Orange; yet her strict intimacy with Count Obdam and his family, from whom I am persuaded she conceals nothing, makes her a very improper person to be talked to upon that subject. This I only hint provisionally to your Lordship, not knowing nor inquiring upon what account she is really gone.

Since I have mentioned the Prince of Orange, I will trouble your Lordship with a short account of what has passed here concerning him, since I wrote last to your Lordship upon that subject. He was to have come here about three weeks ago, but the Pensionary desired M. de Linden that it might be put off till March, without giving any reason for that request. Upon which M. de Linden came and consulted me whether it should be complied with or no. I told him I thought it was necessary to please the Pensionary as much as possible, and to soften him at least (if he was not to be gained) by all imaginable deference to his opinion. M. de Linden accordingly went to Utrecht to put off the Prince's journey for six weeks; but while he was there I received a letter from Prince William of Hesse, wherein he told me he should come to the Hague the first week in March. As I thought it highly improper these two Princes should be here together, knowing very well the ill disposition of the uncle towards the nephew, I immediately wrote to M. de Linden to inform him of it, and to advise him to bring the Prince of Orange here time enough for him to return, before the arrival of his uncle; and to think of some excuse to make to the Pensionary upon that occasion. Upon this M. de Linden settled the Prince's

---

* Jane, daughter of Sir John Temple, of East Sheen, Bart., and widow since 1709, of William, first Earl of Portland. She had been governess to the Princesses, daughters of George the Second.—M.

journey here for Thursday next, the 17th instant, and returned here the next day, and excused it to the Pensionary upon pretence that the Prince of Orange's house here was not big enough to hold him and his uncle at the same time. The Pensionary, to M. de Linden's great surprise, seemed not only satisfied, but pleased that the Prince was to come so soon; which I can only ascribe to this—that as all his projects meet with very strong opposition in the Assembly of the States of Holland, and especially from the town of Amsterdam and the Anti-Stadtholder party, he is not sorry to have the Prince of Orange here to frighten them with a little.

I mentioned to your Lordship some time ago, that measures were taking in a certain Province, to get the Prince declared Stadtholder; that Province was Zealand, where there has been lately a considerable revolution in favour of the Stadtholder party, in the Magistracy of Flessingue and Tervere; and I hope something more may be done in about two months' time.

I am, with the greatest truth, etc.

I hope I may depend upon those letters that I trouble your Lordship with, in my own hand, being kept secret.

XXIV.

TO LORD TOWNSHEND.

Private.

HAGUE, *February* 18, 1729.

The Prince of Orange * arrived here last night. I went to wait upon him, and, as far as I am able to judge from half an hour's conversation only, I think he has extreme good parts. He is perfectly well-bred, and civil to everybody, and with an ease and freedom that is seldom acquired but by a long knowledge of the world. His face is handsome; his shape is not so advantageous as could be wished, though not near so bad as I

* William Charles Henry, Prince of Nassau and Orange, whose name frequently recurs in this Correspondence, was born in 1711, and married, March 25, 1734, Anne, Princess Royal of England. He died suddenly in 1751, and his widow in 1759. His only son and successor was born in 1748.—M.

had heard it represented. The acclamations of the people were loud and universal. He assumes not the least dignity, but has all the affability and insinuation that is necessary for a person who would raise himself in a popular Government.

XXV.

TO LORD TOWNSHEND.

Private.

HAGUE, *April* 19, N.S., 1729.

MY LORD,

The pressing solicitations of a very unfortunate young man, oblige me to give your Lordship this trouble. Mr. Maul, son to the Bishop of Cloyne in Ireland, who had the misfortune about a year ago to kill his own servant, has been in this country almost ever since I have been here ; and, as he represents his case to me, it is, I think, as compassionate a one as a thing of that kind can possibly be. The Bishop, his father, is now come to England to solicit in his behalf, and I suppose has by this time waited upon your Lordship for that purpose, and showed you those depositions and certificates, which, by his son's account, very much mitigate the case. I could not refuse him the justice of assuring your Lordship that his behaviour here carries with it all the marks of a sincere concern and repentance, even almost to a degree of despair, and that I verily believe him to be an object worthy of his Majesty's compassion.

I am with the very greatest truth, etc.

XXVI.

TO LORD TOWNSHEND.

Private.

HAGUE, *April* 29, N.S., 1729.

MY LORD,

As the King's journey to Hanover now draws near, and as I take it for granted your Lordship will attend him there, you must give me leave to solicit, and to endeavour to secure, an honour and a pleasure that I am very desirous to obtain, which is, that if you take this place in your way (as I hope you will) you won't think of lodging in any other house than mine. The accommodation (I own) has little to tempt your Lordship, and the company less; but if, for so little a time, you will bear with some inconveniences, you will do the greatest honour to, and lay the highest obligation imaginable upon,

Your Lordship's most obedient servant.

XXVII.

TO LORD TOWNSHEND.

Private.

HAGUE, *July* 26, 1729.

Count Sinzendorf, the Imperial Minister, left this place last Sunday morning, saying that he was going to see some of these provinces, and might possible go to Spa, but with an air of great mystery, which has occasioned some speculation here; but, for my own part, as I know the gentleman, I do not believe the mystery is upon account of the journey, but I rather believe he takes the journey for the sake of the mystery!

XXVIII.

TO THE HON. MRS. HOWARD.

HAGUE, *July* 26, 1729.

MADAM,

The just apprehensions I had of being entirely forgot were agreeably removed by the honour of your letter of the 8th, and you have made me the only amends you could for so long an intermission of your correspondence.

The account you give me of Lord Herbert's journey to Paris is very satisfactory, and convinces me of the truth of a common observation; that little regard is to be had to history, especially to the causes generally assigned by historians for great events. I confess his Lordship's journey had raised my curiosity, as it did the speculations of all Europe, and has been variously accounted for; but the true reason has not been guessed. Some thought that he was ordered to go and cruize in the Mediterranean till the arrival of the fleets; others thought he was sent to Paris, to show that in him alone we were able to fulfil all our engagements. For my own part, I (who am not apt to refine) concluded that the Court of France only desired to have him there in the absence of Bannières. In short, every one judged according to his hopes or his fears. But no doubt those Powers that were so apprehensive of his motions will think themselves very well off when they shall come to know that for this time his Lordship only meditates the destruction of tied wigs. I can tell him for his comfort, that there is not such a thing in France now as a tied wig, but they all wear either their own hair, or little wigs that they call *des bonnets*.

I assure you, you need not be alarmed at what Lord Albemarle and Mrs. Macartney are pleased to call my magnificence ; for it is nothing like it, and only what is barely necessary ; and as for the expense, I should be very sorry to be a gainer by this or any other employment that the King may ever think fit to give me. Whatever my actions may be, interest shall never be thought to influence them ; and if I can procure any credit to my master or myself, at the expense, not only of what he allows me, but even of my own, I shall think it very well bestowed.

I find, by your account, that Kensington is not at present the seat of diversions. I wish we could find a way of joining companies, which might possibly prove to our mutual advantage ; for the Hague is at present very empty, and we are reduced to two or three families. The women here have one way of animating the conversation, which perhaps might be of use to you at Kensington, that is by quarrelling and scolding one another. We are about twenty that sup constantly together every night ; and a supper never ends without a quarrel between two or three of the finest women there. If the maids of honour did not live in that perfect friendship that they do, you might have that amusement at Kensington too ; but considering their union, it is not to be expected. I hope that during this interval of your diversions I may put in my claim for a part of your idle time ; which, since it affords you no pleasure, I beg you will employ it in bestowing a very great one upon yours, etc.,

I made your compliments to Lady Albemarle, who returns you a great many.

XXIX.

TO GEO. TILSON, ESQ.

UNDER SECRETARY OF STATE.

Private.

HAGUE, *July* 29, N.S., 1729.

SIR,

I have nothing worth troubling the Duke of Newcastle *
with by this post, and I only write this to acquaint you that I
am informed one Monsieur Pellnitz is gone into England, who
has wrote a most scandalous book, entitled *l'Histoire de Cune-
gonde,* and which contains the whole life and history of his
present Majesty's mother.† He had sold a copy of it to a
bookseller at Amsterdam, which I immediately bought, notwithstanding he had assured me before that he would never
publish it. I suppose if he is gone to England it is with a
design of publishing it there, where he sees anything may be
printed with impunity. So that if you could find him out, it
would not be amiss to seize his papers, amongst which, you
would probably get the only copy he has left of it. If I could
meet with the gentleman here, I should go a shorter way to
work with him than you do with your libellers in England, and
I believe the apprehensions of that have made him withdraw
himself from here. He is nearly related to a Madame Pellnitz,
who has been much known at Hanover, and he has at this time
a brother in the King's service there, but he himself is in every
respect a very great scoundrel.

I am, with great esteem, etc.

* The Duke of Newcastle was at this period colleague of Lord Townshend as second Secretary of State.

† Sophia Dorothea of Zell, the unhappy consort of George the First
and mother of George the Second, had been for thirty-two years immured
in the castle of Ahlen. Her demeanour in early youth to Count Konigs-
mark, a Swedish nobleman on a visit to Hanover, was the motive, or at
least the pretext, of her captivity. She died in November, 1726, only a
few months before her husband.—M.

XXX.

TO GEO. TILSON, ESQ.

Private.

HAGUE, *August* 5, N.S., 1729.

SIR,

I am very much obliged to you for the assurances you give me of your friendship in your letter of the 22nd July, which I received yesterday by Crew, the messenger. I send you by Wiggs, the courier, Mr. Pellnitz's performance to give to the Duke of Newcastle, since his Grace desires to see it. The manner of its being writ is not so blameable, as the stirring of the thing at all is in my mind improper. The author endeavours to shelter himself under the commendations he gives to his present Majesty; but that, I should think, is not sufficient to secure him from the censures he deserves for reviving an affair of that nature. I am extremely glad to hear of her Majesty's perfect recovery; her lingering so long having given me great uneasiness.

I am, with perfect truth, etc.

XXXI.

TO LORD TOWNSHEND.

Private.

HAGUE, *August* 23, N.S., 1729.

MY LORD,

Mr. Hop * having wrote word here from Hanover that the King intended to stay a day or two at the Hague, in his way to England, both the States General and the States of Holland begin to be in a bustle about the manner of his Majesty's reception. They take it for granted, and I believe with reason, that his Majesty will not lodge at the old Court, which belongs to the King of Prussia, as the late King did; wherefore they propose offering him Prince Maurice's house, which is the place where they receive ambassadors when they make a public entry.

* M. Hop was for many years the Dutch Minister at the Court of England. See Lord Chesterfield's letter to his son of June 23, 1752.

Another thing which they are very inquisitive about, is, whether his Majesty will notify his arrival publicly beforehand; if he does, a deputation must be sent him, both from the States General and the States of Holland, which always creates a quarrel between those two deputations, each insisting upon the precedence. In the late King's time, it even came to jostling and scurrilous language. I have been applied to, underhand, to inform them of all these particulars, to which I could give them no answer; but it is really necessary that they should know some time beforehand, they being extremely pleased with the thoughts of the King's coming here, and resolved to receive his Majesty with all possible marks of distinction and respect.

For my own part, I dare not think of offering the house I live in to the King. Your Lordship knows how unfit it is to receive him; besides it is his Majesty's own already, and if he thinks fit to make use of it, he will command it; but if by chance his Majesty should choose to take up with so bad an accommodation, for the sake of avoiding a good deal of troublesome ceremony at Prince Maurice's, I believe I need not say how happy such an honour would make me. It is impossible to be, with a more perfect truth and respect,

Your Lordship's etc.

XXXII.

TO LORD TOWNSHEND.

Private.

HAGUE, August 23, N.S., 1729.

MY LORD,

Your Lordship's goodness in receiving my particular applications to you, encourages me to repeat them, and makes me (it may be) but too troublesome. Most of his Majesty's northern Ministers having obtained his leave to pay their duty to him at Hanover, I think I should be wanting to mine, if I did not endeavour to obtain the same honour, and most humbly ask his Majesty's gracious permission to do so too. But at the same time, however desirous I may be to throw myself at the feet of so gracious a master, I would by no means solicit that honour at the expense of neglecting my duty to his Majesty here. Insignificant as my presence is everywhere, yet should there be any business or likelihood of it here, of which his Majesty is best judge, I would prefer my duty to my inclination, and not think of stirring from hence, nor of adding negligence to the many other imperfections that render me already but too unworthy of his Majesty's goodness to me.

I must therefore beg of your Lordship to mention this affair to his Majesty in whatever manner you think properest, and to let me know his Majesty's orders, which I shall always receive and obey with the utmost submission and satisfaction.—I have the honour to be, etc.

XXXIII.

TO LORD TOWNSHEND.

Private.

HAGUE, *October* 7, N.S., 1729.

MY LORD,

When I had the honour of seeing his Majesty at Helvoet Sluys, I had not time humbly to beg his permission to pay my duty to him in England some time this winter, where not only my own inclinations call me upon that account, but where also my own private affairs render my presence very necessary. I must therefore beg of your Lordship to use your interest with his Majesty, that he will be graciously pleased to give me leave to come to England for some time this winter.* It is now above a year and a half that I have been here, and have not stirred one day from my post; so that I hope his Majesty will not think this request unreasonable; nor, indeed, have I any reason to suppose, that my presence anywhere can be of importance enough for his Majesty's service to suffer in the least by my absence from hence.

If upon the supposition that I shall obtain his Majesty's permission, I may take the liberty of mentioning the time, I

---

* According to Coxe, this permission was solicited by Lord Chesterfield at the secret suggestion of Lord Townshend. The object was to obtain the appointment of the former, as Secretary of State. But Sir Robert Walpole, jealous of such influence, resisted this scheme, and its failure was one main cause of Townshend's own resignation in May, 1730. (*Memoirs of Walpole*, vol. i. p. 335, etc.)—M.

could wish, for the sake of my own business, to be in England about the latter end of this month. If the King is pleased to grant me this request, it will add to the very many marks I have already so undeservedly received of his Majesty's goodness; if not, I shall submit to his orders with the utmost duty and resignation.

If I am troublesome with my frequent applications to your Lordship, you will, I hope, forgive me, when you do me the justice to believe the perfect attachment and inviolable truth and respect with which I have the honour to be, etc.

XXXIV.

À MONS^R. JACQUES DAYROLLES.*

à LONDRES, *ce* 5 *Juin*, V.S. 1730.

MONSIEUR,

Je suis très-sensible à la part que vous prenez aux bontés que le Roi a eu pour moi,† et je voudrois bien qu'elles me donnassent une occasion de vous témoigner, par des effets, la véritable amitié et considération que j'ai pour vous. Votre neveu, qui est très-digne de la tendresse que vous avez pour lui, peut compter sur mes services dans les occasions, et j'avois pensé à cette heure de le faire Secrétaire de l'Ambassade à Paris sous Mylord Waldegrave, qui est destiné à cette commission; mais · malheureusement le Duc de Newcastle avoit justement obtenu du roi cet emploi pour son parent,‡ qui avoit été Sécrétaire du Congrès à Soissons,§ et qui y prétendoit comme

---

* Mr. James Dayrolles (a gentleman apparently of French extraction) had been for many years the King's *Resident* at the Hague. "In him the ambassador found a most useful assistant."—(Maty's *Memoirs*, p. 100.) He died in 1739, (see Letter LXVI.); and his nephew and heir, Mr. Solomon Dayrolles, became Lord Chesterfield's constant friend and correspondent.

† Lord Chesterfield having returned to England, on leave of absence, according to the permission solicited in the last letter, had there received high and distinguished tokens of the Royal approbation. On May 18, 1730, he was elected a Knight of the Garter; he was installed as such at Windsor, on June 18, and on the following day he was appointed Lord High Steward.—M.

‡ Mr. Thomas Pelham.

§ A Congress had been opened at Soissons, in June, 1728, to put an end to the differences between the allies of the Treaty of Hanover (England

de droit. Je ne manquerai pas de parler en faveur de votre neveu à Mylord Harrington, quoique je crois qu'il ne fera pas de changement dans le bureau; et d'ailleurs, s'il en faisoit, je sais qu'il a des jeunes gens qui lui appartiennent. Par rapport à la charge de Grand-Maître * que j'ai, il n'y a à ma disposition que des petits emplois, qui ne lui conviendroient nullement. Mais nous parlerons plus amplement de cette affaire quand j'aurai le plaisir de vous revoir à la Haye, ce qui arrivera bientôt; † en attendant, faites-moi la justice d'être persuadé que je suis plus que personne, votre, etc.

Ayez la bonté d'assurer Madame Dayrolles de mes très-humbles respects.

XXXV.

TO THE PLENIPOTENTIARIES.

(Mahon's *History of England*, Append. vol. ii. p. 72, second ed.)

HAGUE, *September* 15, 1730.

My last letters from Berlin inform me that the King of Prussia had beaten the Princess Royal, his daughter, most un-mercifully—dragged her about the room by the hair, kicking her in the belly and breast, till her cries alarmed the officer of the guards, who came in. She keeps her bed of the bruises she received. Twenty pence a day is allowed for the maintenance of the Prince Royal in the Castle of Custrin; and the inquiry is carried on with rigour, under the direction of Monsieur Grumkow.‡

France and Prussia) on the one side, and the allies of the Treaty of Vienna (Spain and Austria) on the other. The English plenipotentiaries to this Congress were William Stanhope, Stephen Poyntz, and Horace Walpole, and "although," as Coxe observes, "nothing material was transacted, yet the negotiations were managed on the part of the Hanover allies in such a manner, as to create a division between the Courts of Vienna and Madrid." (*Memoirs of Walpole*, vol. i. p. 303.) Of this the fruits appeared by the Treaty of Seville.—M.

    * Lord High Steward of the Household.

    † Lord Chesterfield returned to his post at the Hague, in the August following.—M.

    ‡ The ill-treatment, by the King of Prussia, of his eldest son (afterwards Frederick the Second) and of his eldest daughter (afterwards

XXXVI.

TO LORD HARRINGTON.*

Private.

HAGUE, *September* 19, N.S., 1730.

MY LORD,

I was honoured by the last post with your Lordship's private letter of the 1st, N.S., by which I am sorry to find the resolution that seems to be taken about Mecklenburg. It appears to be no less than perpetuating the commission, at least for this Duke's life; for if he is too wild and extravagant at his age to be treated with at all, I presume he will hardly ever become more *traitable*. As to the dissatisfaction his Majesty expressed with relation to the Pensionary's ideas, I have justified him, and very truly, in my other letter to your Lordship by this post, for I really had not informed him of all his Majesty's demands, thinking it improper, in the infancy of this affair, to frighten him with a catalogue of pretensions, that might make him consider the very thing I was employing him to transact as impracticable.

However, I look upon our negotiation with the Emperor as begun; † but I look upon it, too, as very far from being ended,

Margravine of Bareith) is detailed at length in the *Memoirs* of the latter. It is also confirmed by Voltaire, who especially commemorates :" une contusion à la Princesse au-dessous du teton gauche, qu'elle a conservée toute sa vie comme une marque des sentimens paternels, et qu'elle m'a fait l'honneur de me montrer ! "—M.

* On the resignation of Townshend, and the ascendancy of Walpole in the Cabinet, the office of Secretary of State was conferred upon William Stanhope, lately created Lord Harrington. He was a kinsman of Lord Chesterfield, being descended from Sir John Stanhope, younger brother of the first Earl. From early life, he had served in Spain, first as a soldier, and next as a diplomatist. After holding the Seals of Secretary for many years, and being in 1741 promoted to an Earldom, Lord Harrington succeeded Lord Chesterfield in 1746 as Lord Lieutenant of Ireland. He died in 1756.—M.

† To explain the state of foreign affairs at this period, and the aim of Lord Chesterfield's exertions, it must be observed that on the 9th of November, 1729, a Treaty was signed at Seville, of peace and union, and mutual defence, between England, Spain and France. "This Treaty" says Coxe " stipulated the introduction of six thousand Spaniards (instead of neutral troops, as specified by the Quadruple Alliance) into Tuscany,

and I foresee the many difficulties that will arise in the course of it. The King thinks the guarantee so great a concession, that it entitles him to ask anything or everything. The Emperor considers it in a different light; and, though desirous to obtain it, will not purchase it too dear. He knows it is almost as much our interest as his; he sees our situation with France, and he apprehends little from the concurrence of such jarring particles as our present alliance is formed of. These difficulties, which to me are obvious ones, will certainly spin out the negotiation to a considerable length, though not break it off; for the good of it is, that when once begun, and the demands of England and the Republic meeting with little difficulty, as I am persuaded they will, it will be impossible to break it off, for the sake of some certain conditions that your Lordship and I know of. But as these difficulties will take up a good deal of time, and probably not be discussed here, or, if they were, as I am both unfit and unwilling to be concerned in them, I submit it to your Lordship, whether it is not time to think of a successor for me here, who will require some time to get ready, and who it may be proper should be here before I go. There is now a little more than three months to the sitting of the Parliament; and since I am to be back by that time, I confess I should be glad it were as soon as possible. I therefore beg your Lordship will mention this affair to the King, in what way you think properest, whether as from yourself or me.

It is with the utmost pleasure I reflect that I can address

Parma and Placentia, for securing to Don Carlos the eventual succession to those Duchies, in case the reigning Sovereigns should die without issue male; and if the Emperor would not acquiesce, forcible means were to be used for effecting the introduction." (*Memoirs of Walpole*, vol. i. p. 303.) It was therefore a matter of first-rate importance to obtain the Emperor's acquiescence without recourse to arms; and the Hague, as a central and comparatively neutral post, became, in a considerable degree, the pivot for negotiations. King George was willing to guarantee the " Pragmatic Sanction," that is, the succession of the Austrian States to Maria Theresa, eldest daughter of the Emperor, but he expected, in return, a concession not only to the public demands called for for the welfare of his kingdom, but also to various petty points in Mecklenburg and elsewhere, tending to the aggrandizement of his Electorate. It was amidst those complicated difficulties, caused both by friends and foes, that Lord Chesterfield's abilities for negotiation were long conspicuous and at last successful.—M.

myself in this manner, at the same time to a friend and a minister, and subscribe myself with as much sincerity to the one as respect to the other, etc.

XXXVII.

TO GEO. TILSON, ESQ.

Private.

HAGUE, *December* 12, N.S., 1730.

SIR,

I beg you will acquaint Lord Harrington that I don't answer his last letter *apart* in expectation of his next, that I may give him but one trouble.

I am sorry the answer from the court of Vienna is not satisfactory at first, for I am persuaded it will be so at last, but it is asking too much of the Emperor to ask him to do what none of his family ever could do, *agir de bonne grace.* For my own part I see no other way of getting out of this scrape. I think it is pretty plain France will not help us out of it, at least, without drawing us into a worse. Monsieur Fénélon* takes immense pains to persuade the people here of *la droiture scrupuleuse,* as he calls it, of his Court, but to very little purpose. I know 'tis a bold word, but I really think him the silliest Minister in Europe.

The King of Prussia in the oath he prepared for the Prince to swallow, among many other things, has made him swear that he will never believe the doctrine of Predestination! A very unnecessary declaration in my mind for any body who has the misfortune of being acquainted with him to make, since he himself is a living proof of free-will, for Providence can never be supposed to have pre-ordained such a creature!

I find I shall have the pleasure of seeing you soon in England. Without pretending to be fatigued with business, I have had enough on't to desire no more, and to be very glad to be quiet in St. James's Square,† where I shall always have a pleasure in assuring you that I am with real esteem, etc.

* The French ambassador at the Hague, nephew and heir of the author of *Télémaque.*—M.

† Lord Chesterfield's house in London.

XXXVIII.

TO DEAN SWIFT.*

HAGUE, *December* 15, N.S., 1730.

SIR,

You need not have made any excuse to me for your solicitation; on the contrary, I am proud of being the first person, to whom you have thought it worth the while to apply since those changes, which, you say, drove you into distance and obscurity. I very well know the person you recommend to me, having lodged at his house a whole summer at Richmond. I have always heard a very good character of him, which alone would incline me to serve him; but your recommendation, I can assure you, will make me impatient to do it. However, that he may not again meet with the common fate of Court-suitors, nor I lie under the imputation of making Court-promises, I will exactly explain to you how far it is likely I may be able to serve him.

When first I had this office, I took the resolution of turning out nobody; so that I shall only have the disposal of those places that the death of the present possessors will procure me. Some old servants, that have served me long and faithfully, have obtained the promises of the first four or five vacancies; and the early solicitations of some of my particular friends have tied me down for about as many more. But, after having satisfied these engagements, I do assure you, Mr. Launcelot shall be my first care. I confess, his prospect is more remote than I could have wished it; but, as it is so remote, he will not have the uneasiness of a disappointment, if he gets nothing; and if he gets something we shall both be pleased.

As for his political principles, I am in no manner of pain about them. Were he a Tory, I would venture to serve him, in the just expectation that, should I ever be charged with

---

* Dean Swift had written to Lord Chesterfield (November 10, 1730) recommending for some appointment in the office of Lord Steward "an honest man whose name is Launcelot." The answer of the Earl as here given, appeared evasive to the Dean, and he wrote again with some displeasure and much irony (January 5, 1731). Nevertheless Lord Chesterfield was perfectly sincere in his good intentions, and very soon found an opportunity of providing for Mr. Launcelot. Swift's two letters may be seen in his *Works*, vol. xvii. pp. 345 and 365, Scott's edition.—M.

having preferred a Tory, the person, who was the author of my crime, would likewise be the author of my vindication.

I am, with real esteem, etc.

XXXIX.

TO LORD HARRINGTON.

Private.

HAGUE, *December* 19, N.S. 1730.

MY LORD,

I am in such a hurry to dispatch the courier to Vienna as soon as possible, that, had it not been for your Lordship's commands in your letter of the 4th (*apart*), I should have deferred giving you this trouble till next post. I confess I have my doubts about the success of our Vienna treaty, at least about the dispatch it will meet with there, and I am persuaded it will employ couriers some time longer. When I saw the plan transmitted to your Lordship by Mr. Robinson,* I was concerned to find it clogged with conditions which they could never imagine would be agreed to; such as the guarantee of Brunswick, the Duke of Holstein's affair, etc., and consequently seemed to be intended delays.

Prince Eugene's behaviour to Mr. Robinson would naturally give one hopes of success; but when I consider how much that gentleness is out of character, I own, I refine enough to suspect it. The treaty sent to Vienna, as far as it relates to England and the Republic, is such as the Emperor, I think, in prudence ought to agree to; but considering his haughtiness and obstinacy, and the knowledge he certainly has of the distrusts and jealousies among the Allies, I fear it is uncertain whether he will or no.

I hope Monsieur Dieden's † demands will not prove an obstruction to this affair; but I cannot comprehend what can be meant by an additional security of the King's Electoral dominions, which are already guaranteed over and over by all the powers upon earth, and by the whole empire, as being part of it; so that I suspect additional security to mean additional

---

* At that time British Minister at Vienna, in 1754 appointed Secretary of State, and in 1761 created Lord Grantham.—M.

† The King's Minister at Vienna as Elector of Hanover.—M.

dominions, which can only be by dismembering Mecklenburg, upon a pretence of paying in that manner the expenses of the commission. And this, I think the Emperor never can, and the empire never will, consent to; it being a total subversion of all the fundamental laws of the empire.

I am very willing to stay here till this affair be determined one way or other, and the more so, because should the Emperor agree, I foresee there will be some difficulties in finishing here, where, from the nature of the government, every wrong head or heart has a right of opposition, and can do hurt, though not good. I am, etc.

XL.

TO LORD HARRINGTON.

Private.

HAGUE, December 26, N.S. 1730.

MY LORD,

You will give me leave to trouble you with this letter, to ask your advice both as a minister and a friend. Mr. Finch* has writ me word, that he embarks next Monday in the yacht that is to attend me here; and I propose making it wait till I have some answer from Vienna. If the treaty comes back signed, to be sure I will stay here till I have got the Republic into it. But supposing the answer should be doubtful and dilatory, and plainly show that at least it will take up a good deal more time, I beg both your advice and instructions what I should do in that case, which I am apt to think will exist. For having told Count Sinzendorf, in general, that I had forwarded a courier to Vienna, who would one way or other determine affairs, in about three weeks time, he said, that let it be what it would that the courier carried, even though it were acceptable, yet he knew from the constant dull delays of his Court, that they would take at least a month to consider of anything final; and that he hoped I should not look upon such a delay, so natural to the Imperial Court, as any design to amuse or gain time. I told him I certainly should, and that, considering the crisis things were now

---

* The Hon. William Finch, son of the sixth Earl of Winchelsea, was appointed Envoy at the Hague, in succession to Lord Chesterfield.

iu, it was impossible to see it in any other light. If Mr. Finch should come here before I have received an answer from Vienna, I shall not deliver my letters of revocation till I receive one; but if, when it comes, it should be such a one as I apprehend it will, your Lordship will be pleased to instruct me particularly what I ought to do.

I am very apprehensive that the King will have been displeased that I got nothing to send from hence by the courier to Vienna, but I really found it impossible to do it, with the least degree of security for the secret; and I hope your Lordship will contribute to excuse me to the King. I heartily wish this affair may succeed; for if it does not, I think we shall be in a very bad condition. The design of France, to do either nothing or too much, is now too plain to be doubted of, and the jealousies and distrusts among the Allies have taken too deep a root to be removed, with any prospect of future concert. And if the Emperor is obstinate enough to reduce us to return to France, after this jealousy, we shall be obliged to give them fatal pledges of our future fidelity.

I am persuaded there will be nothing ready for the meeting of the Parliament; for even should the Court of Vienna approve of the treaty in general, yet something or other always happens to retard the conclusion of such important affairs beyond the time one wished or proposed. If accidents don't happen, forms and ceremonies supply their place; and such a Court as that of Vienna will undoubtedly make some alterations in the treaty, were it only to say that they have not subscribed a treaty just as it was sent them. Therefore, in my poor opinion, the Parliament should be put off as long as possible, because whatever his Majesty says at the opening of it will be of the utmost and nicest consequence. I am ever, etc.

XLI.

TO LORD HARRINGTON.

Private.

HAGUE, *January* 2, N.S. 1731.

MY LORD,

I doubt I grow very troublesome to your Lordship with my letters *apart*, but I trust both to your patience and your friendship to excuse them. I received, by last post, a letter from Mr. Walpole, with an account of a very extraordinary one intercepted from Monsieur Hop here to his brother in England; and though whatever passes between the two Hops does, in my mind, deserve very little attention, yet as I know that very slight objects will sometimes make very strong impressions, I thought it necessary, for my own sake, to obviate with your Lordship any effects that this silly circumstance might possibly have with you or any body else.

I cannot conceive upon what Monsieur Hop founds his assertion of my being uneasy at being recalled, as he terms it, and of my attributing it to the ill-will of the two brothers, as he is familiarly pleased to call Sir Robert and Horace; I am sure not upon anything I have said to him, for I have conversed with him but once since his return from France, and that was only upon public affairs, and before I had obtained leave to come back; and it seems very surprising that a Minister who has obtained leave to return to his own country should rather choose to have that return attributed to his disgrace, than to his favour, at his own Court. Foreign Ministers frequently pretend to be better than they really are; but, I believe, I should be the first that ever desired to be thought ill at his Court, that was really not so, as I hope I am not.

Your Lordship very well knows that, when I came back here last summer, it was declared by their Majesties, and understood by me and every body else, that I was to return for good and all by the meeting of the Parliament; so that my writing to your Lordship lately upon that subject was only reminding you of a thing fixed, and not desiring any thing new when I came here. I told every body I should return to England after Christmas, and that the employment the King had done me the honour to give me required my attendance in England; so that my return was universally expected here, and is nothing new, nor can consequently be attributed to any of Monsieur Hop's surmises. If Monsieur Hop interprets my saying that I am personally sorry to leave this place, to be discontent, I cannot help it. It is true I have said that to every body here, and it is no more than what common civility, and even truth, requires from me. I have all the reason in the world personally to regret leaving this place, but that is no argument for my being discontented at my return.

As I suppose the King has seen this letter of Monsieur Hop's, I must desire your Lordship will be pleased to set this matter right with his Majesty, who would have very great reason to be offended, if he could believe that while on one side I beg his leave to return, on the other I complain and am dissatisfied with obtaining it. I should be extremely sorry, at my return to England, to meet with any ill-will or suspicions; for I solemnly declare I shall bring none with me. I desire to live in friendship with all that are in his Majesty's service; it was upon that foot that I took the employment I have, and upon that foot only will I keep it. I am ever, etc.

XLII.

TO LORD HARRINGTON.

Private.

HAGUE, *January* 16, N.S. 1731.

MY LORD,

I was extremely glad to find, by your Lordship's letter *apart*, that the trouble I had given both you and myself, about Monsieur Hop's intercepted letter, was unnecessary; and, indeed, I should never have thought it necessary to have taken the least notice of any of that gentleman's surmises, had I not found by Mr. Walpole's letter, that, at least, they had made some impression upon him.

Your Lordship will have seen by this time, from Mr. Robinson's letters, that I guessed pretty right as to our negotiation at Vienna, that it would still require couriers, and that Monsieur Dieden's demands would create the great difficulties; and this I find has exactly happened, though I am very sure the Court of Vienna was resolved to bring all possible facilities to Monsieur Dieden's demands. I should be wanting to the regard and friendship I profess for your Lordship, if I did not lay before you the fatal, but natural, and even necessary consequences that will attend the breaking off of this negotiation upon Electoral points, in which you are more particularly concerned, as being in your department.

This negotiation is already known by many, and suspected by all; should it break off, we must be more in the power of France than ever, who then, knowing that we have no resource left, will use us as they think fit, and insist upon dangerous pledges of our future fidelity; we must either enter into all their destructive schemes, or at best continue a good while longer, in the disagreeable and unpopular situation we are at present in. But this is not the worst neither; for it is impossible that this negotiation, so far advanced, can now break off, without additional acrimony on both sides; and in that case it cannot be expected but that the Emperor will take the natural advantage of declaring to the nation and to this Republic, that the public tranquillity might have been restored, that he had agreed to all the points that related to England and this country, but that Electoral considerations only prevented the conclusion of so desirable a work, and plunged us into so dangerous a war. What effect this will have, I need not say; our enemies will tell us with pleasure. Nor can I answer that, when the Republic shall once know it, as they certainly will know it, they will not conclude a separate peace, or a neutrality upon any terms; such are their apprehensions of a war, and especially of this war. The Pensionary at first apprehended difficulties from these Electoral points, even without knowing them, and only from the outward aspect of affairs in that part of the world, and he thought it would be impossible to adjust them by treaty; but he hoped they would be referred to future negotiations, after the harmony between the two Courts should be restored, and that then the Emperor might connive at what he could not publicly authorise. But if the whole negotiation should break off, upon any or all of these Electoral points, I think it is impossible to describe the fatal consequences that must result from it, both to the King, the Ministry, and the nation.

I find, by the accounts from Berlin, that the King of Prussia is frightened out of his wits, if he ever had any, and wants to be friends with the King; and for that reason desires a Minister may be sent there, which, in my opinion, should not be done; for he takes every instance of complaisance to be an indication of fear, and grows insolent upon it; whereas, if he is really frightened, as I believe he is, there is no imaginable meanness to which he will not stoop for his security; and I should think it would be better to make him take some of those steps first, before he meets with the least return from his Majesty. Grumkow's * conversion, I hope, will be cultivated in a proper manner; a sum of money will be well employed there, and put him too much in our power for him to go back. I am ever, etc.

XLIII.

TO GEO. TILSON, ESQ.

Private.

HAGUE, *January* 30, N.S. 1731.

SIR,

I received yesterday the favour of your letter of the 15th O.S.

I believe you will by this time have been a good deal disappointed with the despatches that Gould brought, but I am apt to think this was the last attempt of the Court of Vienna, to see if they could make any advantage of the disunion they are no strangers to, among the Allies; and that when they find it will not succeed, they will yield. If Mr. Robinson had stuck firmer to the treaty, it would have been better, for complaisance spoils that Court and all others. The secret is now no longer one, and the negotiation is talked of everywhere, which increases the necessity of finishing the affair immediately one way or another. How it came out, I don't know, but I am sure not from hence, where I own it has been better kept than I expected. If at last I should come back with an olive-branch, I doubt, it will not be before the spring is so far advanced, that I might bring a real one if I pleased! Pray make my compliments to Lord Harrington; I condole with him upon his gout, and am ever, etc.

XLIV.

TO GEO. TILSON, ESQ.

Private.

HAGUE, *February* 2, N.S., 1731.

SIR,

The post not being yet arrived, I have no letters to acknowledge from England, and I have nothing to write from hence, so

---

* Grumkow was the principal Minister of the King of Prussia; he died in 1739. See Preuss, *Lebens-geschichte Friedrichs des Grossen*, vol. i. p. 61, ed. 1832.—M.

I desire you will make my excuses and compliments to Lord Harrington.

I expect with impatience, the courier from England in his way to Vienna, and not without hopes that the Imperial Court will be wise enough to agree to what his Majesty shall finally resolve upon. As well as I can judge by Count Sinzendorf, this was a last attempt to try how far they could bring us, and how far France had reduced us to the necessity of being reconciled with them upon any terms; but when they shall receive the King's peremptory resolution and see the Addresses of both Houses of Parliament, which I hope will be as strong as possible, these considerations, together with the augmentation here, I flatter myself will make them think it their best way not to push our patience too far.

I give you many thanks for the pamphlet you sent me. It is well reasoned and clearly writ, but wants strength and spirit. They attack with invectives, and should be answered in the same manner, and we should not content ourselves with reasoning with enemies that fight with poisoned arrows; besides that, all reasoning is thrown away upon the people; they are utterly incapable of it.

I am, with great esteem, etc.

XLV.

TO LORD HARRINGTON.

Private.

HAGUE, February 14, N.S. 1731.

MY LORD,

Though my thoughts upon the treaty sent to Vienna, and upon the reception it will meet with there, very little deserve your Lordship's attention, yet since you command me to trouble you with them, I will tell you that I think the King has gone as far as he can well go, in this last treaty; and that if the Court of Vienna really intends to conclude, they cannot refuse this reasonable opportunity of doing it. But I confess, I very much apprehend the ill consequences that the death of the Duke of Parma and the memorial of Castelar* will have at that Court, that is so

_____

* Don Baltazar Patiño, brother of the Spanish Prime Minister, had been

easily elated by any favourable incident. Castelar's memorial will give them just reason to expect the utmost confusion among the Allies of Seville, and may make them think the opportunity favourable of seizing the tempting morsels that the Duke of Parma's death presents them with. Upon the whole, I fear delays and chicanes, that will be as bad as a refusal. These inconveniences would have been all prevented, if we had taken these measures when I went to England last, and was charged by the Pensionary to recommend them in the strongest manner, which I did, though to no purpose.

I am likewise far from being persuaded that our Electoral demands are made much more reasonable than they were. For why should not Mr. Hattorf have declared it to you, if they were? And by the way, I think there are some good reasons to suspect that he is not very desirous to facilitate the conclusion of this treaty. If the Court of Vienna has really no mind to conclude, but to break off advantageously, they will certainly lay the whole stress upon the Hanover points, which they may easily do, every one of these points being at best but doubtful; and yet it is certain we shall not recede from them all. If that should happen to be the case, and that case become public, as it certainly will, we shall be in a fine situation!

I am ever, etc.

XLVI.

TO LORD HARRINGTON.

Private.

Hague, *February* 16, 1731.

My Lord,

Count Sinzendorf having sent me word yesterday morning that his courier from Vienna was just arrived, and that he was going to forward him immediately to Count Kinski * in England, I went straight to Count Sinzendorf to see what this courier had brought him, besides what Mr. Robinson informed me of. As

created Marquis de Castelar. See his character in Coxe's *Memoirs of Spain*, ch. xxxii. He was at this period Spanish Ambassador at Paris, and had issued a declaration (January 29, 1731), that the king, his master, considered himself free from all the engagements contracted at Seville.—M.

* The Imperial Minister in England.

soon as I came in, Count Sinzendorf spoke to me in these words, with a great deal of surprise and concern: "You have kept the most material point a secret from me, and never told me that this whole affair turns upon the King's Electoral demands, which are such as it is not in the Emperor's power to comply with. The Emperor has showed the utmost facility in everything that concerned himself or depended upon him. He has given up the Ostend trade, by which the Netherlands will be ruined; he has consented to the introduction of Spanish troops into Italy, by which all his possessions there will be in danger; and yet all this is to avail him nothing, unless he engages to do what is not in his power to perform, but depends upon the empire, and to which the empire never can nor will consent. The present King demands ten times more as Elector of Hanover than ever the late King did, and yet everything between England and the Emperor is to be deemed null and void, unless these impossible demands are complied with; as you will see by this declaration of Mr. Robinson's;" and then he showed me a declaration of Mr. Robinson's, setting forth that "unless *tous les points Allemands* (those are the words) be settled to his Majesty's entire satisfaction, every thing else *doit être censé nul.*"

I told him that the King having a German Minister at Vienna to transact those affairs, I was an utter stranger to them, and that, was I to know them, I was too ignorant of the laws and constitution of the empire to be able to judge how far they were consistent or inconsistent with them; but that I took it for granted impossibilities could not be asked. He said, Yes, but they were; and ran into a long detail of the several demands; and then concluded by saying, that it was to no purpose for the Emperor to explain himself so fully as otherwise he might have done, upon the points concerning England only, since they were to be of no effect, unless these impossibilities were granted at the same time.

As Count Kinski in England will receive the same accounts, I submit to your Lordship whether this can be done with any other view than that I have so long apprehended, of declaring to the world that the negotiation broke off only upon Electoral points. Whether it really breaks off upon these points or no, or whether for other reasons the Court of Vienna should have no mind to conclude it, and what effect this will have everywhere, but especially in England, I leave your Lordship to judge.

I inform your Lordship of this affair by this letter *apart* that you may make just what use you think fit of it. Count Sinzendorf showed me a letter from his father-in-law, wherein he expresses not only the desire, but the impatience of his Court, to conclude with the maritime powers. How sincere this is, a little time will now discover; I own I can form to myself no opinion of the event of this treaty. In good politics, I think the Emperor ought by all means to agree to it; but whether his ardent desire of the totality of Italy, joined to some seemingly favourable incidents for him at present, may not make him reject or delay it, which is in a manner the same thing, I cannot determine.

I am ever, etc.

XLVII.

TO LORD HARRINGTON.

Private.

HAGUE, *February* 27, N.S. 1731.

MY LORD,

I received last night the honour of your Lordship's letter *apart* of the 13th, by Browne, the messenger. I am very glad of the orders your Lordship says Mr. Robinson has to sign, abstractedly from the Electoral points, and Monsieur Dieden to refer them to a future negotiation, and I hope these orders will be executed, though I confess I have great doubts upon that affair; there are too many good reasons for and against the Court of Vienna's concluding the treaty, for me to judge which will prevail; but I am sure all reasons concur for us to hope for the conclusion of it.

If Mr. Finch is impatient to come here, I am sure I am not less so to return to England; and if he has a mind to take the trouble of bringing the Republic into the treaty of Vienna, in case it be concluded, I will most cheerfully resign to him both the trouble and the credit of doing it. I have staid here till now, not by choice, but by obedience; and I shall be gladder to see Mr. Finch here whenever he comes, than he can possibly be to come. The

Cardinal's* mistake in the date of the full powers was too small a one not to give just suspicions that he had better information than he ought to have had.

I am ever, etc.

XLVIII.

TO GEO. TILSON, ESQ.

Private.

HAGUE, *March* 9, N.S. 1731.

SIR,

I received on Wednesday last the favour of yours of the 19th past, O.S. As I have had no commands of late from Lord Harrington, and as nothing has occurred here worth mentioning, I shall not trouble his Lordship by this post.

The States received yesterday a courier from Paris, with letters from Mr. Vandermeer, of the 15th Feb., and Messrs. Van Hoey and Hugronie; but as those letters contain nothing but what you will have had directly from Mr. Keene† and Lord Waldegrave,‡ I will not trouble you with repeating any particulars of them.

It seems pretty difficult to determine which of the two ought to be most credited, the King of Spain or Monsieur Patiño.§ His Catholic Majesty says one thing to the French Minister, Monsieur Patiño says just the contrary to ours, and assures us he is to be believed, and not the King. As the one does not know, and the other does not care, what he says, for my own part, I suspend my judgment. The Cardinal has declared to the Dutch Ministers that though our negotiation with Vienna is a violation of our treaties with France, yet he is not at all surprised at it, having never expected better from a nation that always sacrifices all considerations to their own interest. So that neither his Eminency nor I shall be in the least surprised, for I never expected better from him. I am, with great esteem, etc.

* Cardinal Fleury, Cardinal and Prime Minister in France, 1726, born 1653; died 1743.

† Afterwards Sir Benjamin, and British Minister at the Court of Spain, during many years; an active and able public servant.—M.

‡ Ambassador at Paris.—M.

§ Don Joseph Patiño was at this time the Minister highest in favour with the King, and (what was still more essential) the Queen of Spain.—M.

XLIX.

TO GEO. TILSON, ESQ.

Private.

HAGUE, *March* 27, N.S. 1731.

SIR,

Having received no commands from Lord Harrington by yesterday's post, I have nothing to write to him by this, so must desire you will make him my compliments and excuses.

I am very much surprised at not having yet received a courier from Vienna, and the more so, because Mr. Robinson, by his letter of the 14th, acquaints me that everything was adjusted, and Friday the 16th fixed for signing.* Had the Treaty been then signed, I should have received it some days ago. I don't know what to ascribe this delay to, but the natural slowness and trifling of that Court, for I am convinced they are sincere in the main.

The French Ambassador here grows sullen and affects an indifference about the event of this negotiation, though every now and then he betrays his uneasiness at it. He has not mentioned it to me yet nor I to him. The conduct of Spain is too extraordinary, and I admire the frankness of their declarations, that they will have no regard to the ties of faith, honour or solemn treaties, but will join with the Devil if he will but do what they want. I own I credit these professions so much, that I am persuaded we shall soon see something come out of their separate negotiations with France.

I am with truth, etc.

---

* The treaty was signed on that day, and is usually called the second treaty of Vienna, to distinguish it from that which was concluded in 1725. According to Coxe's summary of its terms, "it was a defensive alliance, and stipulated a reciprocal guarantee of mutual rights and possessions; on the part of England, to guarantee the Emperor's succession, according to the Pragmatic Sanction; on that of the Emperor, to abolish the Ostend Company and all trade to the East Indies from any one of the Austrian Netherlands, to secure the succession of Don Carlos to Parma and Tuscany, and not to oppose the introduction of Spanish garrisons. Thus was this great and difficult task of preventing a general war accomplished with an address and secrecy that reflected high honour on those who conducted it." (*Memoirs of Walpole*, vol. i. p. 346.) Lord Chesterfield tells us that in reality it was concluded between himself, the Pensionary, and Count Sinzendorf at the Hague.—M. See p. 620.

P.S. Having been solicited by many people here to procure them some tickets in the lottery if there should be one, I wish you would apply where it is proper, that I may be set down for one hundred.

L.
TO DR. ARBUTHNOT.

(Extract in Mahon's History of England, vol. ii. p. 255.)

HAGUE, *April* 20, N.S. 1731.

I shall come over well prepared to suffer with patience, for I am now in the school of patience here; and I find treating with about two hundred sovereigns of different tempers and professions is as laborious as treating with one fine woman who is at least of two hundred minds in one day.

LI.
TO LORD HARRINGTON.

Private.

HAGUE, *June* 10, 1731.

MY LORD,

I forward this courier to your Lordship with the melancholy account Captain Guydickens sends from Berlin.

I know from other hands, too, that the match with the Prince of Bareith will now be consummated, if his Majesty does not take the Princess Royal for the Prince of Wales without any other condition; but upon this nice subject I do not pretend to give any opinion, one way or another.

I am, etc.

LII.
TO GEORGE TILSON, ESQ.

Private.

HAGUE, *July* 27, N.S. 1731.

SIR,

Having received no commands from Lord Harrington by this post, I will not trouble him with a letter, and, indeed, I am both weary and ashamed of sending him nothing from hence but ridiculous causes and useless complaints of delays. The province of Holland has not yet, in form, confirmed the act of concurrence, because the towns of Dort and Leyden had some notable scruple, which they wanted to consult their principals upon. However, the sentiments of Holland are enough known to point out to the other provinces what they ought to do.* In two or three days Count Sinzendorf expects the arrival of his courier here, and with a satisfactory answer; if so, you may look upon the affair as done. It is impossible for any body, who is not very well acquainted with this form of government, to have a notion of the strange delays and absurd difficulties that have arisen in the course of this negotiation; but to give you some image of it, represent to yourself an English Minister endeavouring to carry a point by the single merit of the point itself, without the assistance of reward and punishments through what our patriots would call an independent and unbiassed House of Commons, that is, an assembly of people influenced by every thing but by the Court; and then judge how soon and how easily it would pass! This is the case of the Pensionary and Greffier; with this difference, too, that here unanimity is necessary. Without the power of either hopes or fears, they must labour to unite a great number of heads, many of them incapable of judging at all, and yet obstinately pretending to it; many of them incapable of judging right, but yet obstinate in the wrong; and others who always lay hold of such public occasions to extort private advantages for their towns, themselves, and their families. This being the nature of this government, it is rather to be wondered at that any thing is done here at all, than that it is long a doing. For my own part, if I would teach any body the Christian virtues of patience, forbearance, and long-suffering, I would send them to negotiate a treaty here!   I am, with great truth, etc.

LIII.

TO GEORGE TILSON, ESQ.

Private.

HAGUE, *September* 11, N.S. 1731.

SIR,

I return you my thanks for the favour of your letter of the 24th August, O.S.

* See this point more fully explained, p. 618.

When once our conferences begin here, I expect abundance of wrangling, ridiculous doubts, and absurd suspicions; but I think we shall at last get the better of them all. I have let fall some insinuations that I think begin to operate; they are extremely sensible of fear here, for which reason I have circulated some lessons that begin to have a good effect.

Madame Fénélon arrived here last week. She was sent by the Court of France to remove the suspicions her husband's drum had occasioned here. This example will, I believe, be a warning to married Ministers not to beat their drum rashly.

Count Golofkin is expected here every day from Paris, with the character of Ambassador Extraordinary. I should be glad to know whether his present Majesty, or the late King, have ever, by any Act, given the title of Emperor or Empress to the Czar or Czarina.

I am, with truth and esteem, etc.

LIV.

TO GEORGE TILSON, ESQ.

Private.

HAGUE, *December* 18, N.S. 1731.

SIR,

I received yesterday the favour of your letter, of the 3rd, O.S.

I reckon our applications in favour of our distressed brethren of Salzburg* will have the common fate of such applications; of being received and not minded. All we can do for them at last, I believe, will be to pray for them.

I am sorry the Emperor's irresolution continues so long, that the courier is not yet come. The points in question are very worthy of the tradesmen that started them here; but, in my mind, are infinitely below the cares of a Prince and Ministry.

I am glad the Duke of Lorraine is to see the King of Prussia; for he will then see what he could never believe without seeing. He will find some difference between his reception in England, and his entertainment in the *corps de garde* of Berlin.

* The Protestants at Salzburg were at this period undergoing persecution from their sovereign, the Prince Archbishop.—M.

I am sorry I can be of no use to your friend Marquis du Quesne, but the contracts are made, as usual, for wine for the next year, and I have long been engaged to others in case of any alteration. I am still more sorry that I cannot serve your nephew, but the place you mention must be filled up by one who is versed in the accounts of the household, and is not an employment for anything of a gentleman. Besides, I had before disposed of it to one Skinner, who had a sort of a right to it.

I am, with great esteem, etc.

LV.

TO THE COUNTESS OF SUFFOLK.*

SCARBOROUGH, *August*, 1733.

MADAM,

I have heard that ladies often command, what they would be sorry to be obeyed in. I do not know whether your command to me to write to you from hence was not of that sort; however, I determined at all events to obey; for if you have really desired to hear from a very faithful servant of yours, I should have been very sorry to have omitted it; and if not, I have at once the excuse of obedience, and the pleasure of revenge, by taking you at your word.

* During the year and a-half which had elapsed since the date of the last letter in this collection, a most important change had occurred in Lord Chesterfield's life. Soon after his return to England, he had in common with several other holders of office, taken part against Sir Robert Walpole's famous Excise Bill. So general was the resistance, that the Minister found it necessary on the 11th of April 1732, to give up his favourite scheme. But he resolved to proceed with the utmost rigour against its opponents. On the 13th of the same month, as Lord Chesterfield was going up the great stairs of St. James's Palace, he was summoned home to receive a message from the Duke of Grafton, and this message proved to be an order from the King to surrender his white staff as Lord Steward. In like manner, Lords Burlington, Clinton, Stair and Marchmont were dismissed from other offices at Court, and the Duke of Bolton and Lord Cobham, holding only commissions in the army, were deprived of their regiments. From this time forward, we find Lord Chesterfield in eager opposition against Walpole, leagued with Pulteney and Bolingbroke, and with his own partners in dismissal, especially Stair and Marchmont.—M. See Lord Macaulay's Essay on "William Pitt, Earl of Chatham."

This preamble being finished, which (by the way) is generally the most difficult part of a letter, my difficulty begins, which is, what to say. Compliments you shall have none; they are sacred to falsehood, and would be profaned by sincerity; so that here is a great and luxuriant branch of epistolary commerce entirely cut off.

The next thing required in a letter is news; but as to that, I may with great truth make use of that short but comprehensive form of words of most letter-writers in the country to their friends in town,—which is, this place is so barren of news, and affords so few materials for a letter, that it would be but trespassing upon your patience, to trouble you with a long scroll from hence. However, you shall have the present state of Scarborough such as it is.

The ladies here are innumerable, and I really believe they all come for their healths, for they look very ill. The men of pleasure are Lord Carmichael,* Colonel Ligonier,† and the celebrated Tom Paget,‡ who attend upon the Duke of Argyle all day, and dance with the pretty ladies at night. Here are besides hundreds of Yorkshire beaux, who play the inferior parts, and, as it were, only tumble, while those three dance upon the high ropes of gallantry.

The grave people are mostly malignants, or, in ministerial language, notorious Jacobites, such as Lord Stair, Marchmont, Anglesea,§ and myself, not to mention many of the House of Commons of equal disaffection. Moreover Pulteney and Lord Carteret are expected here soon; so that if the Ministry do not make a plot of this meeting, it is plain they do not want one for this year.

The people of this town are at present in great consternation, upon a report they have heard from London, which, if true, they think will ruin them. I confess I do not believe it; not but that there is something probable enough in it. They are informed, that, considering the vast consumption of these waters, there is

---

* John, eldest son of the Earl of Hyndford.—M.

† Afterwards Lord Ligonier and a Field Marshal.—M.

‡ Probably General Thomas Paget, ancestor of the Marquis of Anglesey. See a note to the Suffolk Letters, vol. i. p. 8.—M.

§ Arthur Annesley, fifth Earl of Anglesea.—M.

a design laid of *excising* them next Session ; and moreover, that as bathing in the sea is become the general practice of both sexes, and as the Kings of England have always been allowed to be masters of the seas, every person so bathing shall be gauged, and pay so much per foot square as their cubical bulk amounts to. I own there are many objections to this scheme, which, no doubt, occur to you ; but to be sure too there is one less than to the last, for this tax being singly upon water, it is evident it would be an ease to the landed interest, which it is as plain the other would not have been.

We have it here that the Prince of Orange does not come over. I can hardly believe it, but wish I knew whether it be so or no, for I should take my measures accordingly of coming to town.

I wish you may not think from all this stuff that these waters are apt to fly into one's head, which may discourage you from ever coming here, though I am persuaded they would do you a great deal of good ; but, to convince you that at least they have done my head no hurt, I assure you no man living is with greater truth or esteem,

Madam, yours, etc.

I must not forget my compliments to Miss Hobart.*, I make my compliments likewise to those who will open and peruse this letter before you do.†

LVI.

TO THE COUNTESS OF SUFFOLK.

SCARBOROUGH, *August* 17, 1733.

MADAM,

Though I doubted last time whether I had a justifiable excuse for troubling you, I am now sure that the honour of your letter has not only given me a fair pretence, but has even laid me under a very agreeable necessity of doing it.

There is hardly anything (though ever so valuable in itself) that may not receive some additional value from a certain con-

---

* Lady Suffolk's niece, Dorothy Hobart.—M.

† In the correspondence of the most celebrated men of this period, as Bolingbroke, Swift, etc., it is remarkable how frequently apprehensions are expressed or implied of their letters being opened at the Post Office.—M.

currence of circumstances; this is the case of your letter, which, though I should at all times have valued as I ought, yet in this particular juncture I must look upon it as a most uncommon and uncourt-like piece of friendship and intrepidity. It may, for ought I know, have brought you within the statute of Edward III. as aiding, abetting, and comforting the King's enemies; for I can depose that it *comforted* me, and there are enough ready to depose that I am an enemy of the King's; so that, by an induction not very much strained for the law, your generosity has drawn you into high treason. Besides, as to the contents of your letter, did you reflect upon the strict examinations it was to undergo before it reached me; did you consider that it was to be submitted to the penetration of Lord Lovell, and to the more slow, but not less sure sagacity of Mr. Carteret; * that from them a faithful copy of it was to be transmitted to others of not inferior abilities, and known dabs at finding out mysteries; and could you then hope that your allegory of commerce and cribbage could escape undiscovered, especially since the influence of the *pair royal* and the advantage of the *knave*, at those games, give so obvious a key to it ?

By what you intimate, the party will come over at a very convenient time for me, that is, as I suppose, about Michaelmas; by which time all my country excursions will, I hope, be over, and I quietly in my easy chair, by a good fire, in St. James's Square. I leave this place (thank God!) to-morrow, and go to Cobham's † for five or six days, where I shall diligently look for a certain busto that I heard much talked of there last year; if I meet with it, woe betide it; for we certainly shall not part without a distich or two. From thence I shall take London in my way to Norfolk, in which county I (though unworthy) shall presume to stay about a fortnight. Should I be seized there as contraband, I give you fair warning, I shall produce your letter as a passport.‡

---

* Thomas Lord Lovell and the Hon. Edward Carteret were at this time joint Postmasters-General.—M.

† Stowe, then the seat of Lord Cobham, who intended to place Lady Suffolk's bust in his newly-built Temple of Friendship.—M.

‡ An allusion to Sir Robert Walpole as his opponent, and to Lady Suffolk herself as his friend, both of them being natives of Norfolk.—M.

Your Hampton Court recreations, I find, give the lie to those who complain of the uncertainty and instability of Courts, or must at least claim an exception for yours, since the same joyous measures have, for these sixteen revolving years, been steadily pursued without interruption. Commerce must surely have played its cards excellently well, to have kept its ground so long, or —— the first courteous opener of this letter may insert the rest.

I do not think the Duke of Argyle very much the better for these waters; his head shakes extremely, and he is much dispirited. He goes away to-morrow too, and passes the rest of this year at Petersham.

I have not been so long in writing this letter as I have been trying, but in vain, to finish it with some ingenious paragraph, that should neatly introduce my being, with the utmost regard and attachment,

Madam, yours, etc.

P.S.—I am obliged in gratitude to repeat my compliments to Miss Hobart, as the only person that has blushed on my score these many years.

LVII.

TO ALEXANDER, EARL OF MARCHMONT.*

LONDON, October 5, 1733.

MY DEAR LORD,

I received your letter of the 13th September by the post, and just now Lord Grange † has delivered to me that of the 29th August. I will not take up your time with any compliments to you upon the part you are so good as to take in whatever concerns me; ‡ anything of that kind, I am persuaded, will be as

---

* Alexander, Earl of Marchmont, was born in 1675, and was Member in the Scottish Parliament for Berwickshire, when the Act of Union passed. In 1716, he was named British Minister at the Court of Copenhagen, and in 1725, one of the Ambassadors to the Congress of Cambray. He was now, like Lord Chesterfield, engaged in active opposition against Sir Robert Walpole.—M.

† The Honourable James Erskine, brother to the Earl of Mar, who headed the rebellion of 1715; a Lord of Session.—M.

‡ On the 5th of September, Lord Chesterfield had married Melusina, in her own right Countess of Walsingham.

unnecessary with you, as it is inconsistent with that real zeal and truth with which you know I belong to you.

I am glad the prospect of your elections is so good, but I hope it will not be bragged of. The Court should, if possible, be lulled into a security upon that score; and I could wish our friends would rather seem to despond than discover their strength, which the Court has always means in their hands to lessen when they once know where it is. The Ministry are exceedingly perplexed, both with their foreign and domestic affairs; their elections promise ill for them everywhere. The Duke of Newcastle will probably be beaten in Sussex; the Duke of Dorset * most certainly will in Kent; and so of very many other places, where the Court used formerly always to carry it.

Their foreign affairs are still worse; the French are at last most certainly in earnest, and have lately concluded an offensive alliance with the King of Sardinia.† The Spanish armament is avowedly intended for Italy; and by this time, I believe, the French army has passed the Rhine. France, Spain, and the Emperor severally claim our guarantees, each asserting the other to be the aggressor. In this difficult situation the Ministers will, I believe, call the Parliament pretty early in November, in order to have their sanction for whatever part they take, and to have it supposed to be by the advice of Parliament—a point which very well deserves our consideration how to act in it.

In these circumstances, the Ministers, I think, cannot hold it long, unless they are again supported by those miracles that hitherto have been wrought in their favour upon every crisis.

I know very little of Lord Grange, who will give your Lordship this letter, and his general character is a very good one; however, I must acquaint you, that he has been frequently with the Ministers, and, I am informed, is by no means ill with Lord Isla.‡ You will make what use of this hint you think proper,

* Lionel Cranfield, seventh Earl and first Duke of Dorset, Lord Lieutenant of Ireland, and Lord Warden of the Cinque Ports.—M. See next letter.

† These alarms refer to the short war produced by the death of the King of Poland (February, 1733), and the election of his successor.—M.

‡ Lord Justice-General in 1710 for life; Keeper of the Privy Seal of Scotland in 1721; and of its Great Seal in 1733. He long managed the affairs of Scotland, and became Duke of Argyle by the death of his

either to try him more, or trust him less; but I beg you will not mention it as coming from me.

If the Parliament should meet before Christmas, I take it for granted you will be in town for the first meeting; but if it should not meet till the usual time after Christmas, I still think we ought all to be in town a fortnight or three weeks before, to take our measures together.

I am, with the greatest truth and respect, etc.

LVII.

TO ALEXANDER, EARL OF MARCHMONT.

LONDON, *June* 15, 1734.

MY DEAR LORD,

I received the honour of your letter of the 8th, by the courier that arrived here last Thursday. Though it did not bring me the news I hoped for, it brought me the news I expected.* You had not the necessary arms for victory, for you had only justice on your side, which in Scotland, as well as here, is not alone sufficient. Lord Carteret, Mr. Pulteney, and myself, the only three of your friends now in town, have met and considered all the papers, upon which I refer you to Carteret's

brother in 1743. The following epigram on his "Improvements near Hounslow Heath" is among Lord Chesterfield's pieces of poetry (p. 203. ed. 1778).—M.

" Old Isla, to show his fine delicate taste
In improving his gardens purloined from the waste,
Bid his gardener one day to open his views,
By cutting a couple of grand avenues;
No particular prospect his Lordship intended,
But left it to chance how his walks should be ended.
With transports of joy he beheld at one view-end,
His favourite prospect, a church that was ruined!
But alas! what a sight did the next view exhibit!
At the end of the walk hung a rogue on a gibbet!
He beheld it and wept, for it caused him to muse on
Full many a Campbell that died with his shoes on.
All amazed and aghast at the ominous scene,
He ordered it quick to be closed up again,
With a clump of Scotch fir by way of *a screen*!"

* Of the Election of the Scots Representative Peers, and of Lord Marchmont's defeat on that occasion.—M.

answer, that I may not trouble you with an unnecessary repetition of what you will have better from him; all I will say upon the subject is, that whatever you may think proper to do, and in whatever shape, I will support and labour to the utmost of my power. I should think it might be very possible to get some of the lowest of your venal Peers to come to our bar and confess the money they took to vote for the Court list—which, if it could be obtained, would be such strong evidence, as would be hard to be resisted. I am told there is a Lord ——, that Duke Hamilton might possibly prevail with, and a Lord ——, that the Duke of Montrose might persuade. If that were possible, it would be worth while to make them lusty promises, and even to give them some little money in present; for two witnesses who have actually taken money and voted for it, are worth ten who have only been offered and refused it.

You will likewise receive from other hands a thought that occurred to Pulteney, and which Carteret and I approved of, and which I am so fond of, that I cannot help mentioning it to you, however; it is, that some Scotch Commoner, well armed with facts and proofs, should get up in the House of Commons and impeach Isla of high crimes and misdemeanours, which no doubt the corrupt influencing of elections amounts to. This would be a capital stroke, and affect the master as well as the man, and I should think exceeding practicable, considering the open and impudent proceeding of that worthy Lord.

The elections of your Commons have gone better than I expected, and I take a particular part in the success of your family. I shall always be extremely desirous of showing Lord Polwarth * and Mr. Hume the esteem and regard they both so well deserve, and which, even if they did not, they would always find from me upon your account. You should certainly have your petition presented the very first day of the Session in our House, and be ready with all the proofs that are necessary to support it, as well as with all the circumstances that may conduce to blacken their cause; for, though I am sorry to say it, ' fear you must expect more justice from your appeals to the rest of mankind, than from

---

* Hugh Lord Polwarth and his twin brother Alexander Hume (Campbell), sons of the Earl of Marchmont, first came into Parliament at the general election of 1734.—M.

your appeals to our House, where now our strength is so much diminished, and by the loss of that part of it which, without any compliment to you, we could the least afford to spare.

Everything here is in the situation you left it. The President * is as contemptible and subservient as ever; Dorset, you may imagine, is so too; notwithstanding which, he is so ill at Court, that I verily believe, and I am sure I hope, that he will be laid aside with only his Wardenship of the Cinque Ports. Had people any spirit or honesty, now would be the time to exert it, for we have certainly two hundred and fifty in the House of Commons; which number, if well conducted and united, cannot long remain a minority.

I must not omit mentioning to you, that it will surely be very necessary for your Lords to attend and solicit your petition in town at the opening of the Parliament, for solicitations *vivâ voce*, and of the persons themselves concerned, have much more weight than remote applications by letter, or the intervention of friends. I really think this absolutely necessary, abstractedly from my own private wishes of seeing those people for whom I have the most sincere regard.

You see in the public newspapers all I know or can tell you in relation to foreign affairs. What the French will think fit to do after they have taken Philipsbourg,† I know no more than our Ministers; but this I know, that they have it all in their hands, and may do whatever they please, for neither the wisdom of our councils nor the terror of our forces will check them in their career.

I forgot that this letter grows to an excessive length, while I am indulging the pleasure I have in conversing with you. You must excuse, however, the trouble you have, from that perfect esteem and regard with which I shall ever be, etc.

* Spencer, Earl of Wilmington.

† Surrendered on the 18th July following to the French, under D'Asfeld, the Duke of Berwick, who commanded the siege, having been killed. Prince Eugene could not attempt to relieve the place on account of his inferiority of force.

LIX.

TO SOLOMON DAYROLLES, ESQ.*

LONDON, *June* 23, O. S. 1734.

MY DEAR CHEVALIER,

I won't make you any excuses for this application, because I am very sure you are always glad to help an old friend. My business is, in short, this : I want four dozen of shirts; two dozen of them to be of Holland that comes to about ten shillings the English ell; the other two dozen, about fourteen shillings the English ell. Take the money of Monsieur Vanneck, and give him a bill upon me for it. Though I have great regard for your judgment in most things, yet in linen I believe it will not be amiss, if you can get the assistance of Madame Dayrolles,† to whom I would not apply directly myself, because, knowing her politeness, I was sure it would be putting her to the trouble of an answer; which trouble I thought it civiller to save her by your means. I desire you will make my best compliments to her and your uncle, who, I hope, are both in perfect health.

Do you divert yourself pretty well at the Hague? Do the suppers and parties of pleasure go on in the Welderen family as they used to do? A friend of theirs and yours, Lady Denbigh, has had bad diversion here, for she has lost every thing she had in the world, which she had unfortunately left in her house at Twickenham.‡

* Mr. Solomon Dayrolles was nephew of James Dayrolles, Esq., the King's Resident at the Hague, who died in 1739. He attained the same post in 1747, by Lord Chesterfield's influence; and he was afterwards Minister at Brussels, but for many years before his death he had come back to reside in England. On his appointment at the Hague, Horace Walpole (ever caustic and often unjust) describes him as follows : " This curious Minister has always been a led-captain to the Dukes of Grafton and Richmond; used to be sent to auctions for them, and to walk in the Park with their daughters, and once went dry-nurse to Holland with them. He has belonged too a good deal to my Lord Chesterfield." (To Sir H. Mann, May 19, 1747.)—M.

† His aunt, Mrs. James Dayrolles.

‡ Lord Denbigh had lent to Monsieur de Chavigny, the French minister then in England, his house at Twickenham, which, during M. de Chavigny's occupation, was by some accident burnt down to the ground. He had married some years before a Dutch lady, Isabella, daughter of Peter de

I hope you continue well with your uncle and aunt. The regard you have always had for them, I am sure, very well deserves their kindness, as their kindness to you deserves your acknowledgments; I wish you all the good that can happen to you, and am, with great truth and esteem, etc.

LX.

TO THE COUNTESS OF SUFFOLK.

ISLEWORTH, *July* 15, 1734.

MADAM,

You will be surprised at this letter; but as I took it into my head that it might possibly be of use to one that both you and I interest ourselves for, I would not omit it.

My hero * is now entirely out of the question, for the place of Master of the Horse, and to my certain knowledge the Duke of Richmond† will soon be declared. This will be the second time that he will have been put by what every body has looked upon to be his right, for the sake of two people of such infinite consequence as Lord Godolphin‡ and the Duke of Richmond. And I will prophesy that this will not be the last time of his being served so, if he takes this patiently; I should therefore think it would be very right for him to renew his applications with vigour where he had made them before, and also to apply directly to the Queen, to whom, I am told, he has not yet mentioned it, and there to insist upon it as his right. I know very well this application will signify nothing as to the place of Master of the Horse, which is as good as given to the Duke of Richmond; but the effect I propose from it is, that his insisting strongly will convince those who cannot love but can fear, that he will resent it as strongly when it is disposed of to another, and make them think it necessary to satisfy him by something else; which they may easily do

Yong, of Utrecht, who is described by Lady Mary W. Montagu, in 1725 as " entertaining enough,

" ———extremely gay,
Loves music, company, and play."
                    (*Letters*, vol. ii. p. 172, ed. 1837.)—M.

* Probably Lord Pembroke "who is more than once in this correspondence called *the hero*." (Note to *Suffolk Letters*, vol. ii. p. 74.)

† Charles, second Duke.   ‡ Francis, second Earl.

if they please, by taking away the gold key from that cypher, Lord Godolphin, and continuing him his pension, with which he will be as well satisfied, and sleep on the Court side. But this is what my hero can never expect to obtain from any motive but their fears, which will rise in proportion to his insisting upon it before it is given away, and to the resentment that he will show afterwards.

You will make what use you please of these thoughts of mine; you may either show them as mine, or hint them as your own, according as you approve of them, or think best as to him. All I desire is, that you will not mention me in this matter to any body but him.

I am persuaded you will not think that I mean by this to exasperate him, in hope of getting him over to the Opposition; for in my mind it would not be the way; since I am convinced that this is the only way, and even a likely way of getting him to be Groom of the Stole; whereas without this method they would go on to use him so ill, that we should be sure of him at last. I can assure you it is only my value and friendship for him that makes me suggest these means as the most likely to procure him what he would like, and what, with regard to the world, considering his rank and long services, he ought in decency to have.

> I am, with the utmost truth and respect, etc.

Pray prevail with him to speak to the Queen herself, without which there is nothing to be done; and to mention in that audience the manner in which he was put by for Lord Godolphin and his own acquiescence at that time.

LXI.

A M. SOLOMON DAYROLLES.

à Londres, *ce* 19 *Aout*, V.S. 1734.

Mon cher Chevalier,

J'ai reçu votre lettre, avec le compte y-joint. Monsieur Vanneck écrit par cet ordinaire à son frère à la Haye, de vous fournir tel argent que vous lui demanderez; de sorte que vous prendrez pour payer la toile, la façon, &c. Je crois que le retour de Monsieur Finch pourra être une bonne occasion de les envoyer, car il revient ici bientôt.

Si vous pouviez persuader à votre oncle de solliciter Mr. Walpole,* pour qu'il pût se démettre de son emploi en votre faveur, bien entendu qu'il recevroit lui tous les appointemens sa vie durant, cela vous l'assureroit en tout cas; et Monsieur Walpole pourroit très facilement le moyenneur, s'il vouloit. Car sans cette précaution, je crains ce Monsieur Pelham qui est avec lui, et qui ne manqueroit pas de s'y fourrer, en cas que votre oncle vint à manquer.

Si vous pouvez porter votre oncle à agréer cette proposition, qu'il fasse en sorte que Monsieur Van Borsele, et quelques-uns de la Régence, s'intéressent en votre faveur, auprès de Monsieur Walpole; car dans la conjoncture présente, il aura de grands égards pour la recommandation de ces messieurs.

Adieu, Chevalier. Craignez Dieu, divertissez-vous, et buvez frais autant que faire se pourra.

Je serai toujours, votre, etc.

LXII.

TO ALEXANDER, EARL OF MARCHMONT.

LONDON, August 27, 1734.

My DEAR LORD,

As this courier carries you the three papers that contain the joint opinions of the Duke of Montrose,† Mr. Pulteney, and myself, which likewise concurred with Lord Carteret's, though we did not see him, and as you will receive at the same time letters from the Duke of Montrose and Pulteney, explaining our sentiments upon all points referred to us better and more fully than I am able to do it myself, there remains very little for me in this letter but to thank your Lordship for the honour of yours of the 12th, and to assure you very sincerely of the sense I shall always have of your friendship. However, you will give me leave to

---

* Horace Walpole, the elder, brother of Sir Robert, and created, in 1756, Lord Walpole of Wolterton. He was now appointed to succeed Mr. Finch at the Hague, but with the rank of Ambassador.—M.

† The Duke of Montrose had the Great Seal of Scotland, but was dismissed for opposing Sir Robert Walpole on the Excise Bill in 1733.—M.

touch upon the three principal points contained in our joint papers, since I know that, at so great a distance, things can never be too fully explained or too often repeated. The advantage conversation gives one of debating, objecting, and replying, is wanted in writing, and must be supplied as well as one can.

The first point of taking up the matter of the election * originally in our House, without any application from your Lordships, is absolutely impossible; for you very well remember that, in our inquiries into the affairs of the South Sea, the strong objection of the Court was, that there was no application from any of the parties concerned, and therefore it was to be presumed that none of them were aggrieved; to which we replied, that the parties were too numerous to concert an application, and many of them, such as minors, orphans, etc., are not in circumstances to be able to do it, and that what was everybody's business was nobody's.

But in this case, the same objection of the Court would be much stronger, without admitting in any degree of the same reply; for here the parties are few, the method of complaint is pointed out by precedents, and even your own protests seem to imply a future application to Parliament. Suppose, for instance, one should try to take it up originally in our House, what would be the event of it? We should certainly be answered in the manner I have mentioned. The question would be put in two or three hours, which we should lose by a great majority, and the whole matter quashed at once, without any facts appearing to the public; whereas, upon a petition, whatever may be the main event of it, at least in the course of our proceedings upon it, those infamous practices will be laid open to all mankind, and condemned by everybody but the House.

As to the second point, the petition itself, though I am very far from expecting the effect from it I could wish,—I mean either that of changing the sixteen, or of vacating the election,—both which are certainly impossible, I still expect a good effect from it. It will lay open to the whole world, in an authentic manner, the whole scene of iniquity and corruption. It must fix upon Isla crimes that will beget questions of censure, from which he can only be acquitted by the scandalous partiality of a majority

* Of the Scots Representative Peers.

as corrupt as himself; and it will be necessary to accompany and assist the other step to be taken in the House of Commons. The petition, being conceived in the general terms in which we have drawn it, leaves us wholly at liberty to push those points only, which, from the evidence we have to support them, or from the nature of circumstances at that time, may seem the likeliest to be brought to bear. Lord Tweeddale's * reasonings in his letter to the Duke of Montrose are unanswerable, and plainly prove that no other fruit is to be hoped for from this petition than what I have mentioned. Evidence you certainly have not sufficient to set aside votes enough to give you a majority; and our House is not at present of a complexion to vacate the election, because of some corrupt practices proved upon some of the electors.

Our great hopes, then, arise from the third point,—the impeachment in the House of Commons. This step, taken there with vigour, the same day that your petition is lodged in our House, will strike both the agent and his master, and may have (as such unexpected steps often have) a greater effect than can be foreseen. There will certainly be evidence enough to fix the high crime of corruption upon Isla, though there is not enough to retrieve the mischiefs that have been occasioned by it. From the turn this takes in the House of Commons we must regulate our conduct as to the petition in our House. They must help one another; and from one, or other, or both, I own I expect some good will arise.

What stand we can make this Session must be in the House of Commons, where we are much stronger than we were last Session; our numbers are a good two hundred and forty, which, if well conducted, cannot, in my opinion, remain long a minority. In the House of Lords our strength is so much decreased, that we must wait for accidents and circumstances from without doors, before we can hope to do anything.

You see in the public newspapers the wretched situation of our foreign affairs, as well as I could inform you. The Ministers, who, I am persuaded, are determined at all events not to engage in a war, are labouring at all the Courts in Europe to bring on some negotiations, or something like a Congress, in order to hold out

* John, fourth Marquis of Tweeddale. He was afterwards Secretary of State for Scotland.— M.

a fallacious prospect of peace at the opening of the new Parliament. But, I believe, their endeavours will be very ineffectual; for I cannot suppose that the Allies * will restore by treaty what they have got, or the Emperor yield what he has lost.

I am extremely glad to hear that I shall have the pleasure of seeing you and others of our friends in town some time before the meeting of the Parliament; it is really very necessary that we should meet in time, and concert measures; besides that a matter of this nature should be countenanced by the appearance of as many of the persons concerned as possible.

I am ashamed of having troubled you so long, and, persuaded that you do me the justice to believe much more than I could say to you, will only add that I am, etc.

May I beg my compliments to Lord Tweeddale and Lord Stair, when you see them?

LXIII.

TO THE COUNTESS OF SUFFOLK.

BATH, *Nov.* 2, 1734.

MADAM,

A general history of the Bath since you left it, together with the particular memoirs of Amoretto's† life and conversation, are matters of too great importance to want any introduction. Therefore, without further preamble, I send you the very minutes, just as I have them down to help my own memory; the variety of events, and the time necessary to observe them, not having yet allowed me the leisure to put them in that style and order in which I propose they shall hereafter appear in public.

Oct. 27.—Little company appeared at the pump; those that were there drank the waters of affliction for the departure of

---

* France, Spain, and Sardinia.

† The Hon. Robert Sawyer Herbert was second son of the eighth, and brother of the ninth, Earl of Pembroke. From the General Election of 1722, until his decease in 1769, he represented the Borough of Wilton in Parliament. He had married Mary, daughter of Speaker Smith, but left no issue.—M.

Lady Suffolk and Mrs. Blount.* What was said of them both I need not tell you; for it was so obvious to those that said it, that it cannot be less so to those that deserve it. Amoretto went upon Lansdowne to evaporate his grief for the loss of his Parthenissa,† in memory of whom (and the wind being very cold into the bargain) he tied his handkerchief over his hat and looked very sadly.

In the evening the usual tea-table met at Lyndsey's, the two principal persons excepted; who, it was hoped, were then got safe to Newbury. Amoretto's main action was at our table; but, episodically, he took pieces of bread and butter, and cups of tea, at about ten others. He laughed his way through the girls, out of the long room into the little one, where he *tallied* till he swore, and swore till he went home, and probably some time afterwards.

The Countess of Burlington,‡ in the absence of her Royal Highness, held a circle at Hayes's, where she lost a favourite snuff-box, but unfortunately kept her temper.

Oct. 28.—Breakfast was at Lady Anne's, where Amoretto was with difficulty prevailed upon to eat and drink as much as he had a mind to. At night he was observed to be pleasant with the girls, and with less restraint than usual, which made some people surmise that he comforted himself for the Lady Suffolk and Parthenissa, by the liberty and impunity their absence gave him.

Oct. 29.—Amoretto breakfasted incognito, but appeared at the ball in the evening, where he distinguished himself by his *bons mots*. He was particularly pleased to compare the two Miss Towardins, who are very short and were a dancing, to a couple of totums set a spinning. The justness and liveliness of this image struck Mr. Marriott to such a degree, that he begged leave of the author to put it off for his own, which was granted him. He declared afterwards, to several people, that Mr. Herbert beat the whole world at similes.

Oct. 30.—Being his Majesty's birthday, little company appeared in the morning, all being resolved to look well at night.

* Martha (or Patty) Blount, Pope's friend.
† Patty Blount.
‡ Lady Dorothy Savile, daughter and co-heir of the last Marquis of Halifax.—M.

Mr. Herbert dined at Mrs. Walter's with young Mr. Barnard, whom he rallied to death. Nash * gave a ball at Lyndsey's, where Mrs. Tate appeared for the first time, and was noticed by Mr. Herbert. He wore his gold laced clothes on the occasion, and looked so fine, that, standing by chance in the middle of the dancers, he was taken by many at a distance for a gilt garland. He concluded his evening, as usual, with basset and blasphemy.

Oct. 31.—Amoretto breakfasted at Lady Anne's, where, being now more easy and familiar, he called for a half-peck loaf and a pound of butter—let off a great many ideas ; and

*   *   *   *   *

The Countess of Burlington bespoke the play, as you may see by the inclosed original bill ; the audience consisted of seventeen souls, of whom I made one.

Nov. 1.—Amoretto took a vomit in the morning, and then with a clear and excellent stomach dined with me, and went to the ball at night, where Mrs. Hamilton chiefly engrossed him.

Mrs. Jones gave Sir Humphrey Monoux † pain with Mr. Browne, which gave Sir Humphrey the toothache, but Mr. Jones has since made up matters between them.

Nov. 2. — Circular letters were received here from *Miss* Secretary Russel, notifying the safe arrival at London with many interesting particulars, and with gracious assurances, of the continuance of a firm and sincere friendship. It would be as

---

* Richard Nash, commonly called Beau Nash, Master of the Ceremonies at Bath. He was born at Swansea in 1674, lived at Bath for more than fifty years, and died in 1761. See " Social Life in Bath," in *Murray's Magazine*, 1891. His full-length portrait was placed by the Corporation in the Rooms between the busts of Sir Isaac Newton and Pope, upon which Lord Chesterfield wrote the following lines :—

> " Immortal Newton never spoke
>   More truth than here you'll find ;
> Nor Pope himself e'er penned a joke
>   Severer on mankind.
> This picture placed the busts between,
>   Gives satire all its strength ;
> Wisdom and Wit are little seen,
>   But Folly at full length ! "

† Fourth Baronet of the name, and at this period M.P. for Stockbridge.
—M.

hard to say who received the strongest assurances, as it would be to determine who credited them the worst.

Mrs. Hamilton bespoke the play at night, which we all interested ourselves so much to fill, that there were as many people turned back as let in : it was so hot that the Countess of Burlington could not stay it out.

You now see, by this week's journal, how much you have lost by leaving the Bath so soon; at least I can assure you we feel what we lost by your leaving it before us. We are all disjointed, and so weary, that I have prevailed with my brother and Charles Stanhope * to start from hence with me on Tuesday se'nnight, which will just complete the two months I was ordered to stay. We set Mr. Herbert down at Highclere † in our way. This day fortnight I hope to have the pleasure of finding you at St. James's, much the better for the Bath; where, over a hot roll with Mrs. Blount, I propose giving you the next week's journal by word of mouth.

After having troubled you so long already, it is only in compliance to the form of letters that I add so unnecessary and so known a truth, as the assurance of the respect and attachment with which I am,

Madam, yours, etc.

LXIV.

TO SOLOMON DAYROLLES, ESQ.

À Londres, ce 8 Decembre, 1784.

MON CHER CHEVALIER,

Je reçois dans ce moment votre lettre; et le capitaine Brett m'a fait dire que dans deux ou trois jours je recevrai les autres deux douzaines de chemises. Je suis très-content de celles que j'ai déjà, et je vous suis très-obligé de la peine que vous avez prise à ce sujet; quoi-qu'à dire la vérité, vû la bonté de la toile,

---

* Charles Stanhope was the elder brother of the first Earl of Harrington. He had been much connected with Lord Sunderland, and had thereby incurred the personal resentment of George the Second, who steadily refused in 1728 to appoint him to a Lordship of the Admiralty, or to any other post of honour and emolument. (Coxe's *Walpole*, vol. i. p. 300.) He died in 1760.—M.

† Near Newbury; now the seat of the Earls of Carnarvon.—M.

et le bon marché, je crois en être redevable aux soins de Madame Dayrolles, à qui vous voudrez bien faire mes complimens et mes remercîmens.

Vous dites que le mariage est un mal épidémique à la Haye; prenez y donc bien garde, mon ami, et ne faites point de sottises. Aimez la princesse en question tant qu'il vous plaira, mais point d'un amour conjugal, s'il vous plait. Badinez, badinez; mais restez en là. Un honnête homme aime bien une jolie personne; mais ce n'est qu'un nigaud, qui l'épouse uniquement parcequ'elle est jolie.

Adieu, mon cher Chevalier; je suis sur mon honneur très-véritablement   Votre, etc.

Mes complimens à votre oncle.

LXV.

TO THE COUNTESS OF SUFFOLK.

BATH, *November* 14, 1737.

MADAM,

Your commands were too obliging not to be immediately and thankfully complied with, by one who would pay the most willing obedience to any you could lay upon him. If all Ladies and Kings (the great rulers of this world) would command in your way, how popular would their governments be with their subjects, and how easy to themselves! At least I would advise Kings to practise it, as the only method they have left to revive passive obedience. You commanded me to do what I had most a mind to do myself; and what would otherwise have wanted an excuse has now the merit of obedience.

I must tell you, then, that the health you were so good as to interest yourself in, is as much mended in this one week as I expected I could be in the six weeks I am to stay here. I have recovered the stomach I had lost, am quite free from the complaints in my head, and have in a good degree regained my spirits, which, I am sure, must be entirely owing to the waters, and not to the company here; for though this place is very full, here are very few with whom I either am or desire to be acquainted. As for quality, we have the very flower of it in the

august persons of the Duchesses of Norfolk * and Buckingham,†
who, thank God, are well enough together to avoid the fatal
disputes about rank, which might otherwise arise between the
first Duchess of the Kingdom and a Princess of the Blood. Your
kinswoman, the Duchess of Norfolk, had like the other day to
have been the innocent cause of Mrs. Buckley's death. Mrs.
Buckley was bathing in the Cross Bath, as she thought, in
perfect security, when of a sudden her Grace, who is considerably increased in bulk even since you saw her, came, and, like
the great leviathan, raised the waters so high, that Mrs. Buckley's
guide was obliged to hold her up in her arms to save her from
drowning, and carry her about like a child.

You will, I am sure, expect from me *l'histoire amoureuse* et
galante of Mr. Herbert; but I am very sorry, both for our sake
and his, that it makes but a very small volume this year. He
lies in bed till between ten and eleven, where he eats two break-
fasts of strong broth; then rides till one or two; after which he
dines commonly pretty plentifully with me, and concludes the
evening at billiards and whist. He sometimes laughs with the
girls, but with moderate success. He had distinguished at first
Mrs. Earle, daughter-in-law to Giles Earle,‡ a very handsome
woman, till a little man about half his height, one Mr. Harte,
like a second David, had the impudence to attack, and the glory
to defeat, him. Since which he has contented himself with a
little general waggery, as occasion offers, such as snatching the

---

* Probably the Duchess Dowager, Mary Shireburne, remarried to Mr.
Widdington. See a note to the *Suffolk Letters*, vol. ii. p. 162.—M.

† The Duchess of Buckingham was daughter of James the Second, by
Catherine, daughter of Sir Charles Sedley, created Countess of Dorchester.
At the Revolution, Sir Charles, resenting the seduction of his daughter,
joined the Prince of Orange and said ironically, "Since his Majesty has
done me the honour of making *my* daughter a Countess, I cannot do less
in return than endeavour to make *his* daughter a Queen!" On the other
hand, the Duchess of Buckingham kept up a constant correspondence
with *her dear brother*, the Pretender, at Rome, and on all occasions (as
Lord Chesterfield intimates in this letter) affected the tone of a Princess
of the Blood.—M.

‡ Giles Earle represented Chippenham and Malmesbury in several
Parliaments, and from 1727 to 1741, was Chairman of the Committees in
the House of Commons. A specimen of his correspondence is preserved
in the *Suffolk Letters*, vol. i. p. 10.—M.

bread and butter out of a girl's hands, and greasing her fingers and his own; taking away a cup of tea ready prepared for somebody else, and such other like indications of innocent mirth; but he is by no means established to his satisfaction, as when you were here.

For my own part, were it not for the comfort of returning health, I believe I should hang myself. I am so weary of sauntering about without knowing what to do, or of playing at low play, which I hate, for the sake of avoiding deep play, which I love, that I look upon the remaining five weeks which I am to pass here as a sort of an eternity, and consider London as a remote land of promise, which God knows whether I shall ever get to or no. If I do, my first attention, as well as my greatest satisfaction, will be to assure you of the perfect truth and respect with which I am,

Madam, yours, etc.

May I beg my compliments to Mr. Berkeley and Miss Hobart, who, I hope, are both well.

LXVI.

TO SOLOMON DAYROLLES, ESQ.

LONDON, January 23, O.S. 1739.

DEAR CHEVALIER,

I make you no compliments of condolence upon the death of your uncle; for, though I loved him very well, I love you better, and you are now easy and independent. I intended to have executed your commission to Lord Harrington; but I happened first to see Horace Walpole, who I thought might prove more serviceable to you in this affair, than the other: accordingly I spoke to him: and he told me he had received a letter from you to the same effect, and that he would take care of the whole affair. The only difficulty, he apprehended, was with relation to your plate, if it happened to be of foreign make. I told him that, as well as I remembered, it was English.

Pray take care to keep well with your aunt, who, I am informed, has a good deal left in her own power. Tell me what disposition your uncle made, what you have got, what you intend to do, and when you come here; for I interest myself really in whatever concerns you, and am sincerely,

Yours.

LXVII.

TO ALEXANDER, EARL OF MARCHMONT.

LONDON, *August* 15, 1739.

MY DEAR LORD,

I received your Lordship's and Lord Stair's letters the night before I left Tunbridge, from whence I returned here yesterday. As you desire my opinion upon the plan,* of which you sent me a copy, I will give it you as well as I have been able to form it in this short time, and without having anybody to talk it over and consider it with; submitting it, however, entirely to the opinions of the rest of our friends, and determined to act as they shall think fit to resolve. I extremely approve of the first part of it that relates to the House of Commons, both as a thing right in itself, and as a good example, which, I hope, may be followed by many counties, at least in England; but, I confess, I have many doubts about the latter part, which relates to the House of Lords, and which is not necessarily connected with the other, so that the former may very well be put in practice, though this be not. The petition of the Lords would be no more than what was done at the beginning of this Parliament, and with many more favourable circumstances. The grievance was then recent, and talked of by everybody, the corrupt influence offered to be proved by witnesses of rank and credit; and yet you saw it did not shake one single man in our House. The elections of one or two since, though in truth nominations of the Court, cannot regularly appear to be so, since there was no opposition, and the election seemed at least to be unanimous. It is not to be doubted neither, but that there would be at the same time a counter-petition, or representation (call it what you will), signed by a greater number of Lords than would sign yours, which would

---

* This plan, like the one referred to in the previous letter to Lord Marchmont of August 27, 1734, was to lay complaints before both Houses, of the alleged abuses in the election of the Scottish Representative Peers.—M.

justify the House of Lords in whatever censure they might have a mind to pass upon yours. Besides, would it not be natural enough to ask this question: " Why now this is neither immediately after a past grievance, nor immediately before a new one of the same kind is apprehended ? " And I really think, such an application would come much more properly towards the end of the last session of this Parliament. Another circumstance, which I think has some weight, is, that the Duke of Argyle is. not yet ripe for a measure of this kind, and I dare say will not come into it, though very probably some time hence he may. Lords Aberdeen * and Tweeddale, it seems, already declare against it, and you very well know who amongst us will do the same here, which would certainly damp it a good deal; though, I own, that alone would not be a reason for laying it aside, if it were otherwise proper at this time.

This, my dear Lord, is my present opinion, of which, however, I am fully diffident, and consequently not tenacious. I shall act in it as the majority of you all determine; for as we all mean the same thing, I will always concur with those measures which shall be agreed upon by those who mean as well, and can judge much better than myself. I beg you will make my compliments to my Lord Stair, to whom I do not write, knowing that my writing to you is the same thing, and thinking that he may possibly be further off.

I am, with the greatest truth and attachment,

My dear Lord, etc.

LXVIII.

TO THE EARL OF STAIR.†

LONDON, *September* 3, 1739.

MY LORD,

By the return of the messenger, by whom I received the favour of your letter, with the inclosed papers, I writ to Lord

---

* William, second Earl of Aberdeen; died, 1746.

† John, second Earl of Stair. Born, 1673; died, 1747. He was appointed Ambassador to Paris in 1715, and Commander-in-chief, under the King, of the army at Dettingen. His turbulent temper, however, frequently embroiled him with the Court, and at the date of this letter, he was among the most vehement opponents of Sir Robert Walpole.—M.

Marchmont my poor sentiments upon the points in question. I thought it the same as writing to you; but chose to direct it rather to him, because the messenger told me he should see him first. I shall say no more now, by the common post, upon that subject, than that I thought the first part of the plan extremely right, but the latter part rather ill-timed now, and would not have the effect proposed or hoped for.—What do you say to the vigour of our Administration? The sleeping lion is roused; and a hundred and twenty men of war now in commission, and forty thousand land-forces in England, will show our enemies abroad, that they have presumed too much and too long upon Sir Robert's pacific temper. I say this on the supposition and hopes that these land-forces are only raised against our common enemies abroad, and not against Sir Robert's enemies at home; though I know which I believe. It is reported too, but I don't know on what grounds, that this Parliament is this Session to be continued seven years longer, upon pretence that, in this time of danger, the nation is not in a proper temper to meet and choose new representatives.* Violent as this step may seem, I cannot think it is totally improbable, when I combine several circumstances; but this I know, that, if it is taken, there is an end of us, I mean constitutionally. Your visit to Ireland is a sign of your good health and spirits, which I rejoice at, and wish you the long continuance of, as much as any man upon earth can do, being, I am sure, as much as any man on earth can be,

My dear Lord, etc.

LXIX.

TO THE EARL OF STAIR.

LONDON, December 8, 1739.

MY DEAR LORD,

Since I troubled you last, I have three letters from you to acknowledge. As to the two first, you will have heard from all your friends here, that the D(uke) of A(rgyle) is by no means as yet ripe to come into any of those propositions. I both think and hope he will by next year; but, in the meantime, he must be

* This report was wholly groundless.—M. The Septennial Act was passed in 1716.

stroked and not spurred.   The plan inclosed in your letter, which
I received yesterday, is, in my opinion, a perfect right one, and
is now followed by many corporations in England, in their instructions to their members; and ought to have been so by all
the counties, if those who at the end of last Session of Parliament
undertook that province, had not either carelessly or wilfully
neglected it till the assizes were over, which has now made it
impossible for this year.   The Bill, to limit the number of place-
men in Parliament, is to be brought in after the holidays, and
will, I suppose, be as soon rejected; after which, it will be necessary to print the names of those who voted for or against it; and
then fresh instructions from every county or borough, both in
England and Scotland, wherever they can be obtained, and, I
believe, they may from almost every county and a great majority
of the boroughs, will come with still greater weight next year.

As for postponing the money-bills till such a bill be agreed
to, which is what you propose, and what is likewise mentioned in
the instructions of the city of London, I find that will not do;
because, to tell you the plain truth, many of the Opposition do
not in their hearts greatly relish the place-bill itself, which they
think might prove a clog upon their own Administration, and
they will by no means hear of anything like a tack, or a postponing of the money-bills.   If the whole Opposition meant the same
thing as you and I do, they would most certainly entertain this
measure, which is the only one that can recover the constitution;
all others are but temporary palliatives; for while the Houses of
Lords and Commons are absolutely in the power of the Crown,
as they visibly now are, we have no constitution, and the Crown
alone is, without a mystery, the three branches of the Legislature.
But unfortunately, I doubt, this is what many people desire as
heartily as you and I wish the contrary.

Sir Robert's health is thought to be very precarious,* and

* This surmise had more truth than is usual in Opposition rumours.
The health of Walpole was gradually sinking beneath his laborious public
duties.   In the autumn of 1741, he was "in great danger" from an ague
and dysentery (*Walpole's Letters*, vol. i., p. 76, ed. 1840), and on the 19th
of October, in that year, his son Horace writes in confidence, as follows,
to Mr. Mann, at Florence: "He who was asleep as soon as his head
touched the pillow, now never sleeps above an hour without waking, and
he, who at dinner always forgot he was Minister, and was more gay and

there are many of us who already anticipate in their thoughts the joyful moment, which they think not remote, of coming into power; and consequently, far from desiring to make shackles for themselves, are rather willing to continue those upon the people which Sir Robert has forged for them. This, I own, is a melancholy case; but I fear it is too much the case. The persons you allude to, that you think might be prevailed with to act against Sir Robert, are not to be moved. They have been tried, and their own interest in so doing has been manifestly shown them, but to no purpose. They consider money as their only interest, and would not venture the suspension of a quarter's salary, to save the whole nation. This, my dear Lord, is our wretched situation, from whence, I think, little good can arise. Union among ourselves cannot be expected, where our views are so widely different. This Sir Robert knows, and triumphs in. I despair of either doing good or seeing any done; yet, while I live, I assure you, I will endeavour it. I wish my country well, and upon that principle alone must wish you so; but many other considerations concur to make me honour and esteem you as I do, and to form that attachment and friendship with which I shall ever be, My dear Lord, etc.

LXX.

TO THE REV. DR. CHENEVIX.*

LONDON, *February* 15, 1740.

DEAR DOCTOR,

I thank you for both your letters. I would have acknowledged your former sooner; but partly business, and partly dispiritedness, hindered me.

thoughtless than all his company, now sits without speaking, and with his eyes fixed for an hour together. Judge if this is the Sir Robert you knew!"—M. In 1742 Walpole was created Earl of Orford; he died in 1745, aged 69.

* The Rev. Richard Chenevix was of French extraction, his parents having left their native country on the revocation of the Edict of Nantes. His first patron was Lord Scarborough, by whom he was recommended to Lord Chesterfield as his Chaplain in Holland. In 1745, Lord Chesterfield's influence as Lord Lieutenant of Ireland raised him to the Bishopric, first of Killaloe and then of Waterford. Dr. Chenevix always retained a grateful sense of Lord Chesterfield's kindness, and continued his regular correspondent until his death.—M. His grand-daughter and heiress,

We have both lost a good friend in Scarborough; * nobody can replace him to me; I wish I could replace him to you; but, as things stand, I see no great hopes of it.

As for the living of Southwark,† I would not advise you to expect it; for Sir Robert Walpole, I am persuaded, will never let you have it. He carries his resentment to the highest degree, even against the memory of one,‡ who was but too long his friend, and too little a while his enemy. However, when it becomes vacant, I would have you renew your application for it.

I am, with great truth, etc.

LXXI.
TO THE EARL OF STAIR.

(*May,* 1740.)

MY DEAR LORD,

I wish I had anything better than thanks to return you for your several letters; but, unfortunately, I can send you no accounts from hence, that I can write or you read with satisfaction. The Opposition is, in truth, become no Opposition at all—is looked upon already in that light by the Court, and, I am afraid, will soon be so by the whole nation. The views of the individuals are too different for them to draw together. Some few mean the public good, and they are for acting and pushing of constitutional measures; but many more mean only their private interest, and they think public inaction and secret negotiations the most conducive to it. They consider Sir

Melusina Chenevix, was the mother of Richard Chenevix Trench, late Archbishop of Dublin.

* Richard, second Earl of Scarborough, had been called to the House of Lords by writ, in 1715, during his father's life, and appointed one of the Gentlemen of the Bedchamber to the Prince of Wales, afterwards George the Second. On the 29th of January, 1740, in a moment of mental alienation, he put a period to his own existence. He was one of the earliest and dearest friends of Lord Chesterfield, who has paid, in the *Characters,* an affecting tribute to his worth.—M.

† Dr. Chenevix was promised the parish of St. Olave's, Southwark, by Sir R. Walpole, on the recommendation of Lord Chesterfield and Lord Scarborough. On this promise not being kept, Lord Chesterfield complained to the King himself. (From a letter of Dr. Chenevix's quoted by Maty.)   ‡ Lord Scarborough.

Robert's life as a bad one, and desire, by their submission and tameness, to recommend themselves to be his successors. The Court, they say, is too strong to be overcome by opposition; that is, in truth, they think it would be too strong for their impatience for power upon any terms. In this distracted state of the Opposition, you will not be surprised that nothing is done, and that the Court triumphs. Those of your friends here, with whom I am connected, wish, as I do, many things which it is not in our power to bring about, and which would only discover our weakness to attempt. My only hopes are from the spirit of the nation in the next election, where, if we exert, I think, there are hopes of having a better Parliament than this. In your part of the kingdom more may be done with effect in that affair than in this part, where the influence of the Court is more powerful; and I hope, therefore, you will all exert in that last struggle for our constitution. We are to have here next week a general meeting, to settle the elections for the next Parliament, in which, I make no doubt, but those who have ruined the Opposition will use their endeavours to frustrate this design too; but still I hope it will have some good effect, though to be sure not so good a one as if we all meant the same thing. The Place Bill comes in on Tuesday next, and will be thrown out the same day. Some of our patriots will rant that day, *par manière d'acquit*, by permission from the Court, and then the Session is ended! I showed your paper upon that subject to some of my friends, who will endeavour to make what use they can of it.

Your old friend Lord Cathcart * kissed the King's hand yesterday, for the command of the intended expedition. Some say it is against Cuba; others, against Buenos Ayres; but none know, and the secret is inviolably kept. For my own part, wherever it is intended, I have a very bad opinion of the success of it,† when I know that nobody capable of forming a right plan has

---

* Charles, eighth Lord Cathcart. He had been appointed to the command of the land-forces in this expedition, but died at sea, after only a few days' illness, December 20, 1740.—M.

† At the same period (June 3, 1746) Pulteney writes as follows to Swift: "In all probability nothing will be done. I have not the least notion that even our expedition under Lord Cathcart is intended to be sent anywhere." (Swift's Works, vol. xix. p. 322, ed. 1814.) In fact, however, the attack was made on Carthagena, but without success.—M.

been consulted in it, and that no officer able to conduct it is well enough at Court to be employed in it.

As I have writ all this to you *à cœur ouvert*, I beg it may go no farther, it being better that the real wretched state of the Opposition should not be universally known, though, I fear, it is but too well guessed at. It might discourage, and could do no good.

If all meant as well as you do, I should, with more hopes and better spirits, take what little part I am able; but I confess that, in the present situation of things, I rather content myself with not doing ill, than hope to do any good. I will keep my conscience and my character clear, wish what I should, and do what I can; *et pour le reste, alors comme alors.* But in all situations, pleased and proud of being reckoned in the number of those who love and value you as you deserve, and who wish you in a condition of doing your country all the good you are both so desirous and so able to do it! Adieu, my dear Lord.

Believe me, etc.

LXXII.

TO HUGH, EARL OF MARCHMONT.*

LONDON, *September* 6, 1740.

MY DEAR LORD,

As I am persuaded that you are convinced of the truth of my regard and friendship for you, I look upon myself as authorised to give you this trouble, without any further excuse for it. The sincere part I take in everything that relates to you has

---

* Early in 1740, Alexander, Earl of Marchmont, had died and been succeeded by his eldest son, Hugh Lord Polwarth; "that valuable or rather invaluable young man," as Bolingbroke in one of his letters calls him. Thus the young Earl had lost his seat in the House of Commons, without (as a Scottish Peer) acquiring any in the House of Lords. It appears, however, by his curious Diary published in 1831, that he continued, though out of Parliament, to take an active interest in politics. It was not till 1750, that he was elected one of the Sixteen Representative Peers; and in 1764, he was appointed Lord Keeper of the Great Seal of Scotland. In the House of Lords, however, he made no efforts to maintain the high reputation for oratory which he had gained in the Commons. He survived till January, 1794, when he died in the eighty-ninth year of his age, at his seat, near Hemel Hempstead, in Hertfordshire.—M.

made me hear with the utmost concern of your uneasiness, not to say despondency, at the two * misfortunes which so soon after one another concurred to affect not only you, but your friends, and all the friends to the public. Your grief, I own, is just; I feel it with you; but give me leave to say your despair would be blameable, and would be adding another misfortune to the former little less sensible to your friends or your country.

I know I am an improper instrument of comfort to you upon this occasion, since I cannot think of our late friend† without too much grief of my own to be able to lessen yours. I have lost a friend, whom I could equally depend upon, both in public and in private life—one who, by his directions and advice, supplied my want of knowledge and experience, and to whose honest heart I could without reserve open my own. How much the public has lost, I need not, I cannot say; but that very consideration ought to prevail with all those who are friends, and particularly with all those who, like you, can be useful friends to it, not to forsake the care of it. The more you and our late friend are missed, in the House of Commons particularly, the more your assistance is wanted out of it; and would you, by withdrawing yourself from business, add to the joy of those who have shamelessly rejoiced at the cause of your grief? There are some friends of yours, who think and wish as you do, but who, without your assistance and advice, can be at best but inefficient well-wishers, though with it, they may be able to check, or disturb at least, the dirty mercenary schemes of pretended patriots or avowed profligates. For my own part I protest to you, that without your assistance and instructions I shall give myself no manner of trouble, because I know it would be to no manner of purpose.

I do not mean to compliment you; I hope and believe, you do not suspect me of it; where compliments are deserved, they lose their odious name by becoming truths; and where they are not deserved, I scorn to give them; therefore, my dear Lord, believe it as a truth, that your presence, and your taking a part in business, is absolutely necessary towards doing any good; and as

* The deaths of his father, and of his friend Sir William Wyndham. "What a star has our Minister," writes Bolingbroke, "Wyndham dead, Marchmont disabled! The loss of Marchmont and Wyndham to our country!"—M.   † Sir William Wyndham.

such, give me leave to add, that it is a moral and necessary duty incumbent upon you, and from which no private consideration can dispense you. If you ask me, what prospect, or what possibility, there is of doing any good, I must answer, in truth very little prospect, but still a possibility. The chapter of accidents at least is open ; and even death, which has hitherto been very partial, may at last prove just. Events, however remote or improbable, are to be attended to ; and it is in some degree criminal to withdraw one's self from the possibility of improving them.

I ask pardon for troubling you with these reflections, which your own good head and heart must have better suggested to you, if your grief had given them leave ; let me only add this interested request of my own, to that I have already made you for the public, which is, that I may have some share of that friendship, which you so justly gave entire to our late friend. I am sensible how little my sincere attachment and regard for you can replace his ; but believe me, my dear Lord, it is as real ; and I am, as much as man can be, etc.

LXXIII.

TO HUGH, EARL OF MARCHMONT.

Tuesday.

MY DEAR LORD,

I share the marks of your friendship to Mr. Pitt,* looking upon everything that concerns him as personal to myself. I have not yet had an opportunity of speaking to him upon that subject, and when I have, I shall break it gently, knowing his delicacy ; but, in the mean time, pray encourage her Grace† in so right and generous a resolution. You shall soon be troubled with a letter or a visit from me upon this matter ; in the mean time, I can assure you, I want nobody's recommendation to continue those sentiments of esteem and friendship with which I have so long been, and ever shall be most faithfully, yours.

* William Pitt, afterwards Earl of Chatham.

† Sarah, Duchess of Marlborough ; the "right and generous resolution" was to bequeath Mr. Pitt £10,000, which she did. Lord Chesterfield received another legacy of £20,000, and the reversion of the Wimbledon estate.—M.

LXXIV.

TO HUGH, EARL OF MARCHMONT.

LONDON, *April* 24, 1741.

MY DEAR LORD,

A favourable opportunity tempts me to do what I had a great mind to, and to lay it upon the opportunity. Mr. Hume's* going to Scotland makes me trouble you with this letter, which will consequently get to you unopened, though very possibly you would not have escaped one, had he not gone; for as no distance can remove you from my thoughts, it is not likely that it could protect you from my letters.

You have heard in general (to be sure) of what happened in both Houses upon the Vote of Credit; † but I believe you may be glad to know more particulars. Pulteney gave up the point at once with alacrity in the House' of Commons, seconded by your friend Sandys,‡ who went still further than he, to make his court upon the tender point of Hanover. The next day the King's speech was to be considered in our House, when, before the meeting of the House, Carteret § came up to the Duke of Argyle and myself, and said to us, "You heard what was done in the House of Commons yesterday; we shall do the same here to-day. We answered, that we had not the least intention of doing the same, for that we should certainly oppose the motion; at which he seemed concerned and surprised. Accordingly the Duke of Argyle threw the first stone at the motion for the Address, and I, the second and last. Then Carteret opened himself with all the

* See Letter LVIII., June 15, 1734.

† This vote was for £300,000 in support of the Pragmatic Sanction, and as a subsidy to the Queen of Hungary against the King of Prussia. It passed the Commons without a division, but in the Lords there appeared twenty-five Non-Contents against seventy-six Contents. Lord Chesterfield's account of the debate (in which a brilliant part was borne by himself) may be compared with Bishop Secker's in the Parliamentary History, vol. xii. p. 150.—M.

‡ Mr. Samuel Sandys, who had been M.P. for Worcester since 1717. On the 13th of February, in this year, he had moved an Address to the Crown, for the dismissal of Sir Robert Walpole.—M.

§ John, Lord Carteret, afterwards on his mother's death, Earl Granville. A most able sketch, both of him and his confederate at this period, Pulteney, is given by Lord Chesterfield among his *Characters.*—M.

zeal and heart of a convert, or an apostate, which you please, if a
man can be called either, who has no religion at all.   We divided
the House, not so much to show our own strength, which we
knew, but his weakness; and indeed it appeared upon the division, that he left us *lui troisième et demi* only, that is, himself,
Winchelsea, Roxburgh, and Berkeley of Stratton, who will not
always go with him; the others who left us, such as Northamp-
ton, and Oxford, doing it visibly upon other considerations.

His Royal Highness* behaved sillily upon this occasion, making
Lords North and Darnley vote against us; such was the power
of the *natale solum*.   This has hurt him much in the public.
Our opposition in the House of Lords had like to have spirited
up one in the House of Commons in the Committee, in which
Pulteney would have been brought to the same trial as his friend
Carteret, and, I dare say, would have acted in the same manner;
but I prevented, though with difficulty, that opposition, because
I plainly saw that it would be almost only a Tory Opposition,
and that Pulteney would have carried two-thirds of the Whigs
present along with him; a triumph which I thought it better he
should not have at the end of this Parliament.   Let his triumph,
or his mortification, whichever circumstances may then produce,
begin with the next Parliament; we are resolved to bring it to
the trial, that is, in the supposition that it be worth while to do
anything at all, which I much doubt.   Your friend, the Duchess
of Marlborough, has in your absence employed me as your substitute; and I have brought Mr. Hooke† and her together, and
having done that will leave the rest to them, not caring to meddle
myself in an affair, which, I am sure, will not turn out at last
to her satisfaction, though I hope, and believe, it will be to his
advantage.

I propose setting out for Aix-la-Chapelle in about a fortnight,
from thence to Spa, till the beginning of August, and then to
take a tour for the autumn at least, if not longer, in France.   If
about that time you propose being at Bolingbroke's, I will contrive my affairs so as to meet you there; otherwise I shall take

---

* Frederick Prince of Wales.

† Nathaniel Hooke, author of a "History of Rome," wrote "The Conduct of the Duchess of Marlborough," under her direction, (published in
1742), and for this received £5,000 from her.

D'Argeville,* as it may be most suitable to my plan of rambling in that country. I tell you truly, what I have told to nobody else, that unless the prospect here mends extremely, I shall not be in haste to return, but will make a considerable stay in a country, that will do me a great deal of good, at a time when I can do no country any good at all. The languor and dispiritedness that have made life burthensome to me all this winter, require a better climate, and more dissipation than I can find here; † and I think it is better conversing with the cheerful, natural-born slaves of France, than with the sullen, venal, voluntary ones of England. But as I shall still be glad to hear from those here, who still wish to be free, let me sometimes, my dear Lord, hear from you. While you are in Scotland, inform me of your health only, in which I need not tell you the part I take.

When you come here, you may add whatever your own leisure, and the situation of things allow. Direct for me at my house in town, from whence all letters will be sent me; upon any extraordinary occasion make use of some amanuensis you can trust, and sign "Johnson." The curiosity of knowing what becomes of one's country, and one's friends, is natural; nay, the want of it would be blameable; but beyond that, I protest, the melancholy prospect before us has sunk me into such an indifference as to public matters, that I should neither trouble my friends nor myself about them. I want those two great prevailing springs of action, avarice and ambition; and being convinced that, as the world goes, a man that will enjoy a quiet conscience must lead a quiet life, I most cheerfully embrace an honest, however contemptible obscurity, in which I shall ever be, etc.

Pray make my compliments to Lord Stair, when you see him. These late events will prove to him, how impossible it was to have any concert between Scotland and those here, who had no concert among themselves.

* Lord Bolingbroke's seat near Fontaineblean.

† Although the causes here assigned naturally and sufficiently account for Lord Chesterfield's journey to the South of France, it has also been frequently ascribed to a deep political motive. It is said that his real object was to solicit through the Duke of Ormond (whose guest he was for a few days at Avignon) an order from the Pretender to the Jacobites to concur in all future attacks against Walpole. See Lord Orford's *Memoirs*, vol i., p. 45.—M.

LXXV.

TO THE REV. DR. CHENEVIX.

SPA, *July* 4, N.S. 1741.

DEAR DOCTOR,

It was with real concern that I heard you were ill; and it is with equal truth that I hope this will find you perfectly recovered. That virtue which makes you fit, and it may be willing, to die, makes those who are acquainted with it, as I am, unwilling you should; therefore take care of your health, and let it not be affected by a too great sensibility of those misfortunes that inseparably attend our state here. Do all you can to prevent them, but, when inevitable, bear them with resolution; this is the part I take with relation to my own health. I do all I can to retrieve and improve it; and if I acquire it, I will do all I can to preserve it; my bodily infirmities shall as little as possible affect my mind, and so far at least I will lessen the weight of them.

These waters have already done me so much good, that I have reason to expect a great deal more from them; and I expect still more benefit from passing my autumn afterwards in constant travelling through the South of France. Thus you see I anticipate eventually the good, which is at least so much clear gain, let what will happen afterwards. Do so too, dear Doctor, and be as well, and as happy, as you are sincerely wished to be by

Your most faithful friend and servant.

LXXVI.

TO G. BUBB DODINGTON, ESQ.

SPA, *September* 8, 1741.

SIR,

Having at last found a safe way of sending you this letter, I shall, without the least reserve, give you my thoughts upon the contents of yours of the 30th of May, O.S.

By the best judgment I can form of the list of this present Parliament, and I have examined it very carefully, we appear to be so strong, that I think we can but just be called the minority;

and I am very sure that such a minority, well united and well conducted, might soon be a majority. But,

Hoc opus hic labor est.

It will neither be united nor well conducted. Those who should lead it will make it their business to break and divide it; and they will succeed; I mean Carteret and Pulteney. Their behaviour for these few years has, in my mind, plainly shown their views and their negotiations with the Court: but, surely, their conduct at the end of last Session puts that matter out of all dispute. They feared even the success of that minority, and took care to render it as insignificant as possible. Will they then not be much more apprehensive of the success of this: and will not both their merit and their reward be much the greater for defeating it? If you tell me that they ought rather to avail themselves of these numbers, and, at the head of them, force their way where they are so impatient to go, I will agree with you, that in prudence they ought; but the fact is, they reason quite differently, desire to get in with a few, by negotiation, and not by victory with numbers, who, they fear, might presume upon their strength, and grow troublesome to their generals.

On the other hand, Sir Robert must be alarmed at our numbers, and must resolve to reduce them before they are brought into the field. He knows by experience where and how to apply for that purpose; with this difference only, that the numbers will have raised the price, which he must come up to. And this is all the fruit I expect from this strong minority. You will possibly ask me, whether all this is in the power of Carteret and Pulteney? I answer, yes—in the power of Pulteney alone. He has a personal influence over many, and an interested influence over more. The silly, half-witted, zealous Whigs consider him as the only support of Whigism; and look upon us as running headlong into Bolingbroke and the Tories. The interested Whigs, as Sandys, Rushout and Gibbon,* with many others, are as impatient to come into Court as he can be; and, persuaded that he has opened that door a little, will hold fast by him to

* Sir John Rushout, Bart., and Philip Gibbon. The three gentlemen here named, all became members of the new Board of Treasury, on the fall of Walpole; Sandys as Chancellor of the Exchequer.—M.

squeeze in with him, and think they can justify their conduct to
the public, by following their old leader, under the colours
(though false ones) of Whigism.

What then, is nothing to be done?   Are we to give it up
tamely, when the prospect seems so fair?   No; I am for acting,
let our numbers be what they will.   I am for discriminating,
and making people speak out; though our numbers should, as I
am convinced they will, lessen considerably by it.   Let what
will happen, we cannot be in a worse situation than that we
have been in for these last three or four years.   Nay, I am for
acting at the very beginning of the Session, and bringing our
numbers the first week; and points for that purpose, I am sure,
are not wanting.   Some occur to me now, many more will, I
dare say, occur to others; and many will, by that time, present
themselves.

For example, the Court generally proposes some servile and
shameless tool of theirs * to be Chairman of the Committee of
Privileges and Elections.   Why should not we, therefore, pick
out some Whig of a fair character, and with personal connections,
to set up in opposition?   I think we should be pretty strong
upon this point.   But as for opposition to their Speaker, if it be
Onslow, we shall be but weak; he having, by a certain decency
of behaviour, made himself many personal friends in the minority.
The affair of Carthagena † will of course be mentioned; and
there, in my opinion, a question, and a trying one too, of censure,
lies very fair, that the delaying of that expedition so late last
year was the principal cause of our disappointment.   An Address
to the King, desiring him to make no peace with Spain, unless
our undoubted right of navigation in the West Indies, without
molestation or search, be clearly, and in express words, stipulated; and till we have acquired some valuable possession there,
as a pledge of the performance of such stipulation: such a
question would surely be a popular one, and distressful enough
to the Ministry.

I entirely agree with you, that we ought to have meetings to
concert measures some time before the meeting of the Parliament; but that, I likewise know, will not happen.   I have been

---

* Giles Earle.   See Letter LXV.
† See Letter LXXI. and notes.

these seven years endeavouring to bring it about, and have not been able; fox-hunting, gardening, planting, or indifference having always kept our people in the country, till the very day before the meeting of the Parliament. Besides, would it be easy to settle who should be at those meetings? If Pulteney and his people were to be chose, it would only be informing them beforehand, what they should either oppose or defeat; and if they were not there, their own exclusion would in some degree justify, or at least colour, their conduct. As to our most flagitious House, I believe you agree there is nothing to be done in it; and for such a minority to struggle with such a majority, would be much like the late King of Sweden's attacking the Ottoman army at Bender, at the head of his cook and his butler.

These are difficulties, the insurmountable difficulties, that I foresee; and which make me absolutely despair of seeing any good done. However, I am entirely at the service of you and the rest of my friends who mean the public good. I will either fight or run away, as you shall determine. If the Duke of Argyle sounds to battle, I will follow my leader; if he stays in Oxfordshire, I'll stay in Grosvenor Square.* I think it is all one which we do as to our House; yours must be the scene of action, if action there be; and action, I think, there should be, at least for a time, let your numbers be what you will.

I leave this place to-morrow, and set out for France; a country which, in my conscience, I think as free as our own: they have not the form of freedom, as we have. I know no other difference. I shall pass a couple of months in rambling through the Southern Provinces, and then return to England, to receive what commands you may leave for, etc.

LXXVII.

TO HUGH, EARL OF MARCHMONT.

LONDON, *November* 12, 1741.

My DEAR LORD,

Mr. Hume gave me yesterday your letter of the 25th of September, which, I confess, was a great disappointment to one,

* Since his marriage, Lord Chesterfield had removed from St. James's to Grosvenor Square, until he built the mansion which bears his name.—M.

who both hoped and expected to have found you here in person at this time of the year. He even gave me no comfort upon that point, but said, he did not know that you had fixed any time for coming to your friends in town. I therefore write this in a great hurry, to beg of you to come here as soon as your indispensable private affairs will permit you. I need not tell you, that it is not proper for you, in the light that all mankind sees you, to be buried in Scotland at this extraordinary crisis; * less need I tell you, how agreeable and necessary your presence here will be to all your friends, and how indispensably necessary it is to me, who cannot stir one step without you. The minority is a considerable and a willing one; and if we can frustrate the designs of some few, who want to divide and weaken it, some good, I think, may be done; but I repeat it again, I can do nothing without you, so

Nil mihi rescribas, attamen ipse veni,

is the most earnest request of, etc.

LXXVIII.

A MADAME DE MARTEL.†

[Février, 1742.]

Nos lettres, Madame, ne semblent se croiser que pour donner lieu à la délicatesse de nos soupçons réciproques, et aux éclaircissemens qui les suivent de si près, circonstances qui ne gâtent rien en amitié, non plus qu'en amour. J'avoue que je me trouve flatté de vos soupçons, et je vous jure que chaque fois que je me vois détrompé des miens, qui par parenthèse sont beaucoup mieux fondés, j'en ai une véritable joie. Ces sentimens, qui sont très réels, ne vous montrent-ils l'amitié de mon côté que comme une chimère en perspective, ou plutôt ne vous prouvent-ils pas que

---

* The new Parliament was to meet on the 1st of the ensuing month, and the Opposition, conscious of its strength, was now preparing for those efforts, which drove Sir Robert Walpole from office in February next. Lord Chesterfield's speech on the Address (December 4, 1741), was applauded for its eloquence even by the speakers on the other side.—M.

† "Madame Martel, s'appelait Mademoiselle Coulon; c'était une petite demoiselle de Dauphiné, dont à son arrivée la beauté fit grand bruit; elle était précieuse, affecté, galante, et eut beaucoup d'aventures." (Madame du Deffand, Lettre à Walpole, le 23 Mars, 1777.)—M.

votre château en Espagne est un édifice très solide, et tout fait?
Oui, Madame, soyez persuadée que, si vous daignez souhaiter, ou
même accepter, une amitié aussi peu intéressante qu'est la mienne,
elle vous est déjà toute acquise, et pour toujours ; et sans craindre
les illusions de l'amour propre, vous pouvez vous en fier à votre
propre mérite, comme garant de cette vérité. Je considère donc
notre amitié comme ratifiée par ces présentes, et si bien ratifiée
même, que pour jouir de mes droits je n'userai plus à l'avenir de
politesse ni de ménagement pour vous. Dieu sait même si avec
le tems je n'en abuserai pas au point de vous tutoyer, car on ne
se tient guères au point convenable, et l'amitié est presque
toujours, ou abusée par la familiarité, ou gênée par les façons.
Je commence dès à présent par vous insulter, et je vous annonce
que malgré vos vœux, votre ami, et non pas notre ami,* est parti
aujourd'hui † pour sa terre ; arraché au Roi par la majorité du
Parlement, et en même tems comblé de nouvelles marques de
faveur, comme titre de Comte, pension considérable, charges à
vie pour ses amis, et dépendans. Sa retraite n'a pas la mine
d'être fort tranquille. . . . Il n'y a pas encore un nouveau
ministère déclaré, et comme vous pouvez juger il y a bien du
mouvement à cette occasion : peu de jours en décideront.

Voilà pour les nouvelles, que je ne bannis non plus que vous
de notre commerce, mais dont je fais l'article le moins essentiel,
car par ma foi je me soucie bien moins de ce que font les Rois
que de ce que vous me dites et de ce que vous pensez, et les faits
seront toujours les endroits de vos lettres qui m'intéresseront le
moins. Ce n'est pas au reste un grand compliment que je vous
fais, vû la situation d'esprit, dans laquelle je me trouve : car,
soit philosophie, soit paresse, ou même indolence, je regarde tous
ces évènemens qui agitent tant les autres, avec le même sang
froid que je lis ceux de l'antiquité ; et tous les Rois de l'Europe

---

* Sir Robert Walpole. In this passage Lord Chesterfield, amidst the
party-spirit of the times, does not do justice to Walpole's fortitude and
serenity in his fall. His friend Lord Morton at the same period (February
11) writes as follows to Duncan Forbes, Lord President : "Last week
there passed a scene between him and me by ourselves, that affected me
more than anything I ever met with in my life. He has been sore hurt
by flatterers, but has a great and an undaunted spirit, and a tranquillity
something more than human." (*Culloden Papers*, p. 175.)

† February 12.

sont pour moi les Rois de Perse et d'Égypte. Si pourtant ma destinée, ou mes liaisons, m'obligent à prendre quelque part aux affaires, il faut subir le joug, et remplir mes engagemens, mais ce ne sera pas sans envier le bienheureux sort de ceux qui restent maîtres de leur tems, de leurs actions, et de leurs paroles.

LXXIX.

TO THE REV. DR. CHENEVIX.

LONDON, *March* 6, 1742.

DEAR DOCTOR,

I will not tell you that I am sorry for your Southwark disappointment,* because, as the Irishman said, I think you have got a loss; and considering the charge of removing, and the increase of your expense by living in London, I am sure you would have been no gainer by your preferment, and yet you would have been looked upon by the Court as provided for. I need not tell you, I am sure, how much I wish to be able to contribute to the advantageous change of your situation; but I am sure, too, that I cannot tell you when I shall; for, till I can do it consistently with my honour and conscience, I will not do it at all, and I know you do not desire I should. The public has already assigned me different employments, and among others that which you mention; but I have been offered none, I have asked for none, and I will accept of none till I see a little clearer into matters than I do at present; I have opposed measures not men,† and the change of two or three men only is not a sufficient pledge to me that measures will be changed; nay, rather an indication that they will not; and I am sure no employment whatsoever shall prevail with me to support measures I have so justly opposed. A good conscience is in my mind a better thing than the best employment, and I will not have the latter till I can keep it with the former; when that can be, I shall not decline a public life, though in truth, more inclined to a private

---

* See Letter LXX. of February 15, 1740.

† "Measures, not men, have been always my mark."—Goldsmith: *The Good-natured Man* (1768). Burke, in his *Thoughts on the Causes of the Present Discontents* (1770), attacks the cant of "not men but measures."

one. You did very well to hinder your friend, Mr. Hutchins,* from taking a useless journey. I have heard a very good character of him, and shall be very glad to do for him when in my power; but he must naturally suppose too that I have some prior engagements to satisfy, and you will possibly think it but reasonable that you should be my first care; at least I think so, for I am

Very faithfully yours.

My compliments to Mrs. Chenevix.

LXXX.

TO DR. CHEYNE,† (OF BATH.)

LONDON, April 20, 1742.

DEAR DOCTOR,

Your inquiries and advice concerning my health are very pleasing marks of your remembrance and friendship; which, I assure you, I value as I ought. It is very true, I have, during these last three months had frequent returns of my giddiness, languors, and other nervous symptoms, for which I have taken vomits; the first did me good, the others rather disagreed with me. It is the same with my diet; sometimes the lowest agrees, at other times disagrees, with me. In short, after all the attention and observation I am capable of, I can hardly say what does me good, and what not. My constitution conforms itself so much to the fashion of the times, that it changes almost daily its friends for its enemies, and its enemies for its friends. Your alkalised mercury, and your Burgundy, have proved its two most constant friends. I take them both now, and with more advantage than any other medicine. I propose going to Spa as soon as the season will permit, having really received great benefit by those waters last year; and I find my shattered tenement admits of but half repairs and requires them annually.

The *corpus sanum*, which you wish me, will never be my lot;

---

* A clergyman in Leicestershire, related to Lord Chesterfield.—C.

† George Cheyne, one of the most celebrated physicians of his day, born in 1671. He had retired to Bath for the sake of his health, and died there in 1742, shortly after the date of this letter. His chief works were: *The English Malady, a Treatise on Nervous Disorders, A Treatise on Gout,* and an *Essay on Regimen.*

but the *mens sana*, I hope, will be continued to me, and then I shall better bear the infirmities of the body. Hitherto, far from impairing my reason, they have only made me more reasonable, by subduing the tumultuous and troublesome passions. I enjoy my friends and my books as much as ever, and I seek for no other enjoyments; so that I am become a perfect philosopher; but whether *malgré moi* or no, I will not take upon me to determine, not being sure that we do not owe more of our merit to accidents, than our pride and self-love are willing to ascribe to them.

I read with great pleasure your book, which your bookseller sent me according to your directions. The physical part is extremely good, and the metaphysical part may be so too, for what I know; and I believe it is; for, as I look upon all metaphysics to be guess-work of imagination, I know no imagination likelier to hit upon the right than yours; and I will take your guess against any other metaphysician's whatsoever. That part, which is founded upon knowledge and experience, I look upon as a work of public utility; and for which the present age and their posterity may be obliged to you, if they will be pleased to follow it.

I am, etc.

LXXXI.
À MADAME DE TENCIN.*

À LONDRES, ce 20 *Août*, V.S. 1742.

Combattu par des mouvemens bien différens, j'ai longtems balancé, avant que d'oser me déterminer à vous envoyer cette lettre. Je sentois toute l'indiscrétion d'une telle démarche, et à quel point c'étoit abuser de la bonté que vous avez eue pour moi pendant mon séjour à Paris, que de vous la redemander un autre; mais sollicite vivement par une dame, que son mérite met à l'abri des refus, et porté d'ailleurs à profiter du moindre prétexte pour rappeler un souvenir qui m'est si précieux que le votre, le penchant, comme il arrive presque toujours, a

---

* Madame de Tencin resided at Paris, and was sister of the famous Cardinal de Tencin, and noted both for wit and intrigue. She was the patroness of men of letters; Fontenelle and Montesquieu were among her friends.

triomphé de la discrétion, et je satisfais en même tems à mes propres inclinations, et aux instances de Madame Cleland, qui aura l'honneur de vous rendre cette lettre. Je sais par expérience, Madame, car j'en suis moi-même un exemple, que ce n'est pas la première affaire de la sorte, à laquelle votre réputation, qui ne se renferme point dans les bornes de la France, vous a exposée; mais je me flatte aussi que vous ne la trouverez pas la plus désagréable. Un mérite supérieur, un esprit juste, délicat, et orné par la lecture de tout ce qu'il y a de bon dans toutes les langues, et un grand usage du monde, qui ont acquis à Madame Cleland l'estime et la considération de tout ce qu'il y a d'honnêtes gens ici, me rassurent sur la liberté que je prends de vous la recommander, et me persuadent même que vous ne m'en saurez pas mauvais gré. J'avoue, Madame, que ce seroit vous faire un mauvais retour pour tout ce que je vous dois, que de vous endosser mes compatriotes, gens très peu faits pour répandre des agrémens dans la société, et qui se trouveroient fort déplacés dans celle que votre mérite et votre bon goût forment chez vous, et dont vous êtes en même tems et le soutien et l'ornement. Mais ne craignez rien de ce côté là; je ne pousse pas l'indiscrétion à ce point. Madame Cleland n'est Angloise que de naissance, mais Françoise par régénération, si je puis me servir de ce terme. Si vous me demandez par hasard pourquoi elle m'a choisi pour son introducteur chez vous, et pourquoi elle a cru que je m'étois acquis ce droit là, je vous dirai naturellement que c'est moi qui en suis cause. En cela j'ai suivi l'exemple de la plûpart des voyageurs, qui, à leur retour, se font valoir chez eux, par leurs prétendues liaisons avec tout ce qu'il y a de plus distingué chez les autres. Les Rois, les Princes, et les Ministres, les ont toujours comblés de leurs graces, et moyennant ce faux étalage d'honneurs qu'ils n'ont point reçus, ils acquièrent souvent une considération qu'ils ne méritent point. J'ai vanté vos bontés pour moi, je les ai exagérées même s'il étoit possible, et enfin, pour ne vous rien cacher, ma vanité a poussé l'effronterie au point de me donner pour votre ami, favori, et enfant de la maison; quand Madame Cleland m'a pris au mot, et m'a dit, "Je vais bientôt en France : je n'y ambitionne rien tant que l'honneur de connoître Madame de Tencin; vous qui êtes si bien là, il ne vous coûtera rien de me donner une lettre pour elle." Le cas étoit embarrassant : car, après ce que j'avois dit, un refus auroit été trop choquant à Madame Cleland, et l'aveu que je n'étois pas en droit de le faire, trop humiliant pour mon amour propre; si bien que je me suis trouvé reduit à risquer le paquet, et je crois même que je l'aurois fait, si je n'avois pas eu l'honneur de vous connoître du tout, plutôt que de me donner le démenti sur un article si sensible.

Ayant donc franchi le pas, je voudrois bien en profiter, pour vous expliquer les sentimens de reconnoissance que j'ai, et que j'aurai toujours des bontés que vous m'avez témoignées à Paris; et je voudrois aussi vous exprimer tout ce que je pense des qualités qui distinguent votre cœur et votre esprit de tous les autres, mais cela me meneroit également au delà des bornes d'une lettre, et au dessus de mes forces. Je souhaiterois que M de Fontenelle voulût bien s'en charger pour moi. Sur cet article, je puis dire sans vanité que nous pensons de même, avec cette différence qu'il vous le diroit avec cet esprit, cette délicatesse, et cette élégance qui lui sont personnelles, et seules convenables au sujet. Permettez donc, Madame, que destitué de tous ces avantages de l'esprit, je vous assure simplement des sentimens de mon cœur, de l'estime, de la vénération, et de l'attachement respectueux avec lesquels je serai toute ma vie,

Madame, Votre, etc.

Je crois que vous me pardonnerez si je vous supplie de faire mes complimens à M. de Fontenelle.*

---

* The reply of Madame de Tencin to this letter (dated October 22, 1742), commences with some graceful compliments. "Je voudrois, Milord, que vous eussiez été témoin de la reception de votre lettre. Elle me fut remise par M. de Montesquieu au milieu de la société que vous connoissez. Ce que vous me dites de flatteur m'empêcha quelques momens de la montrer, mais l'amour propre trouve toujours le moyen d'avoir son compte. . . . La lettre fut donc lue. et ne le fut pas pour une fois. 'Ce Milord se moque de nous!' s'écria M. de Fontenelle, qui fut suivi des autres. 'Qu'il se contente, s'il lui plait, d'être le premier homme de sa nation, d'avoir les lumières et la profondeur de génie qui la caractérisent; et qu'il ne vienne point encore s'emparer de nos graces et de nos gentillesses!'—Les plaintes et les murmures de l'assemblée dureroient encore si après avoir convenu bien franchement de vos torts je ne m'étois avisée de rappeller les agrémens et la douceur de votre commerce. 'Qu'il nous revienne donc!' dirent-ils tous à la fois, 'nous lui passerons alors d'avoir plus d'esprit que nous!' "—Maty's Ed., ii. 333.

LXXXII.

A MONS. DE CREBILLON (LE FILS).

LONDRES, *ce* 26 *Août*, V.S. 1742.

MONSIEUR,

En dernier lieu la poste m'a été plus favorable que de coutume, et m'a apporté vos deux dernières lettres * à tems. Si elle m'a rendu justice aussi auprès de vous, vous aurez vu par ma précédente, que j'étois rassuré sur ce que, pendant quelque tems, sa négligence m'avoit fait craindre. À présent même je lui sais bon gré d'une négligence, qui m'a procuré des marques si flatteuses de votre amitié, et de vos sentimens à mon égard. Je puis avec vérité vous assurer du réciproque par rapport à mes sentimens; mais malheureusement le réciproque finit là, et me manque dans le besoin de vous l'exprimer.

Il y a des vérités avantageuses, qui sentent trop la flatterie, faute d'une certaine délicatesse dans la manière de les dire, comme il y a une flatterie qui, moyennant cette délicatesse, ne paroit qu'une simple vérité. Le talent vous en est personnel, et m'a presque fait croire que je mérite tout ce que vous me dites.

J'avoue ma foiblesse pour la flatterie; je l'aime autant que Voltaire peut l'aimer, mais avec cette différence, que je ne l'aime que de main de maître. J'en suis friand, il en est goulu. J'y ai un bon appétit naturel, il en a une faim canine, qui lui fait dévorer avec avidité tout ce que le plus mauvais gargotier lui présente.

Je sens bien que tout ceci est la même chose que si je vous disois; Monsieur, flattez moi tant qu'il vous plaira, j'en serai charmé. J'en conviens, et je n'en rougis point. *Laudari a laudato viro*, a passé de tout tems pour une ambition très pardonnable; et Ciceron, écrivant à un homme comme vous, lui dit plus d'une fois, *orna me*.

Je comprends parfaitement cela; mais je ne comprends pas comment on n'est pas indigné de la flatterie de ceux dont l'approbation réelle seroit à mon avis humiliante.

Voltaire † m'a récité l'année passée à Bruxelles plusieurs

---

* These two letters are printed in Maty's Ed. of Lord Chesterfield's Works, vol. ii. pp. 312–322.

† Voltaire was born in 1694, and died in 1778.

tirades de son *Mahomet*, où j'ai trouvé de très beaux vers, et quelques pensées plus brillantes que justes; mais j'ai d'abord vu qu'il en vouloit à Jesus-Christ, sous le caractère de Mahomet, et j'étois surpris qu'on ne s'en fût pas apperçu à Lille, où elle fut représentée immédiatement avant que j'y passasse. Même je trouvai à Lille un bon Catholique, dont le zèle surpassoit la pénétration, qui étoit extrêmement édifié de la manière dont cet imposteur et ennemi du Christianisme étoit dépeint.

Pour les scènes décousues, et les morceaux déplacés, si vous n'eu voulez pas, vous ne voulez pas de Voltaire. Avec lui, il n'est pas question de son sujet, mais des pensées hardies, brillantes et singulières qu'il veut donner au public, n'importe où ni comment.

Passe encore pour cela; il n'est pas le premier auteur qu'une imagination vive ait enlevé au-dessus de la raison et de la justesse; mais ce que je ne lui pardonne pas, et qui n'est pas pardonnable, c'est tous les mouvemens qu'il se donne pour la propagation d'une doctrine aussi pernicieuse à la société civile que contraire à la religion générale de tous les pays.

Je doute fort s'il est permis à un homme d'écrire contre le culte et la croyance de son pays, quand même il seroit de bonne foi persuadé qu'il y eût des erreurs, à cause du trouble et du désordre qu'il y pourroit causer; mais je suis bien sûr qu'il n'est nullement permis d'attaquer les fondemens de la morale, et de rompre des liens si nécessaires, et déjà trop foibles pour retenir les hommes dans le devoir.

Malgré toute la fatuité, tous les égaremens, et les impertinences d'auteur, je ne conviendrai jamais que vous renonciez à ce nom, encore moins au métier. Le public y perdroit, j'y perdrois, et vous y perdriez aussi trop. D'ailleurs, il me semble que plus un corps est sujet à des défauts marqués, plus il est glorieux d'être de ce corps, et en même tems, comme vous, d'être exempt de ses défauts.

Parmi les "animaux écrivants," comme vous définissez les auteurs, l'animal écrivant bien est aussi rare, qu'est parmi les animaux raisonnables, comme on nous définit, l'animal qui se sert de sa raison. Continuez, donc, en dépit des caillettes et des petits-maîtres, à mériter une distinction qui vous est due par tant d'endroits, et ajoutez y même, en ajoutant à vos volumes. Donnez nous seulement assez, je ne me mets pas en peine du reste. *De te nam cœtera sumes.*

Adieu, Monsieur; car je m'apperçois que cette lettre approche presque d'un volume, qui ne ressembleroit nullement à ceux que je vous demande, mais qui vous ennuyeroit fort.

Je suis, avec toute l'estime que vous méritez, etc.

P.S.—Si vous voyez quelquefois Madame Herault, faites la souvenir de moi, en l'assurant de mon respect, et dites lui de plus, que si je n'avois une grandeur d'ame unique, qui me rend incapable d'insulte ou de vengeance, je lui enverrois bien des chansons qu'on a faites ici, sur certains mauvais succès en Allemagne,* et que je traduirois en François, pour l'usage de M. de Séchelles.†

LXXXIII.

TO HUGH, EARL OF MARCHMONT.

LONDON, *September* 8, 1742.

MY DEAR LORD,

The ill fortune, that commonly attends me in everything, has distinguished itself lately in putting me out of your way, every time you have endeavoured to see me. I have as often intended to wait upon you at Battersea, but have as constantly been prevented by some unexpected and ill-timed incident. I have a thousand things to say to you, and to almost only you; for, except one or two more of my friends and yours, whom can one speak to with either satisfaction or safety in these times of perfidy and avarice, when half-a-crown can dissolve the strongest ties of friendship?

I go to-morrow to Nugent's ‡ for a week, from whence, when I return, I shall take up Pope at Twickenham the 19th, and carry him to the Duchess of Marlborough's at Windsor, in our way to

* The ill-success of the French armies during this campaign, in the war against Maria Theresa.—M.

† Probably the father of. Herault de Séchelles, too well known in the worst times of the French Revolution. It is stated in the *Biographie Universelle*, that his grandfather, who had been *Lieutenant-Général de Police*, had died August 2, 1740.—M.

‡ Robert Nugent, afterwards created Earl Nugent. He was a maternal ancestor of the last Duke of Buckingham.

Cobham's, where we are to be the 21st of this month. Should you happen to be at the Duchess of Marlborough's the 19th or 20th, it would be a pleasure, I dare say, to all who will be there those two days, and to none a more sensible one, than to

Your most attached and faithful servant.

LXXXIV.

TO HUGH, EARL OF MARCHMONT.

Thursday, January 5, 1743.

MY DEAR LORD,

Lord Bolingbroke dines with me to-morrow; I do not know whether Lord Marchmont does or not; but I wish he did.

I send you the skeleton of a protest * upon the Hanover troops; it is truly a skeleton yet; I beg you will give it flesh and colour, which nobody can do so well. It is a child which I am by no means fond of; so pray use it with all the severity necessary for its good. Keep it by you a week; insert, cut out what you think proper; and return it me as unlike as possible to what it is now.

I am, my dear Lord, etc.

LXXXV.

TO THE REV. DR. CHENEVIX.

LONDON, *November* 3, 1743.

DEAR DOCTOR,

As this is a begging letter, I think I should begin in the usual style of those epistles, and tell you that past favours embolden me to ask for new ones, and that your ale was so good that I wish you would send me a little more of it. By the time it lasted me, for I drank the last bottle yesterday, you may judge, that I mean literally but a little more; and if you send me more than you did last time, it will only be spoiled before it is drunk.

---

* A motion in the House of Peers against taking Hanoverian troops into British pay was brought forward on the 1st of February ensuing, by Lord Chesterfield's kinsman, Earl Stanhope. But after a long debate (in which Lord Chesterfield's eloquence was highly distinguished) the Ministers prevailed by ninety votes against thirty-five. The protest on its rejection, as being written by Lord Chesterfield, bears his signature as the first on the list.—M.

My brother John told me he left you at Nottingham in perfect health, which I was extremely glad to hear, it being in my mind impossible for a man not to be happy with good health and a good conscience like yours. Money may improve but cannot make happiness; and though I wish it would improve yours, yet in the mean time I am convinced that there are many more people in this kingdom that have reason to envy your situation, than to prefer their own to it.

I have been of late a little out of order with a cold; but bleeding set me right, and I am in hopes of resisting the winter tolerably, which is the trying season to me.

Adieu, dear Doctor, *divertissez-vous, il n'y a rien de tel;* and believe me most affectionately and faithfully yours.

LXXXVI.

TO LADY ——————

Vous feriez bien mieux, Madame,* de vous fier à votre propre jugement que de demander le mien sur les Lettres † en question, aussi bien que sur toute autre chose; mais vous me l'ordonnez, il faut obéir. Il faut donc que j'aie l'honneur de vous dire naturellement, que l'auteur trouvera très-peu de personnes, qui voudront s'engager à payer deux cent francs par an pour deux lettres de la fabrique dont il a donné l'échantillon.

Par exemple, en voulant montrer que ceux, qui ont traité de notre mot *humour*, s'y sont trompés, il ne montre que trop qu'il l'ignore parfaitement lui-même.

La définition pourtant en est assez simple : *humour* c'est une représentation juste et frappante de ce qu'il y a de singulier ou de ridicule dans un caractère, et *a man of humour* est un homme, qui saisit vivement ce singulier, ou ce ridicule, qui distingue ce caractère, et qui le met dans tout son jour. On s'imagine

---

* Maty says that the letter was given to him by the lady to whom it was written, whose name he is not at liberty to mention; and the "author" referred to was Abbé Le Blanc, and his book, the *Lettres d'un François*.

† The *Lettres d'un François*, which gives a clear and amusing account of England, was published at the Hague (chez Jean Neaulme) in 1745. It would seem as if it had been in the first instance designed to be published by subscription; and this letter, written in French to an English lady, was no doubt intended to be shown to the author.—M.

généralement que nous autres Anglois possédons, exclusivement des autres nations, l'*humour ;* mais il n'y a rien de moins vrai. Jamais homme n'en a tant eu que Molière ; son Avare, son Jaloux, son Bourgeois Gentilhomme, en sont des preuves suffisantes ; et la comédie Françoise en fournit encore un millier d'exemples. Si à la vérité, on dit qu'il n'y a pas de pays en Europe, où il y a tant de différens caractères singuliers, je crois qu'on n'aura pas tort. Mais *humour* ne consiste pas en cela. L'homme qui a le travers, ou le ridicule, n'a point d'*humour*, c'est son naturel ; mais c'est l'homme qui saisit, et qui dépeint ce ridicule ou ce travers, qui a de l'*humour*. Je finis cette dissertation déjà trop longue sur l'*humour*, et dans laquelle, peut-être, ai-je donné à gauche autant que votre auteur, et ceux qu'il critique. D'ailleurs, quand on a l'honneur d'écrire à une personne comme vous, il sembleroit assez singulier que trois pages entières ne roulassent uniquement que sur le ridicule des caractères. Des matières plus agréables demanderoient une juste préférence, et votre critique épistolaire y trouveroit bien de quoi critiquer.

J'ai l'honneur d'être, avec les sentimens de la plus parfaite considération.

Votre très-humble, etc.

LXXXVII.

TO THE EARL OF HARRINGTON.
Private.

HAGUE,* February 21, N.S. 1745.

MY LORD,

Having received no commands from your Lordship by the last post, I have little to trouble you with by this.

I thought the keeping of the Dutch ships, an object of consequence enough to give in yesterday the inclosed Memorial, to the States-General, with the report of the Lords of the Admiralty translated and annexed. But I am far from saying, and it may be from hoping, that it will have any effect ; for the

---

* On the 3rd of January, 1745, Lord Chesterfield was appointed Lord Lieutenant of Ireland, but was instructed to proceed previously on a special embassy to the Hague. The object of that embassy, and the course he pursued in it, are explained in his letter to his son, Sept. 29, 1752.—M.

word Necessity is the answer to everything I ask. It is really true that all their Admiralties together cannot fit out another ship in the world; but it is as true too, that this necessity is owing to that long ill conduct and those inveterate abuses, which have near destroyed, and if they go on, as I think they are much more likely to do than to be reformed, will soon totally ruin this Republic.

The Princess Royal and the Prince of Orange arrived last night at their House in the Wood, and I had the honour of waiting upon them this day. Her Royal Highness is declared to be with child. The States-General will, I dare say, soon appoint his Highness General of the Foot, dating his commission on the 2nd of January, 1742, which is the day after the dates of the Commissions of the Foreign Generals that made so much noise here, and that gave the Province of Frise the reason (or possibly only the pretence) of opposing every thing and paying nothing ever since. I hope the Prince will accept of that commission; I do my utmost to prevail with him, but I much doubt of my success. I will venture to say he is very ill advised if he does not, both for his own private and the public interest.

The appointing the Prince of Waldeck to command in chief the Dutch forces this year, has disgusted many of the old Generals here; but in truth they are such as are much better disgusted than employed. This choice is approved of by every body else. They have chosen him here as a spirited mettled officer, fit for the action and vigour which they intend and hope for this campaign. General Cronstrom said beforehand that he would quit, but has since begged to be employed; Ginkel talks in the same way, but I dare say will act in the same manner. Pretorius I really believe will quit this service.

I am ever, etc.

LXXXVIII.

TO THE EARL OF HARRINGTON.

Private.

HAGUE, February 23, N.S. 1745.

MY LORD,

The Greffier has just now brought me a resolution of the States in answer to my Memorial about the ships; but as it is in Dutch and too late to have it translated to-night, I do not send it your Lordship. Moreover it is sent to Monsieur Hop, from whom you will hear enough of it. The substance is to insist upon having ten of their ships back again, to serve for convoys to their fleets of merchant-men. I have not agreed to it, but I fear his Majesty must, or else he will run the risk of losing them all. For they are so set upon this that I think them very capable of recalling the whole twenty, if the ten are refused them. But I think it should be understood that in consideration of his Majesty's consent to part with one half, that he may absolutely depend upon the continuance of the other half, properly victualled and fit for any service he may think proper to employ them in. As they want these ships to protect their trade against the French, I have taken this occasion to ask them what they get by not declaring war against France, since France in effect has declared it against them ? And what they could lose by declaring it, if their trade is equally interrupted ? But arguments have little weight in the present anarchy, and without returning any, their answer is they can't, because they can't, or they won't because they won't.

I am with the greatest truth and respect, etc.

LXXXIX.
TO THE EARL OF HARRINGTON.
Private.

HAGUE, *February* 26, N.S. 1745.

MY LORD,

I could not help troubling your Lordship with this solicitation in favour of one Mr. Lewis Oury, who is now a Lieutenant of Invalids in Jersey. He is brother to Madame Van-haren, the wife to the celebrated Monsieur Van-haren, of Frise, who is a most active, able, and well-intentioned member of this Government; but who, being of a very violent temper, is as easily angered as pleased. His wife, that is himself (for he married her for love and has the surprising good fortune of being in love with her still) solicited me strongly to recommend him to his Majesty's favour for a company of Invalids in Jersey or Guernsey, or any other promotion that his Majesty shall think proper. I could not refuse recommending this to your Lordship to lay before his Majesty; for though the promotion of Mr. Oury may in itself be very insignificant, I am sure it will extremely oblige Monsieur Van-haren, and the disappointment I fear may equally offend him.

I am with great truth and respect, etc.

XC.

TO THE EARL OF HARRINGTON.

Private.

HAGUE, *March* 5, N.S. 1745.

MY LORD,

By a letter I have just now seen from General Wade * to General Ligonier, it seems as if the former expected to be sent to command the British troops again this year in Flanders. It little becomes me, and indeed I am less inclined, to mingle myself in an affair of that nature, in which I have most certainly nothing to do; but as I had your Lordship's orders when I left England to send you the sentiments of people here, upon the subject of another person, I think myself under the same obligation to communicate to your Lordship their unanimous sentiments upon Maréchal Wade. Your Lordship may remember that, in my former letter upon this delicate subject, I told you, that though they thought Lord Stair too warm and enterprising, they would infinitely rather see him at the head of the British troops than Maréchal Wade, of whom, I must say, they have (though I dare say without reason) a very indifferent opinion,

---

* General George Wade, raised to the rank of Field-Marshal in December, 1743. He is now chiefly remembered from the military roads which were executed under his direction through the Highlands. In a letter of September, 1765, the poet Gray refers to travelling by "Marshal Wade's road from Dunkeld to Inverness." Marshal Wade commanded an English army in the rebellion of 1745-46; and at that time the following stanza was added to "God Save the King":—

> "Lord, grant that Marshal Wade
> May, by Thy mighty aid,
>   Victory bring!
> May he sedition hush,
> And like a torrent rush
> Rebellious hosts to crush.
>   God save the King!"

and against whom I have with the greatest difficulty (and possibly not yet quite) stopped a public complaint which they intended to have made to his Majesty, upon the separation of the troops last year.

I find by the same letter to General Ligonier that Lord Stair was to have commanded in Flanders, but that the command given to Count Königseck has obstructed that affair. I hope I have not been to blame in concurring with the States in their offer of that command to Feld-Maréchal Königseck, which I should not have done so readily, had I not known from your Lordship that his Majesty had thought of that General in failure of Prince Charles, and that his Majesty's intentions had been communicated to him, as appeared by his letter to Monsieur Wasner, which your Lordship showed me. As to the dispute of command, or other difficulties of that nature, I am an utter stranger to them; but I took it for granted then, and do still, that Count Königseck could never be thought of in any other light than as Commander-in-Chief of the whole combined army, and not as Commander only of the few Austrian forces that may make a small part of it; and by a letter I have seen from Count Königseck to Baron Reischach, I find he understands it so too himself. From all which, I don't see what new difficulty can have arisen concerning Lord Stair, that was not to be expected from the very first nomination of Feld-Maréchal Königseck. If I have done anything wrong in this affair, I must only beg his Majesty's pardon, it having been merely an error of ignorance; for if in his Majesty's service I could be influenced by any other motive, it would have been by my regard and long friendship for Lord Stair. I must beg your Lordship will manage me in the invidious part which I am so unwillingly obliged to take in this affair.

I am, etc.

XCI.

TO THE REV. DR. CHENEVIX.

HAGUE, *March* 12, N.S. 1745.

I put nothing at top of this letter, not knowing whether the familiar appellation of *dear doctor* would now become me; because I hope that, by the time you receive this letter, you will be, as it were, my Lord of Clonfert. I have the pleasure of telling you, that I have this day recommended you to the King, for the Bishopric of that name, now vacant by the translation of its last Bishop to the see of Kildare. I hope my recommendation will not be refused, though I would not swear for it; therefore, do not absolutely depend upon your consecration, and stay quietly where you are till you hear further from me. I assure you, I expect few greater pleasures in the remainder of my life than that I now feel in rewarding your long attachment to me, and, what I value still more, your own merits and virtues.

Yours sincerely.

XCII.

TO THE REV. DR. CHENEVIX.

HAGUE, *April* 27, N.S. 1745.

DEAR DOCTOR,

I told you at first not to reckon too much upon the success of my recommendation, and I have still more reason to give you the same advice now, for it has met with great difficulties, merely as mine, and I am far from knowing yet how it will end. Pray, give no answer whatsoever to anybody, that either writes or speaks to you upon that subject, but leave it to me, for I make it my own affair, and you shall have either the Bishopric of Clonfert, or a better thing, or else I will not be Lord Lieutenant. I hope to be in England in about a fortnight, when this affair must and shall be brought to a decision.* Good-night to you!

Yours, etc.

---

* "When the King refused his consent to making me a Bishop, he directed Lord Harrington, then Secretary of State, to acquaint Lord Chesterfield that he would comply with his application in favour of any one, except me. His Lordship's answer was, that he would not continue Lord Lieutenant of Ireland, except I had the vacant Bishopric. One of the reasons given by his Majesty was, because he was told I wrote political pamphlets against the administration, which was absolutely false; . . . and Lord Chesterfield never employed me to negotiate for him any political transaction, though Sir Robert thought so, because I used to go to him every morning by eight o'clock and stay till he was dressed." Note by Bishop Chenevix, Maty's edition.

XCIII.
TO BISHOP CHENEVIX.

HAGUE, *May* 12, N.S. 1745.

MY GOOD LORD,

Now you are what I had positively declared you should be—a Bishop; but it is Bishop of Killaloe, not Clonfert, the latter refusing the translation. Killaloe, I am assured, is better. I heartily wish you joy, and could not refuse myself that pleasure, though I am in the greatest hurry imaginable, being upon my journey to Helvoet-Sluys for England.* Adieu!

Yours, etc.

XCIV.
A MADAME LA MARQUISE DE MONCONSEIL. †

À LONDRES, *ce* 24 *Juin*, V.S. 1745.

Il est bien flatteur pour moi, Madame, de voir que vous vous appercevez seulement de mon silence ; et il me l'est d'autant plus

---

* On returning from his embassy, Lord Chesterfield enjoyed the satisfaction of having entirely succeeded in its object. "He has concluded a treaty," writes Mr. Philip Yorke to the elder Horace Walpole, "regulating the contingents of force and expense for this campaign. I wish it could have been for the whole war. The States agree to bring 52,000 men into the field (including their corps on the Lower Rhine) to our 40,000. In sieges they are to furnish one-third, and we the rest. The expense of the land-carriage of artillery is to be borne by the Government in Flanders." —Letter, dated May 16, 1745.—M.

† This lady continued during many years a correspondent of Lord Chesterfield. Her father was Monsieur de Cursay, of whom Madame du Deffand says : "Il était gentilhomme, frère de Madame de Pleneuf." (*Letters to H. Walpole*, vol. iii. p. 239, ed. 1810); and her daughter married the Prince d'Henin (vol. i. p. 109). Horace Walpole mentions Madame de Monconseil, and refers to his having gone several times to her house at Paris. (To the Hon. H. S. Conway, Nov. 12, 1774).

It is stated by Dr. Maty in a note to the previous editions, "The originals of the following letters were sent to me from Paris, by a noble and respectable friend of the lady to whom they were written. I was laid by her and him under the disagreeable restriction of suppressing her name," and accordingly the name has hitherto remained in blank. But on a careful comparison of these letters with other parts of Lord Chesterfield's correspondence (especially the letter to the lady, of August 1, 1751, with that to his son of July 8, in the same year, both of which refer, though in very different terms, to Madame de Cursay's illness) there can remain no doubt whatever as to whom these letters were addressed.—M.

qu'il faut nécessairement que ce soit la justice que vous rendez à mes sentimens, et non ma manière de les exprimer, qui me procure cette attention. Je vous aurois écrit il y a longtems, si un nombre infini de différentes affaires m'eût laissé quelques momens à mon choix ; mais ma part à la régence d'ici, et les affaires d'Irlande, où je vais en six semaines, accablent un paresseux comme moi, qui souhaiterois de passer ma vie dans une tranquillité parfaite, et sans autres soins que ceux de la société et de l'amitié.

Vous m'avez envoyé, Madame, le plus parfait contraste du monde, votre lettre, et le discours de Monsieur le Président C——. La clarté accompagne tout ce que vous dites, et Monsieur le Président relève votre *chiaro* d'un *oscuro* unique. Il faut que ce bon homme se soit donné la torture bien longtems pour parvenir à ce point de perfection dans le galimatias. Dieu n'a jamais eu l'intention que l'homme pensât de la sorte, comme il n'a pas voulu non plus qu'on marchât sur les mains avec les pieds en l'air ; mais, moyennant le travail, il y a des gens qui sont venus à bout de l'un et de l'autre. Avec tout cela, ce galimatias dont on se moque chez vous, et dont on se moqueroit également ici, traduit en Italien ou en Espagnol, seroit l'objet de l'admiration de ces deux nations, où depuis deux cent ans on n'a rien écrit de plus juste, ou de plus clair. Le poème de Voltaire * n'est sûrement pas dans ce genre ; il est d'une grande justesse, et je n'ai pas encore vu de gazette, dans laquelle la liste des morts et des blessés, à la bataille de Fontenoy, ait été plus fidèlement et plus simplement détaillée ; je m'imagine que ce n'est que par hazard qu'une relation si exacte est en vers ; et apparemment Voltaire, comme Ovide, fait des vers sans y penser. Je trouve qu'il a beaucoup mieux écrit les relations des batailles de Narva et de Pultowa en prose, puisque la prose convient beaucoup plus à l'histoire.

Je vous assure que je souhaite la paix tout autant que vous ; et je crois que s'il ne tenoit qu'à nous deux de la faire, elle seroit bientôt faite ; mais comme malheureusement elle ne dépend pas absolument de nous, le moyen de l'avoir ? Vous la voulez à votre mode, ce qui ne nous conviendroit nullement : nous la voulons équitable, vous la voulez avantageuse, de sorte que je crains

* On the battle of Fontenoy.

qu'elle ne soit plus éloignée que jamais. Nous ne cherchons que la liberté, et la sûrete de l'Europe, vous n'y cherchez que votre despotisme; comment donc s'accorder? Laissez seulement à notre Reine * ce qui lui appartient, et que vous lui avez garanti, et ne demandez pas pour la vôtre,† ce qui ne lui appartient nullement, et alors on pourroit s'accommoder.

Me seroit-il permis, Madame, d'abuser de votre amitié, et de vous consulter, de vous employer, et de vous ennuyer, sur une affaire qui m'intéresse très sensiblement? Il me semble que vous me répondez qu'oui; je vais donc au fait; le voici. J'ai un garçon, qui à cette heure a treize ans; je vous avouerai naturellement qu'il n'est pas légitime, mais sa mère est une personne bien née, et qui a eu des boutés pour moi que je ne méritois pas. Pour le garçon, peut-être est-ce prévention, mais je le trouve aimable; c'est une jolie figure, il a beaucoup de vivacité, et je crois de l'esprit pour son âge. Il parle François parfaitement, il sait beaucoup de Latin et de Grec, et il a l'histoire ancienne et moderne au bout des doigts. Il est à présent à l'école, où je compte de le tenir jusqu'au mois de Mai qui vient: mais comme aux écoles ici, et même il faut ajouter, dans ce pays ici, on ne songe pas à former les mœurs ou les manières des jeunes gens, et qu'ils sont presque tous nigauds, gauches et impolis, enfin tels que vous les voyez quand ils viennent à Paris à l'age de vingt ou vingt-et-un ans, je ne veux pas que mon garçon reste assez ici pour prendre ce mauvais pli, dont on ne se défait guères, dès qu'il est une fois pris. C'est pourquoi quand il aura quatorze ans, je compte de l'envoyer à Paris, et le mettre en pension en quelque bonne maison bourgeoise; mais comme il sera alors très jeune, et qu'il n'aura pas à beaucoup près fini les études nécessaires, j'enverrai avec lui un Anglois‡ d'une érudition consommée, qui continuera et augmentera son Latin et son Grec, et qui lui enseignera en même tems sa logique, sa rhétorique, et un peu de philosophie. Ce savant en sera le maître absolu, dans la maison, et toutes les matinées; mais comme il ne sera guères propre à lui donner des manières, ou si vous le voulez le ton de la bonne com-

---

* The Queen of Hungary, the ally at that time of England.
† The Queen of Spain.
‡ The Rev. Walter Harte. See Chesterfield's Letter to his Son, of Oct. 4, 1746, and Index.

pagnie, chose pourtant très nécessaire, et peut-être aussi utile que tout le Grec et le Latin de Monsieur Vadius,* ne pourrois-je pas trouver à Paris quelque homme, ou quelque Abbé, qui (moyennant de l'argent que je lui donnerois volontiers) se chargeroit du soin du garçon depuis quatre heures l'après-midi; qui le meneroit aux comédies, aux opéras, et même chez vous, si vous vouliez bien lui en accorder la permission? Comme j'aime infiniment cet enfant, et que je me pique d'en faire quelque chose de bon, puisque je crois que l'étoffe y est, mon idée est de réunir en sa personne ce que jusqu'ici je n'ai jamais trouvé en la même personne; je veux dire, ce qu'il y a de meilleur des deux nations. C'est pourquoi je lui destine son pédant Anglois, qui est d'ailleurs homme d'esprit, pour l'érudition solide que je lui voudrois, et son précepteur François des après-diners, pour lui donner, avec le secours des compagnies où il pourra le mener, cette tournure aisée, ces manières, ces agrémens, que sûrement on ne trouve qu'en France.

Vous ayant ainsi expliqué mon idée, ayez la bonté de me dire, Madame, si vous croyez qu'il y ait moyen de la remplir, et de m'indiquer comment. Pourriez-vous trouver un tel homme, sur lequel on pourroit absolument se reposer? Voudriez-vous avoir aussi la bonté de vous informer de quelque bonne maison bourgeoise, où il y auroit une famille honnête, pour l'y placer? Et, si j'ose le demander, voudriez-vous bien lui permettre d'être quelquefois votre page chez vous le soir, pour donner les cartes, le café, et les chaises? En ce cas là, ce seroit bien sa meilleure école, mais je n'ose pas seulement y penser. Comme sa naissance pourroit lui nuire chez de certaines gens, je crois qu'il vaut mieux ne la pas déclarer, et le donner pour mon neveu, selon l'exemple des Cardinaux; en cela aussi vous me dirigerez.

Vous voyez bien, Madame, et par la longeur et par le contenu de cette lettre, à quel point je compte sur votre amitié, ou pour mieux dire, à quel point j'en abuse; mais, convaincu comme j'en suis, les excuses seroient déplacées, et si malheureusement je m'y trompois, les excuses ne me serviroient de rien, je ne vous en fais donc point, et je vous donne le bon soir.

* One of the characters in *Les Femmes Savantes* of Molière.

XCV.

À MADAME LA MARQUISE DE MONCONSEIL.

à LONDRES, *ce* 26 *Juillet*, V.S. 1745.

Il n'y a que vous, Madame, qui auroit pû non seulement pardonner mon indiscrétion, mais même vous y prêter. Vous entrez dans mes petits détails comme s'ils vous étoient personnels, et vous recherchez des soins, dont les amis vulgaires trouveroient bien moyen de s'excuser, sans pourtant blesser les apparences de l'amitié. J'y suis d'autant plus sensible, que je suis persuadé que la véritable amitié se distingue plus dans les petites choses que dans les grandes. On n'ose pas manquer aux grands devoirs de l'amitié, on y perdroit trop du côté de la réputation, mais aussi on les remplit souvent plus par intérêt, que par sentiment, au lieu qu'il y a mille prétextes honnêtes pour éviter les petites attentions, qui seroient très embarrassantes et incommodes, si le sentiment ne leur donnoit même des charmes. Je vous avoue que mon affection, ou si vous le voulez, ma foiblesse pour ce garçon, fait que tout ce qui lui arrive m'est infiniment plus sensible que tout ce qui me pourroit arriver à moi-même, et me fera toujours envisager vos moindres bontés pour lui, comme les marques les plus solides et les plus flatteuses de votre amitié pour moi. Par rapport à son arrivée à Paris, cela dépend sûrement, comme vous dites, de la paix, et si elle ne se fait pas dans un an d'ici, il faudra songer à le placer ailleurs en attendant ; et en ce cas là je songe à Genève, mais si la paix se fait avant ce tems là, ce que par mille autres raisons je souhaite, je tiens qu'il n'y a que Paris pour le bien former. Pour la maison où vous comptez de le placer en pension, je m'en remets entièrement à vous, et cela ne sera pas difficile ; mais je conçois bien les difficultés que vous me montrez au sujet du polisseur. Je ne m'obstine nullement ni à un Abbé, ni à un savant ; je demande seulement un homme d'esprit, soit laïque, soit ecclésiastique, qui eût du monde, et qui étant présentable lui-même, pourroit présenter le garçon dans les bonnes compagnies, et lui donner le ton des honnêtes gens. Je serois bien aise aussi qu'il voulût lire avec lui l'histoire moderne, et les ouvrages d'esprit, pour en même tems l'instruire des faits, et lui former le goût. Son Anglois, qui sera avec lui, est un magazin d'érudition Grecque et Latine, et de ce côté là ne déplaira pas à l'Abbé Sallier ; mais il ne pourra jamais l'introduire, ni même l'accompagner chez les gens du monde. A son age il est impossible qu'il y aille seul, surtout aux opéras et aux comédies, où néanmoins il est bon qu'il aille quelquefois. Si un tel homme est à avoir, vous en jugerez mieux que personne, et je m'en rapporte en toute sûreté à votre choix. J'espère qu'il ne se mêlera pas de lui parler au sujet de la religion, puisque ce seroit ruiner le garçon dans ce monde ici, et sûrement sans dédommagement dans l'autre. Je suis entièrement de votre avis que sa naissance soit absolument cachée, et que dans cette vue, il vaut mieux que je passe pour un parent plus éloigné, et son tuteur, que pour son oncle, mais pourtant je ne voudrois pas en imposer à Monsieur de M—— que j'honore trop pour cela, et j'aimerois mieux renoncer à tous les avantages qui résulteroient au garçon d'être le galopin de Monsieur son fils que d'en profiter par abus.

J'ai ordonné à mon écuyer, qui se connoît parfaitement en chevaux, d'en chercher un par toute l'Angleterre, qui réponde autant qu'il est possible aux besoins de Monsieur de Nevers.* Si quelque chose pouvoit ajouter du poids à vos ordres auprès de moi, ce seroit le plaisir de pouvoir être utile dans la moindre chose à une personne du mérite reconnu de Monsieur de Nevers. J'ai mille fois regretté de n'avoir pas eu l'honneur et le plaisir de l'avoir connu personnellement pendant mon petit séjour à Paris ; je me ferai sûrement une affaire de réussir dans sa commission, mais pour trouver un cheval précisément tel qu'il le demande, je crains qu'il faudra le chercher avec une lanterne en plein jour, comme le philosophe cherchoit un homme ; je ne sais pas même s'il ne seroit pas plus facile de trouver une femme pour un autre, qu'un cheval, parceque peut-être elle est moins nécessaire, et qu'on s'en sert moins ! Quand j'en aurai trouvé un, je l'enverrai à Monsieur Wolters à Rotterdam, et vous aurez la bonté immédiatement de faire dire à quelqu'un de s'annoncer au dit Wolters, pour l'homme qui doit recevoir le cheval d'entre ses mains dès qu'il arrivera.

Je pars pour l'Irlande en trois semaines, mais adressez moi les lettres dont vous voudrez bien m'honorer, à Londres, comme à l'ordinaire : elles me font trop de plaisir pour que je ne prenne

* Father of the Duke de Nivernois.

pas toutes les précautions possibles pour n'en pas perdre une. Adieu, Madame ; je vous accable.

XCVI.
TO DAVID MALLET, ESQ.*

DUBLIN CASTLE, *November* 27, 1745.

SIR,

I have just now received the favour of your letter of the 20th, which adds to my shame, for not having sooner acknowledged your former. The truth is, that the business of this place, such as it is, is continual; and as I am resolved to do it while I am here, it leaves me little or no time to do things I should like much better; assuring you of my regard and friendship is one of those things, but though one of the most agreeable, I believe the least necessary.

I cannot comprehend the consternation which 8,000 of your countrymen have, I find, thrown seven millions of mine into; † I, who at this distance, see things only in their plain natural light, am, I confess, under no apprehensions; I consider a High-lander (with submission to you) as Rowe does a Lord, who when opposed to a man, he affirms to be but a man; from which principle I make this inference, that 49,000 must beat 8,000; not to mention our sixteen new regiments, which must go for something, though in my opinion not for much. I have with much difficulty quieted the fears here, which were at first very strong, partly by contagion from England, and partly from old prejudices, which my good subjects are far from being yet above. They are in general still at the year 1689, and have not shook off any religious or political prejudice that prevailed at that time. However, I am very glad I am among them; for in this little sphere, a little may do a great deal of good, but in England they must be much stronger shoulders than mine that can do any good at that bulky machine. Pray let me hear from you as often and as

* David Malloch, a Scotchman, who in England altered his name to Mallet, was the literary executor of the Duchess of Marlborough, and of Lord Bolingbroke. He is included among the poets in Dr. Johnson's Lives.

† The invasion of England by Prince Charles Stuart, then on the march to Derby.

minutely as you have leisure; most correspondents, like most very learned men, suppose that one knows more than one does, and therefore don't tell one half what they could, so one never knows so much as one should.

I am, etc.

XCVII.

TO THE DUKE OF NEWCASTLE.

DUBLIN CASTLE, *February* 18, 1746.

MY DEAR LORD,

Though I threatened you, in my last of the 15th, with a longer letter, this shall not be a very long one; for, besides that I am not, at any time, very fond of my own speculations, all speculations at this distance, and in such a conjuncture, are probably impertinent.* A situation so violent must vary every minute; and will, I dare say, be very different, at the time of your receiving this letter, from what it is now, at the time I am writing it.

I am convinced I need not tell you, that the day after my arrival in London, I shall most certainly resign my employment: as to the manner of doing it, I will receive and observe your directions. But this I think necessary to tell you, which is, that though I believe most people have a good opinion enough of me, to take it for granted, that I intend to quit, yet I have not communicated that intention to any one person living, either here or in England, but leave it entirely to you, to publish or not, as you shall think proper. Let me only know which you do, that I may conform myself here to it.

During the rest of my stay here, which shall be as short as I can possibly make it, though it cannot be half so short as I wish it, I must necessarily send my recommendations to my successor,

---

* This letter refers to the rash intrigue of Lords Bath and Granville, in February, 1746, to overthrow the Ministry, and form one of their own. They had the King completely with them, but found on trial a total want of Parliamentary followers, and were compelled to relinquish their attempt only two days after they had commenced it. See a spirited sketch of their proceedings in Horace Walpole's letter to Mann of February 14, 1746. Lord Chesterfield, it appears, wrote his letter at the news of their attempt, and his postscript at the news of their failure.—M.

whoever he may be; but I will take care that those recommenda-tions shall be of such a nature only, as that, if they prevail, I shall only have a civility but not an obligation to acknowledge. In the mean time my situation is extremely disagreeable; and God knows when it will end, for I have no great hopes that the Council in England will give much attention or despatch to my Irish Bills; so that I may possibly have full leisure to learn the language, if I apply myself.

It seems to me impossible that the two Earls can carry on the business, unless they have a strength in Parliament, which I am not aware of; for, I take it for granted, that, by much the greatest part of your old corps will stick to you; and I cannot think that many of the old Opposition will join them, so that, in my mind, your situation is better than it has been this great while; your way is clearer; you must be called for again, and that upon your own terms.

When that day comes, and I think it cannot be far off, *point de foiblesse humaine, point de quartier,* I beseech you; and let no ill-timed decency, candour, lenity, or heroism, weaken or spoil the best and most solid settlement of an administration, that it was ever in people's power to form. In short, do not be *subjectum lenis in hostem.* Adieu, my dear Lord; you have long known me to be what, if possible, I am now more than ever, etc.

My compliments to the late Chancellor of the Exchequer, and if you please to the whole late Cabinet Council.

P.S. *Tuesday night.* Just as I was sending away my letter by an express, I received Mr. Stone's of the 14th, which showed me that I was no bad prophet. And, to do honour to my spirit of prophecy, I send you the letter itself, by the common post, which you are again master of. Your victory is complete; for God's sake pursue it. Good policy, still more than resentment, requires that Granville and Bath should be marked out, and all their people cut off. Old Archy* ought too, in my mind, to be made an example of, for more reasons than one. Everybody

---

* "Lord Barrington comes into the Admiralty in the room of Lord Archibald Hamilton." Duke of Newcastle to Lord Chesterfield, February 18, 1746; as printed in Coxe's Pelham.—M.

now sees and knows, that you have the power; let them see and know too, that you will use it. The Garters, I should think, ought instantly to be properly disposed of, in one way, and the Finches in another. A general run ought to be made upon Bath, by all your followers and writers. If the rebels had pursued their victory at Preston Pans, they might have come to London, and we had been undone, as they are now, by their own neglect. If we had pursued the victory at Dettingen, Fontenoy had never been. As to your humble servant, all he desires for himself is, despatch to his Irish Bills, of which he will send you another cargo, the latter end of this week.

XCVIII.

TO THE DUKE OF NEWCASTLE.

Private.

DUBLIN CASTLE, *March* 11, 1746.

MY LORD,

My office letter to your Grace by this post being, as I hope, the last that I shall trouble you with from hence this season, contains variety of matters, and those of some importance, with regard to this country. Your Grace will therefore give me leave to explain them to you, with that truth which, wherever I am concerned, I desire his Majesty should most minutely know.

The Council door has not been opened of some years, I think seven or eight, and crowds are pressing at it, as it is really a Board of consequence here, being part of the Legislature. Some new members are really wanting, it being sometimes difficult to make up a quorum; but the greatest difficulty of all was, where to stop. I have at last reduced the number to eight, of which I don't reckon above five effective, which is about the number wanted at the Board.

The Earl of Kildare* applied to me early and strongly; his rank and estate in this country, I thought, left me no room to hesitate, and I readily promised him my recommendation.

The Earl of Kerry† is of a great family, has a great estate, and is a kind of a sovereign in the wild county of Kerry; a

---

* James Fitz-Gerald, twentieth Earl of Kildare, created a Marquis in 1761, and in 1766, Duke of Leinster.—M.

† William Fitz-Maurice, second Earl of Kerry. He died in 1747.—M.

very honest man, and very zealous for his Majesty's Government. He is ambitious of the title, more than of the thing itself; for his ill state of health, which is a palsy, will seldom or never let him attend. I think he very well deserves that mark of his Majesty's favour.

Lord Ikerren* is son-in-law to the Speaker—has a very good estate, is a very honest man; and, the truth is, the Speaker makes it a point.

The Lords Massarene† and Powerscourt ‡ are men of good sense and good estates, and will be of use at the Board. They are both what we call here *Castle-men*—that is, they meddle with no cabals nor parties; but they belong to the Lord-Lieutenant, and as such, in my humble opinion, deserve the favour of the Government in this case; and the more so, as they ask for nothing else.

Lord Limerick§ applies himself much to the business of this country, promotes the manufactures, and is in that way so efficient a man, that it seems as much the desire of most people, as his own, that he should have a place at that Board.

Lord Hillsborough‖ has a very considerable estate in this country, and his relations here, particularly Mr. Hill, his uncle, have credit and influence. They make it their request; and I look upon his admission there to be more nominal than real, as I believe he will be more in England than here.

Lord Viscount Fitzwilliam,¶ who likewise will, I believe, seldom take his seat, I fairly confess I recommend, at the earnest instances of his relations in England, though he has a very good estate here, and is a most unexceptionable person.

I assure your Grace I have no favourite among them, and

---

* Somerset Butler, eighth Viscount Ikerren; in 1748, advanced to the dignity of Earl of Carrick. He had married the daughter of Henry Boyle, Speaker of the Irish House of Commons, and afterwards created Earl of Shannon.—M.

† Clotworthy Skeffington, fifth Viscount, and afterwards Earl of Massareene.—M.

‡ Richard Wingfield, lately created Viscount Powerscourt.—M.

§ James Hamilton, Viscount Limerick, and afterwards Earl of Clanbrassil. See Letters CCCXXV., 29 Jan. 1755.—M.

‖ Wills Hill, second Viscount Hillsborough, and afterwards Marquis of Downshire.—M.

¶ Richard Fitzwilliam, sixth Viscount Fitzwilliam.—M.

my recommendation proceeds singly from the motives I have mentioned.

The Earl of Grandison's * application for a Viscountship for his daughter, Lady Betty Mason, seems to me so reasonable with regard to him, and of so little consequence to anybody else, that I own I have given him some reason to hope for that mark of his Majesty's favour. His estate here is at least eight thousand pounds a year. Mr. Mason, who married his daughter, has four; all which will centre in the son by that daughter. Lord Grandison's present Viscountship goes at his death to Lord Jersey. This request of his, therefore, seems to be a very common, and, so far at least a pardonable, piece of human vanity, often indulged in other cases, and I hope will be so in this.

The new Barrack Patent is a thing of absolute necessity for his Majesty's military service here. I should be a great deal too tedious if I were to state to your Grace a tenth part of that affair. I will therefore only say, that this new Patent, together with some other regulations I am making here, is the only probable method of preventing for the future the enormous abuses of the Barrack Board.

The Dublin Society is really a very useful establishment. It consists of many considerable people, and has been kept up hitherto by voluntary subscriptions. They give premiums for the improvement of lands, for plantations, for manufactures. They furnish many materials for those improvements in the poorer and less cultivated parts of this kingdom, and have certainly done a great deal of good. The bounty they apply for to his Majesty is five hundred pounds a year, which, in my humble opinion, would be properly bestowed; but I entirely submit it.

As to the applications of the Earls of Cavan† and Rosse,‡ and Lord Mayo,§ all I can say for them is, that they have

---

* John Villiers, fifth Viscount and first Earl of Grandison. As recommended by Lord Chesterfield, Lady Elizabeth Mason, was, in April 1746, created in her own right Viscountess Grandison.—M.

† Ford Lambart, fifth Earl of Cavan.—M.

‡ Richard Parsons, second Earl of Rosse.—M.

§ Theobald Bourke, seventh Viscount Mayo.—M.

nothing of their own—that they are part of the furniture of this House of Lords, which if his Majesty thinks proper to put in a little better repair, he will at the same time do a real act of compassion.

The few small pensions are too trifling to mention; they are the usual charities of the Government, and at the same time lay some obligations upon more considerable people who solicit them; and the establishment can very well bear them.

Having now finished, as I hope, all my recommendations for some time, I must beg leave to assure your Grace that they are, every one of them the recommendations of his Majesty's Lord-Lieutenant only, and that I am neither directly nor indirectly, in my private capacity, concerned in any one of them. I have neither retainer, friend, nor favourite among them.

I have one request more to trouble your Grace with, which indeed concerns myself singly, and that is, that your Grace will be pleased to apply to his Majesty for his gracious permission for me to return to England, to lay myself at his feet.* I shall by that time have been here near eight months, during which time I have endeavoured to carry on his Majesty's service. If I have failed it must have been only from want of abilities; for my zeal, I am sure, was not wanting, and I must, with the warmest and most respectful gratitude, acknowledge that his Majesty's indulgence to all my recommendations has given me all the credit and weight I was capable of receiving.

I am, with the greatest truth and respect, etc.

P.S. I have received the honour of your Grace's letter of the 5th, relating to the embargo, and have given the proper orders thereupon.

---

* According to the permission here solicited, Lord Chesterfield set out from Dublin, a few weeks after the date of this letter, and arrived at his house, in Grosvenor Square, on April 30, 1746. It is much to be regretted that the preceding letter is the only one in this collection, giving an account of public business during his Lord-Lieutenancy of Ireland.—M.

The date in the foregoing note is not quite correct; in the official correspondence of Lord Chesterfield in Dublin Castle is a letter to the Lords Justices, dated "Grosvenor Square, 3rd May, 1746," in which Lord Chesterfield says "he arrived safe last night." He continued to be Lord Lieutenant, though residing in England, up to 18th Nov., 1746.

XCIX.

TO THOMAS PRIOR, ESQ.*

LONDON, *June* 14, 1746.

SIR,

I thank you for the favour of your letter, with the inclosed scheme for carrying on the war; which if others approved of as much as I do, and the present situation of the war permitted, would be soon put in execution.

As you are one of the few in Ireland, who always think of the public, without any mixture of private, interest; I do not doubt but that you have already thought of some useful methods of employing the King's bounty to the Dublin Society. The late additional tax upon glass here, as it must considerably raise the price of glass-bottles imported into Ireland, seems to point out the manufacturing them there ; which consideration, with a small premium added to it, would, in my mind, set up such a manufacture. Fine writing and printing paper, we have often talked of together; and the specimen you gave me, before I left Dublin, proves, that nothing but care and industry is wanting, to bring that manufacture to such a perfection as to prevent the exportation of it from Holland, and through Holland from France ; nay, I am convinced that you might supply England with a great deal if you pleased, that is, if you would make it, as you could do, both good and cheap. Here is a man who has found out a method of making starch of potatoes, and, by the help of an engine of his own invention, to make a prodigious quantity of it in a day. But here is an Act of Parliament which

* Thomas Prior was born at Rathdowney, Queen's County, Ireland, in 1680, and educated at Trinity College, Dublin (Sch. 1701, B.A. 1703). The foundation of the Dublin Society—afterwards the Royal Dublin Society—was due to him, and originated at a meeting of thirteen gentlemen in Trinity College on 25th June, 1731. It was established to promote agriculture, manufactures, the arts and sciences. It received a Parliamentary grant of £500 a year in 1749. Prior died 21st October, 1751. A monument was erected to his memory in Christ Church Cathedral, Dublin, with an inscription written by his friend and fellow-student, Bishop Berkeley, in which he is styled " Societatis Dubliniensis Auctor, Institutor, Curator." He wrote pamphlets on The Absentees of Ireland, The National History of Ireland, The Success of Tarwater, etc.

strictly prohibits the making starch of any thing but flour.
Have you such an Act of Parliament in Ireland? If you have
not, and that you import your starch from England, as I take
it for granted that you do, for you import everything that you
can, it would be well worth this man's while to go to Ireland,
and advantageous for you that he should; his starch being to
my knowledge and experience full as good, and abundantly
cheaper than any other.

These are the sorts of jobs that I wish people in Ireland would
attend to with as much industry and care, as they do to jobs of
a very different nature. These honest arts would solidly increase
their fortunes, and improve their estates, upon the only true and
permanent foundation, the public good. Leave us and your
regular forces in Ireland to fight for you; think of your manufactures at least as much as of your militia, and be as much upon your guard against Poverty as against Popery; take my word
for it, you are in more danger of the former than of the latter.

I hope my friend, the Bishop of Meath,* goes on prosperously
with his Charter-schools. I call them his, for I really think that
without his care and perseverance they would hardly have
existed now. Though their operation is sure, yet, being slow,
it is not suited to the Irish taste of *the time present only ;* and I
cannot help saying, that, except in your claret, which you are
very solicitous should be two or three years old, you think less
of two or three years hence than any people under the sun.
If they would but wish themselves as well as I wish them; and
take as much pains to promote their own true interest, as I
should be glad to do to contribute to it, they would in a few
years be in a very different situation from that which they are in
at present. Go on, however, you and our other friends; be not
weary of well-doing, and though you cannot do all the good you
would, do all the good you can.

When you write to the most worthy Bishop of Cloyne,† pray
assure him of my truest regard and esteem, and remember me
to my honest and indefatigable friend in good works, Dr. Madden ;
and be persuaded yourself, that I am, with sincere friendship and
regard,

Your most faithful humble servant.

* Dr. Henry Maule.   † Dr. Berkeley.

C.

TO THOS. PRIOR, ESQ.

LONDON, *July* 15, 1746.

SIR,

I acknowledge the favour of your two letters, of the 3rd and 5th; they were doubly welcome to me, as coming from one, who I know wishes so well to the public as you do, and as they brought 'me good accounts of the progress you make in your public-spirited views. The manufacture of glass-bottles cannot possibly fail, but from want of care and industry; for as the price of glass bottles is risen considerably here, upon account of the new duty, if you would but make them in Ireland, you are sure of sale for them; and I should hope, at least, that considering the close connection there is between bottles and claret, this manufacture, *though your own,* may meet with encouragement. I think you are in the right to do it as quickly as can be, and to give your premiums without publishing them, not to alarm our glass people here; though in truth it could never be thought reasonable, nor would it, I dare say, ever be attempted here to prohibit any manufactures in Ireland, merely for home consumption.

The paper you gave me in Ireland, though good, was not so good as it should, and as I am sure it might be with care. It was too spongy and bibulous, which proceeds only from want of care, in choosing and sorting the best rags. Some premiums for this purpose will have a great effect; and I am convinced that, if this manufacture were carefully and diligently pursued, you might in time not only entirely supply yourselves, but us too, with great part of that paper which we now take from Holland and other countries. But then, indeed, you must make it cheap as well as good, and, contrary to your custom, content yourselves with less present profit, in order to get possession of a future and permanent advantage.

I have not yet taken any step concerning the Charter for the Dublin Society,* and I confess to you I have great doubts about it. Your Society, as it is, does so very well, that I am afraid of

* See the Index, and the note to letter to Dr. Madden, Dec. 12, 1746.

touching it. However, if you and others, who, I am sure, mean well, and can judge well, think upon the whole that a Charter would be beneficial, I will endeavour to get one.

You did extremely right to open the Spaniard's letter to me, and, in consequence of it, to proceed in that humane manner with him. His post was a very considerable one in the West Indies, and is never given but to people of consideration. In that light he deserves to have regard shown him; but still more, in my mind, from being unfortunate. I have writ to him by this post, in answer to his. As you tell me that part of the cargo of the ship is snuff, which I should think must be good, I shall be obliged to you, if, when it comes to be sold, you will send me twenty pounds of the strongest and the deepest coloured, and ask Mr. Lingen for the money.

The death of the King of Spain * must produce good effects in Italy at least.

I received a very kind letter from my Charter-school Apostle, the Bishop of Meath, which I have not time to answer by this post, but I will soon.

I am, with the esteem which you deserve,

Your faithful friend and servant.

CI.

TO THOS. PRIOR, ESQ.

LONDON, *July* 26, 1746.

SIR,

I received by the last post the favour of your letter of the 17th, with the enclosed account of the premiums offered for 1746. I think them all perfectly right, and, as I told you in my last, I think you will do well to pursue the manufacture of glass bottles with as little noise as possible. I heartily wish you success, and am, very truly,

Your faithful humble servant.

* Philip V., King of Spain, died on the 9th of July, N.S.

CII.

TO THOS. PRIOR, ESQ.

LONDON, *September* 23, 1746.

SIR,

A long and dangerous illness has hindered me from acknowledging, till now, your last letters; and though I am a great deal better, I still feel, by extreme weakness, the shock which that illness has given to a constitution too much shattered before.

Pray be under no kind of uneasiness as to the accident that happened to my letter, for I assure you that I am under none myself. I confess, the printing of a letter carelessly and inaccurately written, in the freedom and confidence of a friendly correspondence, is not very agreeable, especially to me, who am so idle and negligent in my familiar letters, that I never wrote one over twice in my life, and am consequently often guilty both of false spelling and false English; but as to my sentiments with regard to Ireland, I am not only willing, but desirous, that all Ireland should know them. I very well recollect the two paragraphs in my letter, which might be objected to by many people; but I recollect them without retracting them. I repeat it again, that there are not many people there, who, like you, employ their thoughts, their time, and their labour, merely for the public good, without any private view. The condition of Ireland sufficiently proves that truth. How different would the state of your lands, your trade, your manufactures, your arts and sciences, have been now from what it is, had they been the objects of general, as they have been of your particular, attention! I still less recant what I said about claret, which is a known and melancholy truth; and I could add a great deal more upon that subject.

Five thousand tuns of wine imported *communibus annis* into Ireland, is a sure, but indecent, proof of the excessive drinking of the gentry there, for the inferior sort of people cannot afford to drink wine there, as many of them can here; so that these five thousand tuns of wine are chiefly employed in destroying the constitutions, the faculties, and too often the fortunes, of those of superior rank, who ought to take care of all the others. Were there to be a contest between public cellars and public granaries, which do you think would carry it? I believe you will allow that a Claret Board, if there were one, would be much better attended than the Linen Board, *unless when flax-seed were to be distributed.* I am sensible that I shall be reckoned a very shallow politician, for my attention to such trifling objects, as the improvement of your lands, the extension of your manufactures, and the increase of your trade, which only tend to the advantages of the public; whereas an able Lord-Lieutenant ought to employ his thoughts in greater matters. He should think of jobs for favourites, sops for enemies, managing parties, and engaging Parliaments to vote away their own and their fellow-subjects' liberties and properties. But these great arts of Government, I confess, are above me, and people should not go out of their depth. I will modestly be content with wishing Ireland all the good that is possible, and with doing it all the good I can; and so weak am I, that I would much rather be distinguished and remembered by the name of the *Irish Lord-Lieutenant* than by that of the Lord-Lieutenant of Ireland.

My paper puts me in mind that I have already troubled you too long, so I conclude abruptly, with assuring you that I am, with the truest esteem, etc.

CIII.
TO SIR THOMAS ROBINSON* (At Vienna).

WHITEHALL, *October* 31, 1746.

SIR,

The King having been pleased, upon my Lord Harrington's resignation, to pitch upon me, though very undeserving, to receive the Seals of the Northern Province, I take this first opportunity of acquainting you with it, and desiring the favour

---

* At the date of this letter, Lord Chesterfield had, against his own inclination,† exchanged the Lord Lieutenancy of Ireland, for the Seals of Secretary of State. An account of this affair is given by Lord Marchmont in his Diary from Lord Chesterfield's own confidential narrative. "He said that his conduct in Ireland had quite softened the King to him, and particularly the letter he writ over here, whereby he put a stop to Lord Kil-

---

† This statement is not borne out by his letters in the Newcastle MSS. in the British Museum; and see Lord Carnarvon's " Memoir."

of your correspondence, assuring you that you shall find me always punctual in signifying the King's commands to you for your guidance, and ready to show you, upon all occasions, with how much truth and esteem I am, etc.

P.S. I send you herewith enclosed an extract of a letter from Mr. Villettes to his Grace the Duke of Newcastle, by which his Majesty sees with great concern the slowness of the Austrians in marching their contingent for putting in execution the important plan of entering Provence, and at the same time observes the resolution expressed by the King of Sardinia for carrying it into execution. It is therefore the King's pleasure that you should forthwith make the strongest representations to the Court of Vienna, pressing them in the King's name to expedite, by immediate and positive orders to their Generals, the operations intended upon the French territories, that this great opportunity may not be lost of striking such an important blow whilst the consternation is so great, and the defence so weak, in those parts of France, and whilst the King of Sardinia is ready and willing to concur in it.

You are likewise to represent to the Imperial Minister that his Majesty is very desirous that Maréchal Bathiany may have orders

dare's regiment, and the other 'mob-regiments' as he called them; and that whilst there all his recommendations had been like so many nominations, not one having been refused; that on his arrival here, the Duke of Newcastle had spoke to him of being Secretary, if Lord Harrington quitted or was turned out; and that he had refused it, saying he would keep Ireland as long as he was in place, for he liked it." Lord Chesterfield then proceeded to relate in detail how Lord Harrington (against whom the King had conceived a strong aversion), actually did resign, and how when the Duke of Newcastle asked the King whom he thought of to succeed him, the King said, "I think it must be Chesterfield." Mr. Pelham also told him "that he (Lord Chesterfield) must accept, or he (Mr. Pelham) could not continue in; and that for this reason he did accept of the Seals, but desired to go into the King alone. . . . He there said, he must take the liberty to capitulate with his Majesty, that as he came in to serve his Majesty, and not himself, he desired that whenever he found his service either not agreeable or not useful to him, he might take the liberty to resign the Seals, without its being taken for an affront or disgust at the particular time; to which the King answered, 'Then take the Seals, for I can believe you'—which expression the King has often repeated since with particular emphasis." (Lord Marchmont's Private Diary, August 30, 1747.)—M.

to repair to the Hague, and to continue there for the settlement and regulation, in concert with his Majesty and the States, of the preparations necessary to be made for the ensuing campaign.

CIV.

TO THE LORDS JUSTICES OF IRELAND.*

GROSVENOR SQUARE, 18 *Nov.*, 1746.

MY LORDS,

His Majesty having done me the honour, most unexpectedly and undeservedly on my part, to appoint me to be one of his Principal Secretaries of State, and having been pleased to appoint the Earl of Harrington to be Lord Lieutenant of Ireland, I cannot take my leave of your Lordships without returning you at the same time my sincerest thanks for your assistance during my residence in Ireland, and for your wise and prudent administration of the government of that Kingdom ever since.

Could anything add to my personal regard and consideration for your Lordships, it would be the conviction I have that your sentiments and affection for the Kingdom of Ireland correspond with mine.

May your Lordships be able to promote effectually what now I can only wish sincerely—the interest and prosperity of a loyal and a brave people; may Industry improve, Trade enrich, and all Happiness attend Ireland.

I am, my Lords, with great respect, your Lordships'
Most faithful and most humble servant.

CV.

TO F. LAWRENCE, ESQ. (AT BERLIN).

WHITEHALL, *November* 21, 1746.

SIR,

M. Andrie† having some time ago represented to the King how agreeable it would be to his Prussian Majesty, if the King would be pleased to remove you from his Court, and employ you

---

* Now first published (1892) from the original in Dublin Castle.
† Prussian Minister in London.

elsewhere, and the said Minister, having now again repeated by order of his Master his instances upon this subject, in the most earnest manner, I am to let you know that his Majesty has thought fit to give the King of Prussia this instance of his willingness to gratify him in the said request, and therefore, that it is the King's pleasure, that upon receiving this letter, you should prepare without loss of time, to leave the Court of Berlin, acquainting, however, Count Podewils first, and the other Prussian Ministers, with these his Majesty's orders now signified to you.

But as his Majesty is pleased to be satisfied with your zeal and diligence in his service, I am at the same time to acquaint you with his Majesty's intentions in consideration thereof, of employing you at the Court of Saxony, and that it is the King's pleasure that you accordingly repair to Dresden, where the King is graciously pleased to intend that you shall continue to enjoy the same appointments which you now have at the Court of Berlin.*

I am, etc.

CVI.

À MADAME LA MARQUISE DE MONCONSEIL.

À LONDRES, *ce* 28 *Novembre*, V.S. 1746.

Je vous remercie, Madame, tout simplement, parce que c'est du fond de mon cœur, de l'intérêt que voulez bien prendre à ma santé, qui est passablement bien rétablie, malgré tous les soins de la faculté, qui m'a traité dans toutes les formes.

Votre ami est relâché sur sa parole, aussi bien que tous les autres officiers, de façon que vous ne m'en avez point d'obligation particulière. Je ne puis pas vous dire s'ils sont encore partis, mais je sais qu'ils n'attendoient pour cela qu'un vaisseau de

---

* For a considerable time afterwards George the Second stubbornly refused to appoint any new Envoy at Berlin. " Lord Chesterfield said to me that our King would not send King Frederick a Minister, calling him a 'fripon,' and wished he was Cham of Tartary! Lord Chesterfield told the King he wished so too, but as he was King of Prussia, the more he was a *fripon*, the more necessary it was to have a Minister who was a spy at his Court!" (Diary of Lord Marchmont, Nov. 29, 1747.)—M.

cartel. Ayez la bonté, Madame, d'assurer Madame de Martel de mes très humbles respects, et de lui dire qu'elle m'a fait un véritable plaisir en me chargeant de ses ordres ; que j'ai envoyé sa lettre dans le moment que je l'ai reçue à Monsieur son fils, l'accompagnant d'une de ma part, pour lui offrir mes services, et pour le prier de ne me pas ménager. Je languis de recevoir les ordres que vous me promettez dans votre dernière, parce que vous me dites que c'est sur quelque chose qui vous regarde personnellement. Bon soir, Madame, je suis obligé bien malgré moi de ne vous plus retenir.

CVII.
À MADAME LA MARQUISE DE MONCONSEIL.

À Londres, *ce* 2 *Decembre*, V.S. 1746.

De la façon que vous vous y prenez toujours, Madame, vous ne laissez à vos amis et serviteurs que le seul mérite de la reconnoissance. J'en suis un exemple ; j'avois la plume à la main pour vous communiquer, comme à la personne du monde à laquelle je souhaite de témoigner par préférence mes premières attentions, le changement de ma destination, quand je reçus l'honneur de votre lettre du 26 passé, qui me marquoit d'une manière si flatteuse la part que vous y preniez. Cette lettre, la plus aimable, et la plus amicale, qui ait jamais été écrite, me causa des mouvemens de plaisir, et en même tems de honte, que je ne puis pas vous exprimer. Il me fallut d'abord changer mon premier arrangement ; prévenu comme je l'étois, et honteux de n'avoir que la reconnoissance, en partage ; pour cette reconnoissance, soyez persuadée, Madame, qu'elle est vraie et vive.

Me voici donc tiré d'un poste honorable, lucratif, et dont les fonctions ne prenoient pas trop sur le tems que j'aime à donner aux douceurs de la société, ou même de la paresse. J'y avois en même tems loisir et dignité, au lieu qu'à present je me trouve placé sur un piédestal public, dans un certain point de vue, que ma figure, qui comme vous le savez bien, n'est nullement colossale, ne pourra guères soutenir, et accablé par-dessus le marché d'un travail également au-dessus des forces de mon corps, et de mon esprit. Faut-il donc me féliciter, ou ne faut-il pas plutôt me plaindre ?

Vous me demandez la paix comme si je l'avois en poche ; je voudrois bien l'y avoir. Si vous voulez la prendre telle que je vous la donnerois, vous l'aurez dès demain ; mais malheureusement vous voulez que nous la prenions de vous telle que vous nous la voulez donner, et voilà ce que nous ne voulons pas plus que vous ne voulez de la nôtre. Dans cette différence de sentiments, je doute fort si les plénipotentiaires à Breda* seront assez habiles pour constater un certain milieu raisonnable ; et il me semble que vous nous forcerez à renvoyer cette négociation à cent quarante mille plénipotentiaires que nous aurons en Flandres, et à soixante mille autres qui vont actuellement négocier en Provence. Je ne doute nullement que vous n'envoyiez à leur rencontre un nombre égal de ministres, que vous croyez aussi habiles qu'eux, et le résultat de ces conférences sera sûrement plus intéressant et plus décisif, que ne le seroit celui des conférences de Breda. Pour dire deux mots sérieusement sur cet article, voici la vérité du fait. J'avoue vos succès en Flandres, avouez moi aussi vos pertes en Italie. Vous voulez une paix sur le pied de vos succès ; une telle paix nous seroit aussi funeste que la campagne la plus malheureuse, et il vaut mieux tenter l'une que de se soumettre à l'autre. Pour faire montre de ma lecture, je vous remarquerai, que c'étoit la maxime des Romains de ne jamais faire la paix que victorieux ; peut-être poussoient-ils cette idée quelquefois trop loin, mais au fond ils s'en sont bien trouvés. Ne croyez pas au reste que je cherche plaies et bosses, au contraire je vous assure que je suis pacifique et que je me croirois bien heureux de pouvoir contribuer à une paix qui fût solide, et qui ne bouleversât pas l'équilibre de l'Europe.

Assurez, je vous en supplie, Madame, de mes très humbles respects, et de ma parfaite reconnoissance, ces personnes également aimables et respectables, qui ont bien voulu se souvenir de moi. Pour vous même, je ne puisque vous réitérer la continuation des mêmes sentimens, que vous me connoissez depuis longtems ; rien n'y peut ajouter ; et le tems, ni l'absence n'y peuvent donner la moindre atteinte.

Bon soir, Madame.

* Conferences for a peace had been recently opened at Breda ; but, as Lord Chesterfield predicted, they led to no useful result.—M.

CVIII.

TO THE REV. DR. MADDEN.*

LONDON, *December* 12, 1746.

Can you forgive me, my dear Dr. Madden, what I can scarcely forgive myself; I mean having so long delayed my acknowledgments for your first very friendly letter? but, though I am blameable, I am not quite so much so as by the length of time it would seem, when you consider my long and dangerous illness, and, since my recovery, the multiplicity of business which the late change of my situation has brought upon me.

I can with the strictest truth assure you, that my sentiments of esteem and friendship for you are in no degree lessened, and I am sure never will be, since they are founded upon your love and zeal for mankind in general, and your country and friends in particular, which I am sure will never end but with your life. I have read your work with great satisfaction; it is full †
*   *   *

A concurrence of circumstances has obliged me to change an easy for a laborious employment, in which too, I fear, it will be

---

* Samuel Madden, D.D., was born in Dublin, December, 1686, graduated in Trinity College, 1705, and became Rector of Drummully, near Newtown Butler, County Fermanagh, in 1721, where he had as curate the celebrated Philip Skelton. In 1729 he published a tragedy, *Themistocles*, which was played with success in London. In 1731 he published " A Proposal for the General Encouragement of Learning in Trinity College," and in 1733, a "Memoir of the Twentieth Century." He promoted a system of quarterly premiums in Trinity College (whence he was called " Premium Madden "), and constantly exerted himself to induce persons of wealth and influence to support plans for the improvement of the country. He assisted Prior in the establishment of the Dublin Society, and it was mainly through his influence that a charter of incorporation was obtained for it. He contributed annually £130, and after some years, £300 in premiums, awarded by the Society for the encouragement of manufactures, etc. He died at Manor Waterhouse (Fermanagh), December, 1765. There is an account of his life, and of the Royal Dublin Society, in the *Irish Quarterly Review*, 1853. His son, S. M. Madden, bequeathed his estate at Belturbet for the founding of a prize, worth £300 a year, to be given at the Fellowship Examination, T.C.D.

† In this, and also in a following passage, a part of the original letter appears to have been accidentally torn.—M.

much less in my power to do good, than it was in my former.
It may seem vain to say so, but I will own that I thought
I could, and began to hope that I should, do some good in
Ireland. I flattered myself that I had put jobs a little out
of fashion, and your own manufactures a little in fashion, and
that I had in some degree discouraged the pernicious and beastly
practice of drinking, with many other pleasing visions of public
good. At least I am sure I was earnest in my wishes, and would
have been assiduous in my endeavours for it. Fortune, chance,
or Providence, call it which you will, has removed me from you,
and has assigned me another destination; but has not, I am sure,
changed my inclinations, my wishes, or my efforts, upon occasion,
for the interest and prosperity of Ireland; and I shall always
retain the truest affection for, and remembrance of, that country;
I wish I could say of that rich, flourishing, and industrious
nation. I hope it will in time be so, and I even think it makes
some progress that way, though not so quick as I could wish;
but, however, there are righteous enough to save the city, and
the examples of you, and many of your friends, will, I hope, prove
happily and beneficially contagious. I did flatter myself, a little
before my removal, that I should   *   *   *

Continue me, dear Sir, your friendship and remembrance, which
I will say that in some degree I deserve, by the sincere regard
and esteem with which I am, etc.

P.S. Pray make my compliments to the worthy Bishop of
Meath, to whom I will write soon, and likewise to my friend
Mr. Prior.

CIX.

TO THOS. PRIOR, ESQ.

LONDON, *January* 10, 1747.

SIR,

The person who will deliver you this letter is a most skilful
mechanic, and has made many useful discoveries. He is going
to try his fortune in Ireland, and desired me to recommend him

to somebody there. I could not refuse him, knowing his ingenuity; and then, whom could I recommend him to so well as to my good friend Mr. Prior, the disinterested and zealous patron of all good and useful things? I really think he may be of use to the Dublin Society, who I know are of very great use to the public. If he should prove so, well and good; so far only I recommend him to you eventually. This obligation, however, I have to him, that he has given me an opportunity of assuring you of the continuance of that esteem and regard with which I am,

Yours, etc.

CX.

TO THE EARL OF SANDWICH.*

Private.

WHITEHALL, *January* 27, 1747.

MY LORD,

I received the day before yesterday your Lordship's letter of the 31st, N.S., and laid it before the King, who has commanded me to send you, in the utmost confidence, the following instructions thereupon.

It is very true, as the Pensionary observed,† that the armistice was mentioned by Monsieur Puisieux in conversation, and not proposed in form; but it is as true, too, that the real intentions of a Court may often be better guessed at by the conversation than by the conferences of its Ministers; and as at this time particularly an armistice, if obtained, would be very advantageous to France, and if only proposed might have some effect upon timid and desponding minds, there is no doubt but that Monsieur

---

* John Montagu, fourth Earl of Sandwich (so well known in after years as First Lord of the Admiralty), had been sent in August, 1746, as Envoy Extraordinary to the States of Holland. He was also the British Plenipotentiary at the conferences of Breda. See Gray's *Letters* and the *Letters of Junius.*

† The Pensionary Slingelandt, the intimate friend of Lord Chesterfield, had died in 1736, and been succeeded by M. Van der Heim. See Coxe's *Life of Lord Walpole of Wolterton*, p. 203. A few years afterwards M. Van der Heim was in his turn succeeded by M. Gilles.

Puisieux, in mentioning the armistice, spoke the real intention of his Court, however carelessly he might seem to drop it in conversation only. Upon this point I can add nothing to his Majesty's orders, which I sent your Lordship in my letter of the 13th inst., which are absolutely to reject any such proposal, whenever it should be made.

The King entirely approves of the answer which your Lordship made to the Pensionary upon the renewal of his instances for specific proposals of peace; and I may acquaint you, in confidence, that his Majesty cannot help being a little surprised at the Pensionary respecting these instances at this juncture. The King knows the abilities and the firmness of that Minister, and therefore ascribes his impatience for specific proposals upon certain points to the importunity of others less able than he to see through the designs of France, and (it may be) less willing to defeat them.

The Pensionary owned to your Lordship, that he thought "that the exact discussion of certain points was not advisable, but still seemed to think some answer necessary." His Majesty, who is as desirous of peace as the Pensionary, and whose disproportionate burthen of the war is an undoubted pledge of his sincere desire to end it, would be very glad if any points could be found out as *materia tractandi*, the discussion of which might produce very good effects, or even not be attended by very ill consequences, in the present important crisis; and the King would make no difficulty of opening himself in confidence to the Pensionary, upon any points upon which his Majesty could himself form an opinion. But in the present situation of affairs, in which every day may produce some material variation, it is as impossible to form a resolution what to ask, or what to take, as it would be imprudent eventually to declare it.

Can anybody say what establishment Don Philip should have in Italy, or whether any, at a time when the French and Spaniards are drove out of Italy, and when the Allies have an army in Provence, the good or ill success of which must necessarily determine that question.

The object of Cape Breton, in which his Majesty's honour and the commercial interests of this nation are so highly concerned, is a point upon which at this time, more peculiarly than at any other during the whole course of the war, it is unreasonable to expect that his Majesty should open himself. Now that affairs have taken so favourable a turn in Italy, and present for the first time so favourable a prospect in Flanders, is it a season for his Majesty to think of yielding up so valuable a possession, acquired singly by his own arms and at his own expense? The reasoning upon this point in Holland seems very unfair; and if an object of equal importance to their commerce were in question, they would not admit that mode of reasoning from any of their Allies. *   *   *

I am, etc.

CXI.

TO THE EARL OF HYNDFORD.*

Private.

WHITEHALL, March 10, 1747.

MY LORD,

Your Excellency will have seen by the copy of my letter to Mr. Guy Dickens, which I sent you two posts ago, that the present designs of France and Prussia are to disturb as soon as possible the tranquillity of the North by the means of Sweden, and that in this view France is actually employing its money, and the King of Prussia his skill, (and the latter is likewise ready to exert his force,) as soon as the Triple Alliance now forming between the Powers above-mentioned, at Stockholm, shall be finally concluded.

*   *   *   *   *

His Majesty suggests whether it might not be proper to sound the intentions of the King of Denmark in particular. That Prince, though at present under a subsidiary engagement with the French Court for two years longer, is by no means in his heart inclined to the French system, but may by degrees be insensibly engaged too far in it if he sees himself neglected by other powers.

* John Carmichael, third Earl of Hyndford (at that time British Minister at the Court of Russia), was born in 1701, and died without issue in 1767.—M.

The Court of Russia is not ignorant that the Duchy of Sleswick, the present possession of Denmark, is guaranteed in the most solemn manner to this last Crown by several great Powers, and, if I mistake not, by Russia in particular.

This therefore being the case, the Great Duke of Russia would renounce very little in renouncing what is already guaranteed to Denmark by Russia itself, and therefore the King has the less reason to suppose that the Imperial Prince will have any difficulty to adopt this measure. But if he should, his dependence still is so great upon Russia, and his interest so considerable in the prosperity of the affairs of that Empire that his Majesty thinks that the Empress may very properly and reasonably require that complaisance from him, and if the King of Denmark by this complaisance on his part could be gained to accede, the King is persuaded that such a system might now be established and consolidated in the North as would effectually serve to secure the peace of these parts, and frustrate and defeat the designs of France and Prussia through Sweden to give any disturbance to it.

It is therefore his Majesty's pleasure that your Excellency should take the first opportunity of mentioning what forms the subject of this dispatch to the Chancellor Bestucheff, in the utmost confidence, and to him only; and you will transmit an account to me, without loss of time, how far that Minister relishes this idea, and whether he will support this measure effectually with the Czarina. And your Excellency may observe to Monsieur Bestucheff upon this occasion that the danger to Russia is greater and nearer than they seem to imagine, and that therefore, if your Court have any regard for their own security, after the many friendly advices which his Majesty has ordered to be communicated to them, it is necessary and incumbent upon them to take measures in time to break the storm which is gathering over them.

I am, etc.

CXII.

À MADAME LA MARQUISE DE MONCONSEIL.

À LONDRES, *ce* 13 *Avril*, V.S. 1747.

Au lieu de vous plaindre de moi, vous devez me plaindre, Madame, de ce que la malice des affaires fait si souvent diversion à mon objet principal, qui est celui de vous assurer de mes respects. Respects ! le terme ne me plait pas, et me semble même injurieux à des sentimens d'amitié aussi vifs et aussi délicats que les miens ; ce sont donc ces sentimens, et non pas mon respect, que je voudrois vous réitérer chaque jour de poste, si mes affaires d'un côté, et ma discrétion à votre égard de l'autre, me le permettoient.

Je cherche encore un cheval pour Monsieur de Nevers, mais jusqu'ici inutilement, et vous croirez bien que ce n'est pas faute de soin, puisque assurément il n'y a pas de peine que je ne me donnasse pour lui procurer le moindre plaisir. A propos de lui, me pardonnerez-vous la liberté que je prends d'envoyer sous votre enveloppe ces deux lettres pour Monsieur le Duc de Nivernois, et Monsieur le Chevalier de Mirabeau, qui m'ont tous deux fait l'honneur de m'écrire les lettres du monde les plus obligeantes ? Je ne sais pas où les addresser autrement ; le port même vous en sera couteux, mais je consens que vous tirez une lettre de change sur moi pour trois livres tournois, pourvu que vous m'en donniez avis par une lettre qui ne se paye pas, comme sont toutes les vôtres.

A propos de lettres, je suis irrité contre vous ; j'ai ouvert une lettre qui m'étoit addressée de votre main, avec mon avidité ordinaire pour tout ce qui vient de vous, et j'y trouve seulement une lettre pour la Duchesse de Richmond, sans un seul mot pour moi-même. J'ai été sur le point de m'en venger en ne la lui envoyant pas ; mais après y avoir pensé un peu, j'ai cru que si elle faisoit la moitié du cas seulement de vos lettres que j'en fais, le coup seroit trop noir.

Bon soir, Madame !

CXIII.

TO THE EARL OF SANDWICH.

Private.

WHITEHALL, *April* 24, 1747.

MY LORD,

I received this morning, and laid before the King, your Lordship's letters to me of the 2nd of May, N.S.

As to the Republic's demand of succours from his Majesty, the establishment of the forces here is so low that it will be very difficult to send over any body of troops; but his Majesty has that matter under his consideration at present, and will, if possible, show his friendship and attention for the Republic in* that respect. But it must be considered, on the other hand, that if his Majesty should weaken himself at home to a degree of tempting an invasion from abroad, the necessary consequence would affect the Dutch so much as us, as in that case the King would be obliged, as he was during the last rebellion, to send for a very considerable number of his troops home for his own defence.

The King entirely approves of your Lordship's thought of protecting, as far as is possible for him to do, the Dutch trade; and his Majesty has accordingly sent orders to the Admiralty that they should order our men-of-war to take under their convoy, when they are to sail with any of our trade, all Dutch ships that are bound their way, and are ready and willing to accompany them.

Your Lordship will be pleased to acquaint the Pensionary, and such other principal Members of the Republic as you shall think proper, with these his Majesty's kind intentions for the service of the States; and his Majesty doubts not but you will give this step its full value in Holland.

The King is very well pleased to observe by your Lordship's letter, that the election of the Prince of Orange for Stadtholder of the Province of Holland, goes so unanimously and so quietly through the several towns of that Province,* and that, in all

* In April, 1747, the advance of the French armies against Holland produced nearly the same effect as nearly the same cause had produced in 1672. The people rose in arms, first in Zealand, and next at Rotterdam and the Hague, and proclaimed the Prince of Orange as Stadtholder and Captain General with such unanimity that the Deputies, however reluc-

probability, his Highness will, in a very short time, be Stadt-holder of all the Seven Provinces, which must naturally not only unite them among themselves, but strengthen the union between his Majesty and the Republic, and remove those causes of distrust and jealousy which have lately been so detrimental to the common cause.

I am, etc.

CXIV.

TO SOLOMON DAYROLLES, ESQ.

LONDON, *May* 4, O.S. 1747.

MR. RESIDENT,

I have finished your affair this morning; * it went easy, and you must go very soon. Come to town immediately upon the receipt of this, and wind up your own private bottoms as well as you can in the meantime, for you must go on Friday. *Je vous en félicite.* Adieu !

CXV.

TO THOS. PRIOR, ESQ.

LONDON, *May* 6, 1747.

MY GOOD FRIEND,

I have been long in your debt, and am ashamed of it ; but I am sure you do me too much justice to suspect me of either fraud or negligence. The truth is, that I have as little command of time as many people have of money, and, though my intentions are honest, I am often forced by necessity to be a very bad paymaster.

I desire that the Dublin Society will dispose of the trifle that I

tant, were compelled to ratify and confirm his nomination. Shortly afterwards a law was passed rendering the dignity hereditary in his house, and even enabling the widow of a Stadtholder to direct affairs in the minority of her son, with the title of *Gouvernante*—a case which actually occurred in Holland only four years afterwards. *Par cette révolution*, says Voltaire, *les Provinces Unies devinrent une espèce de monarchie mixte, moins restreinte à beaucoup d'égards que celles d'Angleterre, de Suède et de Pologne.* (*Siècle de Louis XV.* ch. xxiii.)—M.

* Lord Chesterfield had just succeeded in obtaining for Mr. Dayrolles the post of King's *Resident* at the Hague.—M.

gave them in the manner they shall think proper. They are the best judges, and have shown themselves so by all their past conduct. They have done more good to Ireland, with regard to arts and industry, than all the laws that could have been formed; for, unfortunately, there is a perverseness in our natures which prompts us to resist authority, though otherwise inclined enough to do the thing, if left to our choice. Invitation, example, and fashion, with some premiums attending them, are, I am convinced, the only methods of bringing people in Ireland to do what they ought to do; and that is the plan of your Society.

I am glad to find that your paper manufacture goes on so well; if it does but once take root with you, I am sure it will flourish, for it is the beginning only of things that is difficult with you. You want stock to set out with, and patience for the returns; but when once the profit begins to be felt, you will go on as well as any people in the world.

I am surprised that the high duty upon glass here and the suspension of the manufacture of it in some degree, has not encouraged you to apply yourselves to that part of trade, in which I am sure the profits would be very considerable; and your making your own bottles might be some little degree of equivalent for what emptying of bottles costs you. I wish every man in Ireland were obliged to make as many bottles as he empties, and your manufacture would be a flourishing one indeed.

I am very glad to hear that your Linen Board is to give out no more flax-seed, but only premiums for the raising of it; for that same flax-seed was the seed of corruption, which throve wonderfully in the soil of particular people, and produced jobs one hundred fold.

The snuff you sent me was extremely good, and I am much obliged to you for the trouble you took about it, though I know that you think it no trouble to serve your friends, and hope that you reckon me in that number. I assure you I am, and I should not be the friend that I really am to Ireland, if I were not so to you, who deserve so well of your country. I know few people who, like you, employ both their time and their fortunes in doing public good, without the thoughts or expectations of private advantage; when I say advantage, I mean it in the common acceptation of the word, which, thanks to the virtue of the times, implies only money; for otherwise your advantage is very considerable, from the consciousness of the good you do—the greatest advantage which an honest mind is capable of enjoying. May you long enjoy it, with health, the next happiness to it!

I am, etc.

P.S. Pray make my compliments to the good Bishop of Cloyne, when you write to him.

CXVI.

TO SOLOMON DAYROLLES, ESQ.

LONDON, *June* 2, O.S. 1747.

DEAR DAYROLLES,

I have received your two letters of the 6th and 9th, N.S., and am heartily glad to hear of your safe arrival at the Hague. All you have said to Bentinck and to *L'ami* * was perfectly right; go on upon that tone with them both. *L'ami* is apt to refine, and consequently may be mistaken, both with regard to the suspicion which he supposes Lord Sandwich entertains of you, and that which he thinks Bentinck entertains of me upon account of my letter to Prince Waldeck. However, *il n'en sera ni plus ni moins.* Lord Sandwich, who arrived this morning, † spoke very well of you to me, and did not discover the least discontent at your mission. I am in a great hurry to-night, and can add nothing more now, than that I am most truly and affectionately,

Yours:

Pray tell *L'ami* ‡ that I have received his letters regularly up to the 9th. My compliments to your aunt.

* Mr. Duncan, who was employed to settle the articles of marriage between the Stadtholder and the Princess Royal.—M.

† Lord Sandwich had returned home, on leave of absence, from his post at the Hague.—M.

‡ The following is an extract from the original MS. of Mr. Dayrolles's letter to Lord Chesterfield of June 9, N.S. 1747: "I have delivered your Lordship's letter to Mr. Duncan, and he approves entirely what you are pleased to mention to him. . . . He is of opinion we should never meet but privately, for I find he does not care to be suspected of having any secret transaction with your Lordship; for Bentinck, who does not

CXVII.

TO SOLOMON DAYROLLES, ESQ.

LONDON, *June* 9, O.S. 1747:

DEAR DAYROLLES,

I have received your two last separate letters of the 13th and 16th, N.S., and thank you for the informations they give me. I have long thought that the Duke of Newcastle and Bentinck had a secret correspondence, in which I believe they have now engaged Sandwich. This latter, I have now found out, is much displeased at your being sent to the Hague; but you need not mind it; he shall not be able to hurt you, and on your part don't give him the least cause to complain, nor let him see that you know he is displeased with your being at the Hague.

You did right in putting yourself in the Prince of Orange's way, and at the same time in not obtruding yourself upon him for a private audience. Whenever you have one, give him all possible assurances of my attachment; but keep to generals, unless before that time I should send you some particular instructions. I find by what Ligonier said to you, that the French have that superiority which I apprehended they would have; and I own that I dislike the prospect in Flanders, for I cannot think that Maréchal de Saxe has brought the French King to the army, to be either a spectator of inaction, or to attempt what he has not a moral certainty of succeeding in. The King, I can assure you, approves of your office letters; so continue to write in that manner, and put in every circumstance relative to the affair of the Republic, though seemingly trifling. As for what you hear from other quarters of Europe, you will insert it or not, in proportion as you give credit to it, or as you think it deserves notice. The application concerning the ship *Eendraght* you

love him, would be glad of an opportunity to misrepresent him to the Prince (of Orange). He desires for the time to come, to be always called *L'ami*, least the letters should be opened, for though this has not been practised in Holland for many years, they have now lately begun to do it." In a note to Lord Chesterfield's Works, vol. iv. p. 79, Mr. Dayrolles adds, that "Mr. Duncan was the favourite of the Prince before his elevation to the Stadtholdership and had been employed in London to settle the articles of his marriage with the Princess Royal."—M.

should have put in your office letter, because that now the
memorial will appear in the office without any letter relative to
it; therefore, put all those sort of things for the future in your
office letters. Without complimenting your Honour, you do
extremely well, and an experienced Minister could not have done
better.

> Vos pareils à deux fois ne se font pas connoître.
> Et pour leurs coups d'essai, veulent des coups de maître.*

Tell *L'ami* that I received his letter, and thank him. You will
do right to keep your connection with him as private as possible,
for Bentinck I know hates him, and so does the Princess.† He
tells me he will only converse with you *à la Nicodème,* ‡ which is
certainly best. Adieu! for to-night; I need not tell you that I
love you sincerely, and am convinced of your attachment to

Yours.

CXVIII.

TO SOLOMON DAYROLLES, ESQ.

LONDON, June 16, O.S. 1747.

DEAR DAYROLLES,

I acknowledge at once your two separate letters of the 20th
and 23d, N.S.

You answered the Princess Royal very well, when she recommended Monsieur de la Millerie to you; and, when you have an
opportunity, acquaint her (with my most humble respects) that I
will not fail to put Lord Harrington frequently in mind of her
Royal Highness's orders, but, however, without answering for
the success.

As the Prince has lately spoke to you as freely as usual, it is
very probable that his former coolness was through inadvertency
or *distraction* only. At least, seem to think so.

Far from disliking the dissolution of the Parliament, I approved of, and promoted it, as much as anybody, and do think it
a very right measure, as will appear, I dare say, by the majority
which we shall have in the new one. Our enemies have not time

---

* Corneille's *Cid.*
† The Princess Royal of England, wife of the Prince of Orange.
‡ Like Nicodemus—" by night."

to work, nor money to work with, as they would have had if this Parliament had died a year hence of a natural death.

The news of Lord Sandwich succeeding me was put into the public papers here, whether by design or ignorance I don't know. Many people, I believe, think that *my Brother* * will wear out my patience, as indeed he has most people's; but as I have a good deal I may hold out longer than people think. Besides that, *things may mend.*

If the Dutch will declare war, it will be now that the French have embargoed their ships. I conceive why the Prince does not care to press them to it; but I don't conceive why those who wish well, and who have spirit, don't do it of themselves.

If Van-haren has the lady, † adieu, Bentinck, before it is long, for I am sure her interest will prevail at last. Let me know, if you can, what was said or thought at that Court upon the supposition of my being out.

Don't distrust yourself, for upon my word you do perfectly well. Good night!

P.S. I send you the enclosed from poor Chataigné, my page. If you can do him any service, by speaking in his behalf to any of the Prince's people, pray do.

CXIX.

TO THE BISHOP OF WATERFORD.‡

LONDON, *June* 18, O.S. 1747.

MY DEAR LORD,

I thank you for your letter and for your kind hint, and am heartily glad to hear that you have made up your affair with your predecessor's widow.

What becomes of your intended establishment at Waterford for the reception of foreigners? Does it go on? It would be of great advantage to the town, and a good example to others. How does Mr. Smith's linen manufacture flourish with you?

---

* His colleague as Secretary of State, the Duke of Newcastle.

† "Mr. Bentinck is the Prince's chief favourite, as Van-haren, on the other hand, is the most in favour with the Princess." Mr. Dayrolles to Lord Chesterfield, June 13, N.S. 1747, MS. letters.—M.

‡ Dr. Chenevix, who had been translated to Waterford from Killaloe.

If it prospers, I should think it would both invite and employ foreigners. I wish my country people, for I look upon myself as an Irishman still, would but attend half as much to those useful objects, as they do to the glory of the militia and the purity of their claret. Drinking is a most beastly vice in every country, but it is really a ruinous one to Ireland; nine gentlemen in ten in Ireland are impoverished by the great quantity of claret, which, from mistaken notions of hospitality and dignity, they think it necessary should be drunk in their houses; this expense leaves them no room to improve their estates, by proper indulgence upon proper conditions to their tenants, who must pay them to the full, and upon the very day, that they may pay their wine-merchants.

There was a law, in one of the ancient Governments, I have forgot which, that empowered a man to kill his wife if she smelt of wine. I most sincerely wish that there were a law in Ireland, and better executed than most laws are, to empower the wives to kill their husbands in the like case; it would promote sobriety extremely, if the effects of conjugal affection were fully considered.

Do you grow fat? Are Mrs. Chenevix and your children all well? Are you as cheerful and as happy as your good conscience ought to make you? I hope them all; for upon my word, nobody loves and values you more than

Your faithful friend and servant.

CXX.

TO SOLOMON DAYROLLES, ESQ.

LONDON, June 23, O.S. 1747.

DEAR DAYROLLES,

As the letters of the 30th, N.S. are not yet come in, I have little to say to you by this post; and should hardly have written, but that I love to write to you, because I know that you love to hear from me.

I am glad that the Prince of Orange has begun to talk confidentially to you. Cultivate that growing confidence. When he speaks to you again about the Russian affair, take care to get out of him, *sans faire semblant de rien*, in what proportion and upon what foot he proposes that we should take a share in it. The case is this: By the *resultat*, which I signed two years ago,* we are engaged to pay three-fourths of the *frais casuels de la guerre;* now subsidies come under this head, and consequently we now pay three-fourths of the Bavarian and Hessian subsidies; but the Dutch pay the whole pay of those troops themselves. It will therefore make a very great difference to us in the expense, if the 30,000 Russians be taken into our joint service upon a stipulated pay as troops, or if the whole is to be paid for by one great subsidy; because that, in the first case, we might get off for half, or it may be less, whereas in the latter we must probably pay our three-fourths. Therefore, if the Prince of Orange or Bentinck should enter with you into the particular scheme of engaging these Russians, you may, without seeming to know what I have now told you, endeavour and propose to have them taken upon the foot of pay for the respective corps, alleging, that if it were to be done by way of one gross subsidy for 30,000 men, that number would probably prove deficient, and the deduction from the subsidy difficult; whereas there could be less deceit if they were to be paid according to the musters, like the Bavarians and the Hessians. Though, by the way, I must observe to you, that the Elector of Bavaria and the Landgrave of Hesse have small subsidies, of which we pay three-fourths over and above the pay of their troops, which the Dutch pay by themselves. Prussia will probably require something of this kind too; but, however, the less the subsidy the easier we shall get off.

I expect bad news every day from Italy, and wish more than I hope for good news from Flanders. Something, I think, must soon happen there.

I have had a very satisfactory letter from Mr. Harte, and am convinced there has been no gaming at all in the case. However, when you hear from Monsieur de Bochat † or Madame, in answer to the letter you write, pray send me their letters. *A propos* of Monsieur de Bochat, pray tell me in what way I can reward him, for the lectures that he has read to the boy.‡ Should

---

* At the Hague, in the spring of 1745. See note to Letter XCIII.

† Professor of History and Civil Law in the University of Lausanne.—M.

‡ Lord Chesterfield's son, Philip.

I send him money, how much? If no money, what must I present him with, and to about what value? Tell me without reserve. Make my sincerest compliments to your aunt. Good night!

CXXI.

TO SOLOMON DAYROLLES, ESQ.

LONDON, *July* 3, O.S. 1747.

DEAR DAYROLLES,

I received by the last mail your letter of the 7th, N.S. and though I have very little time to-night, yet I would not omit acquainting you that the hints, which I gave you in one of my former letters, concerning the 30,000 Russians, are now useless. The Prince of Orange writ to me two posts ago to propose the taking of the Russian troops jointly in the service of the Maritime Powers, that is that the Dutch were to take 10,000 into their pay, and we the 20,000 into ours. Nay, more, they would even, I believe, have contributed their fourth part to our 20,000 over and above their own 10,000; but upon mature and *wise* deliberation, it was thought proper to put off this affair till September to wait for events *en attendant*, which God knows, in my mind, we have done but too long already. I represented the distance of the Court of Petersburg, and the necessity of immediately beginning whatever negotiation you would have concluded at that Court even by next spring, but in vain, for the old spirit of delay and indecision prevailed. I fear this delay will be very disagreeable to the Prince of Orange, who I dare say thought that the proposal would have been very welcome here.

I thank you for the account which you sent me from Lausanne, though I can't say that it gives me great comfort. I shall hint nothing of it to the boy, while he stays at Lausanne, that he may neither accuse nor suspect anybody there of being my informer; but, as soon as he is at Leipsig, he shall receive *des mercuriales* upon all those points.

I own I am in great pain for the Dutch frontier, Bergen-op-zoom, Breda, or Bois-le-duc, but chiefly the two first, being, I am convinced, the object of the French, which, if they succeed in, the consequence is but too plain. Pray tell me what you take to be the whole force of Prince Saxe Hildbourghausen's corps.

Burn this letter as soon as you have read it, and don't mention the former part of it to anybody living.

Yours faithfully.

(Separate and Secret Postscript, first printed in Lord Mahon's edition.)

When you deliver my office letter to the Prince of Orange, I dare say he will talk to you about the Russian affair, which it relates to. I daresay, too, that he will be disappointed in finding his proposal so coldly received here, and put off for so long. He will probably express something of this kind to you, which when he does, you will just hint, that you believe that my opinion was for taking the Russians immediately; because you know, that while we are in war, I am for making it vigorously, and with superior force, and not consuming ourselves, by inferior and ineffectual armies.

In the course of this conversation, take an opportunity of showing him my enclosed letter, which I have calculated for that purpose, and in which I have inserted the Lausanne affair, to prevent the least suspicion. But when you do show it, do it with seeming difficulty, and as a mark of your unbounded confidence in the Prince; and enjoin him the strictest secrecy, especially that I may never know that you showed it to him.*

* The further progress of this transaction is related as follows by Mr. Dayrolles, in a secret letter to Lord Chesterfield, dated July 18, N.S. 1747: "Everything has happened in the manner your Lordship imagined when I delivered your office-letter to the Prince of Orange. He not only appeared disappointed, but likewise extremely concerned, and told me that nothing could disconcert his measures more than this; for, as he expected that in England you would have readily come into so reasonable a scheme, he had framed his plans accordingly. . . . I then told him I was very certain this did not come from your Lordship, for that no man in England was so sensible of the necessity of carrying on the war in the most vigorous manner. He answered, he did not imagine that your Lordship could dislike his scheme; upon which I told him, I could easily fix him in that opinion with some proofs I had in my hands, and would even venture to do it, as my confidence in him was unbounded, and I was well persuaded he never would betray me, especially to your Lordship. Upon this, he gave me the strongest assurances of secrecy, and I gave him your letter to read. He appeared to be very well pleased with it,

Both the King and I thought the measure a right one, and that we should get all the force we could; but we can neither of us do what we have a mind to do, and the resolutions of those who neither know how to make war nor peace are to prevail.

Good night, once more!

CXXII.

TO SOLOMON DAYROLLES, ESQ.

LONDON, *July* 17, O.S. 1747.

DEAR DAYROLLES,

I shall take it ill of you, and look upon it as contempt, if you are not in a damned passion at me, for not having writ to you these two posts; but I have really been so entirely taken up with the political puzzle which we have been in, that I have not had a minute's time to pay my separate duty to you.

I can tell you in confidence, that though I received a second letter from the Prince of Orange, upon the subject of the Russian troops, and pressing that measure again, old indecision still prevails, and I am only to order Lord Hyndford to *entamer* that affair, and to prepare it eventually, that less time may be necessary when decision shall come. Things are now, in my opinion, in a most miserable situation, and the taking of Bergen-op-zoom *y mettroit le comble.* I wish I could see a plan for either a vigorous war or a tolerable peace, or rather, a plan eventually for each. I see many things which I will not mention, that make me despair of seeing the war carried on another year with that vigour and superior or at least equal force, which is absolutely necessary for success; and as I think no state so bad as that which we have been in these three years, of neither making war nor peace, I own I am now rather inclined for the latter, if it can be obtained upon reasonable terms, which I much doubt

and as he went on reading repeated several times, *Voyez vous, c'est tout comme je vous disois tout à l'heure.* But now I think, upon recollection, that when he came to the article, that 'upon mature and WISE deliberation it was thought proper to put off this affair till September,'—he did not make the proper application of the word WISE, and seemed to think of the King. As I am not clear upon this point, your Lordship will know best whether it would not be proper for you to procure me soon an opportunity of seeing him again to set him quite right by giving him some hints."—M.

of, especially if Bergen-op-zoom should fall. All this *entre nous* absolutely; for I meddle very little; I execute orders quietly, and give no advice. Let those who puzzle us in puzzle us out if they can. By this conduct I am better and better every day in the Closet.

Lord Sandwich embarks for Holland on Sunday night, or Monday morning at farthest. After his arrival, I cannot find in my heart to refuse you your visit to Ubbergue,* where I wish I could attend you, and where I desire you would present my respects *a tutte quante.* But I would have you contrive to set out on some Wednesday morning, and return to the Hague on the Monday night, or the Tuesday morning following, by which means you will miss but one post. Burn this letter as you did the last; and so we heartily wish you farewell for to-night.

Yours.

P.S.—I have this minute received yours of the 25th, by the last paragraph of which I find you are a little angry, but not angry enough.

(Separate and Secret Postscript, first printed by Lord Mahon.)

Contrive to do by this letter just as you did by the last; your delivering of my letter to the Prince will probably give you an occasion to do it in the same manner. Upon my soul we shall be undone if we have not a peace, for I am sure we should not carry on the war better next year than we have done this. Give the Austrians what we please, they will always be grossly deficient; and let the Dutch take what vigorous resolutions they please, I fear they have not the means of enforcing them. Our means fall short, and our capacity still shorter. *Nous ne sommes pas montés sur le ton de' conquéte.* However, don't declare your opinion either way where you are; but speak cautiously and doubtfully. Sandwich I know has instructions from the Duke of Newcastle to watch you carefully; he goes back much puzzled between his Grace and me; he would be well with both, and sees that it is impossible. The Duke of Newcastle has, I believe, shown him my place *en perspective,* which possibly it may not be in his Grace's power to dispose of.

---

* The country-seat of Count Welderen in the province of Guelders.

CXXIII.

TO SOLOMON DAYROLLES, ESQ.

LONDON, *July* 21, O.S. 1747.

DEAR DAYROLLES,

I received yours yesterday, by which I find my own notion confirmed—which was, that the bulk of the Republic would be frightened into pacific measures, whatever the inclinations of the new Government may be. The lines are, I am convinced, by this time forced, the necessary consequence of which is the taking of Bergen-op-zoom. I own I dread the opening of my next letters from Holland. Pray tell our *friend* that I have received all his letters very safe to his last of the 28th inst. inclusively, and that I thank him extremely for them. As he is so watched, I would by no means have him write to me for some time; but if he has anything of consequence to inform me of, he may tell it you by word of mouth. Advise him from me to be patient, in which case, I dare say, his turn will come again; and if he could get any channel to the *lady*, I think that would be his surest, and would certainly do at last. The seldomer you see him, unless in the utmost secrecy, the better for you both. In great haste, yours faithfully.

CXXIV.

À MADAME LA MARQUISE DE MONCONSEIL.

À LONDRES, *ce* 31 *Juillet*, V.S. 1747.

Je crois avoir à la fin trouvé un beau cheval entier bai de cinq ans, qui a l'encolure magnifique, les épaules libres, et les hanches très cadencées. Je l'ai à assez bon marché, n'ayant coûté que cinquante cinq guinées : pour l'accompagner en chemin, je prends la liberté d'envoyer à Monsieur de Nevers un petit cheval gris de mon propre haras, qui n'a encore que quatre ans, et qui n'a jamais été élevé à la course. Comme il ne me coûte rien, Monsieur de Nevers voudra bien qu'il ne lui coûte rien non plus. Il est échappé du plus beau cheval Arabe que nous ayons eu en ce pays, et Madame sa mère étoit une petite beauté Angloise, qui ne fut pas insensible aux fleurettes énergiques du dit Arabe. Pour un si jeune cheval il est fort doux, et je conseillerois à Monsieur de Nevers de le monter lui-même, plutôt que le cheval entier, qui pourroit lui jouer un mauvais tour. On ne peut guère se fier à ces Messieurs là, qui deviennent méchans du soir au lendemain.

Mademoiselle —— me dit des merveilles de *Bagatelle*.* Nous voudrions tous les deux y être, ce ne seroit pas une bagatelle pour nous; vos bagatelles valent bien le solide des autres. Est-il loin de Paris? car quoique vous tirerez toujours le meilleur parti de tout, je tiens qu'il faut que les honnêtes gens soient à portée de la capitale. Une société aimable est, à la longue, la plus grande douceur de la vie, et elle ne se trouve que dans les capitales. C'est sur ce principe que je me ruine actuellement à bâtir une assez belle maison ici,† qui sera finie à la Francoise, avec force sculptures et dorures.

Il ne reste pas assez de papier pour finir par un compliment d'une longueur convenable, de sorte que je n'en ferai point du tout. Adieu donc, Madame.

CXXV.

TO SOLOMON DAYROLLES, ESQ.

LONDON, *July* 31, O.S. 1747.

DEAR DAYROLLES,

I have received yours of the 4th of August, N.S., but I have. so little to say to you by this post, that it is only the satisfaction, which I have in writing to you, makes me write to-night.

By this time, I suppose, both Sandwich and Booteslaer are at the Hague; they went from hence in very different sentiments, the former very warlike, the latter very pacific. What our real sentiments are here it is impossible for me to tell you; they vary so often. We have no plan for either war or peace; the least favourable event inclines us to the former, the least check to the latter, so that we are always either at the top or at the bottom of the house, and the middle floor is always to be let! Pray let me know in what way Booteslaer talks of us and particularly of me. I think I was well with him.

* The villa of Madame de Monconseil, near Paris, in compliment to which Lord Chesterfield called his country house at Blackheath, Babiole.

† Chesterfield House.

I send Lord Sandwich, by this post, his Credentials of Ambassador, which he has long solicited, but which he is neither to present nor mention till he receive further orders; therefore don't you seem to know anything at all of it. Far from having drawn up his own instructions,* I can hardly say that he has any; such is our indecision still.

I have writ to Mr. Harte to inquire at Lausanne of some of Monsieur de Bochat's friends, in what way to make him a compliment for the trouble he has been at, and to act accordingly, and likewise to make some present to Monsieur Brenles,† when they leave Lausanne, which will now be very soon, for I have ordered them to be at Leipsig by Michaelmas, N.S. As they will therefore leave Lausanne in three weeks, I shall be obliged to you, if you will write to Monsieur Brenles in about a fortnight, to desire that he will send you in the utmost confidence, but with the greatest freedom, the entire analysis of the boy's heart, mind, and manners; which in all this time he must know thoroughly, having seen him every day, and in his unguarded hours. It will be of infinite use for me to know all these particulars. I have not yet mentioned, either to the boy or Mr. Harte, anything of what Madame de Bochat writ to you, that they might not suspect from whence it came, or endeavour to fish it out. But as soon as they are got to Leipsig, they shall hear of it with a vengeance, but so, as that it shall be impossible for them to guess from whence I had it.

I am astonished at the not sending Prince Waldeck's corps into the lines of Bergen-op-zoom, where they would, with those troops that were in the lines before, have formed a strength, which might probably have saved the town; whereas, divided as they are, I fear that neither corps is strong enough separately for any purpose.

I hope Sukey Young is well and kind. Fanny Murray was last night in the Park in perfect health but in very close mourning—for some near relation, I presume, of the illustrious family of the Murrays! Adieu: Yours.

* "We are told here that Lord Sandwich has had the sole framing of his instructions." Mr. Dayrolles to Lord Chesterfield, August 4, N.S. 1747.—M.

† At whose house Lord Chesterfield's son was a boarder, at Lausanne.

CXXVI.

TO SOLOMON DAYROLLES, ESQ.

LONDON, *August* 11, O.S. 1747.

DEAR DAYROLLES,

I was in doubt, whether I should write to you to-night or not, it being doubtful, whether by this time you have a head upon your shoulders or not.* But, upon mature deliberation, I determined to write eventually, knowing that, at worst, my letter would by no means be the first that had been sent to a minister without a head. I confess the hopes which I have, that the French will raise the siege of Bergen-op-zoom, arise from the apprehensions which they may entertain of you and the Bishop of Raphoe; for otherwise, I see no one thing, that should induce them to it.

I suspect that the Bishop of Raphoe has an eye to the Bishoprick of Munster, upon the death of the Elector of Cologne, and means to show that he will do as well as Bernard Van Galen.†

Bentinck's arrival was as you guessed, a meditated secret, and Lord Sandwich, who was surely in it, never mentioned it till he was embarked; but we knew it from the yacht four days before. I informed you wrong in my last when I told you I should by that post send Lord Sandwich his Credentials of Ambassador, for when I carried them afterwards to the King he would not *"pour un diable"* sign them, but has indeed allowed him the full appointment. Don't mention a word of this. If Lord Sandwich does not think proper to speak to you about business don't seem to observe it, but go on *tout de suite*.

I cannot imagine what Booteslaer means by mixing Pelham with his brother, the Duke, in his account of the heat and ignorance of people here; he knows very well that Harry Pelham is in quite different sentiments and entirely of my opinion.

I am persuaded, that the new tax,‡ from which such sums are

* Mr. Dayrolles, in company with Dr. Twisden, Bishop of Raphoe, had just made an excursion to Bergen-op-zoom.—M.

† The warlike Bishop of Munster, who twice laid siege to his capital and took so active a part in the Dutch war of 1672.—M.

‡ "This tax, under the name of *Liberal Gift* or *Don Gratuit*, was raised in a very extraordinary manner. Large cases or trunks were placed in all

expected, will either not be laid, from the opposition it will meet with; or, if laid, will hardly be collected without the assistance of dragoons. In my opinion, when Bergen-op-zoom shall be taken, the consternation will be universal in the Republic, and the tone of the most sanguine will be altered. Williamstadt or Zealand will fall next; and then what ground our troops will have to stand upon, and where they will find quarters, I am at a loss to guess. I am even in pain for their existence, after the town shall be taken.

I have signed your bill of extraordinaries. Pray what becomes of Kreuningen? Is he not frightened out of his wits? Adieu.

Yours faithfully.

CXXVII.
TO SOLOMON DAYROLLES, ESQ.

LONDON, August 21, O.S. 1747.

DEAR DAYROLLES,

I am very glad to find the canon-balls, bombs, shells, and mines, which you went to visit at Bergen-op-zoom, received you só civilly, as to give you all the entertainment they could afford, without playing you those tricks which they are apt to do to those with whom they are more familiar. In short, you are well off, and I am glad of it.

I think, as you do, that the town must fall, and soon, it being impossible for the whole army to march to its relief; at least

the town-houses in the province of Holland, in which all persons, whose whole capital did not amount to less than 2,000 florins, were obliged to deposit upon oath, either in cash, obligations of the State, or plate, to the value of at least *two per cent.* of whatever they possessed, either in cash, land, jewels, plate, pictures, obligations, employments, etc., nothing but household goods and wearing apparel to be excepted. They were also obliged to swear, that in case they should afterwards find out, that they had not paid in their quotas, according to a true and just valuation of all their effects, they would faithfully make it up again, to the best of their knowledge. The sum produced by this heavy imposition was kept a profound secret, and never came to the knowledge of the world with any certainty. However, there is good reason to think, that the amount of the same did not fall short of twenty-two millions of florins, viz. two millions sterling, in the single province of Holland. The public debt of that province alone, at that time, was computed at forty millions sterling."—Note by Mr. Dayrolles in Maty's edition.

the Duke * is convinced of it, though I find that the Prince of Orange is of a contrary opinion. That is not, I doubt, the only point, upon which they differ.

Bentinck's commission here was (between you and me) to prevent or defeat any negotiations of peace, and to engage us in immediate preparations of war for another campaign; in which he has as yet neither quite failed nor quite succeeded, as our natural indecision inclines us one day to the one and another day to the other, as the least good or bad events encourage or frighten us. I think he proposes returning next week.

I see the *two per cent.* tax is not yet laid, and that the States of Holland are separated to deliberate upon it. I own, I much doubt, whether it will be laid, and still more whether it will be levied if laid.

Divertissez-vous bien, craignez Dieu, et buvez frais autant que faire se pourra. Adieu.

CXXVIII.

TO SOLOMON DAYROLLES, ESQ.

LONDON, *August* 25, O.S. 1747.

DEAR DAYROLLES,

I don't at all wonder at Lord Sandwich's proceeding with you, as it is conformable to his conduct with regard to me. His Lordship has for some time made his option between the Duke of Newcastle and myself, and I suppose thinks he has chose the best, in which however he may some time or other find himself mistaken. Bentinck follows his example, and never comes near me nor speaks to me about business, though in my province, but confers wholly with his Grace. But I take no notice of it, and I advise you to do so too. Their great point is to prevent any peace at all, the Prince of Orange thinking as vainly that the Republic has resources, as the Duke of Newcastle thinks that he

* Of Cumberland, then commanding in Flanders. Mr. Pelham writes of him, and of the Prince of Orange at this period, "Our two young heroes agree but little. Our own is open, frank, resolute, and perhaps hasty, the other assuming, pedantic, ratiocinating, and tenacious." To H. Walpole the elder, August 14, 1747.—M.

has abilities to carry on the war. I let them go on quietly, being convinced that events will soon show who is in the right and who in the wrong. Pray do not upon any account discover the least dissatisfaction either with regard to yourself or to me, but remember that *Volto sciolto e pensieri stretti* are often very necessary in business. The taking of the Russians is, in my mind, eventually a right step, provided we make the right use of it; that is, to treat seriously of peace, with force in our hands for war. For I am convinced, that everything that does not tend to a peace, is absurd, and will in the end prove fatal.

I have no opinion of your new tax; and though it may be laid, I believe it will be so lamely collected, that it will not produce anything like what is proposed. Pray tell me what impartial people think of it.

Don't be distrustful of yourself; for everybody here allows, that it is impossible to do better than you have done. So, good night.   Yours.

CXXIX.

A MADAME LA MARQUISE DE MONCONSEIL.

à LONDRES, *ce* 8 *Septembre,* V.S. 1747.

Je vous suis plus qu'infiniment obligé de l'Anti-Lucrèce * que vous avez eu la bonté de m'envoyer, et que Monsieur l'Abbé de la Ville m'a fait tenir le plus poliment du monde. Je l'ai lu avec avidité et plaisir. C'est un ouvrage digne de son auteur; la poésie en est belle, et le Latin sent le siècle d'Auguste; enfin si l'on se dégage des préjugés dans lesquels on est élevé en faveur de l'antiquité, il faut convenir que l'Anti-Lucrèce ne le cède en rien à Lucrèce même, et qu'en fait de philosophie, il l'emporte de bien loin. Nous autres Anglois, à la vérité, nous sommes fâchés que le Cardinal ait donné la préférence au système de Descartes, et qu'il n'ait pas plutôt adopté celui de notre Newton, hors duquel nous ne croyons pas qu'il y ait de salut.

---

* The *Anti-Lucretius* was a poem in Latin by Cardinal de Polignac, in reply to that of Lucretius. The Cardinal had died in 1741, in his eightieth year; but it was published by one of his friends in 1747. The copy sent to Lord Chesterfield was the first that appeared in England; "it was conveyed by a transport from Marshal Saxe to the Duke of Cumberland, directed to the Earl of Chesterfield."

Pour moi, qui ne suis nullement philosophe, et par conséquent nullement prévenu en faveur de quelque systême que ce soit, j'avoue que je trouve que l'attraction universelle de notre Newton a quelque chose d'infiniment plus joli et de plus galant, que ces vilains tourbillons, qui ne me donnent que des idées de fracas et de tumulte, au lieu que l'attraction en fournit de plus douces. Monsieur de Nevers et moi nous sentons tout le vrai du Newtonianisme.

Au reste, Madame, je vous supplie de vouloir bien dire de ma part tout ce que vous pouvez dire de plus poli (et que ne pouvez-vous pas dire de la sorte ?) à Monsieur l'Abbé le Blond. J'ai voulu d'abord lui écrire moi-même, pour le remercier ; mais j'ai fait réflexion, que si je vous en chargeois, il pourroit peut-être croire que je vous avois dicté ce que vous lui diriez, et j'ai mieux aimé profiter d'une erreur si avantageuse pour moi. A propos d'Abbés, comment se porte notre Abbé Sallier ? jouit-il toujours de sa santé, de sa bibliothèque, de son Syriaque, et de tout son grimoire savant ? Ayez la bonté de lui faire bien mes complimens.

Vous ne voulez pas m'accorder le sentiment ; et en même tems, vous et votre Monsieur de Nevers, vous me faites sentir que je ne l'ai que trop, au moins si la jalousie est une preuve du sentiment, comme sûrement elle l'est, et je crois que vous êtes convenus ensemble de m'envoyer sa dernière lettre, pour me faire enrager. C'est assurément une insulte des plus marquées de sa part : les reproches qu'il vous fait de mon triomphe ne font que m'annoncer le sien ; et j'y vois tout le langage d'un rival d'autant plus modeste et discret qu'il se sent victorieux et sûr de son fait. Que faire ? le cœur me dit de me fâcher contre tous les deux, mais l'esprit me dit que vous avez tous deux raison. Que mon rival au moins ne s'attende pas que le petit cheval gris soit beau, car il se trouveroit bien trompé ; il n'est tout au plus que passablement joli, mais il a les allures bonnes, et il sera commode ; il est mince par derrière, mais voilà comme tous nos chevaux de race sont faits.

Les reproches, que vous fait Madame votre mère sur mon sujet, sont bien flatteurs pour moi ; ayez la bonté, Madame, de l'assurer de ma reconnoissance et de mon respect.

Bon Dieu ! quelle lettre ! J'en ai honte, je me cache.

CXXX.

TO SOLOMON DAYROLLES, ESQ.

LONDON, *September* 11, 1747.

DEAR DAYROLLES,

I don't acknowledge separately the several letters which I have received from you since my last, as you are sensible that I must have received them, and have not always time to answer them. *Au reste je n'en pense pas moins.* Charles Bentinck arrived here the day before yesterday; but what his business is, is yet a secret to me, neither his brother nor he thinking it necessary to communicate anything to me, though in my department. The affairs are all transacted secretly with the Duke of Newcastle, Sandwich, and Chabannes. Bentinck talks more extravagantly than ever poor Lord Stair did.* Bergen-op-zoom is no loss; the Dutch have more resources than they want; and though they should lose a province or two this year, they will recover that and a great deal more the next! He goes away next Sunday, and is to be sent Minister from the Republic to the Conferences at Aix la Chapelle, there to try not to promote but to put an end to the negotiations for peace. All this *entre nous seuls. Adieu, mon cher enfant.*

CXXXI.

TO SOLOMON DAYROLLES, ESQ.

LONDON, *September* 22, O.S. 1747.

DEAR DAYROLLES,

I am convinced that you judge very right, † and that the present connection between the two persons you mention is only

---

* "At Lord Chesterfield's, before dinner, Count Bentinck came in to take leave, setting out to-morrow for Holland. . . . Mr. Thomas Villiers came in as Count Bentinck went away, and Lord Chesterfield told him that Bentinck exactly resembled Lord Stair, who would allow no facts or reasoning against his own hopes and schemes."—Diary of Lord Marchmont, September 13, 1747. —M.

† "What your Lordship is pleased to tell me in confidence about the extraordinary behaviour of the two brothers (Bentinck) shows very plainly, that I was not misinformed when I told your Lordship that you did not stand very well in Madam's book" (the Princess of Orange). "I know, my Lord, she looks upon you as one whose schemes will never square

lord chesterfield's letters.

temporary, and for the present purpose. *He* being the only person here weak enough and ignorant enough to support those wild schemes which I fear will end in the ruin of the Republic, and, in consequence, of England. I am concerned for the public which I take to be in a very dangerous situation; as to myself in particular, I am extremely easy. I will continue in public life, while I can do it with honour; and, when I cannot, I shall enjoy private life with pleasure, and I hope some reputation. The Republic talks and looks big; but neither does, nor I fear can act up to it. And how they will repel the dangers of this year, by the force which they are to raise the next, I am at a loss to discover.

I have spoke to Mr. Pelham about your payment, and will take care that you shall be paid as soon as, or sooner than, any other foreign Minister; and more you must not expect, for a very strong reason, which is, that there is not money.

The Parliament will meet the second week in November; till when the town will continue as empty as it is now, and I never knew it emptier. My only amusement is my new house, which has now taken some form, both within and without. There is but one disagreeable circumstance that attends it, which is the expense. Adieu. *Portez vous bien.*

CXXXII.

TO SOLOMON DAYROLLES, ESQ.

LONDON, *October* 2, O.S. 1747.

DEAR DAYROLLES,

Inclosed is a letter for M. de Bochet, which I desire that you will direct properly, and forward to him; for the proper titles are of great importance all over Germany. My letter is an answer to a very civil one, which you sent from him, and at the same time conveys my thanks for his book,* which, as far as I

with hers, and if she seems at present so much attached to the Duke of Newcastle, I am sure it is neither out of friendship nor any particular esteem for him, but only on account of her notions of his mighty interest, and that his politics agree better with her views."—Mr. Dayrolles to Lord Chesterfield, September 26, N.S. 1747. Original MS.—M.

* *Critical Researches into the ancient state of the Helvetic Body, with an Account of the Monuments of Antiquity found in Switzerland.*

have read, is, I think, an excellent one. He gives me in the main a good character of the boy, and he has very kindly wrote to Professor Mascow,* to inform him previously of what the boy does or does not know, of his dispositions, character, etc., all which it is right that the Professor should know beforehand, in order to take his measures the better.

What the Bentincks say with relation to the frequent audiences which the eldest had of the King, is very true, for he had several, in which, I believe, assertions were more numerous than proofs. First, the French could not take Bergen-op-zoom, such prudent, such infallible measures had been taken, to prevent it! When unfortunately it was taken, it was no matter, but rather for the better, as it would animate the Republic so much the more! The Republic, though she called for it, wanted no assistance, but had sufficient resources of men and money! And poor Hop was severely reprimanded by them, while they were here, and complained of to the Stadtholder, for having by express orders from the States-General, delivered a Memorial to me, in which they apply to the King for *prompt et efficace secours*, upon the taking of Bergen-op-zoom. This the Bentincks were wise enough to say, was an admission that the Republic wanted assistance. which they denied to be true; and affirmed that the *prompt et efficace secours* related only to next year. I have a notion that they want to pick a quarrel with Hop, in order to send Charles Bentinck here in his stead. Hop thinks so too, and is very uneasy. If they mean, by my having nothing to say at Court, that my opinion does not prevail there, they are very much in the right; and I should be very sorry that the measures which do prevail, should be supposed to be mine. A little time, I fear, will show the fatal consequences of them. The stake now played for, is no less than the Republic itself; and I see no better prospect of either better cards, or better play next year, than to our cost, we have seen this. However, do you be discreet, and do not let the warmth of your friendship for me, make you say anything that may give *prise* upon you, to those who I promise you, would be glad to have it. For I am too well convinced of the truth and cordiality of your affection for me, to want any new proofs of it.

* See Chesterfield's Letter to his Son, July 30, 1747, and note.

Though things go now smoothly, and to the wish of the Stadtholder in Holland, I suspect that they will not long continue to do so. The heads that govern now, are too hot for the old ones that are to obey; and I foresee that the string will be pulled till it breaks.

Make my compliments to your aunt. Yours most faithfully.

CXXXIII.
TO SOLOMON DAYROLLES, ESQ.

LONDON, *October* 16, O.S. 1747.

DEAR DAYROLLES,

You allow me the privilege of a busy man, which is, not to write, when he has not time to do it; and that of a lazy man, which is, not to write, when he has not a mind to it; but for the two last posts I claim the privilege of a sick man, for I have had confounded rheumatic pains in my shoulder, for which I have been let blood, physicked, and confined, but I am now pretty well again.

Bentinck, I hear, is ill, and Van-haren better than ever he was in his life, by a very good place which he has lately got, and which gives uneasiness to the former. I foresee great discord in that country, and great discontent in the Republic, which will not, I believe, produce that strength for the next campaign that they promise us here, and that we are weak enough to expect.

I suppose that you have received your money, for it has been ordered some time ago.

What becomes of *L'ami?* Is he persecuted or only neglected?

Has Kreuningen paid his two *per cent.* and survived it? Have you seen your old friend Caroline? *Bon soir.*

CXXXIV.
A MADAME LA MARQUISE DE MONCONSEIL.

À LONDRES, *ce* 20 *Octobre*, V.S. 1747.

Sur mon honneur, Madame, vous m'avez déjà fort gâté, et si vous continuez sur ce même ton, vous me ruinerez absolument. J'avale à long traits votre flatterie, vous l'apprêtez si bien que vous en faites un nectar, mais il n'en tourne la tête que plus pour cela.

J'ai montré l'Anti-Lucrèce à quelques savans d'ici qui ont en même tems du goût; ils en sont tous charmés; entre autres notre grand Chancelier * l'a lu deux fois, et a prononcé un décret des plus avantageux. Je donne cinq cent ans à tout le conclave à produire quelque chose qui l'égale.

Revenez donc de *Bagatelle;* il ne faut jamais être hors de la capitale quand une fois il faut faire du feu : il n'y a pas d'autre bon quartier d'hiver que Paris et Londres.

CXXXV.

TO SOLOMON DAYROLLES, ESQ.

LONDON, *October* 23, O.S. 1747.

DEAR DAYROLLES,

. I have just now received your letter of the 31st instant, N.S. The news † which you mention to be sent from hence to your little Court, is, I believe, wished there to be true, and possibly, I wish it more myself, than anybody else does; but yet I will say that it is in nobody's power, but my own, to verify it. How soon I may choose to do it, I cannot now determine; but this I know, that you judge very right in thinking that it must be very disagreeable to tug at the oar with one who cannot row, and yet will be paddling so as to hinder you from rowing. I think, I have had a great deal of patience already, and how much longer it will hold, God knows; to do any good, I would bear a great deal, but as I find that impossible, and that we are to be ruined by incapacity, I do not much care to share in the reproach when I know I am free from the guilt.

I think our friend will never carry his point, of being sent to England, as the lady, I know, hates him cordially, and never yet forgave when she once hated. Bentinck's blind impetuosity and invincible obstinacy suits her better.

I send a packet to you by this courier, who is going to Vienna; it is a stuff for Madame Monconseil at Paris, who tells me that Monsieur Chiquet has allowed her to have it addressed to him, and that he will further it to her. Therefore pray send it to him, and beg of him, to send it on; you may make any use of my name to him, that you please. I have not time to say a word more. Adieu.

* Lord Hardwicke.   † Of his retirement from office.

CXXXVI.

TO SOLOMON DAYROLLES, ESQ.

LONDON, *November* 17, O.S. 1747.

DEAR DAYROLLES,

I mend though slowly, and yet I wish that other things mended as fast. Your politics in Holland are above my comprehension, as well as ours here. In pursuit of chimerical and unattainable views, we are running into certain ruin. Heat, prejudice and obstinacy hurry you on in Holland; incapacity leads or rather misleads here. But enough of this and *entre nous* only.

I received a letter from Kreuningen, full of groans and lamentations; he declares, however, that he will most conscientiously pay his two per cent. If he does, I do not believe that ever man sacrificed more to a quiet conscience. Pray make him my compliments and assure him that if any pamphlet had appeared here worthy even of his ——, I would have sent it him. But I never knew the press so quiet and so uninteresting in my life, as it has been of late.

The two Dutch Plenipotentiaries are, I find, of the nomination of the first (Mr. Bentinck) and will consequently greatly contribute to a general pacification, as Count Maurice's activity will to the defence of Zealand! *Je suis bien las de tout ceci et serois bien aise d'une bonne occasion de me sauver d'une galère sans pilote, et battue de vents contraires. Adieu, mon cher enfant.*

CXXXVII.

TO SOLOMON DAYROLLES, ESQ.

LONDON, *December* 1, O.S. 1747.

DEAR DAYROLLES,

I received but last Sunday yours of the 1st N.S., and there are two more posts due from Holland.

Though your correspondence cannot, in this season of inaction, be so informing as at other times, it is still the correspondence of a friend; and I value much more what the heart dictates, than what occurrences supply. So write on, when you have leisure; and depend upon your letters being equally welcome to me, how-

ever full of, or free from, news. Chetwynd * tells me that you
have some doubts, whether you should regularly write your
office-letters or not, as you have not great variety of materials
for them at present. That is none of your fault, and must necessarily be the case while Lord Sandwich is at the Hague. But,
however, I can tell you that the King reads your letters with
great attention, and is very well pleased with them; therefore
continue by all means, and insert everything that comes to your
knowledge. His Majesty loves to hear the little occurrences of
every place.

Lord Sandwich writes me word in his letter of the 1st, N.S.,
that as soon as the Brunswick troops shall be taken into our joint
pay, of which the Dutch proportion is 3,000 men, the whole
intended augmentation of 30,000 men will want but 1,000 of
being fully complete, though by his former account, about six
weeks ago, he said that there wanted 15,000 to complete that
augmentation. I have not, in the intermediate time, heard of
any new troops being engaged by the Republic. Therefore pray
(without telling the reason why you want it) endeavour to get
me an exact account of all the troops now in the service of the
Republic; distinguishing those that were there before the election of the Stadtholder, and those which have been raised since;
and likewise an account of the prisoners still in the possession of
the French. This account, I know, you can hardly get in any
other shape, but that of battalions and squadrons; but, however,
I desire you will accompany it with the best-grounded conjecture that you can form of the real number of effective men,
to which that whole establishment amounts.

As the world goes, I am not displeased with Monsieur Brenles's
account of the boy; and, to tell you the truth, it is better than
I expected. I agree with you, that Leipsig is not the place to
give him that *bon ton*, which I know he wants; but then consider,
that he can acquire that *bon ton*, nowhere but in mixed companies,
and in the pleasures of people of fashion at Courts, which if he
were to taste of so young as he is now, there would be an end of
all studies. And he still wants a foundation in several sciences,
which he will lay better at Leipsig than anywhere else. He will

* William Chetwynd, Under Secretary of State in the Northern Department.—M.

there make himself master of the German language, the history and constitution of the empire, some Grotius, some civil law, and other things, which he must either learn now or never. It is true, that in all this time he will contract a little German dirt; but that is easier rubbed off, especially at his age, than English dirt. Turin will effectually do that; and Paris shall give, at last, the true varnish.

Harte writes me word, that the boy really works hard, and has barely time to eat, drink and sleep. In all the vacations, he is to go to Dresden; which will do some good to his manners. Adieu.

CXXXVIII.

TO SOLOMON DAYROLLES, ESQ.

LONDON, *December* 14, O.S. 1747.

DEAR DAYROLLES,

I have received your letter of the 19th, N.S. Your account of the inefficiency of the Government in Holland is, I am convinced, very true, and I have the same from various hands. Much talking and very little doing, sanguine folly without force, and obstinacy without judgment. Maréchal de Lowendahl* will, I believe, soon talk in a much more effectual manner to Zealand or Breda, though I should rather think the latter; as it is easier, and with regard to England of more importance.

If Count Nassau will break bones, I presume he will begin with Rodriguez's.† It is a most scandalous article.

I have spoken again about your payment, and have had fair promises.

I have not yet received *Memnon*;‡ have you read *Angola ?* § It is very prettily written. By the first opportunity of a courier, I shall send Kreuningen a cargo of pamphlets, though we have had no good ones of late. *Adieu, mon enfant.*

* Commander of the French army.—M.
† The writer of the Cologne Gazette.—M.
‡ One of Voltaire's philosophical tales.
§ An Indian tale, published anonymously in 1746, by the Chevalier de la Morliere, in the licentious style of Crebillon the Younger.

CXXXIX.

TO SOLOMON DAYROLLES, ESQ.

LONDON, *January* 1, O.S. 1748.

DEAR DAYROLLES,

The beggar's blessing attend you for this and fifty more years! after that, I leave you to take your chance.

I have received your two last letters, and likewise *Memnon*; I always like the former, but, to tell you the truth, I do not so much admire the latter as Kreuningen does, who tells me that he *devoured* it. I have sent him a load of bad books and pamphlets, by his particular order, for none good have appeared here of late. Pray make him my compliments, and my excuses for not having yet answered his letter, which I will do soon.

By what you tell me, and by what I hear from other hands, there is much talking and little doing at the Hague, whereas the French (though they love talking as well as other people) seem to be doing, as I fear we shall soon find. I am called away. Good night, dear Dayrolles!

CXL.

TO SOLOMON DAYROLLES, ESQ.

LONDON, *January* 12, O.S. 1748.

DEAR DAYROLLES,

Three mails, which came in together, brought me two letters from you; the case of good things, of which it is often said, that but two of them come over in three ships. The Abbé de la Ville's letter, for I am sure it is his, is but superficial; he might have made more of the subject; but, however, it is prettily writ.

I have heard from another quarter likewise, what you tell me about Bentinck, and I have long foreseen it, knowing his impetuous and impracticable temper.* The Pensionary is ten times more a man of business, and has shown himself ductile enough;

---

* "Both her Highness and the Greffier are much displeased with Bentinck's vivacities and peremptory manner of deciding upon all occasions, and that his common phrase is *que si on ne veut point suivre les voies qu'il indique, que pour lui il ne veut plus se mêler de l'affaire en question.*" (Mr. Dayrolles to Lord Chesterfield, Jan 12, N. S. 1748. Original MS.)—M.

and Her Royal Highness will certainly prefer the most ductile. Whether the tone of that Court be peace or war, it differs only in point of time; for a peace there will necessarily be; if prudence makes it soon, it will be so much the better; but if sanguine folly delays it, necessity will, before it is long, make it, and make a damned bad one. We have not nor cannot have any force to look the French in the face with, till the middle of the campaign; before which time they will have struck their stroke, and the Republic will beg, instead of refusing a peace.

I have desired Kreuningen to send me any good new French books that come out, and to give them to you, who will pay him for them, and transmit them to me. And I insist upon your sending me the account, that I may pay you. Our booksellers here import no books worth two-pence.

When Lord Sandwich shall be gone to Aix-la-Chapelle, which, God knows when he will, you need not doubt being fully instructed by *somebody* or other.

Bon soir, mon Enfant.

CXLI.

TO SOLOMON DAYROLLES, ESQ.

LONDON, *January* 26, O.S. 1748.

DEAR DAYROLLES,

This letter goes to you, in that confidence, which I always shall, and know that I safely may, place in you. And you will therefore not let one word of it transpire.

What Haslang wrote to Elsacker,* I believe will, nay I am sure must prove true. Neither the state of foreign nor domestic affairs will permit me to continue much longer in my present situation. I cannot go on writing orders, of which I see and foretell the fatal tendency. I can no longer take my share, of either the public indignation or contempt on account of measures in which I have no share. I can no longer continue in a post

---

* "We have here many fresh reports of your Lordship's resignation, which are even strongly affirmed in two letters from Baron Haslang to M. Elsacker. Yet I am determined to be an unbeliever till the confirmation comes to me from yourself." (Mr. Dayrolles to Lord Chesterfield, Jan. 26, N.S. 1748. Original MS.)—M.

in which it is well known that I am but a *Commis;* and in which
I have not been able to do any one service to any one man
though ever so meritorious, lest I should be supposed to have
any power and my colleague not the whole. And lastly, I tell you
very truly, I long for rest and quiet, equally necessary to my
present state both of body and mind. Could I do any good, I
would sacrifice some more quiet to it; but, convinced as I am
that I can do none, I will indulge my ease, and preserve my
character.

I have gone through pleasures while my constitution and my
spirits would allow me. Business succeeded them; and I have
now gone through every part of it, without liking it at all the
better for being acquainted with it. Like many other things, it
is most admired by those who know it the least. And this one
consideration would alone disgust one of it, even if one had the
sole power; which is, that in this country one must, for political
reasons, frequently prefer the most unworthy to the most worthy,
and prostitute to importunity and undeserving greediness the rewards of merits. Thus weary of business, you will easily imagine,
that in retiring from my present business, I shall not engage in
any other; but far from embarking upon any account in cabals
and opposition, whenever I do take any part in the House of
Lords, it shall be in support of the Government. Do not think
neither that I mean a sullen retirement from the world; on the
contrary, my retreat from business will give me both more time
and better spirits for the enjoyment of social life, from which I
will never withdraw myself.

What day I shall resign the Seals is not yet fixed; therefore,
I desire that you will not, upon any account, mention one word
of this letter, or give the least intimation to any one living, that
you know anything of this resolution. As I know the warmth
of your friendship for me, and at the same time the warmth of
your temper, I most earnestly recommend to you, nay, I insist
upon, your being discreet, when this event shall become public.
There are those at the Hague, who will be glad to lay hold of
any little slip of yours, in order to do you an injury: disappoint
them by your discretion, and say nothing more upon it than that
you knew that my health required exercise, and my temper quiet;
and that you know too, that whenever I can, as a private man, be

of any use to the King or to the public, I shall act the same out of place as I should have done in. This conduct I shall look upon as a proof of your friendship, and not of your coolness for me. As I shall always have a satisfaction in hearing from you, write to me from time to time as usual; but remember too, that I shall then be no longer master of the post; therefore let such of your letters as come by it, contain nothing but what will bear an opening previous to mine. But when you can have a safe opportunity of conveying a letter to me, write more fully, and tell me what passes at the Hague, what is said of my resignation, and how things go at your little Court, which, if I do not mistake, will be subject to great variations and frequent ones.

Adieu for this time, my dear Dayrolles; and be convinced that, knowing as I do your merit, your good heart, your truth, and your affection, I shall, though hereafter a very useless one, be ever

Your very faithful friend.

CXLII.

TO SOLOMON DAYROLLES, ESQ.

LONDON, February 9, 1748.*

DEAR DAYROLLES,

Le sort est jetté: you receive this letter from a sincere friend, but not from a Secretary of State; and I know you to be so true a friend too, that I am sure you value it more in the former character than in the latter. Last Saturday † I resigned the Seals into the King's hands, who parted with me in the most gracious manner possible. My health, my spirits, and my character, all concurred in this measure, and made it absolutely necessary for me. I retire without any personal quarrel with any man whatsoever; and if I disapproved of measures, it was by no means upon account of their authors. Far from engaging in opposition, as resigning Ministers too commonly do, I shall, to the utmost of my powers, support the King and his Government; which I can do with more advantage to them, and more honour to myself, when I do not receive five thousand pounds

---

* See letter LIV., of same date, to his son.
† On the 6th of February, O.S.

a-year for doing it.   I shall now, for the first time in my life
enjoy that philosophical quiet, which, upon my word, I have long
wished for.   While I was able, that is, while I was young, I
lived in a constant dissipation and tumult of pleasures ; the hurry
and plague of business, either in or out of Court, succeeded, and
continued till now.   And it is now time to think of the only real
comforts in the latter end of life, quiet, liberty, and health.   Do
not think, by the way, that by quiet and retirement I mean
solitude and misanthropy ; far from it, my philosophy, as you
know, is of a cheerful and social nature.   My horse, my books,
and my friends, will divide my time pretty equally ; I shall not
keep less company, but only better, for I shall choose it.   Therefore do not fear finding me, whenever you take a little turn here,
morose and cynical : on the contrary, you will find me as gentle
as a dove ; but, alas! not so amorous.   At least, whatever else
you find me, you will always find me with the truest affection,

Yours.

P.S.   Pray make my compliments to my Baron, and thank
him both for his books and his letters : I will do it myself very
soon.

CXLIII.

TO SOLOMON DAYROLLES, ESQ.

LONDON, *February* 9, O.S. 1748.

DEAR DAYROLLES,

As you will be asked a million of questions about my resignation, I have wrote you the letter in which this goes enclosed,
by way of brief for you to talk out of ; and moreover, you may
if you please (though with some seeming difficulty), show the
letter itself to the curious.   Various and absurd reports will, I
know, be stirring upon this event ; I cannot help that, and must
pay that tax as well as other people.   One of those reports I am
sure will be, and indeed in some measure already is, that my
ambition was boundless, and that because I could not be everything, I would be nothing ; to which I shall only answer, that if
such were my ambition, staying in Court was a much more likely
way of gratifying it than going out ; and that my chance was far
from being a bad one, if I would have tried it, as an ambitious

mau certainly would have done. But upon my word, I gave you my true motives iu my former letter, I told them to my friends here likewise, and as for the rest of the world, they are welcome to refiue and speculate as much as ever they please for

Yours sincerely.

Point de Vivacité!   Temper, Temper!

The Duke of Newcastle has taken my department (in truth he had it before), and the New Secretary, whoever he shall be, will have the Southern. The difficulty is where to get one; some talk of the Duke of Bedford, to hold it till Lord Sandwich can come from the Congress; but nobody is yet fixed.

Whoever it shall be, I will venture to prophesy that he will not agree with his colleagues so long as I did.

CXLIV.

À MADAME LA MARQUISE DE MONCONSEIL.

À BATH, *ce* 15 *Février*, V.S. 1748.

Vous me reprochez, Madame, un silence que votre esprit ne peut pas regretter. Vos reproches me sont d'autant plus flatteurs que je les dois uniquement à vos sentimens d'amitié; c'est par là seulement que je prétends vous tenir, et quoique vous ne vouliez pas m'accorder des sentimens en général, ayez la justice de faire une exception en votre faveur. Il est vrai, je ne suis pas ami banal; si je l'étois, mon amitié seroit indigne de la vôtre. Il me faut premièrement bien connoître mes gens; je ne veux point un ami sans sentimens, parcequ'il a de l'esprit, comme je ne veux pas nou plus d'un ami à sentimens, qui n'a pas le sens commun. Il faut des sentimens réciproques pour former l'amitié, mais aussi il faut réciproquement de l'esprit pour la conduire. A cette confession de ma foi amicale, jugez, Madame, si vous n'en êtes pas le premier article. Les lettres, il est vrai, sont les messagers et de l'amour et de l'amitié, mais n'en sont pas toujours des preuves, et trop souvent même elles ressemblent plutôt à des ministres qui mentent pour le service de leurs maîtres. Sur ce pied donc, si mes lettres ont été moins fréquentes en dernier lieu, cela ne décide de rien à mon désavantage; la fausseté n'est-elle pas toujours infiniment plus exacte à remplir les devoirs extérieurs que la vérité ? Mais en tout cas, Madame, gare l'avenir, et le loisir que je viens de me procurer. Vos plaintes pourroient bientôt être d'une autre sorte, si votre politesse ne s'y oppose pas.

Il y a à cette heure douze jours que j'ai quitté mon poste de Sécretaire d'Etat ; vous l'aurez certainement su par les nouvelles publiques, mais vous n'en aurez certainement pas su les véritables raisons, que le public sait rarement, et n'allègue jamais : d'ailleurs, elles sont trop simples pour être crues ; elles ne sont donc véritablement que l'amour du repos, et le soin de ma santé, qui en exigeoit. Pour s'acquitter passablement de cet emploi, il faut un travail sans interruption, et une attention sans relâche, deux articles qui ne s'accordent nullement avec ma paresse naturelle, ni avec ma santé délicate. Il y falloit aussi sacrifier toutes les douceurs de la société et de la vie privéa, ce qui convenoit encore moins à mon humeur : enfin, après y avoir mûrement réfléchi, je me suis décidé en faveur du repos, et s'il eût été possible de me faire changer de sentiment, je dois avouer que la manière gracieuse et affectueuse, dont le Roi a tâché de me détourner du parti que j'avois pris, auroit plus que tout autre chose fait cet effet.

Je jouis donc à présent d'un repos qui a d'autant plus de charmes, que je ne l'ai jamais goûté auparavant. Dans ma jeunesse, la dissipation, et le tumulte des plaisirs, auxquels je me livrai sans reserve, ne m'en laissoient point, et pendant ces dernières vingt années, les affaires m'en ont laissé aussi peu ; il étoit donc bien tems d'en jouir, et grace à Dieu j'en jouis pleinement à présent. Il y a six jours que je profite de ma liberté pour boire ces eaux ici, qui ne manquent jamais de me rétablir, et je m'apperçois déjà que mes indigestions commencent à se corriger ; la parfaite oisiveté de ce lieu ne laisse pas que d'y contribuer aussi.

Je languis pour les lettres, qui doivent m'expliquer votre *Quipos* * et autres paroles mystiques dans votre dernière ; je ne les ai pas encore reçues, mais je m'en fie bien aux soins de l'Abbé de la Ville, à qui je suis redevable de mille attentions. Adieu. Madame, tout brusquement, mais pas pour long-tems.

* The strings or threads used, it is said, by the ancient Peruvians to supply the want of writing, and lately brought into notice by Madame de Graffigny, in her *Lettres Péruviennes*, published anonymously in 1747.— See Letter to his son, Feb. 20, 1752.

CXLV.

TO SOLOMON DAYROLLES, ESQ.

BATH, *February* 23, O.S. 1748.

Me voici, mon cher enfant, enjoying liberty and idleness, but attended with a great cold, which I got upon the road, in the coldest weather, and the deepest snow, that I ever remember. This has hindered me from drinking the waters hitherto; but that is no great matter, as I came here more for the sake of quiet, and absence from London, while I was the only subject of conversation there, than for any great occasion that I had for the waters.

Without affectation, I feel most sensibly the comforts of my present free and quiet situation; and if I had much vanity in my composition, of which I really think that I have less than most people, even that vanity would be fully gratified, by the voice of the public upon this occasion. But, upon my word, all the busy tumultuous passions have subsided in me; and that not so much from philosophy, as from a little reflection upon a great deal of experience. I have been behind the scenes, both of pleasure and business. I have seen all the coarse pullies and dirty ropes, which exhibit and move all the gaudy machines; and I have seen and smelt the tallow-candles which illuminate the whole decoration, to the astonishment and admiration of the ignorant audience.

Since my resignation, my brother,* as you will have seen in the newspapers, is appointed Commissioner of the Admiralty, which he never would have been as long as I had continued in, the resolution being taken to exclude all those who might otherwise have been supposed to have come in upon my interest. As I retire without quarrelling, and without the least intention to oppose, I saw no reason why my brother should decline this post; and I advised him to accept of it, and the rather as it was the King's own doing.

George Stanhope † too, I am told, is now to have the rank of Colonel given him, which I could never procure him; so that it seems I have a much better interest out of place than I had in.

* The Hon. John Stanhope.
† Son of the first, and brother of the second, Earl Stanhope.

All goes well at Leipsig; the boy applies and improves more than I expected. Count and Countess Flemming, who saw him there, and who carried him to the Duchess of Courland's, gave me a very good account of him; and assured me, that he was by no means the awkward English oaf, but *passablement décrotté*. He shall stay there a year longer, and then go to Turin. If you should accidentally hear, or can procure, any memoirs of his private character, pray let me know them.

Remember the cautions which I gave you in one of my former letters. When Lord Sandwich goes to the Congress, you will have a great deal to do, and play a considerable part, at the Hague; which I know you are able to acquit yourself of very well. This, I think, will put you *en train d'être Monsieur l'Envoyé*, upon Lord Sandwich's return to his post here, which will be before it is very long; for, however little peace is at present intended, necessity will soon make it by the means of the *Maréchaux de Saxe et Lowendahl;* and then, being upon the place, I think you may reasonably ask, and probably obtain, the character and appointments of Envoy.

The more to facilitate this point, make your court as much as possible to the Prince of Orange,

> "Et sachez qu'en ceci
> La femme* est comprise aussi."

For a word dropped in a private letter from *sister* to *sister*, may be of great use upon that occasion.

May you have all you wish!   Adieu, yours.

CXLVI.

TO THE BISHOP OF WATERFORD.

BATH, *March* 1, 1748.

MY DEAR LORD,

I thank you for your kind letter, by which I am glad to find that you approve of my resignation, and of my resolution to enjoy the comforts of a private life; indeed, I had enough both of the pageantry and hurry of public life, to see their futility, and I

---

* The Princess of Orange, who was probably, as Lord Chesterfield hints, in constant correspondence with her sister in England, Princess Emily.—M.

withdraw from them, *uti conviva satur.* This conviction from experience secured me from regret; those who have only seen the gaudy outside of great stations, languish for their hidden charms, which in my mind soon satiate after possession.*

I am very glad to hear that I shall have the pleasure of seeing you and your family here this summer; I know that I cannot see a truer nor a warmer friend, which, I assure you, you may say too when you see me. I suppose that you will stop in your way in Nottinghamshire to see your son, whom as you return, you will probably take with you to Ireland.

I have been here now a fortnight, and have found good by the waters, not that I had any great occasion for them; but, to say the truth, I came here chiefly to be out of the way of being talked to, and talked of, while my resignation was the only object of conversation in town.

Adieu, my dear Lord; I cannot tell you how sincerely and affectionately I am   Yours.

CXLVII.

TO DAVID MALLET, ESQ.

BATH, *March* 9, 1748.

SIR,

I am very much concerned at the continuance of your complaint, and am afraid that you increased it by the letter which you favoured me with. I shall put your eyes to that trial no more of a good while at least, for I shall be in town next Monday or Tuesday, and I hope for the rest of my life, except now and then a little excursion to this place, which always does me good. I can say to you now, without a compliment, what I could not with truth have said to you some years ago, which is, that I do not know a pair of eyes in which I interest myself so much as I do in yours. I use the word "interest" here very properly, for

---

* "When I had the honour to see Lord Chesterfield, some time after his resignation, one reason he told me why he was glad he had resigned, was because it was very difficult, in the public station he was in, to be entirely free from doing things that were not quite right."—Note by the Bishop of Waterford in Maty's edition.

it is from the use of your eyes that I expect the best employment for my own.

By this time I suppose that I am a little out of fashion, as a subject of political refinements; and that new matter has shoved me off the coffee-house tables. I own I should not have been sorry to have heard, unseen, the various speculations thrown out, and facts asserted concerning myself of late; which I dare say were full as near the truth, as those will be, which some solid historians of these times will transmit to posterity. Not one of them will allow the desire of ease and quiet to have had the least share in my determination; but on the contrary will assert that it was only the pretence of disappointed ambition. Lord Chesterfield would be Cæsar or nothing, says a spirited politician; there is something more in this affair than we yet know, says a deeper; he expects to be called again, says a third; while the silent pantomimical politician shrugs at every thing eventually, and is sure not to be disproved at last. They are all welcome; let them account for my present situation how they please, this I know, and they do not, that I feel and enjoy the comfort of it.

Before I left London I spoke to Mr. Pelham concerning you; he told me that he had been exceedingly pressed by Lyttelton in favour of Thomson and West. I answered that I had a great value for them both, and should be extremely sorry to hurt either, but they had already something, and could therefore, in my opinion, better wait a little than you. Our conversation ended, as all those conversations do, with general assurances on his part, that he would do for you when he could. None but he who gives these assurances can know the real value of them; for he could not say more if he meant to realize them, and he would not say less if he did not; all that I can say is, that he shall not want a remembrancer. The situation of your affairs makes me only more anxious, but not more desirous to serve you than I was before; as it was your merit, which I did know, and not your circumstances, which I did not know, that made me, what I ever shall be,

Your most faithful friend and servant.

CXLVIII.

À MADAME LA MARQUISE DE MONCONSEIL.

À LONDRES, *ce* 15 *Mars*, V.S. 1748.

Revenu des eaux, et établi en ville, me voici en état, Madame, de vous en faire ressentir les effets, par le nombre de lettres dont je vous accablerai. Je suis à présent dégagé de tous les devoirs, excepté ceux de l'amitié, où vous méritez sûrement une préférence marquée; ajoutez aussi, s'il vous plait, à ce devoir, le plaisir que j'ai à le remplir, et vous ne douterez plus de mon exactitude; vous aurez peut-être plutôt sujet de vous en plaindre.

Je suis en vérité bien affligé de la triste fin du Comte de Coigny* surtout par rapport à Monsieur le Maréchal, que j'honore comme il le mérite. Je crains même pour sa vie à l'âge qu'il a; pour résister à de pareils malheurs, il faut la force, et les occupations d'un âge moins avancé que le sien; au lieu qu'à présent il n'a rien pour interrompre la continuité des idées accablantes. Ditesmoi, je vous en prie, Madame, toutes les particularités de cette malheureuse affaire; je m'y intéresse au point d'en demander les circonstances, ce qu'on fait toujours dans les malheurs, quoiqu'elles ne servent ordinairement qu'à en augmenter le poids. J'écris au Maréchal par vos ordres, étant bien sûr que cela convient, puisque vous le dites; sans cela j'aurois cru qu'il auroit mieux valu ne pas percer le voile devant la douleur paternelle.

Ma liberté m'est d'autant plus flatteuse qu'elle me présente une perspective de vous revoir un jour à Paris; quand ce jour, pour lequel je languis véritablement, viendra, je trouverai ma place à mon bureau bien avantageusement troquée contre une place à souper chez vous. Je compte qu'assurément la paix m'ouvrira le port de Calais dans le cours de cette année. Nous ruinons votre commerce et votre marine, vous ruinez nos bons alliés les Provinces Unies; on se lassera de part et d'autre de ces ruines réciproques, et on est viendra à une liquidation.

---

* The Comte de Coigny, son of the Maréchal of the same name, appears to have been killed in a duel. According to M. Villenave, *un propos offensant tenu au jeu à un prince légitimé lui coûta la vie, le 4 Mars*, 1748.—M.

Je n'ai pas encore reçu les *Contes Péruviens ;* je m'impatiente, et en attendant, votre *Quipos* me donne la torture.

Voulez-vous bien avoir la bonté de dire à la Princesse de Montbazon, que j'avois exécuté ses ordres avant même que de les avoir reçus, et que j'avois obtenu la permission du Roi pour que Monsieur le Prince de Montbazon et quelques autres chevaliers de Malte prisonniers pussent faire leurs caravanes. Monsieur le Marquis de Puisieux l'avoit demandée par le canal de Milord Sandwich, et j'ai eu le plaisir de finir les fonctions de mon emploi par là.* Je crois incommoder moins Madame la Princesse de Montbazon, en ne lui écrivant pas, simplement pour accuser la lettre dont elle m'avoit honoré. Adieu, Madame, sans compliment.

Ayez la bonté aussi de donner l'incluse à mon aimable rival Monsieur de Nevers. Je ne la ferme pas, afin que vous voyez que vous ne nous avez pas encore menés jusqu'au cartel.

CXLIX.

TO SOLOMON DAYROLLES, ESQ.

LONDON, *March* 22, O.S. 1748.

DEAR DAYROLLES,

I am now returned from the Bath in a state of health, which I have not known of some years, and which is owing to quiet of mind and exercise of body. I am now master of my own time, and of my own motions. I do whatever I please, whenever I please, and am mightily pleased with it.

I have received your two letters since my last; in one of them you went too far, and seemed to have forgot, that I might pos-

---

* The following is an extract of the letter on this subject from *le Bailli de Froulay de Tessé, Ambassadeur de Malte près S. M. Très Chrétienne,* which was transmitted to Lord Chesterfield. After giving the names of *le Chevalier Louis Constantin de Rohan, Prince de Montbazon, Enseigne de Vaisseau,* and other naval officers in the French service, who had been taken prisoners and allowed to return to France on Parole, he adds, *Ils supplient très humblement qu'il leur soit en outre permis d'aller faire leurs caravanes sur les galères et vaisseaux de Malte, où ils serviront une puissance qui observe inviolablement la plus exacte neutralité dans les différends entre les Princes Chrétiens . . . . . et ils donnent leur parole d'honneur de se représenter toutes et quantes fois ils en seront requis.—*M.

sibly not be the first reader of it. *Soyez sage*, for that will be a better security to you, than anything that Lord Sandwich can say to you, for I do not rely much upon his professions.

I lay no great stress upon Keith's* remaining at the Hague, which I do not think is with any other design but only to be the channel of a certain correspondence between the Duke of New-castle, the Prince of Orange, and Lord Sandwich. *Apropos* of that correspondence, Charles Bentinck is come here to contradict every word that his elder brother said six months ago. He has confessed the impotence of the Republic; has owned that they are disappointed in their levies; and has desired to borrow twelve hundred thousand pounds, or at least a million sterling, without which he says that the Republic must be inevitably ruined. When the King heard the purport of Charles's commission, he said *Chesterfield told me six months ago that it would be so.* As to his loan of a million at least, he has been told, that, if he can get it, *à la bonne heure*, but that it is not very likely that he should, when our own loan is at five *per cent.* discount, and when it is very doubtful whether the further payments will be made at all. At last he came down to beg for God's sake, that we would, at least, take the whole expense of the Russians upon ourselves, for that the Republic cannot possibly pay the share that they had stipu-lated. What answer he has received to that request I do not yet know. Money was never so scarce in the city, nor the stocks so low, even during the Rebellion, as now; which you, as a monied man, certainly know. Twelve *per cent.* is offered for money, and even that will not do. And if there is not a cer-tainty of peace in three or four months at furthest, an entire stagnation of all credit, if not a bankruptcy, is universally ex-pected.

Could you buy me two hogsheads of superlative good claret at Palairet's, or any where else, and send it me over by some English ship, as you know the Act of Navigation requires? I would have it of the first growth, and a strong body. I trust to your distinguishing palate for the quality of it. I am in no sort of haste for it, so that you may take your own time to taste, con-sult, and at last to fix. Only do not send me any, unless you can be sure of sending me what is extremely good.

* Robert Keith, afterwards *Chargé des Affaires* at St. Petersburg, etc.

Make my compliments to our friend when you see him. I am heartily glad of Wolters's new employment.*

Yours affectionately.

CL..

TO SOLOMON DAYROLLES, ESQ.

LONDON, *April* 8, O.S. 1748.

DEAR DAYROLLES,

Since my last to you I have received your two letters with their inclosures, which were a letter and a duplicate from Madame de St. Gille, at Madrid. She wants to have a certain Spanish prisoner exchanged, and, thinking me still in office, applies to me for it. I have, however, got it done, as I inform her in the inclosed; which I desire that you will forward to her some way or other. The safest way, I believe, will be to give it to the Marquis del Puerto's Secretary. It may give you an opportunity, if you have a mind, to send her something tender from yourself; for I remember you was one of her lovers, and went so far at least, as to talk a great deal of ——— to her.

When the Treasury meets after Easter, Mr. Pelham has promised me that you shall be paid every shilling that is due to you, so that then you will be out of debt. I hope you take care to live within your appointments, and to lay up all your own, that in case of any *revers* you may not be a loser by your commission. Pelham told me in confidence that you were in danger soon after I went out, but that now you were very safe again. But Hop told me yesterday, that in the copy of a Resolution of the States which he had received lately, he was sorry to find it said, that that Resolution should be communicated to Mr. Keith. Be that as it will, *laissez faire,* and be quiet; and give them no handle by any complaints on your part, to complain of you; for I have reason to believe, that notwithstanding all the assurances given you, they would be glad to have you out of the way; but if you give them no *prise* upon you, Pelham, I am sure, will protect you against them.

The deliberations about the christening,† and the magnificence

---

* Agent to George II. at Rotterdam.
† Of the Prince of Orange's son, afterwards his successor.

and profusion of it, were surely *déplacés* at this time; at least it is thought so here, unless it proceeded from a resolution of dying merrily. Your end seems to me to be near. Maestricht, I am persuaded, will be taken in a fortnight *de tranchée ouverte;* and after that there is not any one place that can hold out a week. Maréchal Lowendahl's leaving his former destination of Breda and Zealand, in order to join the Grand Army, convinces me, that something more is intended there than the taking of Maestricht; and I dread the next letters from Holland, bringing us an account of the Duke's army being cut off in the whole, or in part. All my predictions are now verifying too fast, as on the other hand, all the assertions of the eldest Bentinck when here, and of Lord Sandwich from the Hague, have proved absolutely false. Our army, which was, according to their calculation, to consist of 192,000 men, is actually weaker than it was last year; and that peace, which the Republic will in a few weeks be obliged to sign upon the drum head, will be such a one, as will prove how much those were in the right, who were for treating last year upon the foot of Maréchal de Saxe's proposal to Ligonier.

Here is a pamphlet come out entitled, *My Apology,* * which I will send to my Baron, with a bundle of other pamphlets, by the first opportunity, and he will show it you. It makes a very great noise here, as you will easily conceive that it must when you read it. Many people really believe, and many desire that it should be believed, to have been written by my direction at least; but, upon my word and honour, so far am I from having any hand directly or indirectly in it, that I do not so much as guess at the author, though I have done all I could to fish him out.

---

* "An Apology for a late Resignation, in a Letter from an English Gentleman to his friend at the Hague." London, 1748, 8vo. It was commonly ascribed to Lord Marchmont, who in consequence, says Horace Walpole, "was very near losing his place." (To Sir H. Mann, Dec. 2, 1748.)—M. Walpole, however, in his *Memoirs of George II.*, calls it "Chesterfield's book," and on the title-page of the copy sold at the Strawberry Hill auction are the words "Lord Chesterfield's," in Walpole's handwriting. The reviewer of Lord Mahon's edition of *Chesterfield's Letters* (*Quarterly Review*, Sept., 1845) considers that it was dictated by Chesterfield, and written by Mallett, and that one reason for his strong denial of the authorship was because (as stated in the next letter) most of his letters were opened.

As to your flame, you have given me two very good reasons for not extinguishing it in matrimony; particularly that of her father's being likely to live these thirty years. As to the family madness, should it break out upon the lady, she would then be but a very little madder than most other women!

Pray do not buy me any claret till you hear further from me; for I am lately informed, that there is great difficulty in importing it here, even in an English bottom. But in the mean time you may be tasting eventually if you please.

Their Graces of Richmond are at their own motion reconciled to Fox,* and Lady Caroline. They were aware, I believe, that in case of any changes, Fox stood foremost; and therefore thought it right and prudent to take him in time, and not to stay till the view of interest would have been too strongly marked.

It is time to finish this letter. Good night then, my dear Dayrolles.   Yours faithfully.

CLI.

TO SOLOMON DAYROLLES, ESQ.

LONDON, *April* 19, O.S. 1748.

DEAR DAYROLLES,

I have received yours of the 19th, N.S. The situation of the Republic is now exactly what six months ago I foresaw and foretold it would be; there was indeed no conjuration in that prediction, nothing having happened since, that was not the necessary effect of causes well known then.

What will the Republic say of those who, well knowing all that time its situation, represented it so falsely, as to encourage us to continue the war this campaign, to bring the now-impending ruin upon the Republic and ourselves? *Those here* who were in that secret, in order to exonerate themselves, now lay all the blame upon *those who brought*, and upon those *who sent* the false accounts of those great resources and irresistible efforts, which we might depend upon on the part of the Dutch this campaign.

* Henry Fox, afterwards (in 1763) the first Lord Holland, who had contracted a clandestine marriage with Lady CarolineLennox, eldest daughter of the Duke and Duchess of Richmond.—M. He was father of Charles Fox; he was born in 1705, and died in 1774.

What reason, say they, had we not to believe those accounts which we received in so authentic a manner; and who could have thought that Mr. Bentinck would have so grossly misrepresented the state of the Republic, in order to engage us in measures, more immediately fatal to Holland than to England? The answer to this is so obvious, that I need not mention it. You cannot wonder, nor do I, that Mr. Keith, who was originally in this mystery of iniquity, is to carry on the rest of it, and that you are excluded; and indeed I think you are not unlucky in being quite clear of it. Our foreign bottoms must soon be now wound up, by a very bad peace which will soon be made, and then I believe you will, for some time at least, be the only English Minister at the Hague, for I take it for granted, that Keith will return from the Hague with Lord Sandwich unless he can get to be made Envoy, which he tried for in Lord Stair's time, but could not prevail; and I can hardly think that the King will be persuaded to make him Envoy. At all events, if they will not let you remain, there is no help for it; but do not give them a handle for it by any unguarded words.

If you should by accident know or hear of a *Van-der-Poll*, pray let the person know that I am very much obliged to him for his correspondence, which is very instructive; and that I beg he will continue it. I do not know who he is; and if you should, do not send me his name in a letter by the post; for I know that most letters from, and to, me are opened.*

I am not yet able to guess who wrote my Apology, which I am the more surprised at, as it must be somebody pretty well informed, all the facts being very near true. An answer to it is advertised, but not yet published. I am impatient to see it, that I may know, as I easily shall when I read it, whether it is written by order or not; if it is not, I shall not meddle with it; but, if it is, it shall have a reply.

Pray tell my Baron, that I have received his letter, and will

---

* It appears from Mr. Dayrolles's MSS. that the letters to Lord Chesterfield signed "Adrian Van-der-Poll," in a disguised hand, and in the French language, were in reality from Mr. Dayrolles himself, as a secure channel of communication. A private letter in his own name, dated August 25, 1748, and sent over by Sir Matthew Decker, further shows that until that period Lord Chesterfield himself was not aware who Van-der-Poll really was.—M.

answer it before it is long.　He will be able to send me all the
little French books that come out, when Maréchal de Saxe, with
his army, shall be at the Hague; for then all the French officers
will be at the Baron's levee, and glad to show him those little
civilities!

The Duke of Devonshire will, I believe, resign soon,* and be
succeeded by the Duke of Marlborough.　Adieu, dear Dayrolles.

Yours sincerely.

CLII.

À MADAME LA MARQUISE DE MONCONSEIL.

À LONDRES, *ce* 3 *Mai*, V.S. 1748.

L'Emploi que je ne quitterai de mes jours, mais que j'exécu-
terai avec zèle, c'est celui, Madame, de votre commissionaire dans
ce pays; et quoique je n'aie plus le pouvoir de faire tout ce que
je voudrois dans cette charge, donnez moi au moins les occasions
d'y faire tout ce que je puis.　Dans le moment que j'ai reçu
l'honneur de votre dernière lettre, je me suis intéressé pour la
liberté de Monsieur le Chevalier d'Albert,† mais heureusement
pour lui et malheureusement pour moi, il y avoit plus de quinze
jours qu'il étoit parti pour aller en France.　Que ne m'avez-vous
chargé de cette affaire plutôt? ou bien je l'aurois fait, ou en tout
cas, j'en aurois pris le mérite; car pour dire le vrai, je souhaite
tant d'en avoir auprès de vous, que ne je ne me ferois pas conscience d'en voler à d'autres.

En accusant tant de vos lettres à la fois, je sens bien que je
m'accuse moi-même, c'est-à-dire que les apparences sont contre
moi; mais au fonds je ne suis rien moins que coupable, car
quoique je n'aie pas eu l'honneur de vous écrire depuis que j'ai
reçu trois de vos lettres, vous ne m'avez pas moins occupé pour
cela.　Au contraire, ayant prévu depuis quelque tems que le paix
se feroit bientôt, j'ai travaillé sans relâche à vous faire des *Quipos,*

---

* William, third Duke of Devonshire, was at this period Lord Steward
of the Household.　His resignation did not ensue until June, 1749, when,
according to Lord Chesterfield's prognostic, he was succeeded by the Duke
of Marlborough.—M.

† A French captain, who commanded the *Magnanime,* a man-of-war of
74 guns, which was taken by two ships of Sir Edward Hawke's squadron,
January 31, 1748.

dont je chargerai le premier gros batiment qui ira d'ici à Calais.
Oh ! la belle et utile invention que les *Quipos !* je ne doute nullement qu'on ne s'en serve déjà à Paris. En vérité celle des lettres
étoit trop usée, elle trainoit les rues, le peuple même s'en servoit,
et il manquoit aux honnêtes gens quelque nouveau moyen de
s'entrecommuniquer leurs idées.   Me direz-vous que vous aurez
de la peine à déchiffrer mes *Quipos ?* Je vous dirai que c'est tant
mieux, et que les beaux esprits d'aujourd'hui ne se laissent tout
au plus que deviner, et cela même assez rarement ; d'ailleurs les
vieilles vingt-quatres ne suffisoient réellement pas pour exprimer
les nouvelles découvertes des modernes, au lieu que les *Quipos*
(sur tout s'ils s'entortillent en chemin faisant) dépeindront bien
plus naturellement la nouvelle quintessence des sentimens qu'on
n'a jamais sentis.   On dit toujours qu'il faut flatter le lecteur en
lui laissant quelque chose à penser ; les *Quipos* donc doivent bien
flatter le lecteur, en lui laissant tout à penser.   Enfin, Madame,
quelque difficiles que mes *Quipos* vous paroissent d'abord, je
compte assez sur votre pénétration pour être persuadé que vous
les comprendrez tout aussi bien que vous avez compris les deux
tiers des livres, qu'on a publiés chez vous depuis dix ans.

Félicitons nous, Madame, réciproquement de la paix faite.*
Je crois qu'elle nous convenoit aussi réciproquement ; nous vous
ruinions par mer, vous nous ruiniez par terre : vous faisiez des
conquêtes sur terre dont vous n'aviez pas besoin, aux dépens de
votre commerce, et de votre marine, pendant que nous prodiguions
sur terre les fruits de l'un et de l'autre.   Il n'a pas tenu à moi
que cette paix ne se fût faite l'année dernière ; soyons plus sages
à l'avenir, et restons bons amis.   Nous connoissons chacun à
présent notre élément, le vôtre c'est la terre, le nôtre c'est la mer,
et nous nous y tiendrons à l'avenir.   Si nous eussions fourni à
nos alliés en argent la moitié seulement de ce qu'ils nous ont coûté
par terre, et que nous eussions employé l'autre moitié de surcroît
par mer, vous auriez été plutôt las de la guerre ; car moyennant
cela, la Reine d'Hongrie auroit eu de plus grandes armées par
terre, puisque ce n'est pas les hommes, mais l'argent qui lui
manquent, et nous aurions eu de plus grosses flottes, qui non
seulement ne nous coûtent rien, mais qui nous apportent des
sommes immenses.   On a fait un calcul, que je crois être assez

* The Peace of Aix-la-Chapelle.

exact, de la valeur des prises que nous avons faites pendant cette guerre, et (le croiriez-vous ?) il monte au moius à cinq millions de livres sterlin. A dire le vrai, quoique la guerre vous ait sûrement été fort glorieuse, nous y avons gagné au fonds plus que vous. Nous avons conservé à la maison d'Autriche tous ces pays qu'au commencement de la guerre on regardoit comme perdus pour elle ; nous lui avons procuré de plus la dignité Impériale : notre commerce et notre marine, loin d'avoir souffert, se sont beaucoup augmentés par la guerre. Il est vrai de l'autre côté que nos armées en Flandres, et les subsides que nous payions, nous ont furieusement coûté. Vous avez gagné un établissement en Italie pour le redoubtable Don Phillippe, vous avez eu trois victoires en Flandres, et vous y avez pris un grand nombre de villes que vous restituez ; mais votre commerce et votre marine y ont souffert au point de ne se pas remettre de bien des années. Voilà les fruits de la guerre de part et d'autre : pour ceux de la paix, le plus beau pour moi est celui de pouvoir un jour vous faire ma cour à Paris ou à *Bagatelle*. Je languis pour ce moment sans pouvoir encore le fixer. Vous connoître comme je le fais, et souhaiter ce moment comme je le fais, ne sont que la même chose. Bon soir, Madame.

CLIII.

TO SOLOMON DAYROLLES, ESQ.

LONDON, *May* 3, O.S. 1748.

DEAR DAYROLLES,

My prophecy, as you observe, was fulfilled *sonica*, which I heartily congratulate both you and myself upon, for, had not that part of my predictions come to pass in the moment that it did, the other part would, which was inevitable ruin. Had not the French politely signed the preliminaries when they did, but resolved to profit of the advantages which they had in their hands, we were undone. Most people here are astonished at the moderation of the French Court, and cannot account for it from any known rules of policy. Deep and profound historians, who must assign some great and political cause for every event, will likewise, I believe, be at a loss to assign such a one for this. But I, who am apt to take things in a more simple light, and to seek for their causes more in the weaknesses than in the wisdom of mankind, account for it in this manner. The King of France is a quiet, unambitious Prince, was weary of the war, and particularly of a camp life, which, as he had once adopted, he could not well lay aside while the war lasted. The French Courtiers are not so unskilful, as not to advise what they know their Prince wishes, no matter whether it be consistent with, or contrary to, the public interest. This very principle, if you do but change the word *Peace* to War, accounts likewise for our continuing the war, so long after it was plain that we were not able to carry it on. But be the causes what they will, our escape is surely great in general, and the escapes of four people in particular, are almost miraculous. The Duke of Cumberland has escaped defeat and disgrace. The Prince of Orange has escaped being deposed, and the Duke of Newcastle and Lord Sandwich, being——.* I do not therefore wonder in the least at the general joy, which you tell me is expressed at the Hague upon this occasion, from the Princess and the Baron, to the fisherman at Scheveling. Must not Bentinck now confess that either he lied like a tooth-drawer while he was here, or else that he knew nothing at all of the state of his own country? And must not Lord Sandwich confess himself a dupe, if he will not acknowledge himself to be something worse?

When you happen to see *l'ami* of Amsterdam, tell him, pray, that I am obliged to him and his *ami*, and that I hope they will continue to let me hear from them. In the hand, and the other circumstances in which they write, the Devil cannot discover them here; all the care that is necessary is only to put their own letters privately into the post.

I believe the King will set out from hence next Saturday seven-night; I suppose that you will be at Helvoet to meet him, where I desire that you will be particularly attentive to do Lady Yarmouth any services that you can; she deserves them from us both, being much my friend, and yours.

Adieu, mon enfant ; portez-vous bien.

* Thus in the MS.—M.

CLIV.

TO SOLOMON DAYROLLES, ESQ.

LONDON, *May* 13, O.S. 1748.

DEAR DAYROLLES,

You answered the Prince of Orange's question, concerning me, perfectly well; far from blaming the peace, I am heartily glad that it is made. I was for making it sooner, and consequently better. I foresaw and foretold our weakness this campaign, and would have prevented, by a timely negotiation last October, those evident dangers to which it must necessarily expose us, and which we have escaped more by our good fortune than our wisdom. I may add, that my resignation made this peace, as it opened people's eyes with relation to the imminent dangers of the war, and made the continuation of it too strong a measure for our Minister to stand. As a proof of this, I resigned on the 6th of February last, and on the 9th Lord Sandwich had orders sent him to make the best peace that he could, but to make any rather than none. The Republic is saved by it from utter ruin; and England from bankruptcy.

The King sets out this night or to-morrow morning for Holland, attended only by Mr. Stone.* It is given out that the Duke of Newcastle is to follow in three weeks; but that is only given out, but not intended; for I have reason to be pretty sure that he will not go at all. The King would not let either of the Secretaries† go to Hanover; but as the Duke of Bedford has strongly solicited to go, in case the Duke of Newcastle did not, it is to be said, that the latter is to go, in order to put off the former without offence.

Sir Matthew Decker goes in the yacht with Stone, and will be sometime at the Hague, where I desire that you will do him all the service, and show him all the civilities, that you can. You may say anything to him, and send me any letter by him

---

* The brother of Dr. George Stone, Primate of Ireland, and who afterwards himself became sub-governor to the Prince of Wales. Horace Walpole calls him "a cold mysterious man, of little plausibility," but "the bosom confidant of the Duke of Newcastle."—*Memoirs.* vol. i. p. 248. —M.

† The Duke of Bedford had succeeded Lord Chesterfield as Secretary of State.—M.

when he returns, for I can entirely depend upon his friendship and secrecy.

Lord Sandwich has asked leave to come over here for a little time upon account (*as he says*) of his own private affairs; that you may believe or not as you please.

I have heard of no new Minister named for the Hague; but I am told there is to be one. I should guess Lord Fane,* who solicits much to go to Spain, but has been refused. The Duke of Richmond, I believe, will go to Paris as Ambassador for the representation part, which part he will certainly do well. Yours most truly.

CLV

À MADAME LA MARQUISE DE MONCONSEIL.

À Londres, *ce* 24 *Mai*, V.S. 1748.

Comme tous nos vaisseaux qui vont en France sont si chargés de bleds† que je n'ai pas encore pu trouver place pour mes ballots de *Quipos*, je vous écris, Madame, à la vieille mode, selon l'invention de Cadmus, qui imagina, dit-on, les lettres il y a deux ou trois mille ans ou plus; mais j'aurois beau me servir des vieilles ou profiter des nouvelles inventions, pour vous communiquer mes pensées, je n'en trouverai pas sûrement quelqu'une qui vous expliquera comme je le voudrois toute la vivacité et la vérité de mes sentimens, et il me faudra toujours vous laisser quelque chose à penser sur cet article; mais j'en suis moins en peine parceque je sais que vous pensez trop juste, pour ne me pas rendre justice. Nous jugeons ordinairement des autres par nous-mêmes, et ceux qui ont des sentimens eux-mêmes, en supposent toujours aux autres, à moins qu'ils n'ayent fait leurs preuves du contraire.

L'invitation que vous me faites de venir Ambassadeur à Paris, auroit été bien tentante il y a quelques années. Le bruyant et

* Charles Fane, second and last Viscount Fane. He was afterwards ambassador at Turin and Constantinople.—M.

† The southern provinces of France were greatly distressed for want of bread, which rose to an exorbitant price at the end of the war; and large quantities of corn were exported to France from England.

le brillant avoient, je l'avoue, des charmes pour moi; mais à present que la douceur de la vie est mon unique objet, je trouverai bien plus mon compte à vous rendre mes devoirs comme petit particulier et voyageur. Milord Chesterfield jouiroit à son aise et sans interruption de la société, et des aimables soupers, de la rue de Verneuil;* au lieu que Monsieur l'Ambassadeur se trouveroit souvent obligé de renoncer à de si doux momens, pour recevoir, et pour expédier des pacquets ennuyeux, essuyer des cérémonies, ou jouer au plus fin avec vos Ministres. Non, Madame, je veux que vous soyez l'unique objet, et non pas l'épisode, de mon voyage à Paris; ce ne sera pourtant pas cette année, mes arrangemens particuliers ne le permettent point, et d'ailleurs, dans la situation présente des affaires, le public, qui cherche, et qui trouve finesse en tout, me supposeroit négociateur secret, et d'autant plus important pour cela.

Voici la paix qui s'arrondit, notre bonne alliée la Reine d'Hongrie y a pris déjà sa place, et votre bon allié Catholique,† sans doute, en fera de même. Tout ceci auroit pu se faire également il y a deux ans, si l'Angleterre et la France l'eussent voulu, et elles y auroient toutes deux gagné; nos alliés reciproques nous ont coûté bien cher; profitons au moins de cette expérience à l'avenir.

Votre élève, dont vous avez la bonté de vous informer, est actuellement à Leipsig, où il restera encore sept mois pour finir un certain cours d'études auquel cette université est très propre, c'est-à-dire la langue Allemande, l'histoire, et le droit public de l'empire. De là il fera un tour, pour six mois, à l'académie à Turin, afin de le décrotter, au point que vous en ayez moins honte, quand il aura l'honneur de vous appartenir à Paris. Oui, Madame, je me sers du terme de vous appartenir, puisque du moment qu'il sera à Paris, j'y renonce; c'est à vous à en ordonner comme vous jugerez à propos, je ne m'en mêlerai plus. Votre amitié m'est garant que vous voudrez bien vous charger de ce soin, et rien au monde ne peut m'être si sensible. Jusqu'ici sa conduite, et les progrès qu'il a faits, me donnent tout lieu d'espérer qu'il ne sera pas indigne de vos soins.

* In the Faubourg St. Germain, the town-house of Madame de Monconseil.—See letter to Mr. Dayrolles, of April 27, 1750.

† The King of Spain.

CLVI.
TO SOLOMON DAYROLLES, ESQ.

LONDON, *May* 30, O.S. 1748.

DEAR DAYROLLES,

As this letter will be safely given to you by Monsieur Hop it shall contain the true state of affairs in this country, as far as they relate to those in yours. It may be useful to you to be *au fait* of them, and I will never omit being of any use to you that I can. Now that the peace is as good as made, I find that Lord Sandwich is for loading the Prince of Orange with all the blame with which he knew that the public loaded him. He affirms, that all the accounts which he sent here, of the immense sums of money, and the incredible number of troops to be raised by the Republic for the campaign of this year, he took from the positive assurances of the Prince of Orange, and that they would have been realized if the Prince of Orange had employed that time in acting, which he threw away in talking, and if he had not lent himself to the advice and insinuations of the enemies of both countries, meaning the Pensionary Gilles and his party. This language the Duke of Newcastle adopts and holds by way of excuse for his own conduct in rejecting all terms of accommodation last winter. The Duke of Cumberland too joins in with them, and lays the whole blame upon his brother-in-law, who I find is excessively ill with him. The King, who by the way, never loved the Prince of Orange, easily received, and now obstinately entertains these notions; as it has appeared but too plainly of late, by his extraordinary reception of the Princess Royal at Mainland Slys, and of the Stadtholder at Utrecht.

But what is more surprising is, that the two Bentincks give into this too; and complain that the Prince of Orange has, to a great degree, withdrawn his favour and confidence from them and placed them in the Pensionary and the Republican party. Upon which they are strongly soliciting here, that Lord Holderness,* who you know married a relation of the Greffier's (who,

---

* Robert D'Arcy, fourth Earl of Holderness, afterwards Secretary of State and Lord Warden of the Cinque Ports. In 1742 he had married the daughter of M. Doublet, member of the States in Holland. The poet Gray and Horace Walpole were entertained by him in Paris in 1739. In 1754, he appointed Mason (Gray's friend) his chaplain. He died in 1778.

by the bye, I perceive is the *ame damnée* of the Bentincks), should be sent Ambassador to the Hague with instructions to support their interests with the Prince of Orange, and to let him know that the King cannot place any confidence in him, unless he places his entirely in the Bentincks and the Greffier. This measure, absurd as it is, we are willing enough to take here; but the difficulty is, whether Lord Holderness is capable of carrying it into execution, so that he is not yet absolutely fixed upon for that commission. Should we take this silly step for the sake of the little Bentinck cabal in Holland, we shall unite all parties there against us, and reduce the Prince of Orange, who is certainly not naturally inclined to it, and the Republican party, which certainly is, to prefer the friendship of France to ours. France will not be negligent in offering it, and has such specious reasons to give for that preference, that those who do not think very deep, or who are provoked, are very likely to be captivated by them. Lord Sandwich, who had pressed for leave to return to England during Monsieur de St. Severin's* absence from Aix-la-Chapelle, was refused, and ordered to go to the Hague during that interval, but he absolutely declined that, saying that he would not have anything more to do with the Prince of Orange. And I believe, that when the definitive treaty shall be concluded, and that he returns here for good and all, he will endeavour to avoid even going through the Hague if he can.

Thus I have told you all that has come to my knowledge concerning these affairs, and what I have told you may possibly enable you to fish out more where you are. You will make that use of these informations, which you may think most for your own advantage, but you will take care not to give any body reason to suspect that you had them from me. As for your own conduct, I think it is obvious what it should be; that is, that you should keep clear of all these cabals and intrigues, and go straight forward with your own business. But at the same time I would advise you to make court to the Prince and Princess of Orange, and to give them to understand that you will belong to them and them only. That will be in my mind the best ground you can stand upon; for the Bentincks, I know, want to get rid of you:

* The French Plenipotentiary at the Conferences of Aix-la-Chapelle.

Keith, if he can get nothing better, will likewise push at you; and Sandwich, whatever he may profess to you, has, I am sure, a stiletto ready for you upon occasion, so that though the Prince and Princess of Orange have not much interest here at present, yet I think they will be your best support. When you shall see the Duke of Newcastle, who will ask you a thousand questions, take care to appear in a great degree ignorant, but by all means absolutely disengaged from, these *brigues;* tell him that you confine yourself entirely to your own business, which you have endeavoured to do to the best of your power, and as you hope, to the King's and his Grace's satisfaction; but that you are ignorant because you are determined to keep clear of all cabals and private intrigues; and that you hope that while you observe that conduct there, you shall have nothing to fear from hence. Lady Southwell,* who as you know is lately arrived here, told one who told it me again that it was thought that you stood upon slippery ground at the Hague, ever since I resigned; that indeed you were very well with the Prince and Princess, but that others had a mind to have you out of the way. I lay no great stress upon what she says, knowing her to be the silliest woman in the world, but as I suppose that she picked up this among people who knew more than herself, I thought it worth informing you of.

The Duke of Newcastle did certainly at first not intend to go abroad; but when he perceived that it was generally suspected that he did not mean to go, and that it occasioned a great deal of talk and ridicule, he determined much against his will, to *brusquer le passage de mer,†* and certainly goes next week. *Il brillera bien dans les pays étrangers!*

I guessed that the letters which I received, signed Van-der-Poll, came originally from *L'ami;* but I showed them here, pre-

---

* Margaret, daughter of A. C. Hamilton, Esq., married in 1741 Thomas George Viscount Southwell.—M.

† The Duke of Newcastle's fear of the sea, as of most other dangers, was excessive. According to Horace Walpole, "he has hired a transport; for the yacht is not big enough to convey all the tables, and chairs, and conveniences that he trails along with him and which he seems to think don't grow out of England,"—(To Sir H. Mann, June 7, 1748.) On another occasion, in 1752, we find: "The King set out for Hanover; the Duke of Newcastle who attended him, would not venture himself in any yacht but the one in which Lord Cardigan had lately escaped a great storm!"—(Lord Orford's *Memoirs,* vol. i. p. 243.)—M.

tending not to guess in the least from what quarter they came, in order to prevent, (knowing that they opened at the Post Office) any suspicion of the quarter from which they really did come; this precaution had its effect, and they are convinced here that those letters really came from Amsterdam. They were very instructive and useful to me; pray tell *L'ami* so, and that I beg the continuation of them, if he can find an opportunity of putting them into the post either at the Hague, or at Amsterdam, unsuspected, for as for here they will not have the least suspicion. In the last sheet I received, the author says that he is *L'ami de L'ami*, which I should think must mean either Torch or Randwych. Let me know when you have an opportunity; but be sure not to answer one word of this letter by post, any more than barely to acknowledge the receipt of it. When any body comes over here, that you can trust with a letter to me, you may explain this and many other things to me; but by the post, remember to say nothing but what you are willing should be read before I read it. Mr. Pelham tells me that you are, and promises me that you always shall be, paid up to the utmost. Adieu!

Yours faithfully.

CLVII.

TO SOLOMON DAYROLLES, ESQ.

LONDON, *June* 10, O.S. 1748.

DEAR DAYROLLES,

I was glad to find by your last that the King and you are so well together; though if you are to be demolished, that intimacy will not serve you. But in my opinion you are very safe, and though you will not be in the secret, I think you will continue in your place as long as you think fit. An Ambassador will certainly be sent to the Hague; but who it will be, I have not yet discovered; nor do I believe that it is settled. Lord Holderness, it is true, has a mind to it, and the Bentincks have strongly pressed for him, but yet I believe it will not do; that business is thought to be above him, as it certainly is. Should it be one person, whom I am apt to suspect, I will answer for your being very well with him, and for his doing you all the service he can.

The Duke of Newcastle will be with you about the same time that this letter will; he relies upon your doing everything for him at the Hague. You may easily guess what a hurry and bustle he will be in, in this beginning of his travels; therefore be officious about him; which you know he loves. But at the same time, *renfermez vous dans votre ignorance;* and tell him that you neither know nor meddle with anything out of your own sphere. And hint to him, likewise, that you hope that he will protect you against any attempts that may be made to remove you, and that you rely wholly upon his protection. This will flatter his silly vanity, and quiet his silly jealousy.

I have had a letter from Sir Matthew Decker full of your praises, and of acknowledgments for your civilities to him. You may write to me by him, when he returns, anything that you have upon your heart.

I am now extremely busy in moving to my new house, where I must be before Michaelmas next; so that between my old house and my new one, I have really no house at all. As my new house is situated among a parcel of thieves and murderers, I shall have occasion for a house-dog; and as Madame's son and heir* puts you to expense of board-wages, it may be a conveniency to us both if you transfer him to me; if you approve of this proposal, write to your gardener (Horace and Boileau both wrote to theirs) to send him to me; and I will take care, that, by your return, you shall have a hopeful son and heir of his to succeed him.

Pray, give or send the enclosed to Sir Matthew Decker, to whom I do not know where to direct. Tell my Baron, that I have received his *Droit public de l'Europe;†* that is, the first volume of it. As far as I have gone yet, I like it mightily. I hope he will send me all the other volumes. I will write to him soon. Good-night.

---

* A dog, which Mr. Dayrolles called after the celebrated Baron Trenck, then at the height of his prosperity. The Baron was born in 1726, and guillotined in Paris, in 1794. See next letter.

† By Abbé Mably.

CLVIII.

TO SOLOMON DAYROLLES, ESQ.

LONDON, *June* 24, O.S. 1748.

DEAR DAYROLLES,

I am very glad of what you tell me has passed between you and his Grace; which, together with the trouble and expense that he has put you to, ties him down at least not to suffer you to be hurt. For by the particular circumstance relating to the Greffier, who he desired should recommend you, it is plain to me, that he knew that a certain party was pushing at you. The poor honest Greffier is the tool of that party, and they make him do whatever they please, for which reason, I suppose, his Grace had a mind to hinder him from engaging against you. I think, you are now quite safe, which certainly before this, you were not; for I know that the Bentincks and Lord Sandwich are so incensed against me, that they would give no quarter to any body whom they thought in the least connected with me. They have, I know, even obliged little Milling to renounce me with the flesh and the Devil, and he now says, that he was mistaken in me, and that I am not now the man he once thought me.

Pray, how was Lady Yarmouth to you? I suppose particularly civil: she has promised me to do you all the service that she can; but that indeed is not much: I wish her power were equal to her good-will.

Lord Delawar* and Lord Anson† talk of nothing here, but of the delicacy of your table, your manner of doing the honours of it, etc. You are in the right to exert upon this occasion; but take care, however, not to run in debt; for times of bad payment may come, and in that case a small debt would soon run up to a great one. You will laugh at my preaching economy to you.

The mob in Holland, I see, has got the better, and abolished the farms; ‡ which will be attended with many inconveniences to

---

* John, Lord Delawar, a general officer in the army; raised to an Earldom in 1761.

† The famous admiral and circumnavigator, who had been created a Peer in 1747.—M.

‡ "The taxes farmed and gathered by the excise-officers, called *Pachters*." —Note by Mr. Dayrolles in Maty's edition.

the Government, though the farms were attended with some relatively to the people. I suppose, that the scheme of the Pensionary Slingelandt will now be taken up; and, it is undoubtedly the best. But be it ever so good, any point, however right in itself, when extorted by the violence of the mob, is a dangerous precedent, and encourages those gentlemen to further demands, which at last can only be refused by regular force. And I prophesy, that you will see, before you leave the Hague, the now-quieted mob in motion again upon some other occasion.

Baron Trenck arrived this morning, and seems to be a very civil gentleman: your gardener, a man of gravity and dignity, assures me, that his taste for mutton has left him; and that there are few Surrey gentleman so well behaved as he is; which I can very easily believe.

I cannot tell you by the post, who the person was, whom I hinted at as a candidate for the embassy to the Hague. Lord Holderness is the person strongly solicited for from your side of the water, but thought rather too incapable on this side; but as that is a trifling objection, and got over in many instances, it may very possibly be got over too in his favour. Should it be he, I think he is inoffensive and would choose to live well with you; but should it be the other, I would be bound for him, that he would be your friend, in consideration of your being mine.

Yours faithfully.

CLIX.

TO SOLOMON DAYROLLES, ESQ.

LONDON, *July* 2, 1748.

DEAR DAYROLLES,

Lord Pulteney will give you this letter: he is going to Leipsig for some time, and will not stay long at the Hague; but during his stay there, you will oblige me in obliging him. Pray, present him to the Prince and Princess of Orange, and air him at the assemblies.

My boy goes next spring to Turin, to be *décrotté*, which I am told he wants a good deal. Sir Charles Williams writes me word that he is very handsome, but very awkward—has a great deal of knowledge, but no manners. *Il faut remédier à cela à Turin, et à Paris après quoi vous y mettrez la dernière main.*

I go to Cheltenham to-morrow for a fortnight or three weeks—not for any present want of health, but by way of preservative against the autumn, when I am apt to have fevers. Good night! Mademoiselle Nassau does not love you in one way better than I do in another. Yours.

CLX.

À MADAME LA MARQUISE DE MONCONSEIL.

À LONDRES, *ce* 5 *Juillet*, V.S. 1748.

Vous me faites tort, Madame; je goûte infiniment les Lettres d'une Péruvienne, et ce n'étoit nullement par rapport à elles que je me plaignois des raffinemens, et des entortillemens à la mode; au contraire, il y a beaucoup de naturel et de sens commun. J'aurois voulu seulement que Zilia, justement outrée du procédé d'Aza, eût épousé Detterville par reconnoissance. Je ne dis pas par amour; l'amour ne se transporte pas si tôt d'un objet à un autre, mais il est sûr que l'amour peut s'éteindre, et s'éteindroit tout à coup, pour un objet qui s'en seroit rendu aussi indigne qu'Aza; alors l'indifférence par rapport à tous les autres objets succède, et non seulemens nous permet, mais même nous porte, à nous livrer aux sentimens de reconnoissance et d'estime. Il est vrai que vos auteurs François se sont appliqués bien plus que les nôtres à étudier le cœur de l'homme. La Rochefoucault et La Bruyère en ont bien développé tous les plis, et les replis; mais leurs successeurs, qui se sont crus obligés, non seulement de renchérir sur eux, mais aussi les uns sur les autres, ont poussé leurs analyses jusqu'au plus fin galimatias.

Vous me pardonnerez, Madame, si je ne suis pas tout-à-fait de votre sentiment au sujet de votre élève; je crois même vous mener au mien. Faites reflexion qu'il est tout couvert de la poussière des collèges de Leipsig, qu'il n'a point du tout de manières, et que malgré une fort jolie figure, il a très mauvais air; et jugez ce qui en seroit, si son premier début étoit dans un monde comme Paris. Ne se sentant pas fait comme les autres, et honteux de ne l'être pas, il éviteroit les bonnes compagnies, qui l'éviteroient aussi à leur tour, et il se refugieroit auprès de ses aimables compatriotes au café Anglois; au lieu que, dans un petit endroit comme Turin, où il y a pourtant une Cour très polie, une académie bien réglée, et bonne compagnie, il se décrottera insensiblement sans se rebuter; après quoi, devenu plus présentable, Paris, vos bontés, et ce qui plus est encore, votre exemple, y mettront la dernière main. J'avoue que je m'impatiente, comme un auteur, pour voir une belle et correcte édition de mon ouvrage, ce qui n'arrivera qu'après que vous aurez bien voulu le corriger.

CLXI.
TO SOLOMON DAYROLLES, ESQ.

CHELTENHAM, *July* 18, O.S. 1748.

DEAR DAYROLLES,

I am very glad to find by your letter that Mr. Keith will soon be out of your way. You are at least so much the safer against misrepresentations; and I suppose that his residence at Vienna, in the absence of Sir Thomas Robinson, will raise him above the residentship at the Hague. I do not find that it is yet determined who is to be Lord Sandwich's successor at the Hague; Lord Holderness desires to be so, and the Bentincks press earnestly that he may. Should that happen, I do not think that he would desire to hurt you, for I think him a good-natured inoffensive man, and I would speak to him very earnestly upon your subject. Your only danger, then, is from the violence and suspicious temper of the two Bentincks, for I do not think that you have one single enemy on this side of the water; and the Duke of Newcastle has, by what he said to you at the Hague, tied himself down not to let you be hurt.

I am very glad that Lord Sandwich's blunder about the day for mutual restitution is set right, and postponed to the last day of October for the Indies; otherwise we might have had a very pretty bill to have paid for the damages which will probably have been done before that time by Boscawen. As the French must have been aware of this, I own I am astonished at their compliance.

I do not see that things tend to quiet in the Republic; the people, having now carried one point,* will want twenty more, of which the Stadtholder must refuse at least nineteen. This use, however necessary, of his power, will exasperate

* The abolition of the *farms*, *vide* letter of 24th June.

those who gave it him; and the confusion which must arrive
from this is obvious. I thank God I am out of the galley; but,
however, I wish it fair weather and a good voyage. I leave this
place in two days for London. I have been here three weeks,
and find myself much the better for the waters. In about a fortnight I shall go for a week to Lord Pembroke's, at Wilton, which
will be my last excursion for this year, and then I shall settle in
my new house, under the protection of Baron Trenck. I hope
that by next summer, when peace shall have taken a certain
consistency, you may get leave to make us both a visit. You
will not, I believe, be sorry, and, upon my soul, I shall be glad.
Good night!   Yours.

CLXII.

À MADAME LA MARQUISE DE MONCONSEIL.

À LONDRES, *ce* 30 *Juillet*, V.S. 1748.

Je reviens d'un voyage que j'ai fait à quarante lieues d'ici,
pour prendre des eaux,* qui m'ont fait beaucoup de bien, mais
qui ont contrebalancé ce bien, en me privant pour quelques jours
de votre dernière lettre. Je fais encore demain une autre course
à la campagne pour quinze jours, pas par choix mais par nécessité,
car actuellement je n'ai point de domicile, je déménage de ma
vieille maison, et je ne puis pas encore entrer dans ma nouvelle,
de façon qu'il me faudra encore quelques semaines vivre aux
dépens de mes amis. Encore si la rue de Verneuil ou *Bagatelle*
se trouvoit entre mes deux maisons, je souffrirois volontiers le
dérangement, qui me fait enrager à cette heure. Dans six
semaines j'espère d'être établi, tant bien que mal, dans mon
hôtel, où à la fin je serai bien logé. J'ai accommodé la plûpart
de mes chambres entièrement à la Françoise. J'ai une grand
cour, et un grand jardin, deux choses très-rares dans cette ville,
quoique très-communes à Paris. Enfin, venez la voir, Madame;
il n'y a qu'un pas de chez vous ici, et j'ose vous assurer, qu'à
l'exception de la bonne chère, de la bonne compagnie, et de tous
les agrémens de la société, vous vous croiriez encore à Paris.

On nous a apporté dernièrement de Paris une petite brochure,

* At Cheltenham.

pas mal écrite, intitulée l'année 1748,* qui prédit, pour le premier du mois prochain, un changement très-considérable ; il ne s'agit de rien moins que de la métamorphose totale et réciproque des deux sexes. Pour moi, qui naturellement ne suis pas trop crédule, j'ai de la peine à le croire, quoique j'y consentirois volontiers à une condition, qui seroit que vous et moi nous changeassions l'un contre l'autre. Il est vrai que vous perdriez bien au change, mais il est aussi vrai, que j'y gagnerois beaucoup, et dans les choses essentielles, qui est-ce qui s'embarrasse de ce que leurs amis perdent, pourvu qu'ils y gagnent euxmêmes ? La décence veut qu'on sacrifie à ses amis de petits objets et qu'on leur témoigne des attentions, qui ne coûtent que peu ou rien ; mais on passeroit pour Iroquois, si on poussoit plus loin que cela les sentimens d'amitié. Plut-à-Dieu donc, Madame, que le premier du mois prochain, je me trouve tout-à-coup vous, et que vous vous trouviez votre très-humble serviteur !

CLXIII.

TO SOLOMON DAYROLLES, ESQ.

LONDON, *August 16th*, O.S. 1748.

DEAR DAYROLLES,

I received your last while I was at Wilton, which place Pem has improved so much, that l hardly knew it again. It is now in my mind the finest seat in England. I am returned to a very empty town, which I can bear with very well ; for if I have not all the company that I could like, I am at least secure from any company that I do not like ; which is not the case of any one place in England but London. Besides, I have time both to read and to think ; the first I like ; the latter I am not, as too many are, afraid of. The rest of the day is employed in riding, and fitting up my house ; which, I assure you, takes a good deal of time, now that we are come to the minute parts of finishing and furnishing.

I am very glad that the Prince of Orange has carried the affair of the *Posteries*,† at Amsterdam : it is a great point gained for the

* *L'année Merveilleuse,* by Abbé Coyer ; an imitation of the *Annus Mirabilis* of Arbuthnot.—M.

† "Till this time, the management and direction of the Post-office were

public, as that revenue must be very great, and much greater than it was ever owned to be while in private hands. If he will only push such points as are of an evident national utility, he will carry them all, notwithstanding the private or public opposition of particular interests. Queen Elizabeth was, in this free country, as absolute as the Sultan is in Turkey; but then the nation was convinced that she only desired and exerted that power for the public good.

I cannot think that the definitive treaty will be concluded so soon as we were told it would; and I cannot help entertaining certain suspicions, from the Queen of Hungary's conduct, which I will not communicate to you by way of letter.

Sir Matthew Decker is expected here next week; I am impatient to see him, because I expect to hear more concerning you, and other matters, from him, than letters admit of. I am in no pain about you now that Keith is gone, for there must always be a Resident at the Hague; and as the Minister, whoever he is that is to go there, will have the secret, you will be quiet and secure. A much safer situation for you, than if you were let into the *arcana* of an Administration that may possibly not last long.

Pray tell my Baron, that I have received his packet of books by Signor Martinelli; and that I am sorry that I put him both to the expense and trouble of sending me the History of the Wars between France and the House of Austria; which is an execrable one, notwithstanding my friend Rousset's panegyric of it in his preface.

Yours sincerely.

CLXIV.

À MADAME LA MARQUISE DE MONCONSEIL.

À LONDRES, ce 22 d'Aout, 1748.

Ayez la bonté, je vous en conjure, Madame, de dire pour moi à Monsieur le Prince de Conti * tout ce qu'en ma place vous diriez vous-même; alors, avec l'esprit qu'il a il croira que j'en ai aussi

---

in the hands of private persons, who had the sole benefit of the profits arising from them."—Note by Mr. Dayrolles in Maty's edition.

* Louis François Prince de Conti, born in 1717; a man of cultivated mind and literary taste.

beaucoup, car je prétends que vous lui souteniez, en même tems, que je vous l'ai écrit mot à mot. Je ne pense pas que vous soyez assez ladre pour me refuser ce petit présent, dont vous ne sentirez pas le besoin, et que je ne demande que de votre surabondance. Au reste, ajoutez, s'il vous plait, que je me flatte de pouvoir en quelque tems d'ici lui envoyer des recrues de cette sort de chiens : on en avoit négligé la race, depuis qu'il n'y avoit plus de loups en Irlande, mais j'ai écrit à quelques-uns de mes amis de m'en faire faire.

Vos guerriers auront, du moins pour quelque tems, loisir de chasser, quoique pourtant il me semble que ce traité définitif ne finit point. Je ne sais à qui en est la faute, puisqu'il a paru assez clairement que vous voulez la paix, et qu'il est très-sûr que nous la voulons aussi ; et il me semble que dès que nous sommes d'accord, il faut bien que nos Alliés respectifs marchent.

Sauriez-vous, Madame, qui l'on destine chez vous pour Ambassadeur ici ? Nous supposons ici qu'il a deux concurrens pour cette commission, Monsieur de Mirepoix, et Monsieur le Maréchal de Belleisle ; pour moi je demande seulement qu'il soit de vos amis, et que par conséquent il pense comme moi sur votre sujet.

Je tâcherai de procurer pour Monsieur votre beau-frère les papières qu'il souhaite, mais à present tous ceux qui seroient en état de me les fournir sont encore en Flandres ; et d'ailleurs, pour vous dire la vérité, je doute beaucoup de l'exactitude de nos militaires dans ces matières-là. Ils se battent bien, il en faut convenir ; mais ils n'ont pas cette attention, et ce goût pour leur métier, qu'ont les vôtres.

Je vois bien que vous ne convenez pas de mes raisons au sujet de votre futur élève : cela n'est pas extraordinaire ; mais ce qui l'est, c'est que je ne me rende point aux vôtres. Il faut en tout des gradations, et les petites villes le prépareront peu-à-peu pour les grandes. Paris fourmille actuellement d'Anglois, que je ne lui donnerois pas volontiers, ou pour modèles ou pour connoissances, mais qui seroient infailliblement l'un et l'autre s'il y alloit présentement ; au lieu que Turin achevera de le dépayser, après quoi, n'étant plus d'aucun pays, il adoptera sûrement le vôtre. Adieu, Madame ; je vous fais grace d'une page entière, recompensez-moi en en ajoutant une à celle dont vous m'honorerez.

CLXV.

TO SOLOMON DAYROLLES, ESQ.

LONDON, *September* 2, O.S. 1748.

DEAR DAYROLLES,

I received very safe, by Sir Matthew Decker, your long letter of the 23rd August, O.S., in which you give me, what I had long desired, *l'Histoire amoureuse de la Haye.* As I am personally acquainted with most of the characters, I am convinced that all the facts are true; and I particularly foresee the ruin of one family, from the ill conduct of the lady, which will not be endured when the honeymoon is over. I am now an unconcerned spectator of the transactions of the gallant, as well as of the busy, part of the world—the first from necessity, the latter from choice; so that I only inform myself of them for my amusement, without being any otherwise affected by them than as a citizen of the world. As such, I am glad that the horrors and devastations of war are now suspended; but as such, too, I am sorry to foresee the moment of their revival so near as I think I do; I mean the death of the King of Sweden.* If you will have my prophetic politics, here they are. I think that the Queen of Hungary has made all these difficulties of coming into the definite treaty, not in the expectation of succeeding in any one of them, but only with the intention of delaying the return of the Russians, and of forming a plan with Russia, and possibly *some Princes* of the empire, for the recovery of Silesia. Upon this supposition, I expect that she will very soon come into the definitive treaty, in order to be able to employ all her force *elsewhere*. The death of the King of Sweden is, in my opinion, to be the signal for this northern war. The Czarina will not suffer the Prince-Successor to succeed. This Prince-Successor is brother-in-law to the King of Prussia, who has lately, in conjunction with France, guaranteed that succession to him. Reinforcements of Russians are marched into Finland; our Russians loiter in Germany; to me the conclusion is plain.

I am glad that my old friend Van der Duyn † has got a pen-

---

* Which, however, did not take place until two years afterwards.

† A Lieutenant-General, brother to M. de Sgravemoer, one of the College of Nobles in the Province of Holland.—M.

sion, but I am astonished at the size of it. A thousand pounds a year sounds like an English pension; *d'ailleurs*, he has a regiment of guards and a government. This is certain, that the money will not stagnate in my General's strong box, but circulate very quickly through the Hague. *A propos* of the quick circulation of species, it is fixed that Lord Holderness is to be our Ambassador to the Republic, out of compliance to the Greffier and the Bentincks, who insisted upon it. He will, I think, do you no harm, if he does you no good; for, as business will certainly not be my Lord's pleasure, pleasure will, I presume, be my Lord's only business. This too, without the least flattery to you, is certain, that when he shall be at the Hague, you will be *à juste titre, le beau Ministre Anglois*.

Adieu for this time; you shall hear from me more fully before it is long. Yours.

CLXVI.

À MADAME LA MARQUISE DE MONCONSEIL.

À LONDRES, *ce 5 Septembre*, V.S. 1748.

Oui vraiment, Madame, j'ai un boudoir, mais il a un défaut, c'est qu'il est si gai et si riant, qu'on n'y pourra jamais bouder quand on y sera seul: c'est un défaut aimable pour qui aime la bouderie aussi peu que moi, mais en tout cas, il est facile de le reparer, en y recevant les gens maussades, fâcheux, et désagréables, que de tems en tems on est obligé d'essuyer. Quand on m'annoncera un animal de la sorte, je courrai d'abord à mon boudoir, comme à mon sanctuaire, l'y recevoir; là il aura moins de prise sur moi, car, de la façon que nous sommes faits, les objects extérieurs ne sont nullement indifférens par rapport à l'esprit, et tel sot qui m'accableroit dans une chambre lugubre, pourra peut-être m'amuser dans un cabinet orné et riant. De tout ceci il resulte, que la véritable étymologie de boudoir est (pour parler Latin) *a non boudare* comme *lucus* un bois *a non lucendo* c'est-à-dire qu'on ne boude point dans l'un, et qu'on ne voit goutte dans l'autre: au reste si ce trait de profonde érudition vous embarrasse, l'Abbé Sallier, que je salue de tout mon cœur, vous l'expliquera, et vous en fera sentir toute la solidité.

Voulez-vous la description, aussi bien que l'étymologie, de ce boudoir? La voici. La boisure et le platfond sont d'un beau bleu, avec beaucoup de sculptures et de dorures; les tapisseries et les chaises sont d'un ouvrage à fleurs au petit-point, d'un dessein magnifique sur un fond blanc; par dessus la cheminée, qui est de *Giallo di Sienna,* force glaces, sculptures, dorures, et au milieu le portrait d'une très belle femme, peint par la Rosalba.* Je vous ferois la description du reste de la maison, mais comme le second Pline a échoué en voulant donner la description de la sienne, où l'on n'entend absolument rien, je n'ai pas pu espérer d'y pouvoir réussir, et vous savez qu'il est de la sagesse de ne pas tenter des choses au dessus de ses forces.

Il faut que vos Cerbères de la douane soient bien plus inexorables que les nôtres, car j'ai bien instruit mon marchand de ne se pas laisser prendre les étoffes, faute d'un certain compliment, auquel ces Messieurs sont d'ordinaire très sensibles. Il faut espérer que Monsieur votre Contrôleur aura la politesse de relâcher des prisonniers qui doivent vous toucher de si près.

Dites moi de grace, Madame, pourquoi votre Parlement de Paris a tant sévi contre un livre que je viens de lire, intitulé *Les Mœurs.* Comme j'avois lu l'arrêt, avant que d'avoir lu le livre, je m'attendois à trouver dans ce dernier toutes sortes d'impiétés, et de relâchement; au lieu de quoi j'y ai trouvé la religion et la loi naturelle fortement établies et inculquées, une morale même rigoureuse, et tous les devoirs de l'homme bien constatés. Il est vrai que l'auteur n'adopte aucune secte particulière, ni culte extérieur en matière de religion, aussi n'étoit-ce pas de son ressort en traitant des mœurs. Je sens bien que les ecclésiastiques de toutes les religions en seront offensés, mais est-ce une raison pour que le Parlement le soit aussi? En vérité je trouve beaucoup de bon dans ce livre, il y a du bon sens, de l'esprit et des portraits bien caractérisés; il est vrai que quelquefois les raisonnements sont plus jolis que forts, et il semble que l'auteur aime souvent mieux orner que pousser son argument. Soupçonne-t-on à Paris qui c'est? pour moi, si je voulois me livrer

---

* This lady, a native of Venice, or as others say Vicenza, distinguished herself by her works in crayons. *Ses tableaux,* says M. Artaud, *furent recherchés dans toute l'Europe.* She died in 1757, having lost her sight two years before.—M.

à des conjectures, j'en soupçonnerois l'auteur des Lettres Persanes.*

Monsieur le Prince de Conti, croit-il que j'ai l'esprit délicat et aimable? C'est-à-dire, Madame, vous êtes-vous acquittée fidèlement de ma commission auprès de lui? En ce cas, que les Rois seroient heureux d'être servis comme moi, puisqu'alors il n'y auroit peut-être qu'une vingtaine de ceux qui les approchent de plus près, qui sauroient qu'ils n'ont point d'esprit!

A propos, le tems est passé sans que la métamorphose que je souhaitois tant se soit faite,† et à présent j'en désespère, car dès que les prophéties ne s'accomplissent pas à point nommé, c'en est fait. Au moins j'ai gagné par l'imposture, et ce que vous me dites sur ce sujet vaut presque la métamorphose même, car je prends tout à la lettre, et je me donne bien garde d'aprofondir cette matière. On est trop heureux d'etre trompé, ou de se tromper soi-même, agréablement: je voudrois bien que vous pussiez m'avoir une pareille obligation, mais le moyen?—vous ne me tiendriez aucun compte de vérités reconnues, et pourtant on n'y peut rien ajouter; vous donnez beaucoup à penser, mais vous ne laissez rien à dire.

CLXVII.

TO THE REV. DR. MADDEN.

LONDON, *September* 15, 1748.

SIR,

I am very sensibly affected with the late mark which you have given me of your remembrance and friendship. I assure you that I deserve them both, as far as the truest regard for your parts and merit can entitle me to them.

Your Poem, of which I have read the first Canto with equal pleasure and attention, has (without any compliment to you) a great deal of wit and invention in it: the characters are perfectly well preserved; and the moral, which it is easy to foresee from the first Canto, is excellent. You cannot doubt of my being

* Namely, Montesquieu. Lord Chesterfield was mistaken in supposing he was the author, as *Les Mœurs* was written by M. Toussaint.—M.

† See the conclusion of the letter to Madame Monconseil, of July 30.

proud to have such a performance addressed to me ; and I should be prouder of it still, if the author's name were to appear ; but as your friend, I must confess, that I think you in the right to conceal it ; for, though the moral be good, yet, as the propriety of characters has obliged you to put some warm expressions in the mouths of Venus and Cupid, some silly or malicious people might lay hold of them, and quote them to your disadvantage. As to the Dedication, I must tell you very sincerely, and without the least false modesty, that I heartily wish you would lower it : the honest warmth of your friendship makes you view me in a more partial light than other people do, or, upon my word, than I do myself. The few light, trifling things that I have accidentally scribbled in my youth, in the cheerfulness of company, or sometimes (it may be) inspired by wine, do by no means entitle me to the compliments which you make me as an author ; and my own vanity is so far from deceiving me upon that subject, that I repent of what I have shown, and only value myself upon what I have had the prudence to burn.

Though my cares for Irelend are ceased, you do me but justice in being convinced that my wishes for the prosperity of that country will cease but with my life. The best wish that I could form for it would be, that half its inhabitants were like you ; nay, I would compound for twenty who would, like you, devote their thoughts, their time, and a proportionable share of their fortunes, to the public good. Your late considerable benefaction to Dublin College will be a perpetual monument of your public spirit, and your love of mankind. How greatly would arts and sciences flourish in Ireland if those who are much better able than you are, would contribute but half as much as you do to their improvement ! You shine, indeed, the more for it ; but I know you well enough to know, that you would rather *prodesse quam conspici.* The Irish may be a rich and happy people, *bona si sua nôrint.* Free from the heavy load of debts and taxes under which the English groan, as fit for arts, sciences, industry and labour, as any people in the world, they might, notwithstanding some hard restraints which England, by a mistaken policy, has laid them under, push several branches of trade to great perfection and profit ; and not only supply themselves with everything they want, but other nations too with many things. But jobs and claret engross and ruin the people of fashion, and the ordinary people (as is usual in every country) imitate them in little momentary and mistaken views of present profit, and in whisky. As to the incorporating by Charter the Dublin Society, I see many advantages that might arise from it; but I must at the same time own, that I foresee some dangers too. Jobs have hitherto always accompanied Charters, however they may have been calculated to prevent them. The Dublin Society has hitherto gone on extremely well, and done infinite good : why? Because, that not being a permanent, incorporated Society, and having no employments to dispose of, and depending only for their existence on their own good behaviour, it was not a theatre for jobbers to show their skill upon; but when once established by Charter, the very advantages which are expected from, and which, I believe, will attend that Charter, I fear may prove fatal. It may then become an object of party, and Parliamentary views (for you know how low they stoop); in which case it will become subservient to the worst instead of the best designs. Remember the Linen Board, where the paltry dividend of a little flax-seed was become the seed of jobs, which indeed produced one hundred fold. However, I submit my fears to your hopes; and will do all that I can to promote that Charter which you, who I am sure have considered it in every light, seem so desirous of. Mr. Macauley, who is now here, has brought over the rough draught of a Charter, which he and I are to meet and consider of next week. I hope your worthy fellow-labourers, and my worthy friends, the Bishop of Meath and Mr. Prior, are well. May you long be so, for the good of mankind, and for the particular satisfaction of

Your most sincere friend and faithful servant.

I hope you will send me the other Cantos by proper opportunities, for I long to see them.

CLXVIII.

TO ALDERMAN FAULKNER.*

LONDON, *September* 17, 1748.

MY GOOD FRIEND,

I am much obliged to you for the marks of your remembrance and friendship which you send me from time to time. The Sermon of Robert Hort, A.M., is certainly of a very singular nature; but as you do not give me your opinion upon it, I shall not give you mine. Possibly, indeed, we . have neither of us formed one. Thus much only, I will say, and that very sincerely, that if Mr. Hort is in the right, I heartily wish that you may live to see and feel, that general *Restoration and Perfection of all things;* as by the one you will recover your natural leg; and by the other, the letter of your Journal will be as black as ink, and the paper as white as snow, which I reckon make up the perfection of a Journal. But whatever may be the state of printing in those days, however black your letter, however white your paper, I observe with concern, that you are not likely to have Mr. Hort's custom or interest, his sermon being printed by S. Powell.† In the meantime, I hope business goes on well, and that you print and sell a great number of books, whether they are read or not. If they become but fashionable furniture, it will serve your purpose as well, or it may be better; for if people bought no more books than they intended to read, and no more swords than they intended to use, the two worst trades in Europe would be a Bookseller's and a Sword-cutler's; but, luckily for both, they are reckoned genteel ornaments.

Here has been lately published the first volume of a History of the Popes, by one Mr. Bower, who was a Jesuit at Rome. It is

---

* Alderman George Faulkner (1699–1775) was a printer and publisher of great note in Dublin. Several of Swift's later letters were addressed to him; and see the other letters of Chesterfield to him for references to the position he held in the world of letters, and his association with "Swift, Berkeley, and all the best authors of the Irish Augustan age" (Letter of Nov. 11, 1752). He published *Faulkner's Dublin Journal* for upwards of fifty years, and was succeeded in his business by his nephew, Thomas Todd Faulkner; on whose death, in 1793, the *Journal* passed into the hands of John Giffard, grandfather of the present Lord Chancellor of England.　　　　　† Another Dublin Printer.

extremely well wrote, and I believe it would be very well worth your while to print an octavo edition of it at Dublin; for our edition here is a large quarto, and consequently, an expensive one. When finished, it will be four quartos. As yet, no lesser edition has appeared here. In this, or any other undertaking, I assure you, that nobody can wish you more sincerely well, than   Your friend and servant.

As I know you often see the Chief Baron, whom I esteem and honour much, pray make him my compliments.

CLXIX.

À MADAME LA MARQUISE DE MONCONSEIL.

À LONDRES, *ce* 22 *Septembre*, V.S. 1748.

C'est que je ne sais plus comment m'y prendre avec vous, Madame, vous rejettez les vérités les plus simples parcequ'elles vous sont avantageuses. Pour les complimens, nous les avions déjà bannis de notre commerce depuis longtems; et si vous voulez seulement entendre parler de vos défauts, il faut vous addresser à quelqu'un qui vous en connoisse. Il est vrai qu'on s'entend dire plus volontiers les choses qu'on voudroit mériter, ou que, par illusion, on croit mériter, que celles qu'on mérite réellement. Un ancien,* je ne sais plus lequel, disoit à Trajan; *la flatterie est épuisée depuis longtems envers vos prédécesseurs; tout ce qui nous reste donc à votre égard, c'est d'oser nous taire.* Voilà donc le parti que je prends.

Que je languis pour vos bras, Madame! L'expression paroît vive et tendre; il faut l'expliquer, en cas qu'on ouvre la lettre. Je languis donc pour ces bras de porcelaine, que vous avez la bonté de m'envoyer par le retour de mon marchand, qui, depuis qu'il est au monde, n'a jamais été attendu avec une impatience égale à la mienne. Je m'en fie bien à votre goût, et je ne m'embarrasse pas de la couleur; j'ai déjà toutes les couleurs du monde dans ce boudoir, de façon que vos bras n'y peuvent pas être déplacés, de quelque couleur qu'ils soient. Je vous en remercierai donc, Madame, de tout mon cœur, et tout simplement. Voiture

---

* Pliny, the younger:—"Simul cum jampridem novitas omnis adulatione consumpta sit, non alius erga te novus honor superest, quam si aliquando de te tacere audeamus."—*Panegyr.* lv. 3.

n'auroit pas sitôt quitté un si beau sujet pour son esprit, ni le Chevalier d'Her— * pour ses épigrammes.

Votre homme à feu est employé dans le grand feu d'artifice qu'on doit tirer ici au sujet de la conclusion de la paix ; je crains seulement que sa poudre ne se moisisse, et que ses préparatifs ne se gâtent, avant que la traité définitif qui ne finit point ne se finisse. Je serois charmé de rendre service à votre artiste, mais vous me pardonnerez, j'en suis sûr, si en entrant d'abord dans ma nouvelle maison, je ne lui donne pas l'occasion de la faire sauter ou bruler, ou d'en enfumer même les meubles ; suites ordinaires du voisinage d'un feu d'artifice. Pour votre compositeur Adolphati, je vous dirai naturellement que je n'augure rien d'avantageux pour lui dans ce pays ; l'opéra, que nous devons avoir cet hiver, étant entièrement sous la direction d'un seul *impresario* qui vient d'Italie, et qui mène avec lui, et sa troupe, et son compositeur, de sorte que de ce côté là il n'y a pas d'ouverture pour notre *virtuoso*. Du côté des oratorios, des motets, et de cette sorte de musique, il y en a encore moins ; Handel, qui sans contredit est le plus grand compositeur de l'Europe, en ayant tant donné qu'on en est las, qu'on n'y va plus. Il suffit qu'il me vienne de votre part pour que je fasse tous mes efforts pour le servir ; mais franchement je crains que ce ne soit inutilement.

Bon soir, Madame ; aussi la longueur de cette lettre pourra bien y contribuer.

CLXX.

TO SOLOMON DAYROLLES, ESQ.

LONDON, *September* 23, O.S. 1748.

DEAR DAYROLLES,

I thank you for your promise of a second tome of your, *Histoire Amoureuse,* when an occasion shall present itself ; for, upon my word, Petronius † nor Bussy ‡ could not write a better

---

* The *Lettres du Chevalier d'Her—* were written by Fontenelle when very young, but never owned by him.—See Lord Chesterfield's Letters to his Son, of December 24, 1750.

† A licentious writer at the Court of Nero, died A.D. 66.

‡ Count Bussy wrote a satirical account of the gallantries of the Court of Louis XIV., and was banished for reflections in it on that monarch.

than your first. The winter, which will assemble every body at the Hague, will probably furnish you materials.

Your towns and provinces seem to be running a race to the goal of slavery; and they put me in mind of the Nobles and Commons in Denmark, who, in the last century, strove which should first get rid of their liberties. Your Stadtholder must have great self-denial, or great timidity, if he is not very soon as absolute over the Seven Provinces as Louis XV. is in France. For my own part, not being a Dutchman, and having no thoughts of living in Holland, I have no objection to this new-erected despotism; which, for aught I know, may make the Seven Provinces a better barrier for us against France than they were before, as an absolute government is more military, and generally in a better state of defence, than a free one. And upon this principle, were I to cut and carve out Europe to my mind, I would add the other ten provinces to the present seven, and so revive the Duchy of Burgundy;* which, I am sure, would make a better barrier against France, than ever those ten provinces, in the hands of the House of Austria, will prove. *A propos* of Austria, the conjectures which I have formed these four months, and which I lately hinted to you, begin, I think to be verified. The Russians stay in Germany, which is the first point; they will certainly some how or other be juggled out of our pay and service, which is the second point; and then the third is pretty plain. *Ce n'est pas mon affaire.* Let the northern bears worry each other as much as they please, the gazettes will be but the more entertaining, and amuse me the more, *dans mon petit boudoir;* which (by the way) will be the prettiest thing you ever saw. Nothing in the world so gay. *Il sera impossible d'y bouder; d'ailleurs, comme vous savez, je n'y suis pas naturellement trop porté.*

I have spoken to Mr. Pelham about your pay; which I believe, will be ordered very soon. However, *Bride en main;* do not run out, *et n'y mettez point du vôtre. Vous n'en seriez pas plus gras d'un côté, mais vous en seriez bien plus maigre d'un autre.*

The town is now so empty, that I have no tittle-tattle to send

---

* As was actually done in 1815 by the creation of the kingdom of the Netherlands.

you. The house of Kildare* comes here from Ireland next month; and then, I presume, that your friend, who by this time has got the full ascendant over her husband, will open her campaign with *éclat*, though these are very bad times for the female quality and gentry. . . .

Things go to the full as well as I could wish, and much better than I expected, at Leipsig;† we are absolutely masters of Latin, Greek, French, and German, the last of which we write currently. We have *le Droit public de l'Empire*, history and geography very ready; so that, in truth, now we only want rubbing and cleaning. We begin for that purpose with Berlin at Christmas next; Vienna at Lady-day; and the Academy at Turin, at Midsummer; for a whole year. Then to Paris, *et si cela ne nous décrotte pas, il faut que le diable s'en mêle*. If at any of these places it should fall in your way, by letter or verbal recommendation, to help us, I am very sure that you will; for I never doubt of any marks of your friendship to the most faithful of your friends.

CLXXI.
TO SOLOMON DAYROLLES, ESQ.

BATH, *October* 11, O.S. 1748.

DEAR DAYROLLES,

I received your letter of the 11th, N.S., just as I was setting out for this place. I had been much out of order for above a month; languors and vertigos succeeded each other, the latter attended with sickness at my stomach. I underwent the discipline of the faculty to little purpose; who, at last pronouncing that the seat and source of my disorder was my stomach, sent me here. I have already received advantage from these waters, though I have drunk them but four days; which convinces me that they will set me quite right.

I am persuaded, that your first setting out at the Hague must have put you behind-hand; but I hope that you will take care to retrieve; for the credit of living a little better will not do you

---

* Lady Emily Lennox, born in 1731, and married in 1747 to James, then Earl of Kildare, and afterwards Duke of Leinster.

† The reference is to his son at Liepsig, and his progress in his studies.

so much good, as contracting a considerable debt will do you harm. If you can get leave to come here for three or four months, when Lord Holderness shall be settled at the Hague, which I should think would be no difficult matter, that suspension of your expense would, I suppose, go near to set you right. But, in the mean time, should you want money, draw upon me *sans façon :* for I will not have you run in debt to anybody else ; and you and I can, I believe, trust each other.

By all I can hear now, and by all that I knew before, the Republic is so far from being settled, that I do not consider it as a government or a nation. More money is wanted than is to be found, and even the methods of collecting what is there to be found will not be easily fixed. The people will not have *pachters.** Collectors, without the powers of the *pachters,* will collect nothing, and with those powers they become *pachters* themselves, in the most odious and oppressive sense of that word. The Prince of Orange has got more power than by the constitution he ought to have ; and if he does not get all the rest, he will lose what he has got. *Il n'y a point de milieu :* power must either be constitutional or unlimited. Losing gamesters will not leave off while they have anything left, and will never be quiet till they have lost all. When Cæsar had once passed the Rubicon, he well knew that he must be Cæsar or nothing. And this is now the Prince's case.

I now plainly see the prelude to the Pyrrhic dance in the north, which I have long foretold ; the return of Comte Biron and the Duke of Brunswick to Petersburg announces destruction to the Holstein family. The Prince-Successor of Sweden will be the first instance of it, upon the death of that King, which I take to be very near. The next will be, setting aside the Imperial Prince of Russia, and declaring little Czar Iwan the successor. In these transactions, the King of Prussia will necessarily be implicated, which has all along been *l'intention de l'auteur ;* that is of the Court of Vienna, which absolutely governs that of Petersburg, *moyennant* some pecuniary assistance from *another quarter.* But be all this as it will, my *boudoir* and my library, which are my two objects, will be never the worse for it. And I maintain that both of them will be, in their different kinds, the

* See the note to the letter of June 24, 1748.

completest things in England, as I hope you will soon have ocular proof of.

Baron Schmitburg was not arrived when I left London. My compliments to my Baron, to whom I will write very soon. Adieu; *Je vous aime véritablement.*

CLXXII.

TO SOLOMON DAYROLLES, ESQ.

BATH, *November* 4, O.S. 1748.

DEAR DAYROLLES,

I have received yours of the 5th, N.S.; and am glad to find, that your landed estate pays so well as to make up the arrears of the treasury. As soon as I go to town, which will be next week, I will quicken Mr. Pelham to pay his debts; but *en tout cas*, I repeat it again, upon any emergency, draw upon me, for, upon my word, such sums as you can want will be no inconveniency to me to advance. You are besides very responsible, whether considered as a monied or as a landed man; so that, if you should be backward in payment I should forthwith seize Henley Park.*

A propos of money; as I believe it is much wanted by many people, even of fashion, both in Holland and Flanders, I should think it very likely that many good pictures of Rubens, Teniers, and other Flemish and Dutch Masters, may be picked up now at reasonable rates. If so, you are likely to hear of it as a *virtuoso ;* and if so, I should be glad to profit of it, as an humble *dilettante.* I have already, as you know, a most beautiful landscape by Rubens, and a pretty little piece of Teniers; but if you could meet with a large capital history, or allegorical piece, of Rubens, with the figures as big as the life, I would go pretty deep to have it, as also for a large and capital picture of Teniers. But as I would give a good deal for them if they were indisputably eminent, I would not give threepence for them unless they were so. I have pretty pictures enough already; but what I want to complete my collection, is only two or three of the most eminent Masters, of whom I have none now. I can trust entirely to your taste and skill; so that if you meet with such a thing, do not miss it for fifty pounds, more or less.

* The seat of Mr. Dayrolles, near Guildford.

The packet of *brochures,* and flourished ruffles, which you sent me by Hop, waits for me in town. I am sure, by the former, which you sent me, I shall like these : *je m'en fie à votre bon goût.* I shall go to them in about ten days, though, I doubt, not quite restored by these waters, which have not had their usual effects upon me this season. My vertigos still chicane and teaze me, though not quite so frequently as formerly, but still enough to make me fear passing a languid and uncomfortable winter. Patience : I might have more painful complaints, and I will comfort myself by the comparison.

I have some reasons to believe, that what my Baron mentioned to me of a new successor to Sweden, is by no means groundless. I am very sorry for it, as I think it can only be attended with very ill consequences for this country. Reflect upon the tenure and situation of Bremen and Verden, and upon the amicable disposition of two certain brothers* towards each other, and those consequences will immediately occur to you.

I look upon your Republic as a chaos, in the situation which it is now in ; some order may spring from it, but as yet God knows what. The ancient government certainly does not exist; and I see no new one established in its stead. Abject court, it is true, is made to the Prince of Orange, from fear on one hand, and hopes on the other; but still, while he has more power than he should have for the late form of government, and yet less than is necessary to carry on any other, it is no government at all. This was the great difficulty under which Cromwell, one of the ablest men in the world, laboured, and which he was sensible of, when he wanted to be declared King; for he was above minding the title. But he knew that his government wanted that form and consistency which were necessary for its effect and authority.

The peace is, upon the whole, better than could have been expected, from the circumstances and hurry in which it was made ; but the article relating to the hostages,† and that wherein France only renounces the Pretender and his family, by reference

---

* This is said ironically, and appears to allude to the differences between the Prince of Orange and the Duke of Cumberland.—M.

† At the conclusion of the peace of Aix-la-Chapelle, two British noblemen, the Earl of Sussex and Lord Cathcart, were sent to Paris as hostages for the restitution of Cape Breton.—M.

to one in an old obsolete Treaty, shock me, as injurious and personally insulting to the King.

I fear you will not get a furlough this winter, for I do not find that Lord Holderness is yet making any preparations for his embassy. *Bon soir, aimons-nous toujours.*

CLXXIII.

À MADAME LA MARQUISE DE MONCONSEIL.

À LONDRES, *ce* 21 *Novembre*, V.S. 1748.

Je reviens, Madame, depuis quatre jours seulement des Bains, auxquels mes vieilles indispositions m'avoient obligé d'avoir recours. Pendant mon séjour là, des vertiges et des migraines rendoient ma tête très-indigne de vous dire la moindre chose, et elle n'étoit guères en état de vous expliquer les sentimens de mon cœur : ce qui m'en consoloit, c'étoit que vous les connoissiez depuis longtems. En attendant, je me trouve endetté de quatre lettres, que j'ai reçues de vous par différens canaux ; c'est une dette que je ne pourrai jamais payer en espèces de même valeur, et je prétends seulement m'en acquitter par mon obéissance à vos ordres.

Il faut convenir que le théâtre François l'emporte en tout genre sur tous les autres, et même sur les anciens, avec tout le respect que je leur dois.

Je suis charmé des honneurs, dont Monsieur de Richelieu est comblé ; il les mérite, ou bien les auroit mérités à Gênes, s'il eût été question de la défendre, mais, graces à nos bons Alliés les Austro-Sardes, cette ville n'a pas seulement été assiégée. Il est vrai qu'il y avoit une soidisante armée devant la ville, mais pas plus nombreuse que la garnison même, et manquant absolument de tout ce qui étoit nécessaire pour faire un siège. Voila comme nous avons été soutenus par-tout de nos Alliés ; trente mille Autrichiens en ont représenté soixante, qui devoient se trouver en Flandres, et que nous payons comme complets. Heureusement la paix a mis fin à tous ces abus, et il est inutile de regarder en arrière.

Je n'ai pas encore les bras, pour lesquels je m'impatiente si fort, mais ils sont arrivés et je les attends à tous momens ; c'est tout ce qui manque à présent à mon boudoir, qui d'ailleurs est fini, et charmant ; j'y entre à Noël.

Adieu, Madame, pour cette fois ; ma lettre se ressent de ma tête, et je vous assure que ma tête se ressent déjà de ma lettre.

CLXXIV.
TO THE REV. DR. MADDEN.

LONDON, *November* 29, 1748.

SIR,

A return of my old complaint of vertigos and pains in my head, which sent me to Bath, from whence I am but lately arrived here, and that with less benefit than I hoped for, delayed till now my acknowledgments for your last friendly letter, which accompanied the remainder of your poem. I read it with great pleasure, and not without some surprise, to find a work of that length continued to the end with the same spirit and fire with which it begins. Horace's great rule of *qualis ab incepto* was, I believe, never better observed. If the public receive the same pleasure from it that I have done, you will have the satisfaction of having discharged every office towards mankind that a private citizen of the world is capable of. Your example, your fortune, and your genius, will all have been devoted to the service, the improvement, and the rational pleasures, of your fellow creatures.

I make no doubt but that the Charter for the Dublin Society, when once you have formed it properly among yourselves, will be granted here ; and, upon the whole, I am much for it, and will promote it to my power ; not but that I foresee some danger on that side of the question too. Abuses have always hitherto crept into corporate bodies, and will probably, in time, creep into this too ; but I hope that it will have such an effect, at first, as to make the future abuses of less consequence. The draught which Mr. Macauley showed me here of the Charter, seems to have all the provisions in it that human prudence can make against human iniquity.

Good health and long life attend you, my good friend, for the sake of mankind in general, and of that country in particular which will ever have a great share of the warmest wishes of

Yours, etc.

CLXXV.

TO SOLOMON DAYROLLES, ESQ.

LONDON, *December* 6, O.S. 1748.

DEAR DAYROLLES,

By the death of poor John, you have lost a true friend, and I a most affectionate brother and friend into the bargain. The gout fell upon his bowels and head, and threw him into the convulsions of which he died.

I acknowledge now your last of the 6th, N.S., together with your former letters, which my brother's illness and a hurry of other affairs hindered me from answering sooner.

Mr. Pelham has faithfully promised me, that before Christmas you shall be paid up as high as any Minister in the King's service, which I hope will prevent any anticipations.

Lord Sandwich is, I know, impatient to come over, and I know that nobody is ready to go from hence; so that I cannot expect to see you for some months; and in the mean time the whole business of Holland will be in your hands, except what may be separately transacted between Bentinck there and his Grace* here. This, I think, is a lucky circumstance for you, as it will put you in possession of the business to a certain degree at least, and consequently strengthen the claim which you mentioned to his Grace. Though Lord Holderness is strongly insisted upon by the Bentincks, and will therefore, I suppose, be sent at last, yet I know that his distinguished incapacity for business staggers a good deal those who are to send him. *Tant mieux* if he goes, you will be of the more importance, which is my only object, for I have done with business, but not with you.

The prices of Van Huysen's flower-pieces, notwithstanding the scarcity of money in Holland, is owing only to that local phrenzy which always prevails in Holland for some pretty trifling object; tulips, hyacinths, and pigeons, have all had their day, and now Van Huysen has his. But while these high-finished finical pieces bear such high prices, the bold and masterly pieces of the last and the foregoing century are slighted, and more likely to come reasonably. Do not, by any means, suffer that capital picture of Rubens, which you say is to be sold at Brussels, to slip through

* The Duke of Newcastle.

your hands, by the delay of sending me a drawing of it, if you can but be sure that it is an original, and not damaged. Three hundred guineas cannot be dear, and anything under that must be cheap. Wherefore, upon the two conditions of its being an undoubted original and not damaged, buy it me as soon as you can, or some other body may step in between.

Captain Irwine,* whom I believe you know, son to the old General, goes by the next packet-boat to Holland : he has got a furlough from his father for a year, during which time he intends to see as much as he can abroad. I think him a good pretty young fellow ; and, considering that he has never been yet out of his native country, much more *presentable* than one could expect. Pray, carry him to Court, and into some companies, where I think you will not be ashamed of him, which will seldom be your case with my countrymen. I promised him that I would recommend him to you. *Adieu, mon cher enfant !* I am so hurried by lawyers, appraisers, and creditors, that I can say no more now.

P.S. *A propos*, do not mention to anybody that the picture is for me, or what it may cost.

CLXXVI.

TO SOLOMON DAYROLLES, ESQ.

LONDON, *December* 23, O.S. 1748.

DEAR DAYROLLES,

My former was almost an answer, beforehand, to your last letter, which I received the day after I had wrote mine ; I mean, with regard to the Rubens, which I desired you not to let slip. But I am now more confirmed in that opinion, by the drawing, which you sent me, and by the assurances that you give me of the picture being a capital one, and in high preservation. There-

---

* Captain Irwine afterwards Sir John Irwine, K.C.B., and Commander-in-Chief in Ireland. "He began the world as page of honour to Lionel, Duke of Dorset, by whose interest he was pushed forward in the army, and obtained a regiment. He afterwards married, and lived in a style of vain extravagance, which ended by involving him in pecuniary diffi-culties." (Note to Madame du Deffand's Letters, vol. i. p. 240.) Madame du Deffand says of him : " Il me parait comme un assez bon homme."—M.

See Lord Chesterfield's letter to Captain Irwine, of April 4, 1749.

fore, secure it as cheap as you can; but give the three hundred, rather than not buy it; the subject, as you observe, might have been a more pleasing one, but this admits of great expression.

The family-piece, which you mention by Vandyke, I would not give six shillings for, unless I had the honour of being of Sir Melchior's family. The several portraits are, I dare say, finely painted; but then where is the action, where the expression? The good man and his wife generally sit serene in a couple of easy chairs, surrounded by five or six of their children, insignificantly motionless in the presence of Papa and Mamma; and the whole family seem as insipid, and weary, as when they are really together. Their likenesses may indeed be valuable to their own posterity, but in my mind to nobody else. Titian has done more skilfully in his fine picture of the Cornaro family, which he has put in action.

The Venus and Adonis of Vandyke, of which you likewise sent me the drawing, I do not care for, as it is a subject already *rebattu* by still greater masters, and in my mind better, as far as I can judge by the drawing; for Adonis, when he tears himself away from Venus, seems fierce and angry, which I see no occasion for. He is determined, indeed, to leave her for his field sports; but should, in my opinion, soften the rudeness by all possible complaisance in his words and looks.

So much for *virtù*, which, when I shall have bought this picture, I have done with, unless a very capital Teniers should come in your way. You will draw upon me for the money as soon as ever you please.

I am really sorry for my Baron's accumulated misfortunes; his terrors must be unspeakable; his wife, if she died, would be a great loss to him, not indeed in a carnal, but in a domestic sense, and his son turning out a rascal, fills up the measure. Make my compliments to him when you see him.

This wind which keeps the Duke still in Holland, keeps you in breath, and Lord Sandwich in a fever, who longs to be here, *pour s'orienter*, a little at home. He and *His Grace** were lately by no means well together, and even strong expressions in writing, had passed between them. But all that may come right again, for politicians neither love nor hate. Interest, not senti-

* The Duke of Newcastle.

ment directs them. If Bentinck pouts, he may possibly carry a present point by it, from people, who it may be, do not yet care to break openly with him; but he will lose their favour, and even incur their secret hatred. An able man will do whatever he does *de bonne grace quoique le Diable n'y perd rien.* Half anger and half confidence, are the most imprudent things in the world.

Could you send me in some of your letters, some seed of the right Cantelupe melons? I should not know what to do with more than a dozen, or at most twenty, of them; so that all the seed I shall want will neither increase the bulk nor weight of a letter. The Cantelupes, are, in my opinion, the best sort of melons; at least they always succeed best here. It is for Blackheath that I want it, where you can easily judge that my melon-ground is most exceedingly small. I am obliged to keep that place for seven years, my poor brother's lease being for that time; and I doubt I could not part with it, but to a very great loss, considering the sums of money that he had laid out upon it. For otherwise, I own that I like the country up, much better than down the river.*

As I promised to send Captain Irwine a couple of letters to the Hague, for Paris, I must put you to the expense of inclosing them to you, and to the trouble of giving them to him, not knowing how to direct them for him.

Yours faithfully.

CLXXVII.

TO SOLOMON DAYROLLES, ESQ.

LONDON, *December* 23, O.S. 1748.

DEAR DAYROLLES,

I have received yours, with the inclosed drawing of the Vandyke, which must certainly be a very fine one, if the execution,

---

* This villa at Blackheath afterwards became Lord Chesterfield's constant summer residence. He purchased a prolongation of the lease, built a handsome gallery and other additions to the house, and, with respect to the gardens and hothouses, was, as he says himself, strongly seized with the *furor hortensis.* After his death it passed in succession through several other hands, but being built on Crown-land has finally become the Ranger's Lodge, and is given with the office of Ranger of Greenwich Park. Still, however, it frequently goes by the name of Chesterfield House.—M.

as doubtless it is, be answerable to the disposition : but, however, I continue my negative to it, for the reasons which I gave you before, the price, and that it is a portrait, however fine a one. The Rubens, of which I have a great notion, must and shall, for a time at least, content me, unless I strain a little for the Teniers, which you hint at, which if it be a capital one, I will ; and then have done. My great room will be as full of pictures as it ought to be ; and all capital ones.

I gave you by my last letter a very unnecessary trouble, which I now retract. I had forgot that you had some time ago stocked me with excellent Cantelupe melon-seed, which I have since remembered and found, and given to my gardener to sow at the proper season. I hope to give you some of them in perfection next summer ; for I do not flatter myself with the hopes of seeing you here before that time.

I am really sorry for poor Kreuningen, and cannot conceive what will become of him. You gave him the best advice with regard to his son, but yet I doubt it will not do, for either a good or a bad reputation outruns and gets before people wherever they go. I do not write to the father myself, not knowing what to say to him, but pray make him my compliments, and assure him of the sincere part that I take in whatever concerns him.

Adieu, dear Dayrolles. I am hurried by a complication of most disagreeable affairs,* but always,   Yours.

CLXXVIII.

À MADAME LA MARQUISE DE MONCONSEIL.

À LONDRES, *ce* 26 *Decembre*, V.S. 1748.

Ils sont arrivés sains et saufs, Madame, je les ai, j'en suis charmé ; le goût en est parfait ; vous jugez bien qu'il est question de vos bras, dont il n'y a pas un doigt de cassé. Ils flatteront

---

* "The families of Devonshire and Chesterfield have received a great blow at Derby, where on the death of John Stanhope they set up another of the name. One Mr. Rivett, the Duke's chief friend and manager, stood himself and carried it by a majority of seventy-one. Lord Chesterfield had sent down credit for ten thousand pounds."—H. Walpole to Mann, Dec. 26, 1748.—M.

sûrement les yeux de tout le monde, mais à moi, ils me flatteront
encore plus le cœur. La main délicate de l'ouvrier sera ce que
j'envisagerai le moins; mais ce sera le souvenir et l'amitié de la
personne, qui me les a envoyés, qui leur donneront leur véritable
prix. Ils m'ont jetté pourtant dans un certain embarras; tirez
m'en, Madame, par vos conseils; c'est que je voudrois bien m'en
servir, et en même tems je crains de m'en servir. J'en suis
glorieux comme d'une belle maîtresse; mais j'en suis aussi
jaloux; si je ne les produis point, ma vanité en souffrira; et si je
les produis, que sait-on ? Ils sont fragiles, d'autres les toucher-
ont, les casseront peut-être, du moins je craindrai furieusement
pour eux dans mon absence. Décidez donc ce que je dois faire.
Ils vont aux deux côtés de la cheminée de mon boudoir, comme
s'ils étoient faits exprès, je les ai mis, et je les ai ôtés, de sorte
que l'affaire est encore dans son entier, et je ne demande pas
votre conseil comme on le demande ordinairement, après avoir
pris son parti.

La maladie, en ensuite la mort, d'un frère que j'aimois tendre-
ment, joints à ma propre indisposition, dont je ne suis pas encore
tout-à-fait quitte, m'ont mis enarrière avec vous en fait de lettres,
mais aussi, qui ne l'est pas vis-à-vis de vous en fait de tout?
En cela mon sort est commun, mais ne croyez pas pour cela que
mes sentimens le soient aussi; au contraire, c'est le seul point
que je disputerai avec tous vos serviteurs.

P.S. Les complimens de la nouvelle année sont sous-entendus;
aussi je crois qu'il vaut mieux les sous-entendre que de dire ce
qui s'est dit depuis six mille ans.

CLXXIX.

TO SOLOMON DAYROLLES, ESQ.

LONDON, *December* 27, O.S. 1748.

DEAR DAYROLLES,

I received this morning your letter of the 3rd of January,
N.S., with the two parcels of melon-seed, which as I told you in
my last, I might have saved you the trouble of sending me, if I
had but remembered how plentifully you had supplied me before;
but since I have so carelessly put you to that trouble, all I can

now do, is to have it sowed the latest, so that you may be sure
to taste the fruits of it when you shall be here, which I do not
expect will be till autumn. A new Minister will not, before that
time, be well settled at the Hague; and till then you will not,
nor should I wish you to, leave it. I can account for a certain
person's* having changed his opinion and desiring to remain
now where he is. Things are much altered, and the prospect
which a little while ago he had here is vanished; his Grace †
speaks of him very differently from what he used to do, and their
epistolary quarrels are, I believe, remembered with equal resentment on both sides. In my opinion if his Grace could get
off his engagement to Lord Holderness and his friend, on your
side of the water, he would be glad enough to let the present
Minister remain there as long as he pleases, for he dreads his
influence over his brother Grace; ‡ and not without reason. Tom
Villiers,§ who has succeeded my brother in the Admiralty, goes
Ministre de Confiance to Vienna, which commission he would not
accept of without having the Admiralty in hand first. Where
this will shove Keith, I cannot guess; only I should not like his
coming back to the Hague to Lord Sandwich.

As to my Rubens, for I now call it mine, you have acted with
your usual prudence and economy. But if it turns out such as it
is represented to you, I do not expect that you will get any considerable abatement of the first price of £300. As to the method
of getting it over safe here, I refer myself to your abilities;
many officers' baggage will be coming, Ligonier's especially, into
which you may possibly thrust it. Draw upon me, in an
amicable way I mean, how and when you please; for I do not
take your finances to be in a situation to allow long and large
advances.

Your Leipsig acquaintance is setting out for Berlin. He has
applied himself extremely, and with great success, at Leipsig,
having made himself perfect master, as I am assured by his
master, of Greek, Latin, the Laws of Nations and of the empire,
and of the German language to boot; which, by the way, he writes

---

* Lord Sandwich.   † Of Newcastle.   ‡ Of Bedford.

§ Afterwards first Earl of Clarendon, of the second creation. Horace
Walpole speaks of him as "a very silly fellow."—To Sir H. Mann, December 26, 1748.—M.

as well as any German I ever knew. I am therefore no longer in the least pain about the learning part, of which he has now got such a stock, that he will have a pleasure, instead of a toil, in improving it. All that he wants now, is *les Graces*, in pursuit of which he goes, as soon as the roads will permit, from Berlin to Turin, there to remain for at least a year. I know no Court that sends out at least *des gens plus deliés*. I do not know what those may be, whom they keep at home; but by the samples I judge well of them.

The Prince of Wales will, I believe, buy Vandyke's Sir Melchior and company. I have given him the drawing you sent me; and Mr. Laurenzy is wrote to by this post to speak to you about it.

Yours very sincerely,

CLXXX.

À MADAME DE ———.*

À LONDRES, *ce* 1 *Janvier*, V.S.

MADAME,

Je ne suis pas diseur de bonne aventure, ains au contraire ; car je vous annonce que ces quatre billets,† que j'ai choisi avec tant d'attention, et que j'estimois, l'un portant l'autre, à vingt mille pièces au moins, se sont avisés d'être tous blancs.

Je ne me console de votre malheur que par les belles réflexions qu'il me fait faire, et par la morale utile que j'en tire, pour le reste de mes jours.—Oui ! Je vois bien, à présent, que toute la prudence humaine, les mesures les plus sages, et les projets les mieux concertés sont frivoles, si la fortune, cette Divinité inconstante, bizarre et *feminine*, n'est pas d'humeur à les favoriser. Car que pouvoit-on faire de plus que je n'ai fait, et qu'en pouvoit-il arriver de moins ?

Se donnera-t'on, après cela, du mouvement, formera-t'on des plans, et s'inquiétera-t'on, pour les choses de ce monde ? J'oser dire, que si ces réflexions, aussi judicieuses que nouvelles, font la

---

* This letter, and that of the 9th of February, are printed in the "Miscellaneous Pieces" at the end of Mrs. Eugenia Stanhope's edition of Chesterfield's Letters to his Son, but the name of the person, and the year are not given.

† In the Lottery.

même impression sur votre esprit qu'elles ont fait sur le mien, elles vous vaudront plus, que tout ce que vous auriez pu gagner dans la loterie.

Vous êtes bien querelleuse, Madame; jusqu'à m'accorder un talent, que je n'ai pas, pour pouvoir, après, me reprocher de ne le pas employer avec vous; et je m'épuise, dites vous, en *bon ton*, avec Madame de Monconseil. Quelle accusation injuste, et denuée de toute vraisemblance! Un Milord Anglois avec le bon ton! Ce sont deux choses absolument contradictoires; ou pour m'expliquer plus clairement et simplifier mon idée; ce sont deux êtres hétérogènes, dont l'existence d'un implique, nécessairement, la privation de l'autre.

Me voici donc justifié dans toutes les formes de la logique; et si vous n'en êtes pas contente, Madame de Monconseil, qui a en main mes pièces justificatives, pourra vous en convaincre. Au reste; si j'en possédois tant soit peu, ce nouvel an me fourniroit une belle occasion de l'étaler. Et quoique depuis plus de cinq mille ans, toute la terre ait traité ce sujet; je vous dirois quelque chose de nouveau, de galant, et d'obscur, dont on ne s'est jamais avisé auparavant: votre mérite, et les sentimens de mon cœur, y seroient alembiqués, jusqu'à la plus fine quintessence:

CLXXXI.

TO SOLOMON DAYROLLES, ESQ.

LONDON, *January* 20, 1749.

DEAR DAYROLLES,

Last post brought me yours of the 24th, N.S. My old disorder in my head, which has of late plagued me, hindered me from acknowledging your two former letters. I am now much better, thanks to a good blister, which I clapped upon my head, on the part offending.

Since the Rubens is secured, I am in no haste to receive it, for I could not hang it up yet, its place not being ready. The way you mention of sending it by the sloop is, I think, the best; and pray let it be directed to Mr. Hotham, one of the Commissioners of the Customs, who will take care of it, and pay the duty for me. You will take care to have it so safely packed up, that it may receive no damage *en chemin faisant*.

If Lord Sandwich did not really know (which by the way I can hardly believe), that Tom Villiers was to go to Vienna, he must be very little in the secret of affairs here, for it is very well known that Villiers refused going to Vienna, unless he had the Admiralty down first in hand. But I do believe that Lord Sandwich is not upon very good terms with *his Grace*, as my Baron calls him. He arrived here on Tuesday night. The town talks him out of the Admiralty, and the Duke of Cumberland into it; but I do not believe either. You have convinced me that you need not fear the return of Keith, who will look higher.

I am astonished at your being so much behind-hand, for I was most strongly promised that you should, before this time, be cleared off to last Michaelmas at least. I will speak to Mr. Pelham again about it; though after what I have already said to him, and he to me, upon that subject, I fear that it will be to little purpose.

I am glad that I have prevailed with my Baron to return to his old house, for the first warm weather must have suffocated him where he now is. If he escapes dying of the first fright when he goes back, all the rest will do very well, and go on just as it used to do. His *beaux sentimens pour la défunte,* I dare say, will not kill him.

I am rejoiced to hear that I shall have another *tome* of the *Histoire Amoureuse,* for now that (thank God) I have no business, that kind of reading amuses me. The *Histoire Politique* of the United Provinces would at present be but a gloomy one. I see no Government there at all; but I see power without authority, and expense without the possible means of supplies. The Prince of Orange wants a Sully instead of a Bentinck. The reduction of the troops will be a decisive point; if it is a considerable one, the Prince of Orange is nobody; and if it is not, the Republic is undone.

I have read Lord Sandwich's farewell speech, in which I think there are some things more boldly asserted than clearly proved, for it does not by any means appear to me that the Republic was stronger last year, when the enemy was at its gates, than it was three or four years before, when the French were no nearer than Tournay; nor am I as yet sensible of the great advantages which the change of the Government in the Republic has produced with regard to England, when the former cannot in the whole Seven Provinces raise one hundred thousand ducats to pay its share of the Russians, but is obliged to borrow that trifling sum of the latter. But these reflections are entirely out of my present province, and have nothing to do with my house and garden, which employ both my thoughts and my time. I am at work about them all day, and shall take possession of them in about a month. There I shall be impatient to see you, and there I believe you will not be sorry to see Yours.

CLXXXII.

À MADAME LA MARQUISE DE MONCONSEIL.

À LONDRES, *ce* 26 *Janvier*, V.S. 1749.

Comme je respecte vos décisions, Madame, infiniment plus que celles des Papes et des Conciles, fussent-ils même œcuméniques, vos bras sont arborés dans mon boudoir, et y font l'effet que vous pouvez bien croire : mais, à ne vous rien cacher, deux autres motifs ont contribué à m'y déterminer ; le premier, que les questions qu'on me fera à leur sujet me donneront tous les jours occasion de parler de vous ; l'autre, que ma vanité trouvera son compte à dire que je les tiens de vous. Croyez-vous que la vanité n'entre pour rien dans les sentimens les plus délicats de l'amitié, et même de l'amour ? Au moins je vous avoue que je ne tiens pas contre la vanité qui me résulte des marques de votre amitié, et bien vous en prend même, qu'il n'est question que de l'amitié, car ma foi je ne répondrois pas de ma discrétion, s'il étoit question de quelque chose de plus. Nous ne mettons jamais les préférences marquées, de la part de certaines gens, que sur le compte de notre propre mérite ; et c'est en partie sur ce principe que j'érige vos bras comme les trophées du mien.

J'ai lu avec attention la pièce * que vous avez eu la bonté de m'envoyer, et d'autant plus qu'elle paroît avoir votre approbation. Vous m'ordonnez de vous en dire mon sentiment ; si je pouvois vous obéir à regret, ce seroit dans cette occasion, dans laquelle je vois que mon sentiment est différent du vôtre. Je vous avouerai donc naturellement, Madame, que la pièce n'a pas répondu à mon

* Crebillon's tragedy of *Cataline;* Voltaire composed his *Rome Sauvée* in opposition to it.

attente, ni à l'idée que je m'en étois formée, tant par rapport à l'auteur, que par rapport au tems qu'il a travaillé. Je conviens qu'il y a des beaux vers, des endroits brillans, du sublime, et que le caractère de Catilina est achevé ; mais après cela, la conduite de la pièce me choque. Quand une tragédie est faite sur une histoire, ou peu connue ou douteuse, comme quand il est question d'un grand Mogol, d'un Sultan, d'un Soliman, d'un Orosmane, il est très-permis à un poëte de l'accommoder à ses besoins, et la véritable histoire étant ignorée, le poëte devient en quelque façon l'historien : mais de violenter, au point que fait Monsieur de Crébillon, une histoire si connue, si constatée, que celle de Catilina, et peut-être la seule histoire ancienne sur laquelle tous les différens auteurs sont d'accord, c'est en vérité abuser des droits du cothurne. Tullie étoit à la bavette quand Catilina fut tué, et Catilina n'eut garde de se tuer lui-même, pour satisfaire à l'unité du tems et du lieu de Monsieur de Crébillon, mais voulut éprouver premièrement le sort d'une bataille, où il fut criblé de coups à la tête de son armée. Si, par exemple, on vous eût donné une tragédie de Monsieur de Cinq Mars,* dans laquelle, pour la commodité du poëte, cet infortuné se seroit tué lui-même, au lieu de mourir, comme il le fit, sur l'échafaud ; où il auroit été aimé, trahi, et dénoncé par Madame de Combalet, et où le Cardinal de Richelieu n'auroit paru sur la scène que pour déclarer qu'il avoit une peur horrible, et qu'il ne savoit au monde que faire, qu'en diriez-vous, Madame ? et pardonneriez-vous au poëte un tel outrage fait à la vérité historique ? Je ne le crois pas ; et pourtant l'histoire de Monsieur de Cinq Mars n'est pas plus généralement connue, ni mieux constatée que celle de Catilina. J'allois même dire qu'à peine étoit-elle plus récente, puisque les livres qu'on a presque toujours à la main la renouvellent incessamment. Ciceron, il faut l'avouer, étoit naturellement irrésolu et timide ; mais, malheureusement pour le poëte, la seule occasion où il brilla, et où il témoigna véritablement de la fermeté et du courage, est justement celle où il en fait un linge mouillé ; et le Consul, qu'on admire dans l'histoire, fait seulement pitié dans la pièce. Caton paroît sur la scène, uniquement pour gronder et dire pis que pendre des Romains, car tout ce qu'il fait ne mène à rien dans la

---

* In 1642 he was condemned and beheaded with de Thou, son of the historian, for a plot against Richelieu.

pièce. Je me serois passé aussi volontiers de la présence de son
Excellence Monsieur l'Ambassadeur Sunnon, qui ne se produit
que pour donner aux François d'aujourd'hui le plaisir de savoir
que les Gaulois, il y a dix-sept cens ans, étoient bien les meilleures
gens du monde. Je ne puis pas démêler le caractère de Tullie;
aime-t-elle véritablement Catilina? ou en fait-elle seulement
semblant, pour mieux découvrir ses desseins, et sauver la patrie?
Cela n'est pas assez marqué. Si elle aime véritablement Catilina,
et en même tems sa patrie, et son papa, déchireé par des sentimens si opposés, et pourtant si forts, sa situation devroit être si
violente que tout le monde y prendroit intérêt, au lieu que pour
moi, franchement je ne m'en inquiette point, et je la laisse faire.
Pour le caractère de Catilina, il est beau, grand et soutenu
jusqu'à la fin, et on l'aime en dépit de ses crimes: mais permet-
tez-moi aussi d'ajouter, que je fais de cela même un crime au
poëte, qui n'auroit pas dû choisir un sujet si opposé au véritable
but de la tragédie, qui est de rendre le crime haïssable et non
pas aimable. Un de nos meilleurs poëtes Anglois reproche, et
pas sans raison, à Milton, que le diable est en effet le héros de
son poëme, puisqu'il est par-tout habile, intrépide, même aimable,
et qu'il vient à bout de son dessein, qui étoit de damner le genre
humain. Il ne faut pas choisir des sujets qui entrainent nécessairement de telles suites. Voila, Madame, ma petite critique.

Au reste, je vous en prie, gardez pour vous seule ces idées
hasardées. Si elles sont justes, je ne voudrois pas qu'elles fussent
connues, pour l'amour de Monsieur de Crébillon, dont je respecte
le génie et le caractère; et si elles sont fausses, ce qui me paroît
le plus vraisemblable, puisqu'elles né sont pas conformes aux
vôtres, je ne voudrois point qu'elles fussent sues pour l'amour de
votre très-humble serviteur, qui ne s'érige nullement en critique,
et qui aime bien mieux trouver des beautés que chercher des
défauts.

A propos de tragédies, Denys le Tyran, par Monsieur de Mar-
montel, qu'on m'assure n'avoir pas encore vingt-trois ans, annonce
un grand poëte tragique; du moins son coup d'essai me paroît
presque un coup de maître. Envoyez-moi, je vous en prie,
Madame, la traduction de l'Anti-Lucrèce; quelque médiocre
qu'elle soit, elle aura toujours du mérite, si elle conserve seulement un peu du sens de l'original.

CLXXXIII.

TO SOLOMON DAYROLLES, ESQ.

LONDON, *February* 3, O.S. 1749.

DEAR DAYROLLES,

I have honoured your bill, as they call it; but properly speaking I have done better, for I have paid it. I think you have brought me off very cheaply, and so much so, that I shall not own it, when I show the picture, but intimate a much higher price; for you *virtuosos*, I know, often take the price into your consideration, in forming your judgments as to the value of a thing. I sincerely forgive you the three florins, which your curiosity costs me, and will never demand that sum of either you or your heirs, administrators, or assigns. Besides that I really think, that a gratification of three florins is by no means unreasonable for the trouble you have been at. I can tell you by the way, that when my pictures, bronzes, and marbles, shall come to be properly placed, as they will be in my new house, the collection will not appear a contemptible one. There will be nothing, that is not excellent of the kind. I hope you will be here time enough to direct me in the arrangement; for Lord Holderness is now preparing in good earnest for his embassy, and talks of going soon, that is, in two or three months. He has appointed Parson Tindal, who translated Rapin, and well, to be both his chaplain and his secretary; he goes first, as I hear, without Madame, who is to follow him some time afterwards. But though, as you will easily believe, I am impatient to see you, I would not advise you to ask leave to come over immediately upon his arrival, but to stay a couple of months at least after it.

I had a letter the other day from my Baron, by which he seems to be pretty well comforted, and to thirst again for pamphlets, of which I have sent him a fresh cargo. Pray, when you see *L'ami*,* make him my compliments, and assure him of my esteem and friendship. I suppose *qu'il n'est pas question de lui à la Cour.* As for your Republic, it is undone, and I think of it no more. *Conclamatum est.* Adieu.

* See Letter of June 2, 1747, and note.

CLXXXIV.

À MADAME DE ———.*

À LONDRES, *ce* 9 *Fevrier*, 1749.

Adieu donc toute coquetterie, de part et d'autre, et vive la vraie et solide amitié! Heureux ceux qui peuvent y atteindre: c'est le gros lot, dans la loterie du monde, contre lequel il y a des millions de billets blancs.

S'il pouvoit y avoir quelque chose de flatteur dans mon amitié; je dirois, que nous pourrions nous flatter que la nôtre seroit également vraie et durable; puisqu'elle est à l'abri de tous ces petits incidens qui brouillent la plûpart des autres. D'abord, nous sommes de différent sexe, article assez important; et qui nous garantit de ces défiances et de ces rivalités, sur les objets les plus sensibles, et contre lesquels la plus belle amitié du monde ne tient point. En second lieu, il n'entre point d'amour dans notre fait; qui, quoique, à la vérité, il donne un grand feu à l'amitié, pendant un certain tems, la flamme de l'un venant à s'eteindre, on voit bientôt les cendres de l'autre. Et enfin (ce qui me regarde uniquement) nous ne nous voyons pas trop. Vous ne me connoissez que par mon bon côté; et vous ne voyez pas ces moments de langueur, d'humeur, et de chagrin, qui causent, si souvent, le dégout ou le repentir des liaisons, qu'on a formé, et qui font qu'on se dit à soi-même; L'auroit-on cru? Qui l'auroit dit? Comme on peut se tromper aux dehors! Et la perspective, dans laquelle vous me voyez, m'est si favorable, qu'elle me console un peu *della lontananza* où je suis obligé de vous chercher.

Une caillette a beaux sentimens, critiqueroit impitoyablement ceux-ci comme très *indélicats;* mais en sont-ils moins naturels pour cela? Et ne sommes-nous pas, pour la plûpart, redevables de nos vertus à des situations et des circonstances un peu fortuites? Au moins j'ai assez d'humilité pour le croire; et (si je voulois dire toute la vérité) assez d'expérience de moi-même pour le sçavoir. En tout cas, tel que je suis, je vous suis acquis, et vous voyez que je suis de trop bonne foi pour vous surfaire dans le prix de l'acquisition que vous avez faite.

Vous avez beau faire les honneurs de votre pays, et désavouer

* See note to Letter CLXXX.

votre propriété exclusive des Graces ; il faut convenir, pourtant, que la France est leur séjour, ou plûtot leur pays natal. Si elles pouvoient se fâcher contre vous, dont il y a peu d'apparence, elles seroient piquées, au point de vous quitter, de ce que vous les envoyez promener dans un pays, où elles ne connoissent, ni ne sont connues de personne : et si par hasard je les connoissois, ce ne seroit que pour les avoir vues si souvent chez vous.

Il est bien sûr que les Graces sont un don de la nature, qu'on ne peut pas acquérir ; l'art en peut relever l'éclat, mais il faut que la nature ait donné le fond. On voit cela en tout. Combien de gens ne dansent-ils pas parfaitement bien, mais sans grace ; combien il y en a qui dansent très mal avec beaucoup ; combien trouve-t-on d'esprits vigoureux et délicats, qui instruits et ornés par tout ce que l'art et l'étude peuvent faire, ne plaisent pourtant guère, faute de ces graces naturelles, qui ne s'acquièrent point ! Chaque pays a ses talens, aussi bien que ses fruits et ses denrées particulières. Nous pensons *creux*, et nous approfondissons ; les Italiens pensent *haut*, et se perdent dans les nues : vous tenez le milieu ; on vous voit, on vous suit, on vous aime.

Servez vous, Madame, de tout ce que cet esprit et ces graces, que je vous connois, peuvent faire en ma faveur, et dites, je vous en supplie, tout ce qu'elles vous suggèreront, à Monsieur de Matignon, de ma part. Mon cœur ne vous désavouera pas sur tout ce que vous pourrez lui dire de plus fort, à propos du mariage de Mademoiselle sa fille : mais ne vous bornez pas à ce seul article, car il n'y en a pas un, au monde, qui peut le regarder, auquel je ne prendrois pas également part. Ce seroit abuser de sa bonté que de lui écrire moi-même : une messagère comme vous me fera bien plus d'honneur, et à lui plus de plaisir.

Adieu, Madame. Je rougis de la longueur de ma lettre.

CLXXXV.

TO SOLOMON DAYROLLES, ESQ.

LONDON, *February* 24, O.S. 1749.

DEAR DAYROLLES,

The picture is arrived, and is, in my mind, the best I ever saw of Rubens ; but as yet I have only my own opinion for it, as I have not shown it, nor will not, till it is in perfect order.

A little of the varnish, in some immaterial parts, was rubbed off in the carriage, but the painting not the least damaged. I have given it to Anderson, who is a very safe man, to take off that crust of varnish, with which they are so apt to load their pictures in Flanders and Holland; and, when this picture shall be delivered of it, it will be quite another thing. The figure of the Virgin is the most graceful and beautiful that I ever saw, and not so Flemish-built as most of his women are. In short, the whole is excellent. The frame though not a fashionable is a handsome one, and shall, with the addition that I will make to it, be a fine one. I do not dislike something a little *antique* in the frame of an old picture; provided it be rich, I think it is more respectable. As soon as the supreme connoisseurs shall have sat upon it, I will let you know their verdict, not that for my own part I shall care twopence about it, for I distrust the skill of most, and the truth of all, of them. They pronounce according to the pictures that they either have or have not, or that they want to buy or sell, of the same hand. You are an excellent *commissionaire;* and my most dutiful thanks attend you for your care and trouble.

Pray do not let your *maladie du pays* hurry you into any *étourderie.* The Ambassador's *inefficiency* may very possibly make your stay at the Hague more necessary than you are aware of, and you of more importance, which circumstance may hereafter be of great use to you. Upon his arrival at the Hague, exert yourself to get the best and freshest informations, and write them immediately, and add now and then a few reasonings of your own upon them. By these means your despatches will be the material ones from the Hague. By-the-by, your Court there is by no means well with the Court here, therefore beware of panegyric on the one hand as well as of censure on the other. Blame all unnecessary expenses, and remark that those sums would be better employed upon the Civil and Military Government, *car tel est le ton présent d'une certaine Personne.** Keep however well with the Ambassador, but tell him nothing but what he knows before, and God knows that will be very little. When you shall thus have shown yourself to be the efficient man there, ask leave *à la bonne heure* to come over here; but

---

* The King.

then take care to establish such correspondences as may enable you to inform the Ministers here, of what shall be doing in Holland, better than the Ambassador, though upon the spot.

Pray tell my Baron, that I took particular care to send him the *Inquiry into the Conduct and Principles of the Two Brothers;* * so that it must necessarily have been taken out of the packet. Possibly they have no mind that it should be dispersed abroad. I will send it him again the first opportunity. Rutter is now out of town; the moment he comes, I will deliver Mr. Slingelandt's † message to him.

We say here, that it is quite over with the two Bentincks. Is it so? Say nothing for or against them, in your public despatches, but impartially relate matters of fact concerning them; for they are yet well *here*.

Adieu. Yours faithfully.

CLXXXVI.

TO SOLOMON DAYROLLES, ESQ.

LONDON, March 9, O.S. 1749.

DEAR DAYROLLES,

I do not absolutely admit of all the reasonings of your last; for though I agree that Lord Holderness will from his relation to, and connexion with, the Greffier, have the best informations, yet I think he will put them very ill together, and with good materials make but scurvy letters; moreover, you may depend upon it, that he will only write what that Cabal would have him write, so that his accounts will be partial; whereas yours, as far as they go, will be fair, and give the whole. I cannot see neither why the utmost of your hopes should go no farther than the additional £300 a year, nor why you should not in time be *Monsieur L'Envoyé,* somewhere or other. Many have enjoyed, and some do enjoy, that character who in every respect deserve it less. When I see you we will talk these matters over more fully than we can write upon them. Lord Holderness has not yet kissed the King's hand, and of course will not go soon:

---

* Mr. Pelham and the Duke of Newcastle.
† Son of the late Pensionary.

therefore I do not expect to see you till the end of July or August. Upon my soul I long to see you for two reasons, which I have not for longing to see many people; they are, that I love you, and that I know you love me. I shall keep a little room for you at Blackheath, where I will refresh you with the best ananas * and melons in England.

Pray tell Monsieur Slingelandt that I have spoken to Rutter about the horse in question; and the better to know whether he was gentle enough for him, I asked him whether he was enough so for me; to which Rutter could not answer in the affirmative, so that I bid him not send him. I take it for granted that Monsieur Slingelandt, who is a civil quiet gentleman as well as myself, chooses, as I do, a horse like Père Canaye's *qualem me decet esse mansuetum,* † which serene kind of beast is still more necessary in Holland, in the midst of canals, and windmills, than here.

Kreuningen's son, he writes me word, is coming to England, which I am sorry for upon account of Trevor, ‡ whom it embarrasses extremely. It does not embarrass me, because I am resolved to be totally ignorant of all that has passed, and to invite him to dinner, as if nothing had happened. But Trevor cannot plead that ignorance, and Hop, I believe, will not receive him, so that I fancy his stay will not be long here. I should think that Russia would be the best, as it is the remotest, place for him, and possibly Comte Golofkin could get him into that service. Kreuningen *le Père* tells me that he has some thoughts of coming here himself next summer; I should be glad of it for my own sake, but sorry for his; complaisance for singular characters being by no means the natural turn of this country. His oddnesses would be indulged by few, but laughed at by many; so that I think he would pass his time ill here, which would mortify him. I am now three letters in his debt, which I will pay off as soon as I can; but I am so hurried and unsettled

---

* Lord Mahon's note here is :—"The word 'pine-apple' has not yet, it appears, come into common use"; but it occurs in Letter of August 1, 1754; and is found as early as Locke.

† An allusion to the *Conversation du Maréchal d'Hoquincourt avec le Père Canaye*, by St. Evremond.—Note by Dayrolles.

‡ Robert Trevor, who had some years before been Envoy to Holland.—M.

at present, being to remove to my new house this day se'nnight, that I have hardly time to write, or table to write upon.

It is said here, that our Ministers are altogether by the ears, and I believe that there is some degree of truth in the report. There is certainly no love lost between their *two Graces.* Lord Sandwich holds with, or rather governs, his Grace of Bedford; Fox is mutinous, and all the parts of the Ministerial machine disjointed. What order will at last spring out of this confusion, I neither know nor care. The new discipline which is to be established in both Fleet and Army by Act of Parliament,* has caused great debates and long sittings in the House of Commons, has given great dissatisfaction to those two bodies of men, and great alarm to everybody else. This measure is thought to be His Royal Highness, the Duke's; which has added so much to his former unpopularity, that the most scandalous libels imaginable are published every day upon the subject.

Bentinck may possibly have still some remaining credit at your Court, but I am sure not very much power; for I know his turn well enough to know, that if he had much power he would not suffer the Pensionary to be tolerably received there, much less consulted.

I forgot to tell you before, that I cannot for my soul explain the riddle which you sent me sometime ago. The A. E. I. are to me impenetrable. Pray send me the solution. *Bon soir, mon ami.*

CLXXXVII.

À MADAME LA MARQUISE DE MONCONSEIL.

À Londres, *ce* 12 *Mars,* V.S. 1749.

J'ai reçu, Madame, la traduction † de l'Anti-Lucrèce que vous avez eu la bonté de m'envoyer. Monsieur l'Abbé de la Ville, avec sa politesse ordinaire, l'a accompagnée d'une lettre très-obligeante. Nous étions à la fois amis et ennemis à la Haye,

---

* This was a proposal for making all half-pay officers subject to martial law. It was carried as to the military, but not as to the naval service.—M.

† By M. Bougainville, Secretary of the Academy of Belles Lettres at Paris. See Letter of 8 Sept., 1747; and letter to him in June, 1755.

et il n'a pas tenu à nous que la paix ne se soit faite il y a quatre ans; son souvenir m'a flatté, car je l'estime beaucoup. Je trouve la traduction très-bonne; les beautés de l'original y sont aussi bien rendues que la prose le permet; mais un beau poëme perd nécessairement beaucoup à être traduit, même en vers. Je ne puis pas m'empêcher de regretter, qu'un des plus beaux morceaux de l'original, qui selon moi est le sixième livre, tienne à une philosophie si fausse et si pitoyable que celles des automates de Monsieur Descartes, qui certainement ne l'a pas crue lui-même.

Monsieur de Mirepoix viendra-t-il ici, ou se sera-t-il rebuté de certains incidens assez déplacés à mon avis? Je n'ai pas l'honneur de le connoître personnellement, mais ce que tout le monde dit de lui me fait souhaiter qu'il vienne. Madame de Mirepoix est bien aimable; j'ai eu l'honneur de la connoître à Paris; si je pouvois leur être bon à quelque chose ici, j'en serois charmé, et je m'acquitterois de mon mieux des commissions dont ils voudroient bien me charger. Ayez la bonté, Madame, de me procurer, si vous le pouvez, l'emploi de leur commissionnaire.

Je ferai tous mes efforts pour obtenir de Milord Crawford,* ce que souhaite Monsieur votre beau-frère; mais j'avoue que je doute un peu si je réussirai, car j'ai demandé la même chose il y a quelque tems à un autre de nos officiers, qui me l'a refusé tout net; disant qu'il ne savoit pas s'il étoit en droit de le faire, et qu'il pourroit peut-être lui-même donner quelque jour des mémoires de la dernière guerre: enfin, l'Anglois n'est pas naturellement communicatif.

Je suis à présent dans une situation ridiculement violente; j'entre en deux jours dans ma nouvelle maison, qui n'est pas encore à demi meublée, quoique celle où je suis soit tout-à-fait démeublée. Je ne vis que des aumônes de mes amis, et j'écris cette lettre, faute de table, sur un livre sur mes genoux. Je la finis pourtant pour l'amour de vous, mais ce n'est pas pour me tirer d'une attitude gênante, à laquelle on ne pense pas quand on s'entretient avec vous.

* John Lindsay, eighteenth Earl of Crawford, a distinguished general officer. He died in December, 1749.—M.

CLXXXVIII.

TO SOLOMON DAYROLLES, ESQ.

LONDON, *March* 31, O.S. 1749.
HÔTEL CHESTERFIELD.

DEAR DAYROLLES,

I showed your letter to Hop, to whom it gave great satisfaction, and who thinks himself much obliged to you for the part which you take in his affairs. He was uneasy before, and is not quite easy yet, for he fears that if the Bentinck party prevails, they will send some dependent of their own here in his stead, either to mark out their credit, or to carry on their secret; and he has taken such a fancy to this country, that I do not believe he would change his destination here for any other in the world. He refused the embassy to Paris, which he was even pressed to accept.

I can tell you nothing, with any degree of certainty, of the squabbles among our Ministers. That there are some, is undoubtedly true; but then, in the reports, they are either magnified or lessened, according to the wishes or the interests of the reporters. Their two Graces are evidently very ill together, which I long ago knew, and said, could not fail. Mr. Pelham is cordially well with neither of them, though affectedly well with his brother. The Duke of Bedford, governed in general, but not in every particular, by Lord Sandwich, is pretty strong, *moyennant* the Gower family and others whom he brings into Parliament. He likewise gains ground with the Duke of Cumberland, who is, in truth, Minister as well as General, of which you will easily imagine his Grace of Newcastle is horribly jealous. These are, I believe, pretty near the outlines of the present Ministerial piece. Mr. Pelham, who really means well, has the least power, and possibly for that very reason.

But, upon the whole, *que le chien mange le loup, ou le loup le chien*, I am got into my new house, from whence I shall be a most unconcerned spectator of those silly scenes. I have yet finished nothing but my *boudoir* and my library : the former is the gayest and most cheerful room in England, the latter the best. My garden is now turfed, planted, and sown, and will in two months more make a scene of verdure and flowers not common in London.

Anderson has restored the Rubens perfectly well, by taking off that damned varnish with which it was loaded, and fetching out the original painting. The *connoisseurs* have sat upon it, and, what is extraordinary, are unanimous in declaring it one of the best in England. Many have guessed it at £800, none less than £500. *Je les laisse dire, et je ne dis rien.*

I do not care for the Teniers you mention, both my picture-rooms being completely filled—the great one with capital pictures, the cabinet with *bijoux.* So that I will buy no more, till I happen to meet with some very capital ones of some of the most eminent old Italian masters, such as Raphael, Guido, Correggio, etc., and in that case I would make an effort.

I will look out for a horse fit for Mr. Slingelandt, of which I think I am a better judge than a better horseman. You may tell him I shall not much regard the beauty of it, but the intrinsic merit. I desire he should be safe, for I love him, both upon his own account and his father's.

I am glad to hear for his own sake that young Kreuningen does not come here, where I find he would have been in general very ill. Hop was determined not to receive him, and Trevor not to present him anywhere.

I agree with you that my Baron, far from travelling into other countries, will never more see his own, or put on a coat. He will think that he has escaped infection so providentially now, that I am apt to think he will endeavour to trust Providence no more.   Yours, etc.

CLXXXIX.

TO SOLOMON DAYROLLES, ESQ.

LONDON, *April* 4, O.S. 1749.

DEAR DAYROLLES,

Since my last to you, I have received your two letters of the 8th and 11th, N.S., together with the pamphlet in Dutch, which you sent me by General Elliot, * who delivered it to me very safe. It has made me rub up my almost forgotten Dutch, and I

---

* A Lieutenant-General in the Dutch service.—M.

think I understand the meaning of it perfectly. It is extremely well written, and I daresay the facts are all as true, as the reasonings upon them are just. It coincides with, and confirms, all the notions I had formed of the present state of affairs in the Republic. I should be obliged to you if you would inform me, who is either the real, or supposed, author of it. Whoever he is, he is well informed. I am very much obliged to you for sending it to me. I have laid it by carefully, with my own predictions of general bankruptcy and confusion, which I fear a little time more will accomplish.

General Elliot *est un dégourdi, et du bon ton.* I have not seen any Englishman more degenerated by being abroad than he is. I met him at Hop's before I knew who he was, and I was astonished to find a man who spoke English so well, behave himself so well.

I differ with you in opinion about the King of Prussia's two very different letters to the two poets, for I am persuaded that they are both genuine. They are in character, seeking at once to please and to deceive. Should the two poets happen to compare notes, such is human vanity, and still more such is poetical vanity, that each would be convinced that the other was the dupe, and himself his Majesty's most favoured poet. *S'il fait bon battre les glorieux, il fait aussi bon les tromper.* In the first case they do not complain ; in the second they do not even see.

We do not comprehend here any more than you do in Holland why Lord Holderness has not yet kissed the King's hand, though he talks of setting out from hence in a month. Some of his friends here are uneasy at his undertaking, in this critical situation, a commission to which they think he would be unequal in any, and have, I know, tried to dissuade him from it. This is certain at least, that, considering his relations and connections in Holland, he will always be looked upon as a party in all their domestic factions and cabals : a light in which a Foreign Minister, to serve his own country well, should never appear, however deeply engaged privately. Moreover, he will be involved in the disgrace of the Bentincks, which, notwithstanding their present favour, I will venture to prophesy is not very remote. If what I have heard be true, her Royal Highness *la leur garde bonne, quelque mine, qu'elle faise à présent.*

Yours, etc.

CXC.

TO CAPTAIN IRWINE (AT PARIS).

LONDON, *April* 4, O.S. 1749.

SIR,

I send you the letter of recommendation to Mr. Villettes, *
which you desired, by yours to Mr. Grevenkop; but I fear that
he will be gone from Turin before you arrive there. But in that
case you will find a young academician and his governor there,
who will be very glad to do you any service, and to whom I
have sent orders upon that subject. They will take the Carnival
at Venice, in their way, where you will likewise probably meet
them, for I take it for granted that you will contrive to see that
uncommon ceremony. It is worth your while. There will be a
much greater ceremony next Christmas at Rome, which, at all
events, I think you ought to see: that is, the grand Jubilee,
which is celebrated but once in fifty years. So that, young as
you are, if you do not see it then, you probably never will; and,
upon so extraordinary an occasion, I cannot suppose that your
father will refuse to prolong your leave of absence. For my own
part, I think it so well worth seeing, that I send my young
traveller there, though it very much shortens the stay which I
originally intended that he should make at the Academy at Turin.
I return you my sincere thanks for the favour of your letter, with
the inclosed speech of Monsieur de Richelieu, which is perfectly
in character, and, I dare say, all his own!

Any instance of your friendship and remembrance will always
be agreeable to one, who is, with those sentiments of esteem with
which I am,

Yours, etc.

CXCI.

TO THE REV. DR. MADDEN.

LONDON, *April* 15, 1749.

SIR,

You are, I am sure, too well persuaded of my sincere regard
and friendship for you, to impute my late silence to negligence or

* Arthur Villettes, Envoy at Turin.—M.

forgetfulness; but two concurrent causes have hindered me from acknowledging your two last letters : the one was the ill state of my health; the other was the unsettled state of my person, in my migration from my old house to my new one, where I have hardly yet got pen, ink, paper, and a table. This latter has, I believe, been attested to you by your son, who saw me unfurnished in my old house, and since unsettled in my new one. I have (as I told him that I would) executed your orders with regard to my booksellers. I have told them, more fully than I can tell you, my thoughts of the work, and have raised their impatience for some of the copies, for which they will treat with your printer. How they will sell (considering the whimsical and uncertain decision of the public in those matters) I do not know; but how they ought to sell, if the public judges right, I well know—for I never saw more wit, fancy, and imagination, upon any one single subject. Every one of your alterations are, in my opinion, for the better, excepting those which you say you have made in my favour, and in which I fear the public will too justly differ from you. Your partiality to me had carried you but too far before.

I congratulate both you and Ireland most heartily, upon the increasing fruits of your labours for the public good; for I am informed from all hands, that a spirit of industry diffuses itself through all Ireland; the linen manufacture gains ground daily in the south and south-west, and new manufactures arise in different parts of the kingdom. All which, I will venture to say, is originally owing to your judicious and indefatigable endeavours for the good of your country. You know the nature of mankind in general, and of our countrymen in particular (for I still think and call myself an Irishman), well enough to know, that the invitation by premiums would be much more effectual than laws, or remote considerations of general public good, upon which few people reason well enough to be convinced that their own solid private interest essentially depends. The Dublin Society, and, in particular, my good friends the Bishop of Meath and Prior, have seconded you very well; and it is not saying too much of them to say, that they deserve better of Ireland than any one other set of men in it; I will not even except the Parliament. The premiums for flax-seed raised, instead of the former iniquitous distribution of it, have, I am told and believe, had very good consequences for the linen manufacture; and, as there was an infamous job got the better of, I am in hopes that all jobs will be hindered from creeping into that excellent establishment of the Protestant Charter-schools, which, if it be kept pure but for some years, will have a prodigious effect as to the religious and political state of Ireland; but if once Protestant children slip into those schools, as was attempted in my time, the end of their institution ceases.

I hope the University of Dublin, that enjoys a share of your premiums, deserves them. Our two Universities, at least, will do it no hurt, unless by their examples, for I cannot believe that their present reputations will invite people in Ireland to send their sons there. The one (Cambridge) is sunk into the lowest obscurity; and the existence of Oxford would not be known, if it were not for the treasonable spirit publicly avowed, and often exerted there. The University of Dublin has this great advantage over ours; it is one compact body, under the eye and authority of one head, who, if he is a good one, can enforce order and discipline, and establish the public exercises as he thinks proper; among which the purity and elegance of the English language ought to be particularly attended to, for there you are apt to fail in Ireland. But I trouble you too long upon subjects of which you are a much better judge than I am, and upon the spot to observe. My thoughts are only *Quæ censet amiculus*, and I give them you, *Ut si cæcus iter monstrare velit*. My wishes for the prosperity of your country are as warm and as sincere as the sentiments of regard, esteem, and friendship, with which I am,

Yours, etc.

CXCII.

TO SOLOMON DAYROLLES, ESQ.

LONDON, *April* 25, O.S. 1749.

DEAR DAYROLLES,

I am now three letters in your debt, which I would have paid more punctually, if I had any tolerable current species to have paid you in: but I have nothing but farthings to offer, and most of them, too, counterfeit; for being, thank God, no longer concerned in the coinage, I cannot answer for the weight of the coin. I hear, as everybody does, more lies than truth, and am not in a situation of knowing which is which. It is said, for example, that our great men are reconciled, and I believe that they say so themselves; but I believe at the same time *que le diable n'y perd rien.* One *Grace* * is too jealous not to suspect his best friend, and the other *Grace* † too obstinate to forgive or forget the least injury. Lord Sandwich, who governs the latter, and detests the former, who in return abhors him, takes care to keep this fire alive, so that he may blow it into a flame whenever it may serve his purpose to do so; and I am much mistaken, if he does not make it blaze often.

The Prince of Wales gains strength in Parliament in proportion as the King grows older; and Mr. Pelham loses ground there from the public conviction that he has but little power, which indeed I believe is true; the Army being entirely in the Duke of Cumberland, the Navy in Lord Sandwich, and the whole Church in the Duke of Newcastle. All other employments are scrambled for; and sometimes one Minister, and sometimes another, gets one. The situation of things little enables Mr. Pelham to satisfy the hungry and greedy rascals of the House of Commons, and consequently creates schisms and subdivisions in the Court party. The next Session will produce events.

However disjointedly business may go on, pleasures, I can assure you, go roundly. To-morrow there is to be, at Ranelagh Garden, a masquerade in the Venetian manner.‡ It is to begin at three o'clock in the afternoon; the several *loges* are to be shops for toys, *limonades, glaces,* and other *rafraichissemens.* The next day come the fireworks, at which hundreds of people will certainly lose their lives or their limbs, from the tumbling of scaffolds, the fall of rockets, and other accidents inseparable from such crowds. In order to repair this loss to society, there will be a subscription masquerade on the Monday following, which, upon calculation, it is thought, will be the occasion of getting about the same number of people as were destroyed at the fire-works.

---

* Newcastle.   † Bedford.
‡ See a full description of this masquerade in Horace Walpole's Letters to Mann, May 3, 1749.—M.

I hear nothing yet of Lord Holderness going to Holland, and therefore do not ask you when I may hope to see you here; for I suppose that his arrival must be previous to your departure: moreover, I am told that you are so busy in moving from one house to another, that you could not yet move from one country to another. Where is your new dwelling at the Hague?

I am glad to hear that Madame de Berkenroodt goes Ambassadress * to Paris; she will pass her time well there, and she deserves it. Pray make her my compliments of congratulation, and tell her that I am strongly tempted to pay my respects to her at Paris myself; but that, if I cannot, I will at least do it by proxy this winter twelvemonth, and send her an Ambassador about forty years younger, and consequently forty times better than myself. My boy will then be at Paris; he is now at Venice, goes to Turin till November, and then to Rome till the October following, when I shall emancipate him at Paris. I hear so well of him from all quarters, that I think he will do. *Adieu; portez vous bien, et aimez moi toujours.*

CXCIII.

À MADAME LA MARQUISE DE MONCONSEIL.

À LONDRES, *ce* 1 *Mai*, V.S. 1749.

J'ai actuellement devant mes yeux, Madame, trois de vos lettres, dont je n'ai pas encore accusé une seule. Vous jugez bien que j'en rougis, cela est vrai; mais vous jugez bien en même tems que j'avois des raisons valables. Cela est bien vrai aussi; mais je ne vous les détaillerai point, pour ne vous ennuyer que le moins qu'il me sera possible.

Venons à présent au fait, c'est-à-dire, aux ordres dont vous m'avez chargé, auxquels je me fais gloire, et un véritable plaisir, d'obéir. J'ai arrêté donc, pour Madame de Mirepoix, la maisonnette, plutôt que la maison, qu'a eu Monsieur l'Ambassadeur de Venise l'année passée, à un mille d'ici. Le payement en commencera la semaine prochaine, qui est de trois guinées par semaine. Le propriétaire n'a pas voulu attendre plus long-tems, vû que c'est à présent la saison que ces petites maisons se louent

* From Holland.

ordinairement pour les six mois d'été. Au reste, que Madame de Mirepoix ne s'attende pas à des chambres spacieuses, bien meublées, à des sophas, et à des chaises commodes; tout cela n'est pas le ton de nos petites maisons; mais pour la simple propreté, elle y est, et voilà tout.

Quant au pauvre Adolphati, je vous dirai très-naturellement, que je pourrois tout aussitôt débiter cinquante mille de ses *trios* que cinquante : on est excédé, accablé, assommé ici de musique; on est tout-a-fait rebuté du grand nombre de souscriptions qu'on sollicite pour des cantates, des sonates, et tout ce qu'il vous plaira, en faveur de compositeurs très-habiles, établis ici depuis quelque tems, et qui s'y sont fait même quelques amis, au lieu que notre Adolphati est absolument inconnu ici, et en Italie. Entre nous soit dit, ceux qui ont entendu sa musique ici ne l'ont nullement goûtée. J'ai prié quelques bons connoisseurs pour l'entendre chez moi, où il a joué de ses compositions, qu'on a trouvées bien ennuyeuses. Je suis bien fâché de ne pouvoir pas lui faire plaisir à cet égard, parce qu'il me paroit bon enfant, et encore plus parce que vous vous y intéressez; mais en vérité la chose est impossible, et je suis persuadé que Madame de Richmond vous en dira autant.

Monsieur le Marquis de Centurioni et moi, nous nous sommes cherchés inutilement l'un l'autre jusqu'ici, nous croisant toujours. Je m'impatiente de le voir, indépendemment de tout le mérite qu'il peut avoir, parce qu'il me vient de vous, qu'il vous connoit, par conséquent qu'il vous honore, et qu'il me parlera beaucoup de vous.

CXCIV.

TO SOLOMON DAYROLLES, ESQ.

London, *May* 4, O.S. 1749.

Dear Dayrolles,

The stroke is struck, I find at last; * and, if I am not much mistaken, he who struck it will have reason to repent it before

---

* This passage refers to the sudden dismissal from his office of the Pensionary Gilles. Mr. Dayrolles writes upon it as follows: "The Pensionary's fall, and the manner in which he was obliged to resign his post, seems to affect prodigiously the old Republican party, and, though they

it be very long. It is true, that it marks out his power; but, at the same time, it makes him the mark of resentment and jealousy, especially of the jealousy of *one person*, who will not bear even the appearance of a rival. Moreover, he cannot carry on the machine himself, he has neither temper nor knowledge sufficient for it. He must call for help, and then he will be in the case of the Horse, who called the Man to his assistance. Comte Groensfeldt will, in my opinion, be that man, who will soon get astride upon that Horse. He is industrious, temperate, and able; and can work under, still better than above, ground. If he is brought into the *Corps des Nobles*, as they say he is to be, it will be, considering all circumstances, such a glaring and decided proof of his personal favour, that everybody will look up to him; and the public opinion of his power will contribute to increase it. This scramble for power, in your little Court, and in your ruined Republic, puts me in mind of Lord Rochester's image of contending Ministers. He compares them to schoolboys, who, at the hazard of their necks, climb for crabs, which, if they were upon the ground, solid pigs would disdain. How the Pensionary could be ignorant of the favour intended him, as it is reported that he was when he received the message, is what I cannot conceive; for I knew it above a month ago. The manner in which he took it, and spoke the next day in the Assembly, was wise and skilful; but his accepting the pension,* for it is merely a pension, since he is excluded all Assemblies, is dirty, and vilifies him. If I had been he, I would sooner have lived all my life, as Van Beuningen did, by way of experiment, one year, upon six and thirty florins. Though his diet would have been but low, his character would have been high.

I have seen Laurenzi, who, I believe, must observe that diet

don't dare speak out, yet one may easily see by the gloominess of their countenances how it works upon them. It appears as if before this event they had never conceived a true notion of the Prince of Orange's power, which they now find to be as unlimited almost as that of the King of France. And after all I don't see any harm in its being so, and I dare say that the Stadtholder with an absolute power will be able to retrieve the affairs of this country much sooner than if his hands were tied up like those of his predecessors."—To Lord Chesterfield, May 23, N.S., 1749. From the original MS.—M.

* "Of 8,000 florins, about £730 "—Note by Mr. Dayrolles.

too, unless he can get an increase of his appointments, which he is labouring for; but I much doubt of his success. He confirms the accounts I had had before from many, of *la délicatesse et le bon goût de votre table*. Marquis d'Havrincourt was worthy of it, excelling as he does, not only in the theory, but in the practical part, of the table. He dined with me once or twice, and I think I never saw a more vigorous performer. He is a very pretty man, and has *l'extrêmement bon ton de la parfuitement bonne campagnie*, which is at present the short but comprehensive *éloge d'un honnête homme*.

I am in debt, at least three, if not four, letters to my Baron, who is a most excellent correspondent. I will pay him soon in much better coin than my own letters; for I shall send him by the first opportunity a good cargo of good books and pamphlets. Pray, make him my compliments, and tell him that I will write to him soon.

I hear nothing yet of Lord Holderness's going to Holland.

Yours most faithfully.

CXCV.

TO SOLOMON DAYROLLES, ESQ.

LONDON, May 9, O.S. 1749.

DEAR DAYROLLES,

The person who will give you this letter, is the nephew of Monsieur Boissier, a rich, and, for all that, a very honest merchant of the city, from whom I have received many civilities. He is a Swiss, and probably you know him by name and reputation. This nephew is desirous to get into the service of the Republic; and I wish that you could be useful to him in that view. I do not mean, nor does he, that you can procure him a commission; but we think that you may be able to point out to him *le moyen d'y parvenir*, whatever that may be. If it be solicitation, you will tell him where to address it; if a private tip, you will tell him where to apply it. In short, I am sure that, from the part I take in him upon his uncle's account, you will do him what service you can.

By the way, do not apprehend from this, that I shall plague you often with recommendations of this kind, for I have refused them to several people, and shall continue to do so to nine in ten. They desire impertinent, unreasonable, or impossible things; and then desire that I will recommend them to you, because they are sure that I have great interest with you. My answer to which is, that I verily believe I have interest with you, and for that very reason will not recommend to you an impertinent or an impossible thing.

I am now assured that Lord Holderness, though he has not yet kissed the King's hand, will go in three weeks at farthest: so that in six I hope to see you here. I need not tell you how glad I shall be of it. We have not been so long asunder since we loved one another; as we still, I believe, do. Adieu!

CXCVI.

TO SOLOMON DAYROLLES, ESQ.

LONDON, *May* 16, O.S. 1749.

DEAR DAYROLLES,

Lord Holderness sets out for the Hague the beginning of next week at farthest, so that I hope to see you here before it is long. However, do not press importunately for leave to return, because that would imply that a superior Minister at the Hague rendered you unnecessary there, which I would not have thought here. I mention this here upon account of a conversation that passed lately between Mr. Pelham and myself concerning you. He asked me, whether I thought you would care to remain at the Hague after the arrival of Lord Holderness? Though I guessed immediately the meaning of that question, I seemed not to do it, and asked him whether they had a mind to employ you anywhere else. He answered, no; but that he did not know whether you would care to act a subordinate part under Lord Holderness. I told him that I was persuaded you would make no difficulty of that, for that you took your post in those very circumstances under Lord Sandwich. "Why then," said he, "he must e'en stay, and it is only an unnecessary expense to the Government." I answered, that I did not look upon the expense of a Resident at the Hague as an unnecessary one by any means—that there had almost always been one, and that I believed that a Resident was, at least, as necessary with

Lord Holderness as with any other Minister that had ever been there. This he acknowledged, and added, that there were certainly no thoughts of removing you, unless of your own desire. His object, I know, was public economy, which, as he cannot practice where he pleases, he wants to do where he can. But, however, after what passed between us, I will answer for it that he will do you no harm.

On the other hand, I know that the Duke of Newcastle recommended you strongly the other day to Lord Holderness, and advised him to have the utmost confidence in you ; so that you seem to be very safe. But, however, I would not have your post, especially by your own admission, pass for an absolute sinecure, and an unnecessary expense to the Government; therefore I would advise you, when you ask leave to come here for two or three months, on account of your own private affairs, to say that the several details of your post are not so many at this time of the year, and will not be so teazing to the Minister upon whom they will devolve by your absence. Lord Holderness, I must acquaint you, has the pride that all little minds have : flatter that, and you may do what you will with him. Far from a jealousy of business, I think he will be very willing that you should do it all, if you please. If I were you, I would tell him, that now he was at the Hague, all the important business would doubtless be carried on by him only, and that I looked upon myself as no longer concerned in it;—that I had, therefore, nothing now to write but the common occurrences of the Hague, but that I would constantly show his Lordship my letters, if he would give himself the trouble to read them. This offer his laziness and pleasures will never let him accept; but it will give him a confidence in you, and then you will continue to write the best accounts you can get; and, without a compliment to you, I will venture to say that your letters will be the letters of business from the Hague, excepting those particular ones which the Greffier may, upon some important and secret points, dictate to Lord Holderness. We will talk more fully upon this subject when I see you.

It is reported here that Grovestein is disgraced. Is that true ? I should not wonder at it. I am called away of a sudden.

Yours faithfully.

CXCVII.

TO SOLOMON DAYROLLES, ESQ.

LONDON, *June* 9, O.S. 1749.

DEAR DAYROLLES,

As I find, by your last, that your stay in Holland will now be but short, my letters will be so too. We can talk more fully as well as more freely than we can write. You have set out well with our new Minister,* and I believe will go on so. He is one of those people whom a man of sense will not quarrel with, but humour; *cela ne coûte rien.*

Hop showed me yesterday the print of your fireworks; they seem to be so fine and so expensive, that, considering the present necessitous condition of the Republic, they put me in mind of a good *fanfaron* motto upon a French standard, *Peream, modo luceam.* I should have told you first, that the device was a bursting grenado.

My boy, who was going to the Carnival at Venice, was suddenly seized with a violent inflammation upon his lungs, at a miserable post-house, two posts beyond Laybach, in Carniole,† where he remained in great danger for twelve days. He is now recovering at Laybach; and, by this time, I hope, out of all danger. However, as soon as the heats are over, that is, at the latter end of September, I intend to send him to Naples, the best place in the world for tender lungs, and his are so yet. I shall send him a letter of recommendation to Marquis Fogliani, who is the only person I know there; and, as there is no Neapolitan Minister here, that will be the only letter I can give him. Could you easily get a letter or two for him from Monsieur Finochetti? If you can, you may bring them with you here; and I can send them to him time enough from hence. You will remember to call him my nephew. I am told that the Princess Strongoli and General Mahoni's are the two best houses there.

The Parliament is to be prorogued next Tuesday, when the Ministers will have six months' leisure to quarrel, and patch up, and quarrel again. Garrick and the Violetti will likewise, about the same time, have an opportunity of doing the same thing, for

---

* Lord Holderness.

† See Letter to his Son of June 6, 1751, and note.

they are to be married next week.* They are, at present, desperately in love with each other. Lady Burlington was at first outrageous, but upon cooler reflection upon what the Violetti, if provoked, might say or rather invent, she consented to the match, and superintends the writings. *Adieu ; je languis de vous voir.*

CXCVIII.

A MADAME LA MARQUISE DE MONCONSEIL.

À LONDRES, *ce* 13 *Juin*, V.S. 1749.

C'est que le ton grondeur vous va au mieux, Madame, et vous l'apprêtez d'une façon que vous lui donnez un goût flatteur. De tels reproches donnent l'exclusion à l'indifférence, et on est charmé de les recevoir, quand on est bien sûr de ne les avoir pas mérités ; et je suis dans ce cas. Moi! aller à Aix-la-Chapelle sans vous faire ma cour à Paris, ou en allant, ou en revenant! c'est en vérité un soupçon aussi injurieux à mon goût qu'à mes sentimens. Je pourrois peut-être me servir du prétexte d'aller à Aix-la-Chapelle, pour satisfaire à mon envie d'aller à Paris, mais je n'ai garde d'en faire ou l'unique, ou le véritable, objet d'un trajet de mer. Non, Madame, si je fais un pélérinage, ce sera pour faire mes dévotions dans la rue de Verneuil ou à Bagatelle, et y renouveller les vœux d'une amitié respectueuse et sincère ; mais pour cette année, il m'est impossible de sortir d'Angleterre. Un engagement tendre, et plusieurs affaires sérieuses m'y retiennent ; l'engagement tendre est celui de ma nouvelle maison, dont je n'ai pas tout-à-fait joui encore, et c'est un grand item en fait de tendresse. Elle me refuse ses dernières faveurs, jusqu'à ce que je l'aie entièrement nippée ; ce qui ne sera fait que vers l'hiver, car mes deux plus belles pièces ne sont rien moins que finies. · Mes engagemens nécessaires sont des arrangemens de famille,† où par conséquent la chicane entre pour quelque chose, et les délais pour beaucoup.

Votre Marquis de Centurioni a réellement de l'esprit, et de l'acquis, mais quand même il n'en auroit point eu, votre recommandation seule les lui auroit bien valu auprès de moi. Vous le

---

* See Horace Walpole's Letter to Mann of June 25, 1749.—M.

† Consequent on his brother's death.

reverrez bientôt, puisqu'il part d'ici cette semaine : le seul défaut que je lui trouve, c'est qu'il veut absolument être François et petit-maître ; et ne l'est pas qui veut. Le petit-maître François a des graces, avec tous ses défauts, et il plait en dépit de la raison, qui sûrement n'autorise point sa conduite ; mais cette étourderie brillante, cette pétulance aimable, se trouvent très déplacées, quand un Italien, un Allemand, ou un Anglois veut s'en parer : il n'y a que l'original qui plait, toutes les traductions en sont pitoyables.

A propos de traductions, je tâche de faire actuellement traduire en Italien votre futur élève, votre enfant adoptif : il est en Italie, et il doit passer son hiver à Rome. J'ai une grace à vous demander sur son sujet, c'est de vouloir bien le recommander à Monsieur le Duc de Nivernois votre Ambassadeur ; j'aurai l'honneur de lui écrire moi-même, pour satisfaire au respect et à l'estime que je lui dois : cela n'est que pour les formes ; mais c'est de votre recommandation que j'attends tout le solide. Je conçois bien que Monsieur de Nivernois, par la politesse qui lui est si naturelle, le prendroit à diner ou à souper deux ou trois fois pendant son séjour à Rome, et voila où finissent les recommandations ordinaires, mais ce n'est pas là mon fait : et je souhaiterois que Monsieur de Nivernois en fît son galopin, qu'il le regardât comme un petit François de sa suite, et qu'il fût si domestique dans son antichambre, qu'il eût, moyennant cela, de tems en tems des occasions d'étudier le caractère d'honnête homme, sur le meilleur modèle que je connoisse. Ce bonheur ne peut lui arriver que par votre moyen ; et permettez moi de vous dire que vous êtes intéressée à le lui procurer. Plus il sera formé, avant que de vous appartenir en propre, moins il vous sera à charge ; et quelques leçons à l'hôtel de Nivernois vous épargneront bien de la peine après. Je compte qu'il sera à Rome vers le milieu de Décembre ; et dans une année, ou une année et demie après, il sera à Paris ; ou pour mieux dire, cinq ou six heures du jour chez vous, je ne lui demande pas d'autre Paris que cela. J'y serai peut-être son avant-coureur, au moins je le souhaite, et c'est le seul souhait qui me reste. L'age éteint tous les souhaits de l'amour ; la raison et l'expérience ceux de l'ambition ; ceux de l'amitié vous sont bien dus, Madame, et je vous les adresse très véritablement.

CXCIX.

TO SOLOMON DAYROLLES, ESQ.

LONDON, *June* 23, O.S. 1749.

DEAR DAYROLLES,

I have this instant received your letter of the 27th, N.S., which I am very little able to answer, having been ill of a fever ever since Sunday last, and this being the first day that I have been allowed to go out of my bed-chamber. I am very weak, partly from the distemper itself, and partly from being starved. On Monday, I shall go to Blackheath for a week, which I hope will restore me. But I would not delay making you easier than you seem to be at present, about the event of your letter to the Duke of Newcastle. I happened to meet him last Saturday at Boden's country-house, where he told me that Stone had that morning delivered him a letter from you, asking leave to come here for a very short time. I told him that I supposed you would obtain it; to which he answered: Most undoubtedly. So that your having yet had no answer to it, I am convinced, proceeds only from his Grace's usual hurry and negligence. I believe he has at present business enough upon his hands; for in order to strengthen himself against the Dukes of Cumberland and Bedford, and Lord Sandwich, he has been negotiating with Lord Granville, who in consequence of that negotiation had the Garter given to him yesterday. He has refused the Lieutenancy of Ireland, which was offered him about three weeks ago; but he wisely chose rather to remain upon the spot without a place, than to go to Ireland for one. His Grace will very soon find, that, instead of calling in an auxiliary, he has taken a master.

I thank you heartily for the letters you have procured the boy for Naples; he is now so well recovered that he is gone to Venice, where he will stay till the middle of September, and then proceed to Naples. My head will not allow me to write any more; it is my heart adds, that I am faithfully,

Yours.

CC.

À MADAME LA MARQUISE DE MONCONSEIL.

à BABIOLE, *ce 8 Juillet*, V.S. 1749.

Vous voulez donc absolument, Madame, que je vous croye solidement fâchée contre moi ; je le veux bien, votre colère m'est trop glorieuse pour la refuser, et mon innocence fait que je n'y suis sensible que du bon côté. Une belle, qui manqueroit à un rendez-vous, où d'ailleurs elle auroit souhaité de se trouver, seroit bien fâchée si son amant ne l'étoit point. Il gronde, il s'emporte, elle se justifie, il s'appaise. Elle a prouvé sa bonne volonté, lui son empressement, et ils n'en sont que mieux après. Il en est de même dans l'amitié que dans l'amour, quoique d'ailleurs ces sentimens ne se ressemblent guères. Je soutiens que nous sommes actuellement mieux ensemble que jamais, et je suis charmé que vous soyez contente des étoffes qu'à la fin vous avez reçues ; elles se sont fait trop longtems attendre : il y a un point d'attente qui pique, mais il y en a un autre qui lasse.

A propos du bagage de notre Ambassadeur,* je puis vous assurer que l'Ambassadeur même est très sensible à toutes vos politesses, dont il m'a entretenu une heure de suite.

Mon nom seul, sans doute, sera plus efficace que toutes vos recommandations auprès de Monsieur le Duc de Nivernois ! Cela est très-poli de votre part, mais Monsieur de Nivernois ne vous en auroit guères d'obligation : en tout cas, faites comme si cela n'étoit point, et recommandez-lui fortement votre élève, je vous en supplie, au mois de Novembre prochain, puisqu'il sera à Rome au commencement de Décembre. Plus il fréquentera Monsieur de Nivernois, moins vous en rougirez quand il sera sous vos soins à Paris. Il ne lui manque que les manières, car pour la lecture et le savoir, il en a à revendre. Au reste, ne croyez pas que c'est son arrivée à Paris qui décidera de la mienne ; au contraire, je ne voudrois pas pour chose au monde le voir avant qu'il eût été bien formé et poli à Paris, car si je le trouvois ou Allemand ou Italien, et il doit naturellement être un composé de ces deux, j'en prendrois du dégout pour le reste de mes jours : ces deux nations, quoique par des raisons très-différentes, n'ayant pas l'honneur de me plaire infiniment.

* Lord Albemarle.—M.

Je reviens depuis quinze jours d'une fièvre chaude, dont j'ai pensé ne pas revenir du tout : c'est votre étoile, Madame, qui m'a sauvé, et qui n'a pas voulu que vous perdissiez encore un si fidèle serviteur. Procurez-moi, je vous en prie, pour quelque tems, la continuation de cette influence, car si vous le trouvez bon, je voudrois encore vivre dix ou douze ans, pour vous mieux prouver la constance de mon amitié. Je suis actuellement, pour me rétablir, à une très petite maison, que j'ai à cinq petites milles de Londres, et que j'aurois appellé *Bagatelle*, si ce n'eût été par respect pour la vôtre ; mais que j'appellé *Babiole*, pour en marquer la subordination, et pour laisser à *Bagatelle* la préférence qui lui est due. *Babiole* est située dans un des parcs du Roi, à cent pas de la Tamise, où l'on voit tous les jours une cinquantaine de gros vaisseaux merchands, et quelques vaisseaux de guerre, qui vont et qui viennent : les promenades sont les plus belles du monde, il y fait toujours sec, et l'air y est extrèmement fin. Il y a cinq cents ans qu'il n'auroit presque rien coûté à quelque fée ou magicien de nos amis, de transporter dans un moment *Babiole* au bois de Boulogne, pour faire sa cour à *Bagatelle*, mais à présent on ne sait à qui s'adresser pour ces sortes de choses là ; il est vrai, comme l'on dit, que le siècle n'en est pas digne, la foi y manque. Au moins, sans mettre votre foi à de grandes épreuves, vous me croirez bien le plus zélé et le plus attaché de vos serviteurs.

CCI.

A MADAME LA MARQUISE DE MONCONSEIL.

À LONDRES, *ce* 7 *Septembre*, V.S. 1749.

C'est que j'ai battu la campagne depuis plus d'un mois, comme un Juif, sans avoir de séjour fixe. Vous comprenez bien, Madame, ce que cela veut dire ; d'ailleurs, qu'aurois-je pu répondre à votre dernière, qui a pensé tourner ma tête ? Je n'en ai ma foi échappé que moyennant certaines réflexions assez humiliantes, que, malgré mon amour propre, j'ai fait sur moi-même, mais que je n'ai garde de vous communiquer. Si vous êtes réellement dans l'érreur, cette erreur m'est trop flatteuse pour que je tâche de vous en désabuser ; et si vous voulez seulement m'en faire accroire, vous le faites avec trop d'esprit et trop d'agrémens, pour que je me prive du plaisir de me voir, pour un moment, dans le miroir trompeur que vous me présentez. Voila comme nous sommes faits, un moment d'illusion agréable nous charme, toute illusion que nous la sachions; la réflexion nous désabuse après, mais elle n'empêche pas que nous ne nous prêtions avec la même facilité à une nouvelle, ou souvent à la même illusion, dès qu'elle se présente avec les graces et la séduction dont vous savez bien l'accompagner. Enfin il en est de l'esprit comme de tout le reste; nous vivons dans une alternative perpétuelle de péché et de pénitence.

Milord Albemarle vous a dit, plutôt ce que je souhaitois faire, que ce que je pouvois faire, quand il vous a dit que j'aurois l'honneur de vous voir cette année à Paris. La volonté au moins y étoit, et il n'y a que la nécessité qui puisse jamais l'emporter sur la volonté; mais cette nécessité s'y est trouvée, nécessité d'autant plus désagréable qu'elle résulte d'une infinité de détails, et d'arrangemens domestiques, que je déteste, et auxquels je ne suis guères propre. A propos de notre Ambassadeur, en êtes vous contens chez vous? Pour votre beau paladin, et votre aimable petite paladine,* ils font à merveille ici. C'est un grand état, une belle dépense, leurs manières marquent bien leur naissance et leur usage du grand monde; ils s'accommodent à tout, et jurent qu'ils sont charmés de tout; ils me permettent de les fréquenter, et j'en profite jusqu'à l'abus. Je cherche, et je trouve chez eux les agrémens de la société, que je chercherois inutilement chez plusieurs de mes compatriotes.

J'ai reçu en dernier lieu une lettre du petit Centurioni, que j'aime beaucoup; mais l'étourdi ne m'y a pas donné son adresse. Oserois-je vous prier, Madame, de vouloir bien lui faire tenir l'incluse? Il me dit qu'il m'a fait une tracasserie avec vous, en vous découvrant mon indiscrétion au sujet de vos bras. Je conviens du fait; mais qui n'en auroit pas fait autant? L'indifférence est ordinairement la mère de la discrétion, de sorte que vous avez tout à craindre de ma part d'un sentiment contraire.

* The Maréchal and Maréchale de Mirepoix, the French Ambassador and Ambassadress in London.—M.

CCII.

À MADAME LA MARQUISE DE MONCONSEIL.

à LONDRES, *ce* 28 *Septembre*, V.S. 1749.

Je suis bien-aise, Madame, de n'avoir appris la maladie de Mademoiselle votre fille qu'en même tems avec sa convalescence. J'aurois pris part à vos alarmes, comme j'en prends actuellement à votre joie, et comme j'en prendrai éternellement à tout ce qui vous touche. Je conçois bien que votre sang et vos soins doivent nécessairement avoir formé une fille digne de vos plus tendres inquiétudes. Cette occasion lui en aura fait sentir toute l'étendue et la délicatesse, et vous vous serez réciproquement plus chères, l'une à l'autre, par le danger où vous avez été toutes deux d'une séparation, dont peut-être ni l'une ni l'autre n'avoit encore senti toute la rigueur. Nous ne connoissons jamais tout le prix d'un bien, que quand nous nous voyons au moment de la perdre. Puissiez vous longtems, Madame, jouir d'un bien si cher que vous venez de sauver! Je ne compte pas non plus pour rien la conservation de sa beauté: les dévots et les philosophes ont beau parler sentences contra la beauté, je soutiens qu'elle est un avantage réel, puisqu'elle orne, et qu'elle recommande même l'esprit le plus juste, et le mérite le plus solide; je m'en rapporte à vous, vous devez bien savoir si j'ai raison ou non.

Je ne sais pas par quelle fatalité cela ne va pas si bien que je l'aurois cru, entre Milord Albemarle et vos gens. Je le trouve très-aimable, et poli; il aime les plaisirs et la volupté, c'est là aussi le ton chez vous, et pourtant cela ne s'agence point. Notre Ambassadeur a un avantage sur le vôtre, il vous a trouvée à Paris, et j'ose assurer Monsieur de Mirepoix qu'il ne vous trouvera pas à Londres.

Votre garçon sera à Rome en deux mois, de façon que vous n'avez qu'à écrire à Monsieur de Nivernois aussitôt que vous n'aurez rien autre chose à faire; mais ayez la bonté de le prévenir sur un article, qui est, qu'il doit s'attendre à voir un jeune homme, qui n'a ni tournure ni manières, mais qui est encore incrusté de la crotte Angloise, épaissie même de celle de l'université de Leipsig. Il est si fort appliqué à ses études, qu'il ne s'est pas donné le tems, quand même il en auroit eu les occa-

sions, de prendre l'air et les manières d'un honnête homme :
j'espère que l'air de l'hôtel de Nivernois lui sera favorable.

CCIII.

À MADAME LA MARQUISE DE MONCONSEIL.

À LONDRES, *ce* 23 *Octobre*, V.S. 1749.

Vous défendez les gentillesses, Madame ; ayez donc la bonté
de les définir, afin que je n'en dise pas sans y penser. J'ai insinué
qu'il étoit possible que Mademoiselle votre fille pût être jolie,
vous soutenez qu'elle ne l'est point. Voici une question de fait,
et j'en veux la décision, mais le moyen, direz vous ? le voici, et
je crois, ce qui n'arrive guères, que nous en serons tous deux
contens. Je m'en rapporte à Mademoiselle elle-même ; sa
bouche décidera en votre faveur, son cœur en la mienne. A
vous, Madame, à cette heure. Je ne vous ai vu, dites-vous, que
changée et dépérie, et par conséquent je dois croire que vous
avez toujours été fort désagréable. *Nego*, Madame, comme dit
élégamment Thomas Diafoirus ; * je vous intente procès là dessus,
et je vous laisserai même le choix de vos juges ; j'aurai le
triomphe, et vous aurez le plaisir, de vous voir condamnée avec
frais et dépens.

Je suis fâché que notre ami† qui pourroit plaire s'il le vouloit,
ne le veuille point ; j'ai su depuis long-tems son attachement
pour la Sultane ‡ à laquelle il sacrifie ses soirées, c'est-à-dire sa
vie, à Paris ; mais j'espérois qu'il lui feroit ses sacrifices le matin :
c'étoit au moins autrefois la belle heure des sacrifices.

Je ne vous dis rien, ni à Monsieur de Nevers non plus, au
sujet des lettres que vous avez écrites à Monsieur de Nivernois
en faveur de votre élève. Chez vous deux, les politesses et les
amitiés coulent de source, on s'y attend toujours, on ne s'y
trompe jamais, et elles paroissent si fort dans l'ordre, qu'il faut
quelque réflexion pour vous en avoir de l'obligation. On ne sait
presque pas gré à une bonne pendule pendant qu'elle va juste,
et on n'y fait attention que quand elle manque, parcequ'alors
on est surpris. Ce devroit pourtant être tout le contraire ; l'un
est très difficile, et il n'y a rien au monde de si facile que l'autre.

---

* In Moliere's *Malade Imaginaire*.   † Lord Albemarle.

‡ Mademoiselle Gauchet, a former Columbine.—See H. Walpole's Letter to Mann, of May 19, 1750.—M.

Je voudrois bien que votre élève cût fini ses affaires en Italie,
afin que j'en fusse quitte, et que je le visse dans des meilleures
mains que les miennes ; car sachez que du moment qu'il arrive à
Paris, je n'ai plus rien à faire avec lui, il vous appartiendra en
propre, et vous me répondrez de ses manières de sa politesse, et
même de ses sentimens. Gentillesse à part, je sais que vous en
pourrez faire tout ce que vous voudrez. Il vous sera livré par la
poste à Paris, du mois de Mai en un an.

CCIV.

TO CAPTAIN IRWINE (AT DUBLIN).

LONDON, *October* 26, 1749.

SIR,

You judge very right in believing that I take a part, in what
concerns Ireland; I do, and always shall, though an unavailing
one. You judged as right too, in thinking that no accounts of
that country could come to me from a more welcome hand than
yours. Nothing can be better or more clearly stated than your
account of the present *important* transactions relative to Charles
Lucas,* apothecary at Dublin, who, I believe, is the first apothecary that ever was voted an enemy to his country. That apothecary's stuff—of which, till now, only the recipes were printed—
will henceforwards be universally taken, and make a part of the
Dublin Dispensatory. In the Book of Holy Martyrs there are
many Charles Lucases, whose names would hardly have been
known in their own times, but certainly never transmitted down
to ours, if they had not been broiled a little; and the obscure
Dr. Sacheverell's fortune was made by a Parliamentary prosecu-
tion, much about the same time that the French prophets† were

---

* "The discontented in Ireland had been headed by one Lucas, an
apothecary, who was soon after banished from that kingdom, and turned
physician in London, where he wrote controversy in his own profession."
(Lord Orford's *Memoirs*, vol. i. p. 244.)—M. Lucas returned to Dublin and
was elected M.P. for that city in 1760. He established the *Freeman's Journal*,
the first number of which appeared on the 10th of September, 1763. He
was born in 1713, and died in 1771.

† " Ces Prophètes (du Languedoc) allèrent ensuite en Angleterre. . . .
Ils offrirent de ressusciter un mort, et même tel mort que l'on voudroit
choisir . . . La scène finit par mettre au pilori les Prophètes."—*Siècle
de Louis XIV.*, ch. xxxii.—M. See Letter of 26 January, 1766.

totally extinguished by a puppet-show. Great souls are sometimes desirous to purchase fame at the expense of their bodies.
If Charles Lucas, apothecary, is one of those, one should congratulate him upon this occasion; but if his views were, as from
his profession I should be very apt to think they were, of a much
lower nature, one ought to condole with him upon the suspension
of them—at least, for some time. In this uncertainty, I withhold
my compliments of either kind to Charles Lucas, apothecary.

But let us come to a better subject. Pray are you Major, or
only Captain still? For greater security, I direct this to you by
the latter title; but if, in so doing, I injure you, I will publish my
recantation upon the back of my next. But, in either case, I
hope you have not laid aside the thoughts of going abroad again.
You have travelled a little with great profit; travel again, and it
will be with still greater. The knowledge of the manners, the
language, and the government of the several countries of Europe,
is well worth two years' delay of military promotion, supposing
that should be the case. I am, with great truth, Yours, etc.

CCV.

À MADAME LA MARQUISE DE MONCONSEIL.

À LONDRES, *ce Decembre* 4, V.S. 1749.

Monsieur de Nevers, et Monsieur de Nivernois, ne se dé-
mentent ni l'un ni l'autre; il ne se peut rien de plus obligeant
que la lettre du dernier au premier, que vous avez eu la bonté,
Madame, de m'envoyer. Evertuez-vous, je vous en supplie, pour
dire de ma part à l'un et à l'autre tout ce que je devrois leur dire
à cette occasion, et que vous direz bien mieux que moi.

Dans la lettre que j'ai pris la liberté d'envoyer à Monsieur de
Nivernois par votre garçon, je l'ai appellé, à la mode des Papes,
mon neveu, titre qui ne dégrade pas à Rome : si après cela il
découvre la petite supercherie, je me flatte qu'il ne s'en offensera
pas. Il faut, comme vous le dites, ménager les préjugés établis,
et c'est justement là que les petites ruses sont permises pour les
éluder, puisqu'on ne doit pas espérer de les détruire. Mon neveu
donc n'aura l'honneur de vous faire sa cour à Paris qu'au mois
de Mai en un an; c'est que je veux qu'il ait tout appris avant

que d'y aller ; dès qu'à cet âge on a goûté les plaisirs et la dissipation de Paris, adieu toute attention sérieuse, toute application
aux études un peu difficiles.   Au reste, Madame, mon voyage à
Paris ne dépend aucunement du sien ; au contraire, nos âges ne
se conviennent pas assez pour nous y trouver ensemble, et nous
y serions déplacés vis-à-vis l'un de l'autre.

Au sujet des chaises pour les goutteux, j'aurai l'honneur de
vous dire qu'il y en a ici de mille différentes sortes, mais je n'en
ai pas vu de la sorte dont vous parlez, qui roulent moyennant une
manivelle : la meilleure que j'aie vu, c'est une chaise que feu
Monsieur de Broglio avoit fait venir de France, et dont il fit
présent à la feue Reine.   L'on s'y roule soi, même par le moyen
de deux roues assez grandes, une de chaque côté, qu'on tourne
très-facilement des deux mains ; elle sert aussi fort bien dans un
jardin, où le terrein est uni ; mais pas où il y a des montées et
des descentes.   Si, à cette description, Monsieur de Nevers croit
qu'une telle chaise lui conviendra, je me ferai un véritable plaisir
de lui en envoyer une.   Je m'en suis acheté une en dernier lieu,
ayant été enrôlé, depuis un mois, dans le nombre des goutteux.
L'attaque a été courte, il est vrai, mais assez vive à la main
gauche ; je n'en suis nullement fâché, dans l'espérance qu'elle me
garantira des autres maladies, et sur-tout de celles de la tête.   La
vieillesse commence à exiger ses droits, et j'aime mieux en payer
un considérable en forme de goutte, que d'être chicané par la
levée de plusieurs moindres tributs, sous les noms de migraines,
vertiges, maux de cœur, langueurs, etc.   A propos d'incommodités,
vous en avez actullement une, dont vous ne m'avez pas fait part,
et à laquelle pourtant je m'intéresse, c'est votre grossesse.   Je
vous supplie de la terminer par l'heureux accouchement d'un fils,
car je ne veux pas que l'esprit, et les talens, qui vous distinguent
de votre sexe, tombent en quenouille.   Détachez en quelque
petite province pour dot à Mademoiselle votre fille ; mais je veux
que ce soit un fils qui hérite votre empire.   Puisse-t-il vous causer
le moins de douleur qu'il est possible à son début dans ce monde
ici, et toute la joie qu'il est possible dans ses progrès !

CCVI.

TO THE BISHOP OF WATERFORD.

LONDON, *December* 28, 1749.

MY DEAR LORD,

This is to most people, and in most places, the season of lies, dignified and distinguished by the name of compliments; with me it is a season of truth, when I assure you that I wish you, and all who belong to you, whatever you wish for yourselves or for each other, more particularly health, with which nobody need be unhappy.

Though you would not tell me how soon and how generously you provided for Dr. Young's son,* he did, and with all the profession of gratitude which he owed you. I am as much obliged to you as he can be. I am glad that the young man has a good character, which you know I made a *conditio sine quâ non* of my request; and I hope that my recommendation interfered with no views of your own in favour of any other person.

Lord Scarborough's picture will be finished this week, and sent to Mrs. Chenevix. I think it is very well done, and indeed ought to be by the time Barret has taken to do it in; but he has taken it into his head, and I cannot say that I have discouraged him, that a great painter should also be a poet—that the same warmth of imagination equally forms both—and, consequently, when I expect him to bring me home a very good copy of a picture, he frequently brings an execrable copy of verses instead of it. The melon seeds shall go by the same opportunities of the picture and candlesticks; which I suppose will be time enough, since they are not to be sown till February.

I have not yet been able to get the workmen out of my house in town, and shall have the pleasure of their company some months longer. One would think that I liked them, for I am now full of them at Blackheath, where I am adding a gallery. *Il ne faut jamais faire les sottises à demi.* I am, my dear Lord,

Yours, etc.

* "I must observe here, that Lord Chesterfield never recommended any one to the ecclesiastical preferments in my gift, but Mr. Young. When he did, it was in the handsomest manner, by telling me twice in his letter, 'Remember that I do not recommend, but if you approve of his character you will do a good-natured action.'"—Note by the Bishop of Waterford.

CCVII.

À MADAME LA MARQUISE DE MONCONSEIL.

à LONDRES, *ce* 1 *Janvier*, V.S. 1750.

Ce jour-ci, qui est à Paris, à Versailles, et à Londres, la fête des mensonges, est pour moi un jour de vérité, n'y ayant rien de plus vrai ni de plus sincère que les vœux que je fais pour votre santé, et pour votre bonheur—C'est là le commencement d'une lettre de Rousseau,* que par hasard je viens de lire dans le moment, et que j'adopte, Madame, du fond de mon cœur, en vous écrivant ce premier jour de notre année. Ces vœux, depuis que j'ai eu l'honneur de vous connoitre, n'ont jamais manqué ou de vérité, ou d'ardeur ; mais il me semble que cette année y a ajouté de la vivacité, à cause de la situation dans laquelle elle vous trouve; situation inquiétante pour vos amis, mais, ne vous en déplaise, nullement ridicule pour vous. Quoi ! faut-il donc être toujours grosse, ou bien jamais grosse? ou bien, faut-il un certain nombre de grossesses anniversaires fixé par la mode? Que voulez-vous dire avec vos quarante-trois ans? Est-ce que les loix de la nature, de pays, ou de la bienséance, ont établi cette époque pour la stérilité? Au contraire, je soutiens que votre grossesse actuelle est une grossesse de bienséance et de devoir. Vous aviez trop peu travaillé pour la société; vous lui deviez encore de votre race, et vous recommencez à présent à vous acquitter de ce devoir. Je vous en annonce encore quarte ou cinq de suite. Au reste, puisque ni vous ni Mademoiselle votre fille ne voulez absolument pas que cet enfant soit un fils, en cas de ce malheur envoyez-le moi, je l'adopterai volontiers, et je me ferai gloire même de dire qu'il est à moi. Ce sera un ouvrage de réflexion, vous avez pris bien du tems à le composer, et je passerai pour l'auteur d'un chef-d'œuvre ; il y a des plagiaires pour bien moins que cela.

Votre lettre, et celle de Monsieur de Nevers, ont fait tout l'effet que je pouvois souhaiter auprès de Monsieur de Nivernois, en faveur de votre élève; j'en ai reçu une lettre avant-hier de Rome, dans laquelle il me marque que Monsieur et Madame de Nivernois l'ont accablé de politesses, et qu'il y est comme enfant, même gâté, de la maison. S'il ne mérite pas ces attentions, du moins il les reconnoit, et vous en attribue une bonne moitié.

* Jean Baptiste Rousseau.

Faites-moi savoir, je vous en supplie, Madame, par deux lignes de la main d'un valet, ou d'une fille de chambre, votre heureux accouchement aussi-tôt qu'il arrivera, car en vérité je m'intéresse trop à un moment si important pour vous, pour en attendre la nouvelle, jusqu'à votre convalescence. Adieu, Madame, encore. *Molti e felici.*

CCVIII.

À MADAME LA MARQUISE DE MONCONSEIL.

À LONDRES, *ce* 18 *Janvier*, V.S., 1750.

J'ai l'honneur de vous envoyer, Madame, trois ananas qui ne valent rien, premièrement parceque ce n'en est pas la saison, et ensuite parcequ'il a fallu les cueillir avant qu'ils fussent mûrs, sans quoi ils auroient été en compôte à leur arrivée à Paris. Je les envoye par un courier jusqu'à Calais, où ils seront livrés au directeur des postes, selon l'adresse que vous m'avez donnée. Comme les envies des femmes grosses se contentent plus par le nom que par le mérite des choses, j'espère que ces ananas tiendront lieu de bons, auprès de Madame la Dauphine ; * mais le fait est qu'ils sont mauvais ; la véritable saison n'est que depuis le mois de Juin jusqu'à celui d'Octobre.

Cette lettre, qui va par un courier, les dévancera, j'espère, assez pour vous préparer à toutes les cérémonies requises. Au moins ne croyez pas que ces ananas soient de *Babiole*, vous feriez trop de tort à mon jardinage. Les miens sont bien autre chose, mais j'ai eu ceux-ci du seul homme en Angleterre, qui les fait venir dans cette saison. Si vous me promettez d'en venir goûter à *Babiole* au mois d'Août prochain, je promets de venir vous chercher à *Bagatelle* au mois de Mai.

J'ai reçu la lettre du monde la plus obligeante de la part de Monsieur de Nivernois, en réponse à celle que votre élève lui a apportée de la mienne ; je n'y ai pas repliqué, et cela par discrétion, puisque, fait comme il est, c'eût été lui donner la peine d'écrire encore ; mais ayez la bonté d'insinuer cela auprès de Monsieur de Nevers, en même tems que vous voudrez bien l'assurer de ma parfaite reconnoissance.

---

* Marie Josèphe de Saxe, mother of Louis XVI., Louis XVIII., and Charles X.—M.

Continuez, Madame, à m'honorer de vos ordres, quand je pourrai vous être bon à quelque chose, car je vous proteste que rien ne peut égaler le plaisir que j'ai à vous prouver mon attachement inviolable.

CCIX.

À MADAME LA MARQUISE DE MONCONSEIL.

À LONDRES, *ce* 8 *Mars*, V.S. 1750.

Je vous ai fait quartier, Madame, depuis quelque tems, mais, soit que vous m'en teniez compte, ou soit que vous m'en blâmiez, je n'y entre pour rien, également exempt de mérite, ou de crime. J'ai été accablé de migraines, et excédé d'affaires ; d'affaires de famille j'entends, et de détails qui demandoient un arrangement, auquel je ne suis ni naturellement trop porté, ni trop propre. Mes migraines m'ont quitté, et je vous envoye les prémices d'une tête qui n'est pas encore bien rétablie ; ils auront apparemment quelque goût du terroir ; mais les sacrifices ont toujours été reçus plus ou moins favorablement, selon les moyens et les intentions de ceux qui les faisoient, et point sur le pied de leur valeur intrinsèque. Recevez donc, Madame, mes offrandes, quelque médiocres qu'elles soient en elles-mêmes, comme celles d'un cœur qui vous est tout dévoué.

Je suis charmé d'apprendre que les ananas aient si bien réussi ; mais assurément il ne leur falloit pas moins que l'envie d'une femme grosse, pour les faire trouver bons, et le goût que Madame la Dauphine y a trouvé, me paroit une preuve incontestable de sa grossesse ; dans cette supposition, vous pourrez peut-être avoir sauvé à la France un Duc de Bourgogne, et je serai trop heureux d'avoir pu contribuer au mérite que vous en aurez.

J'ai parlé à —— au sujet des plans et des manuscrits de feu son oncle, mais il n'a pas voulu se prêter à la moindre communication de ces papiers. C'est un jeune homme élevé au métier des armes, entêté du mérite supérieur de son oncle, et qui croit posséder exclusivement, dans ces paperasses, des trésors immenses et uniques.

Nous avons eu ici ce matin un second tremblement de terre, plus vif encore que celui d'aujourd'hui il y a un mois. Toutes les maisons de Londres en ont été ébranlées, et quelques cheminées sont tombées ; c'étoit à cinq heures et demie ce matin. J'étois profondément endormi, mais la force de la secousse m'a réveillé en sursaut, et j'ai cru voir le moment où je serois écrasé. L'avez-vous senti chez vous, ou avons-nous joui privativement de ce phénomène ? En tout cas, j'espère qu'il ne vous aura pas effrayée dans votre situation présente ; vos ouvrages méritent bien d'être portés au dernier point de perfection.

Je doute fort si j'aurai le plaisir de vous faire ma cour cette année ; ce ne sera pas au moins, comme vous jugez bien, la volonté qui manquera, mais c'est que j'envisage bien des circonstances peu favorables à ce voyage. Je tâcherai pourtant de les écarter, s'il m'est possible, n'y ayant rien que je souhaite plus ardemment que le plaisir de vous assurer encore une fois en personne de la vérité de mes sentimens, et de l'attachement inviolable avec lequel je serai toujours, etc.

CCX.

TO SOLOMON DAYROLLES, ESQ.

LONDON, *March* 30, O.S. 1750.

DEAR DAYROLLES,

Your signs of life came very seasonably to convince me, that the concern you were in at leaving your *dear country** had not put an end to it. I happened to relate very properly the agonies I saw you in at leaving England, in company, where a lady seemed to think that she was the cause of them. She inquired minutely into the degree and nature of them; spoke of them with tenderness and compassion, though she confessed a quarrel with you for three days before you went away, which had broke off all communication between you. To this I answered like your god-father, that to part with her would have been sufficient cause for your grief; but to part with her offended and incensed, more than justified the despair I observed in you. I obliged her at last to confess, that she wished she had seen you the day before you went. Make your most of these informations in your next letter to her.

* Mr. Dayrolles had been in England on leave of absence between July, 1749, and March, 1750.—M.

You found Holland just as you left it, that is to say, in the same state of insolvency and confusion. I fear it will be soon worse, if my suspicions are founded; for I have good reason to suspect, that your rulers are wild enough to think of engaging in a new war. It is now beginning in the North; and, though publicly it is discouraged, privately it is encouraged, not only in Holland, but *elsewhere*. The Czarina will, I am convinced, soon strike the first blow. The Court of Vienna hopes that the King of Prussia will strike the second, and give them a pretence to the third. If France does not interpose, the King of Prussia is demolished. If France does, it can only be by way of diversion, in falling upon the Queen of Hungary; and that will necessarily be in Flanders, which, it is *hoped* and believed, will force the Maritime Powers to take a part. Bentinck, now at Vienna, could tell us more of this, if he pleased.

I have not heard one word about Mr. Harte,* which makes me believe that I shall not. He shall be no loser, however, and other people no gainers, by the refusal.

Mr. Durand brought me a letter from my Baron, full of complaints of his health. Make him my compliments, and tell him that he shall hear from me soon.

On Thursday sevennight the Parliament rises; and the Tuesday following his Majesty sets out for Hanover. The Regency is at last settled, and the Duke not to be one.

Adieu, mon cher enfant; soyez persuadé que je vous aimerai toujours.

CCXI.

TO SOLOMON DAYROLLES, ESQ.

LONDON, *April* 14, O.S. 1750.

DEAR DAYROLLES,

I could not refuse this recommendation of a *virtuosa* to a *virtuoso*. The girl is a real prodigy; but sometimes a prodigy without a puff will not do. Your hearing her once, and your puffing her afterwards, is all that she desires. The great point is to get the Princess of Orange to hear her, which she thinks will *make her fortune*. Even the great Handel has deigned to

---

* Lord Chesterfield had lately applied to obtain for Mr. Harte a prebend of Windsor.—M.

recommend her there; so that a word from your Honour will be sufficient. Adieu! Yours faithfully.

CCXII.

À MADAME LA MARQUISE DE MONCONSEIL.

À Londres, *ce* 19 *Avril*, V.S. 1750.

Me voici hors d'inquiétude, Madame, puisque vous voilà hors d'affaires. Vous vous étiez trop long-tems désaccoutumée d'un métier, qui demande de l'habitude pou être facile, et je vous avoue que je craignois pour vous, plus que je ne pouvois, ou que je ne voulois vous dire. Si vous comptez de continuer la fabrique des enfans, n'y mettez plus, s'il vous plait, un si long intervalle, mais faites les tout de suite, et sur-tout ayez à l'avenir un peu plus d'attention au genre masculin. Il semble que vous ne peuplez que pour les Amazones; mais je veux absolument, pour l'honneur de mon sexe, que vous nous donniez un fils qui vous ressemble. Au reste, Mademoiselle la première, dont les vœux ont été exaucés en dépit des miens, par l'arrivée de Mademoiselle la seconde, a tort, et elle regrettera, avec le tems, le succès de ses vœux, car je me trompe fort si Mademoiselle la seconde ne sera pas Mademoiselle Benjamin; au lieu qu'un frère ne l'auroit éclipsée que pour un tems, et son interposition entre elle et vous auroit bientôt fini pour l'armée ou les affaires.

Vous me reprochez mon malheur, comme s'il y avoit de ma faute; cela n'est pas généreux, Madame, et je ne vous y reconnois point. Il m'est assez sensible de ne pouvoir pas avoir le bonheur de vous faire ma cour cette année, sans que vous y ajoutiez la mortification d'en soupçonner ma volonté. Pour m'en dédommager un peu, je vous enverrai un ambassadeur extraordinaire, muni de mes pliens pouvoirs, auquel je vous prie d'ajouter foi en tout ce qu'il vous dira de ma part. C'est votre élève, qui sera à Paris vers la St. Michel, établi à l'académie de La Guérinière. J'espère que son dernier séjour à Rome l'aura un peu formé, mais en tout cas je compte sur Paris, c'est-à-dire sur vous; s'il est gauche ou impoli, je vous supplie de ne lui rien passer, mais de lui en parler très-sérieusement, et de tems en tems lui lâcher des traits de ridicule, qui font souvent plus d'effet sur les jeunes gens, que les remonstrances sérieuses. Je lui ai déjà fait savoir qu'il vous appartient en propre, que je vous ai transporté tous mes droits sur lui, et que son crédit et sa faveur auprès de moi dépendront uniquement des rélations que j'en recevrai de votre part. C'est un esclavage bien doux et bien utile que je lui destine; et s'il a le bon sens qu'on m'assure qu'il a, il le trouvera tel, et aura pour vous les sentimens de considération, d'estime, d'amitié, et de respect avec lesquels je vous donne actuellement le bon soir.

CCXIII.

TO SOLOMON DAYROLLES, ESQ.

LONDON, *April* 27, O.S. 1750.

DEAR DAYROLLES,

I am two letters in your debt; but as I knew that you were rambling, I did not know where to tender the payment.

By this time it is probable that you are re-established at the Hague. Had an unhappy foreigner been obliged to pass as many days at Plymouth as you passed at Calais, how admirably he would have diverted himself, and how politely he would have been received! Whereas, I dare say, you passed your time very well at Calais, in case you were not too much an Englishman to think so.

It is very true, that, after a series of difficulties, which, I believe, were never made before upon so trifling an occasion, Mr. Harte has at last got a prebend of Windsor. I am most extremely glad of it; for, that debt being now paid, I owe no man living anything. As it is necessary that he should come over here to take possession of his stall, I have directed him to bring the boy to Paris, and to fix him in La Guérinière's academy there, *pour le dégourdir, le dégraisser et le décrotter.* Some proper steps have been already taken towards that at Rome. * * *

When he arrives at Paris, I will send him a letter of recommendation *à Son Excellence Madame de Berkenroodt; valeat quantum.* In all events, it will be a good house for him to frequent. *Vous y mettrez du vôtre aussi, s'il vous plait,* by writing a word or two in his favour to the lady, or her husband, or both. Pray buy me six dozen of pints of the Cape wine you mention, and have it carefully packed up, and directed *à Madame la Marquise de Monconseil, dans la rue de Verneuil, Faubourg St. Germain, à Paris,* and then send it with a note to *Messieurs Testas*

Père et Fils, à Amsterdam, recommending to their care to forward it to her. Draw upon me for what more you shall disburse, than the twopence of mine now in your hands.

Comte Obdam's sale, I suppose, draws near, at which pray buy me such bustoes and vases as you shall find are universally allowed to be both antique and fine, at such rates as you shall think reasonable; in the whole, you may go as far as two hundred pounds, if the objects are curious and worth it.

Shall you not be surprised, if, at your return here, you find a *pendant* for your Rubens, full as large, and by a still greater master? I have reason to believe that will be the case, and then I shall undoubtedly have two of the most capital pictures in England of those two great masters. For the *virtuosi* here now unanimously confess, that all the Rubenses in England must strike to mine.

I believe, as you say, that you found things in the United Provinces just as you left them, a great deal talked of, and nothing done. However, they would do well to consider, that, in their situation, not to advance is to go backwards. You may depend upon it, that, whatever you may have heard said to the contrary, war was the original design, and the Prussian bear-skin was again scantled out upon paper; but the strong declarations, and indeed preparations, of France on one hand, and the apprehensions which Russia, on the other, had just reasons to entertain of the Turk, have respectively obliged *certain powers* to put water in their wine; and I now verily believe that the North will clear up, and settle for some time in peace.

Lord Harrington is arrived here from Ireland; bonfires were made and a thousand insults offered him at his departure.

Pray, make my compliments to my Baron, to whom I owe a letter; which I have not paid for mere want of specie. Is he got to his own house again? Surely it has undergone lustrations enough to be sufficiently purified for his reception. *La Belle Cécile se sauvera bientôt ou bien séchera sur pied pour l'amour de Monsieur le Capitaine.* Everything here is just as you left it. I am, and ever shall be so, with regard to you; *c'est tout dire; bon soir, mon enfant.*

END OF THE SECOND VOLUME.